Lecture Notes in Computer Science 12717

More information about this subseries at http://www.springer.com/series/7408

Ferruccio Damiani · Ornela Dardha (Eds.)

Coordination Models and Languages

23rd IFIP WG 6.1 International Conference, COORDINATION 2021
Held as Part of the 16th International Federated Conference
on Distributed Computing Techniques, DisCoTec 2021
Valletta, Malta, June 14–18, 2021
Proceedings

 Springer

Editors
Ferruccio Damiani (ID)
University of Turin
Turin, Italy

Ornela Dardha (ID)
Sir Alwyn William Building
University of Glasgow
Glasgow, UK

ISSN 0302-9743 ISSN 1611-3349 (electronic)
Lecture Notes in Computer Science
ISBN 978-3-030-78141-5 ISBN 978-3-030-78142-2 (eBook)
https://doi.org/10.1007/978-3-030-78142-2

LNCS Sublibrary: SL2 – Programming and Software Engineering

This Springer imprint is published by the registered company Springer Nature Switzerland AG
The registered company address is: Gewerbestrasse 11, 6330 Cham, Switzerland

Foreword

The 16th International Federated Conference on Distributed Computing Techniques (DisCoTec 2021) took place during June 14–18, 2021. It was organised by the Department of Computer Science at the University of Malta, but was held online due to the abnormal circumstances worldwide affecting physical travel. The DisCoTec series is one of the major events sponsored by the International Federation for Information Processing (IFIP), the European Association for Programming Languages and Systems (EAPLS) and the Microservices Community. It comprises three conferences:

- *COORDINATION*, the IFIP WG 6.1 23rd International Conference on Coordination Models and Languages;
- *DAIS*, the IFIP WG 6.1 21st International Conference on Distributed Applications and Interoperable Systems;
- *FORTE*, the IFIP WG 6.1 41st International Conference on Formal Techniques for Distributed Objects, Components, and Systems.

Together, these conferences cover a broad spectrum of distributed computing subjects, ranging from theoretical foundations and formal description techniques to systems research issues. As is customary, the event also included several plenary sessions in addition to the individual sessions of each conference, which gathered attendants from the three conferences. These included joint invited speaker sessions and a joint session for the best papers from the three conferences. Associated with the federated event, four satellite events took place:

- *DisCoTec Tool*, a tutorial session promoting mature tools in the field of distributed computing;
- *ICE*, the 14th International Workshop on Interaction and Concurrency Experience;
- *FOCODILE*, the 2nd International Workshop on Foundations of Consensus and Distributed Ledgers;
- *REMV*, the 1st Robotics, Electronics, and Machine Vision Workshop.

I would like to thank the Program Committee chairs of the different events for their help and cooperation during the preparation of the conference, and the Steering Committee and Advisory Boards of DisCoTec and its conferences for their guidance and support. The organization of DisCoTec 2021 was only possible thanks to the dedicated work of the Organizing Committee, including Caroline Caruana and Jasmine Xuereb (publicity chairs), Duncan Paul Attard and Christian Bartolo Burlo (workshop chairs), Lucienne Bugeja (logistics and finances), and all the students and colleagues who volunteered their time to help. I would also like to thank the invited speakers for their excellent talks. Finally, I would like to thank IFIP WG 6.1, EAPLS and the Microservices Community for sponsoring this event, Springer's Lecture Notes in Computer Science team for their support and sponsorship, EasyChair for providing the reviewing framework, and the University of Malta for providing the support and infrastructure to host the event.

June 2021   Adrian Francalanza

Preface

This volume contains the papers presented at COORDINATION 2021, the 23rd International Conference on Coordination Models and Languages, organized online by the University of Malta in Valletta during June 14–18, 2021, as part the federated DisCoTec conference.

The COORDINATION conference provides a well-established forum for the growing community of researchers interested in coordination models and languages, architectures, verification, and implementation techniques necessary to cope with the complexity induced by the demands of today's software development. For the third year in a row, COORDINATION has called for tool papers describing experience reports, technological artefacts, and innovative prototypes, as well as educational tools in the scope of the research topics of the conference. Tool papers were selected according to the combination of an extended abstract and a short video demonstration, after which full papers were produced to be included in these proceedings following a light-weight review. In addition, seeking to further reinforce the practical applicability aspects of the COORDINATION community research, we have explicitly included among the topics of interest the industry-led efforts in coordination and industrial case studies.

The Program Committee of COORDINATION 2021 comprised 32 researchers from 14 countries. We received 16 full paper submissions, 7 short paper submissions, and 8 tool paper submissions. Each paper was evaluated by three reviewers and this process was supplemented by an in-depth discussion phase during which the merits of all the papers were considered. The contributions published in this volume were selected according to their quality, originality, clarity, and relevance. The final program comprises 8 full papers, 2 short papers, and 7 tool papers. The program also included an invited tutorial and an invited talk. The invited talk was given by Mira Mezini from TU Darmstadt, Germany. A short abstract of this talk is included in this volume under the title "Let it Flow: Reactive Computations for Consistent-by-Design Distributed Applications".

We are grateful to all authors who have submitted their work, to the members of the Program Committee and their sub-reviewers for their help in evaluating the papers, and to all the participants for their interest in the conference. We would particularly like to express our gratitude to Giorgio Audrito and Silvia Lizeth Tapia Tarifa, the chairs of the Tool Track; to Stephanie Balzer and Anastasia Mavridou, the organizers of the special topic on digital contracts; to Maurice ter Beek and Hugo Torres Vieira, the organizers of the special topic on configurable systems; and to Ivan Lanese and Larisa Safina, the organizers of the special topic on microservices. Their strong involvement was a key enabling factor for the preparation of the conference. Furthermore, we wish to thank the Steering Committee of COORDINATION and the Steering Board of DisCoTec for their support.

For the second year in a row, DisCoTec – the federated conference whereof COORDINATION is part – took place during the COVID-19 pandemic with many countries having imposed travel restrictions and some of the participants being in lockdown. In the name of all COORDINATION 2021 participants, we thank the Organizing Committee chaired by Adrian Francalanza for allowing the conference to proceed smoothly despite the inherent difficulties of holding it online. Personal thanks go to Duncan Paul Attard, Christian Bartolo Burlo, Caroline Caruana, and Jasmine Xuereb for their help with the conference publicity and running the website.

Finally, we would like to thank the International Federation for Information Processing (IFIP) WG 6.1 for the financial support, Springer for their sponsorship and Anna Kramer, personally, for the support during the production phase of the proceedings, EasyChair for the paper collection, reviewing, and proceedings preparation environment, the University of Malta for providing the infrastructure, and the microservices community and the European Association for Programming Languages and Systems (EAPLS) for the additional publicity they provided.

April 2021   Ferruccio Damiani
                                                                         Ornela Dardha

Organization

Program Committee Chairs

Ferruccio Damiani	University of Turin, Italy
Ornela Dardha	University of Glasgow, UK

Steering Committee

Gul Agha	University of Illinois at Urbana Champaign, USA
Farhad Arbab	CWI and Leiden University, Netherlands
Simon Bliudze	Inria, Lille, France
Laura Bocchi	University of Kent, UK
Wolfgang De Meuter	Vrije Universiteit Brussels, Belgium
Rocco De Nicola	IMT School for Advanced Studies Lucca, Italy
Giovanna di Marzo Serugendo	Université de Genève, Switzerland
Tom Holvoet	KU Leuven, Belgium
Jean-Marie Jacquet	University of Namur, Belgium
Christine Julien	The University of Texas at Austin, USA
Eva Kühn	Vienna University of Technology, Austria
Alberto Lluch Lafuente	Technical University of Denmark, Denmark
Michele Loreti	University of Camerino, Italy
Mieke Massink (Chair)	CNR-ISTI, Italy
José Proença	ISEP, Portugal
Rosario Pugliese	University of Florence, Italy
Hanne Riis Nielson	Technical University of Denmark, Denmark
Marjan Sirjani	Mälardalen University, Sweden
Carolyn Talcott	SRI International, USA
Emilio Tuosto	Gran Sasso Science Institute, Italy
Vasco T. Vasconcelos	University of Lisbon, Portugal
Mirko Viroli	Università di Bologna, Italy
Gianluigi Zavattaro	Università di Bologna, Italy

Program Committee

Zena M. Ariola	University of Oregon, USA
Robert Atkey	University of Strathclyde, UK
Giorgio Audrito	University of Turin, Italy
Stephanie Balzer	CMU, USA
Simon Bliudze	Inria, Lille, France
Laura Bocchi	University of Kent, UK
Roberto Casadei	University of Bologna, Italy

Tool Track Chairs

Special Sessions Organizers

Configurable Systems in the DevOps Era:

Microservices:

Techniques to Reason About Interacting Digital Contracts:

Stephanie Balzer   CMU, USA
Anastasia Mavridou   SGT Inc./NASA Ames Research Center, USA

Additional Reviewers

Davide Basile   Ai Liu
Vincenzo Ciancia   Dominic Orchard
Michael Coblenz   Yann Regis-Gianas
Said Daoudagh   Rudolf Schlatte
Gianluca Filippone   Martina Sengstschmid
Fabrizio Fornari   André Souto
Saverio Giallorenzo   Martin Steffen
Gerson Joskowicz   Bernardo Toninho
Eduard Kamburjan   Gianluca Turin
Ajay Krishna   Adriana Laura Voinea

Sponsors

Let it Flow: Reactive Computations for Consistent-by-Design Distributed Applications (Abstract of Invited Talk)

Mira Mezini

Technische Universität Darmstadt
mezini@cs.tu-darmstadt.de

Abstract. Ubiquitous connectivity of millions of powerful (mobile) devices to each other and to web and cloud computing platforms via programmable networks has fostered globally distributed computing systems – the information power grids of the 21st century – and the development of different kinds of massively distributed applications such as social networking apps (e.g., instant messengers, multiplayer games, etc.), collaborative workflows (e.g., Google Docs, Figma, Trello, etc.), real-time businesses (e.g., collaborative condition monitoring, real-time cross-organizational workflows, etc.), decentralized data ecosystems (e.g., for processing data owned by different stakeholders), etc.

Today, distributed applications often rely on centralized solutions for consistency management. However, centralized management is not a good fit for massively distributed applications regarding offline availability, low latency, or user-controlled data privacy. Decentralized architectures are a better match, but in this setting applications developers must consider partial failures and need to trade-off between availability and strong consistency, ideally employing different consistency levels for different application parts. While there are storage systems that support hybrid consistency, the difficult and error-prone decision about selecting the right consistency levels is left to application developers.

In this talk, I argue for language-based solutions to automate consistency decisions. With such solutions, it is the responsibility of the language machinery to reason about consistency levels and to make use of hybrid consistency as needed by the application semantics. As a result, such languages offer developers well-defined and formally-proven consistency guarantees "out-of-the-box". I will briefly overview some language-based solutions and will elaborate more on the effectiveness of reactive programming in enabling automated concurrency control and fault-tolerance with clear consistency guarantees. I will present the ideas in the context of REScala (rescala-lang.com) - a library-based extension to Scala - that we have designed and implemented in my lab. In REScala, applications are modeled as compositions of reactive abstractions, which denote time-changing values resulting from computations with reactive application semantics (i.e., computations get executed whenever their inputs change). We have reinterpreted and extended this programming model, thereby adopting multi-version consistency control, conflict-free replicated data types, and invariant-based reasoning to enable language-integrated handling of consistency in concurrent and distributed settings with well-defined guarantees.

Contents

Modelling: Structures and Implementations

Microservices

Tutorial

Modeling and Analyzing
Resource-Sensitive Actors: A Tutorial
Introduction

Rudolf Schlatte$^{(\boxtimes)}$ (iD), Einar Broch Johnsen(iD), Eduard Kamburjan(iD),
and Silvia Lizeth Tapia Tarifa(iD)

University of Oslo, Oslo, Norway
{rudi,einarj,eduard,sltarifa}@ifi.uio.no

Abstract. Actor languages decouple communication from synchronization, which makes them suitable for distributed and scalable applications with flexible synchronization patterns, but also facilitates analysis. ABS is a timed actor-based modeling language which supports cooperative scheduling and the specification of timing- and resource-sensitive behavior. Cooperative scheduling allows a process which is executing in an actor to be suspended while it is waiting for an event to occur, such that another process in the same actor can execute. Timed semantics allows the specification of the temporal behavior of the modeled system. Resource-sensitive behavior takes a supply and demand perspective of execution, relating cost centers which provision resources to processes which require them. These modeling concepts have been used in ABS to model cloud computing, e.g., data-processing applications running on the Hadoop platform and microservices running on containers orchestrated by Kubernetes. In this tutorial, we present ABS and its execution environment, and discuss the use of cooperative scheduling and resources in modeling cyber-physical systems and applications deployed on virtualized infrastructure.

Keywords: Resource-sensitive behavior · Cloud computing ·
Distributed actor systems

1 Introduction

Models of modern distributed applications often require that we not only describe the interactions between endpoints, but also precisely specify how the application uses system resources and how its timed behavior depends on these resources. In contexts such as cloud systems, the resource usage may be the critical property to be analyzed with the model. The resource model, the concurrency model and the performed computations all interact and cannot be analyzed in isolation. To model systems that incorporate all these aspects, we need modeling

This research is supported by the Research Council of Norway via the SIRIUS research center (Grant 237898).

F. Damiani and O. Dardha (Eds.): COORDINATION 2021, LNCS 12717, pp. 3–19, 2021.
https://doi.org/10.1007/978-3-030-78142-2_1

languages that are rich enough to express (a) timed behavior, (b) resource usage, (c) interactions between distributed components, and (d) complex computations.

This tutorial shows how these aspects of distributed applications can be combined in resource-sensitive models using the *Abstract Behavioral Specification* (ABS) language [19], which has been successfully applied in several industrial case studies of such systems (see Sect. 7). ABS is based on object-oriented programming principles. Its basics are easy to learn for anybody with basic programming experience in mainstream programming languages, such as Java. This tutorial gives a brief language overview and mainly focuses on the usage of its advanced features for modeling timed and resource-sensitive behavior. For a full overview of the language, we refer to the user manual [1].

Beyond an overview over the modeling features for timed and resource-sensitive behavior, we also address the practical questions of usage. We describe how to use the compiler and simulator, as well as additional features such as the built-in visualization and debugging capabilities: how to compile ABS models, how to run them, how to visualize their executions as interleaved scheduling decisions, and how to replay a specific scheduling. We suggest useful patterns for distributed resource modeling.

All example files in this paper are available at https://github.com/abstools/ absexamples/tree/master/collaboratory/tutorials/discotec-2021. For a detailed tutorial on other aspects of ABS, we refer to Hähnle [17] on the layered semantics of ABS and to Clarke et al. [11] for variability modeling.

Overview. Section 2 gives an overview of ABS and shows how to compile and execute a simple example. Section 3 goes into more depth on how to specify time and resource behavior, and Sect. 4 shows some typical patterns of larger distributed systems. Section 5 discusses visualization and external control of simulations, while Sect. 6 shows how to deterministically record and replay simulations. Finally, Sect. 7 gives pointers to further case studies and tools. Instructions on how to download and use the compiler toolchain of ABS can be found in Appendix A.

2   The ABS Language

ABS decouples communication and synchronization of processes running on actors via its use of (1) asynchronous method calls, (2) futures and (3) cooperative scheduling. *Asynchronous* method calls do not synchronize between caller and callee. Instead, the caller receives a *future*, which resolves once their callee process terminates later. Futures, thus, allow synchronization between processes on different actors (objects). Futures are first-class constructs in ABS, i.e., they can be explicitly represented and manipulated. Different processes inside one actor synchronize using *cooperative scheduling*: on each actor, only one process runs at a time, with scheduling happening at explicit release points. Schedulability of processes at the release point may depend on the state of a future, or on a Boolean condition over the state of the object the process runs on. ABS also includes a side-effect-free *functional layer* that is used to define functions and algebraic datatypes. This section presents ABS by way of example; for detailed reference, see the manual [1].

2.1   A Simple ABS Model

```
1  module Hello;
2  interface Hello {  Bool printMessage(); }
3
4  class Hello(String name) implements Hello {
5      Bool printMessage() { println(`Hello $name$!`);  return True; }
   }
6  // Main block:
7  {   Hello hello = new Hello("world");
8      Fut<Bool> f = hello!printMessage();
9      await f?;
10     Bool r = f.get;
11     println("Main block finished."); }
```

Fig. 1. A small ABS model

Figure 1 shows a very small ABS model. All ABS models consist of one or more **module** definitions, containing zero or more definitions of interfaces, classes, functions, or datatypes. An optional *main block* defines the behavior of a model.

The example defines an interface (Line 2) followed by a class implementing that interface (Line 4). (Note that since classes are not types in ABS, classes and interfaces may share the same name.) The main block starting at Line 7 first creates an object, then asynchronously sends it a `printMessage` and awaits for (i.e., synchronizes on) the resulting process to terminate, and finally retrieves the value stored in the future before printing a message. When removing Lines 9 and 10, the order of the two lines of output is nondeterministic. This is because the two `print` statements are executed in processes running on different actors (but usually the message from the main block will be printed first).

ABS models can be compiled to execute on Erlang with the command `absc -erlang` *filename* `.abs`. After compilation, models can be simulated using the command `gen/erl/run`.

Observe that during the execution of Lines 8–10 the message `print Message()` is put in the message pool of the object `hello`, then the `await` statement *suspends* the caller's execution process (in this case the main block) until the return value of that method `printMessage()` has been processed and stored in the future `f`. At this point, the calling process becomes schedulable again, and proceeds to retrieve the value stored in the future using a `get` expression. (A `get` expression without a preceding `await` *blocks* the process until the future is resolved, i.e., no other process will be scheduled.)

Suspending a process means that the object can execute other messages from its message pool in the meantime. ABS demands that each process suspends itself explicitly via **await** or termination. I.e., it is *not* possible that two processes (if the method is called twice) executing **printMessage** overlap. The method **printMessage** contains no **await** statement, so one process starts, prints and terminates before another one does the same.

ABS supports the shorthand **await o!m(args)** (where o is an object, m a method and **arg** the arguments to the method) for the statements **f = o!m(args); await f?;** and **o.m(args)** for **f = o!m(args); r = f.get;** which *blocks* the caller object (does not release control) until the future **f** has been resolved (i.e., the future has received the return value from the call). The statement **this.m(args)** models a synchronous self-call, which corresponds to a standard call to a subroutine (no blocking mechanism).

3   Specifying Time and Resource Behavior

Timed ABS [9] is an extension to the core ABS language that introduces a notion of abstract time. It allows the modeling of an explicit passage of time, to represent execution time inside methods. This modeling abstraction can be used to model, in addition to the functional behavior, the timing-related behavior of real systems running on real hardware. In contrast to real systems, time in an ABS model does not advance by itself. Instead, it is expressed in terms of a **duration** statement (as in, e.g., UPPAAL [27]). Timed ABS adds a clock to the language semantics that advances in response to **duration** statements, as in Line 7 in Fig. 4. Time is expressed as a rational number, so the clock can advance in infinitesimally small steps.

Deployment is modelled using *deployment components* [22]. A deployment component is a modelling abstraction that captures locations offering (restricted) computing *resources*. ABS also supports cost annotations associated to statements to model resource consumption, as in Line 6 in Fig. 4. The combination of deployment components with computing resources and cost annotations allows modeling implicit passage of time. Here time advances when the available resources per time interval have been consumed.

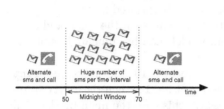

(a) The New Year's Eve client scenario.

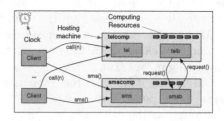

(b) The telephone company scenario.

Fig. 2. A scenario capturing client handsets and two telephone services with cooperating load balancers.

When integrating the time model and the resource consumption model, the global clock only advances when all processes are blocked or suspended and no process is ready to run. This means that for time to advance, all processes are in one of the following states: (1) the process is awaiting for a guard that is not enabled (using `await` statements); (2) the process is blocked on a future that is not available (using `get` expressions); (3) the process is suspended waiting for time to advance (using `duration`); or (4) the process is waiting for some resource (using cost annotations). In practice this means that all processes run as long as there is "work to be done," capturing the so called run-to-completion semantics.

In the rest of this section we present a simple example, adopted from [21], to showcase the behavioral specification of time and resource consumption.

3.1   Example: Phone Services on New Year's Eve

```
1 def Bool isMidnightWindow(Int interval) =
2   let Rat curr = timeValue(now()) % interval
3   in curr > 50 && curr < 70;
4
5 class Handset (Int interval, Int cyclelength, TelephoneServer ts,
  SMSServer smss) {
6   Bool call = False;
7   Unit run() {
8     while (timeValue(now()) < 250) {
9       if (isMidnightWindow(interval)) {
10        Int i = 0;
11        while (i < 10) { smss!sendSMS(); i = i + 1; }
12        await duration(1);
13      } else { if (call) { await ts!call(1); } else { smss!sendSMS();
   } }
14      call = !call;
15      await duration(cyclelength); } } }
```

Fig. 3. The client handset in Timed ABS.

At midnight on New Year's Eve, people stop making phone calls and instead send text messages with seasonal greetings. Inspired by this observation of human nature, we model a workload, depicted in Fig. 2a, in which people in a "normal" behavior alternate between a phone call and a message, but change their behavior during the so called "midnight window" to only sending a massive amount of messages. This behaviour is modeled by the handset clients implemented in Fig. 3. The handset makes requests to the two services. The normal behaviour of the handset is to alternate between sending an SMS and making a call at each time interval. When it makes a call, the client waits for the call to end before proceeding (synchronous call). The handset's spike occurs between the time window starting at time 50 and ending at time 70 that represents the

```
1  interface TelephoneServer  { Unit call(Int calltime);}
2  class TelephoneServer implements TelephoneServer  {
3    Int callcount = 0;
4    Unit call(Int calltime){
5      while (calltime > 0) {
6        [Cost: 1] calltime = calltime - 1;
7        await duration(1);}
8      callcount = callcount + 1;} }
9
10 interface SMSServer { Unit sendSMS();}
11 class SMSServer implements SMSServer  {
12   Int smscount = 0;
13   Unit sendSMS() { [Cost: 1] smscount = smscount + 1;} }
```

Fig. 4. The mobile phone services modelled in Timed ABS

"midnight window", and checked by the function isMidnightWindow in Fig. 3. During the spike, the handset sends 10 SMS requests at each time interval.

Telephone and SMS are the two services handling the method calls from the Handset. The services are deployed on dedicated virtual machines, as depicted in Fig. 2b. The abstract implementations of the services in Timed ABS are given in Fig. 4. The telephone service offers a method call which is invoked synchronously (i.e., the caller waits for the callee), with the duration of the call as parameter. The SMS service offers a method sendSMS which is invoked asynchronously (waiting from the callee is not needed). Cost are accrued for each time interval during a call and for each sendSMS invocation to model the computing resources that handling calls and messages consume.

The model also considers resources and includes dynamic load balancing, which enables the two virtual machines hosting the telephone and SMS services to exchange resources during load spikes. This is captured by the Balancer class in Fig. 5, whose instances run on each service. The Balancer class implements an abstract balancing strategy, transfers resources to its partner virtual machine when receiving a request message, monitors its own load, and requests assistance when needed. The class has an active process defined by its run method, which monitors the local load. The ABS expression thisDC() returns a reference to the deployment component on which an object is deployed, and the method call load(Speed, n) returns the average usage (0–100%) of processing speed in the previous n time intervals. If the load is above 90, the balancer requests resources from its partner. If a Balancer receives a request for resources, it will consider if it has enough resources and it is not overloaded, and if so, transfer part of its available computing resources to its partner, this guarantees that the capacity is always maintained above a minimum (see Line 16 in Fig. 5).

The configuration of the system, depicted in Fig. 2b, is given in the main block shown in Fig. 6. The two deployment components model the hosting virtual

```
1  class Balancer(String name, Rat minimum) implements Balancer {
2    Balancer partner = null;
3    Rat ld = 100;
4
5    Unit run() {
6      await partner != null;
7      while (timeValue(now()) < 250) {
8        await duration(1);
9        ld = await thisDC()!load(Speed, 1);
10       if (ld > 90) {await partner!requestdc(thisDC());} } }
11
12   Unit requestdc(DC comp) {
13     InfRat total = await thisDC()!total(Speed);
14     Rat ld = await thisDC()!load(Speed, 1);
15     Rat requested = finvalue(total) / 3;
16     if (ld < 50 && (finvalue(total)-requested>minimum)) {
17       thisDC()!transfer(comp, requested, Speed);} }
18
19   Unit setPartner(Balancer p) {partner = p;} }
```

Fig. 5. The balancer in Timed ABS

```
1  { Rat minimum = 15;
2    DC smsdc = new DeploymentComponent("smsdc",map[Pair(Speed, 80)]);
3    DC teldc = new DeploymentComponent("teldc",map[Pair(Speed, 80)]);
4    [DC: smsdc] SMSServer sms = new SMSServer();
5    [DC: teldc] TelephoneServer tel = new TelephoneServer();
6    [DC: smsdc] Balancer smsb = new Balancer("smsb",minimum);
7    [DC: teldc] Balancer telb = new Balancer("telb",minimum);
8    await smsb!setPartner(telb);
9    await telb!setPartner(smsb);
10
11   new Handset(100,1,tel,sms);   // start many clients
12   new ....
13 }
```

Fig. 6. The main block configuration Timed ABS

machines; objects are created inside deployment components via the [DC: id] annotations. After compilation, it is possible to simulate the example with the command gen/erl/run -l 100 -p 8080. Here -l 100 allows to run the model until simulated time 100, and -p 8080 allows to observe the load in the deployment components using a browser (via http://localhost:8080/, see Sect. 5 for more details about visualization).

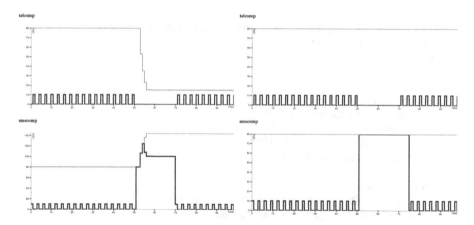

Fig. 7. Running the example with (to the left) and without (to the right) load balancing. Here red lines capture the available resources per time interval in the deployment components and blue lines capture the amount of used resources by the services per time interval. With load balancing the overload of the SMS service is quickly overcome after time 70, without load balancing the SMS service is overloaded until time 75. (Color figure online)

Figure 7 shows two simulations of the example, one with and one without active resource balancers (by commenting out Lines 6–9 in Fig. 6). Observe in particular the changing resp. constant total capacity of the two deployment components, and the duration of overload of the SMS component during and after the midnight window.

4   Advanced Synchronization Patterns

So far, we have seen asynchronous method calls that produce futures, and how to read the resulting value from such a future. This section shows some advanced synchronization patterns that an ABS model can employ to coordinate among a number of independent worker objects and their processes. We use as an example a model of MapReduce as originally described in [12]. The ABS source file is at https://github.com/abstools/absexamples/blob/master/collaboratory/tutorials/discotec-2021/MapReduce.abs.

4.1   Coordinating Multiple Processes via Object State

Our model of MapReduce employs a pool of worker machines, each modeled as an ABS object, and one coordinator object that creates `invokeMap` and `invokeReduce` processes on the workers, awaits the results, and calculates intermediate values and the final result.

```
1 Set<Worker> workers = set[];
2 Worker getWorker() {
3   Int maxWorkers = 5;
4   if (emptySet(workers) && nWorkers < maxWorkers) {
5     nWorkers = nWorkers + 1;
6     DeploymentComponent dc = new DeploymentComponent(
7       `worker $nWorkers$`, map[Pair(Speed, 20)]);
8     [DC: dc] Worker w = new Worker(this);
9     workers = insertElement(workers, w);
10  }
11  await size(workers) > 0;
12  Worker w = take(workers);
13  workers = remove(workers, w);
14  return w;
15 }
16 Unit finished(Worker w) {
17   workers = insertElement(workers, w);
18 }
```

Fig. 8. A worker pool in ABS with maximum size 5.

The coordinator implements the worker pool, as shown in Fig. 8, as an object field called workers. The two methods getWorker and finished coordinate via this field. (Remember that multiple processes of getWorker and finished can run at the same time.)

The method finished simply adds a worker back into the pool. The method getWorker, on the other hand, can only return workers that are currently in the pool. In case fewer workers than the maximum have been created, the condition in Line 4 evaluates to True and a new worker on a fresh deployment component is created and added to the pool.

Multiple processes can hit the await condition in Line 11; one of them will be woken up and return a worker object to the caller each time a worker is added to the pool via the finished method. Note that the worker itself can call finished after completing its task, thereby adding itself back to the pool, so the coordinator does not need to keep track of worker status.

```
1 foreach (item in items) {
2   Worker w = this.getWorker();
3   String key = fst(item); List<String> value = snd(item);
4   Fut<List<Pair<String, Int>>> fMap = w!invokeMap(key, value);
5   // Worker.invokeMap calls 'finished' after finishing the task
6   fMapResults = insertElement(fMapResults, fMap);
7 }
8 foreach (fMapResult in elements(fMapResults)) {
9   await fMapResult?;
10  List<Pair<String, Int>> mapResult = fMapResult.get;
11  // process results of this map task ...
12 }
```

Fig. 9. Distributing tasks among a pool of workers and collecting their results.

4.2 Synchronizing on Multiple Processes via Futures

Figure 9 shows how to distribute tasks among workers in such a worker pool and collect results afterwards. The set `fMapResults` holds the futures of the `invokeMap` processes. Tasks are distributed among worker instances obtained via `getWorker`, ensuring that each worker processes only one task at a time. After all tasks have been distributed, Line 8 and onward collect all results for further processing. It is easy to see that this constitutes a *barrier*; the subsequent `reduce` phase of the MapReduce model (not shown) will only start after all results from the `map` phase have been received by the coordinator.

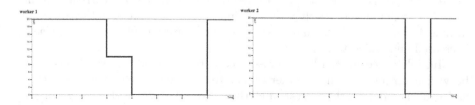

Fig. 10. Machine load during map and reduce phases. Reduce begins at time $t = 7$.

Figure 10 shows the load over time on the deployment components of two of the worker objects (the other three workers process tasks over the whole simulation run). It can be seen that the load on these workers starts dropping before time $t = 7$, where all `map` tasks are finished and the `reduce` phase begins. The graph shown is the default visualization implemented by the Model API (see Sect. 5).

5   Visualizations via the Model API

This section describes the Model API, a way to communicate with a running ABS model via HTTP requests. The Model API can be used to retrieve data from a model and to insert asynchronous method calls. At compile time, HTML and Javascript files can be added to a model to implement bespoke visualizations.

5.1   Exporting Objects and Methods

Objects and methods are made accessible for the model API via annotations. Figure 11 shows the use of the `HTTPCallable` annotation to mark the method `getText` in Line 3 as callable via the Model API, and the use of `HTTPName` in Line 9 to make the object `t` visible via the name `text`.

```
1 module Example;
2 interface Text {
3     [HTTPCallable] String getText();
4 }
5 class CText(String message) implements Text {
6     String getText() { return message; }
7 }
8 {
9     [HTTPName: "text"] Text t = new CText("This is the message");
10 }
```

Fig. 11. A Model API Example.

To use the Model API, the model is started with a parameter `-p xxxx`, where `xxxx` is the port number where the model listens for requests. After starting the above model with `gen/erl/run -p 8080`, calling the `getText` method from the command line results in a JSON-formatted result as follows:

```
$ curl localhost:8080/call/text/getText
{
  "result": "This is the message"
}
```

Full documentation of the Model API can be found in the ABS manual at https://abs-models.org/manual/#-the-model-api.

5.2   Adding a Custom Visualization

When a model is started with the parameter `-p xxxx`, it is possible to connect with a web browser to the URL `http://localhost:xxxx/` (where `xxxx` is a port number). By default, this URL shows a simple visualization of the load and total availability of the CPU resource of all deployment components in the model. It is possible to replace this visualization with custom, model-specific visualizations. This is done by compiling the model with the parameter -modelapi-index-file and giving the name of a HTML file which will then be displayed by the browser. Additionally, the parameter -modelapi-static-dir can be used to include a directory of static assets (Javascript libraries, graphics files, CSS stylesheets, etc.) into the model. These files are accessible within the Model API with /static/*filename*.

For space reasons, this paper does not show an example of this technique. We have prepared a worked example of a water tank controller and a simulated water tank which can be found at https://abs-models.org/documentation/examples/single-watertank/.

6   Record and Replay of Simulations

As already discussed, the semantics of the ABS language are nondeterministic wrt. scheduling of processes. This section discusses a feature of the ABS simulator that makes it possible to *record and replay* simulator runs, such that the scheduling decisions taken during record are faithfully reproduced during replay. This section only shows how to use this feature; a technical discussion can be found in [32].

```
1 module Example;
2 interface Printer {
3     Unit printMessage(String message);
4 }
5 class CPrinter implements Printer {
6     Unit printMessage(String message) {
7         println(`The message is: $message$`);
8     }
9 }
10 {
11     Printer printer = new CPrinter();
12     foreach (m in list["Hello", "Hola", "Hallo", "Hei"]) {
13         printer!printMessage(m);
14     }
15 }
```

Fig. 12. A nondeterministic ABS program.

Consider the ABS code in Fig. 12, which will print four different greetings in arbitrary order when run. Running the example with the command gen/erl/run -t trace.json will produce a file trace.json. Afterwards, running with the command gen/erl/run -r trace.json will print the same interleaving of messages as observed during the recording run.

7   Case Studies and Other Analysis Tools

Fredhopper Cloud Services provides search and targeting facilities for e-commerce retailers as a service (SaaS) [3]. Their software is under constant development and relies on automated configuration [16], continuous monitoring and testing. Using ABS-models allows changes to be analyzed prior to deployment. This includes low-level effects such as consuming the resources of a DC.

For the Fredhopper case study, a general replay tool for logs from the production system was built [6]. The replay tool interacts with the simulator via the Model API and enables simulating real-world scenarios from Fredhopper's system logs. This was used to validate the correlation between the model and the actual system, and for predicting the effects of changes in the system.

ABS-YARN is a case study showing how ABS may be used for modeling applications running on Apache's Hadoop YARN framework with different configurations [30]. Hadoop is a popular cloud infrastructure system and YARN (Yet Another Resource Negotiator) provides a platform for job scheduling and for cluster resource management for Hadoop configurations.

Simulation shows that the ABS framework can accurately reflect the behavior of YARN and can efficiently compare different deployment decisions. This work was extended to Hadoop Spark Streaming [28] and used to study different instance purchasing options provided by Amazon Web Services [20].

The HyVar toolchain is a framework that targets context-dependent software upgrades for car ECUs (Electronic Control Units). The framework collects information from a fleet of cars, analyzes this information to decide how to update the software running on the different cars, and sends software updates back to the cars when needed. The objective of the Timed ABS simulations was to efficiently analyze the *scalability* of the toolchain [29].

Multicore Memory Systems. This case study focussed on how a model of multicore memory systems [8], formalized in structural operational semantics, could be implemented as a simulator of memory operations on a multicore architecture in ABS. The focus of this work was on correctness preserving transformations of operational rules with pattern matching synchronization conditions at the SOS level to a decentralised and asynchronous actor model [7]. The await-statements of ABS were crucial to ensure a granularity of interleaving between processes which corresponded to the SOS model.

Kubernetes. This case study develops a formal model in Timed ABS of a containerized orchestration system for cloud-native microservices, which are loosely-coupled collections of services designed to be able to adapt to traffic in very fine-grained and flexible ways. The model focussed on resource consumption and scaling of microservices deployed and managed by Kubernetes [18].

This work performed experiments on HPC4AI, a cluster for deploying high-performance applications, in order to compare the observed behavior of real systems to corresponding observations of instances of the model [31].

Compugene is a case study that models transcription of mRNA in the context of computational biology[1]. To do so, the effect of different rates of degradation in neighboring cells has been taken into account. The time model of ABS is crucial to model biological processes.

The simulation is used to compare the mathematical model (expressed in ABS) with experimental results, with the aim to reduce the need for the more time-consuming experiments.

FormbaR is a case study that models the railway operations rulebooks of the main German railway infrastructure company [24]. Using an executable model, changes in the rulebooks can be prototyped with quick feedback cycles for their maintenance. The time model is needed to faithfully mirror train driving.

The simulator was leveraged for analyzing the effects of rule changes. A special visualization tool using the Model API is used to interact with the simulation without modifying the ABS code and to summarize the results of the execution [26]. In a more general context, this shows how the model API enables *debugging tools* where the user can inject faults and observe the outcome.

Other Tools

Several static analyses tools have been developed for ABS and we list them here together with bigger case studies that use them, as they offer further insights into modeling with ABS in practice. For tools and case studies of other Active Object languages we refer to the survey by de Boer et al. [10]. Many static analyses, such as deadlock checkers, are bundled in the SACO [2] suite and its extensions [23].

Systematic Checking. Systematic testing explores all execution paths in a program and is implemented for ABS in the SYCO tool [4]. SYCO has been applied to check properties of Software defined networks [5], a paradigm to dynamically and flexibly adapt the policy of network-switches using a central controller and the C-to-ABS [33] framework, a tool that translates C into ABS code to analyze safety properties of C code with underspecified behavior.

Deductive Verification. Deductive verification checks safety properties, such as object invariants, using logical reasoning and as such can reason about unbounded systems and unbounded inputs. Two deductive verification tools are available for ABS: KeY-ABS [13], which has been used to verify a Network-on-Chip packet switching platform [14] and Crowbar [25], which has been applied to a case study in the C-to-ABS framework described above.

A   Installing the ABS Compiler

The ABS compiler is contained in a file `absfrontend.jar`; the latest released version can be found at https://github.com/abstools/abstools/releases/latest. To run the compiler and the generated models, a Java development kit (JDK) version 11 or greater, and Erlang version 22 or greater must be installed.

---

[1] https://www.compugene.tu-darmstadt.de.

Then, to compile an ABS file `model.abs`, use the command `java -jar absfrond.jar -erlang model.abs`. The compiler creates a subdirectory `gen/`, the compiled model can be run with the command `gen/erl/run` (or, on Windows, `gen/erl/run.bat`).

More detailed installation instructions, including links to the necessary software, is at https://abs-models.org/getting_started/local-install/.

Models that do not use the Model API can also be written and run in a web-based IDE based on EasyInterface [15]. To run the collaboratory locally, install docker[2] then run the following command: `docker run -d -rm -p 8080:80 -name collaboratory abslang/collaboratory:latest` and connect a browser to `http://localhost:8080/`. On the start page, you can access ABS documentation and examples, and go to the web-based IDE. To shut down the collaboratory, run the command `docker stop collaboratory`.

References

1. ABS Development Team: ABS Documentation. Version 1.9.2. https://abs-models.org/manual/
2. Albert, E., et al.: SACO: static analyzer for concurrent objects. In: Ábrahám, E., Havelund, K. (eds.) TACAS 2014. LNCS, vol. 8413, pp. 562–567. Springer, Heidelberg (2014). https://doi.org/10.1007/978-3-642-54862-8_46
3. Albert, E., et al.: Formal modeling and analysis of resource management for cloud architectures: an industrial case study using Real-Time ABS. Serv. Oriented Comput. Appl. **8**(4), 323–339 (2014)
4. Albert, E., Gómez-Zamalloa, M., Isabel, M.: SYCO: a systematic testing tool for concurrent objects. In: CC, pp. 269–270. ACM (2016)
5. Albert, E., Gómez-Zamalloa, M., Isabel, M., Rubio, A., Sammartino, M., Silva, A.: Actor-based model checking for software-defined networks. J. Log. Algebraic Methods Program. **118**, 100617 (2021)
6. Bezirgiannis, N., de Boer, F., de Gouw, S.: Human-in-the-loop simulation of cloud services. In: De Paoli, F., Schulte, S., Broch Johnsen, E. (eds.) ESOCC 2017. LNCS, vol. 10465, pp. 143–158. Springer, Cham (2017). https://doi.org/10.1007/978-3-319-67262-5_11
7. Bezirgiannis, N., de Boer, F., Johnsen, E.B., Pun, K.I., Tapia Tarifa, S.L.: Implementing SOS with active objects: a case study of a multicore memory system. In: Hähnle, R., van der Aalst, W. (eds.) FASE 2019. LNCS, vol. 11424, pp. 332–350. Springer, Cham (2019). https://doi.org/10.1007/978-3-030-16722-6_20
8. Bijo, S., Johnsen, E.B., Pun, K.I., Tapia Tarifa, S.L.: A formal model of data access for multicore architectures with multilevel caches. Sci. Comput. Program. **179**, 24–53 (2019)
9. Bjørk, J., de Boer, F.S., Johnsen, E.B., Schlatte, R., Tapia Tarifa, S.L.: User-defined schedulers for real-time concurrent objects. Innov. Syst. Softw. Eng. **9**(1), 29–43 (2013)
10. de Boer, F.S., Serbanescu, V., et al.: A survey of active object languages. ACM Comput. Surv. **50**(5), 76:1–76:39 (2017)

---

[2] https://www.docker.com/products/docker-desktop.

11. Clarke, D., Muschevici, R., Proença, J., Schaefer, I., Schlatte, R.: Variability modelling in the ABS language. In: Aichernig, B.K., de Boer, F.S., Bonsangue, M.M. (eds.) FMCO 2010. LNCS, vol. 6957, pp. 204–224. Springer, Heidelberg (2011). https://doi.org/10.1007/978-3-642-25271-6_11

12. Dean, J., Ghemawat, S.: MapReduce: simplified data processing on large clusters. Commun. ACM **51**(1), 107–113 (2008)

13. Din, C.C., Bubel, R., Hähnle, R.: KeY-ABS: a deductive verification tool for the concurrent modelling language ABS. In: Felty, A.P., Middeldorp, A. (eds.) CADE 2015. LNCS (LNAI), vol. 9195, pp. 517–526. Springer, Cham (2015). https://doi.org/10.1007/978-3-319-21401-6_35

14. Din, C.C., Tapia Tarifa, S.L., Hähnle, R., Johnsen, E.B.: History-based specification and verification of scalable concurrent and distributed systems. In: Butler, M., Conchon, S., Zaïdi, F. (eds.) ICFEM 2015. LNCS, vol. 9407, pp. 217–233. Springer, Cham (2015). https://doi.org/10.1007/978-3-319-25423-4_14

15. Doménech, J., Genaim, S., Johnsen, E.B., Schlatte, R.: EASYINTERFACE: a toolkit for rapid development of GUIs for research prototype tools. In: Huisman, M., Rubin, J. (eds.) FASE 2017. LNCS, vol. 10202, pp. 379–383. Springer, Heidelberg (2017). https://doi.org/10.1007/978-3-662-54494-5_22

16. de Gouw, S., Mauro, J., Nobakht, B., Zavattaro, G.: Declarative elasticity in ABS. In: Aiello, M., Johnsen, E.B., Dustdar, S., Georgievski, I. (eds.) ESOCC 2016. LNCS, vol. 9846, pp. 118–134. Springer, Cham (2016). https://doi.org/10.1007/978-3-319-44482-6_8

17. Hähnle, R.: The abstract behavioral specification language: a tutorial introduction. In: Giachino, E., Hähnle, R., de Boer, F.S., Bonsangue, M.M. (eds.) FMCO 2012. LNCS, vol. 7866, pp. 1–37. Springer, Heidelberg (2013). https://doi.org/10.1007/978-3-642-40615-7_1

18. Hightower, K., Burns, B., Beda, J.: Kubernetes: Up and Running Dive into the Future of Infrastructure. O'Reilly (2017)

19. Johnsen, E.B., Hähnle, R., Schäfer, J., Schlatte, R., Steffen, M.: ABS: a core language for abstract behavioral specification. In: Aichernig, B.K., de Boer, F.S., Bonsangue, M.M. (eds.) FMCO 2010. LNCS, vol. 6957, pp. 142–164. Springer, Heidelberg (2011). https://doi.org/10.1007/978-3-642-25271-6_8

20. Johnsen, E.B., Lin, J.-C., Yu, I.C.: Comparing AWS deployments using model-based predictions. In: Margaria, T., Steffen, B. (eds.) ISoLA 2016. LNCS, vol. 9953, pp. 482–496. Springer, Cham (2016). https://doi.org/10.1007/978-3-319-47169-3_39

21. Johnsen, E.B., Owe, O., Schlatte, R., Tapia Tarifa, S.L.: Dynamic resource reallocation between deployment components. In: Dong, J.S., Zhu, H. (eds.) ICFEM 2010. LNCS, vol. 6447, pp. 646–661. Springer, Heidelberg (2010). https://doi.org/10.1007/978-3-642-16901-4_42

22. Johnsen, E.B., Schlatte, R., Tapia Tarifa, S.L.: Integrating deployment architectures and resource consumption in timed object-oriented models. J. Log. Algebr. Methods Program. **84**(1), 67–91 (2015)

23. Kamburjan, E.: Detecting deadlocks in formal system models with condition synchronization. Electron. Commun. Eur. Assoc. Softw. Sci. Technol. **76**, (2018)

24. Kamburjan, E., Hähnle, R., Schön, S.: Formal modeling and analysis of railway operations with active objects. Sci. Comput. Program. **166**, 167–193 (2018)

25. Kamburjan, E., Scaletta, M., Rollshausen, N.: Crowbar: behavioral symbolic execution for deductive verification of active objects. CoRR abs/2102.10127 (2021)

26. Kamburjan, E., Stromberg, J.: Tool support for validation of formal system models: interactive visualization and requirements traceability. In: F-IDE@FM, EPTCS, vol. 310, pp. 70–85 (2019)
27. Larsen, K.G., Pettersson, P., Yi, W.: UPPAAL in a nutshell. J. Softw. Tools Technol. Transf. 1(1–2), 134–152 (1997)
28. Lin, J., Lee, M., Yu, I.C., Johnsen, E.B.: A configurable and executable model of Spark Streaming on Apache YARN. Int. J. Grid Util. Comput. **11**(2), 185–195 (2020)
29. Lin, J.C., Mauro, J., Røst, T.B., Yu, I.C.: A model-based scalability optimization methodology for cloud applications. In: IEEE SC2, pp. 163–170. IEEE Computer Society (2017)
30. Lin, J.-C., Yu, I.C., Johnsen, E.B., Lee, M.-C.: ABS-YARN: a formal framework for modeling Hadoop YARN clusters. In: Stevens, P., Wąsowski, A. (eds.) FASE 2016. LNCS, vol. 9633, pp. 49–65. Springer, Heidelberg (2016). https://doi.org/10.1007/978-3-662-49665-7_4
31. Turin, G., Borgarelli, A., Donetti, S., Johnsen, E.B., Tapia Tarifa, S.L., Damiani, F.: A formal model of the Kubernetes container framework. In: Margaria, T., Steffen, B. (eds.) ISoLA 2020. LNCS, vol. 12476, pp. 558–577. Springer, Cham (2020). https://doi.org/10.1007/978-3-030-61362-4_32
32. Tveito, L., Johnsen, E.B., Schlatte, R.: Global reproducibility through local control for distributed active objects. FASE 2020. LNCS, vol. 12076, pp. 140–160. Springer, Cham (2020). https://doi.org/10.1007/978-3-030-45234-6_7
33. Wasser, N., Tabar, A.H., Hähnle, R.: Automated model extraction: from nondeterministic C code to active objects. Sci. Comput. Program. **204**, 102597 (2021)

Communications: Types and Implemenations

Manifestly Phased Communication via Shared Session Types

Chuta Sano$^{(\boxtimes)}$, Stephanie Balzer, and Frank Pfenning

Carnegie Mellon University, Pittsburgh, USA

Abstract. Session types denote message protocols between concurrent processes, allowing a type-safe expression of inter-process communication. Although previous work demonstrate a well-defined notion of subtyping where processes have different perceptions of the protocol, these formulations were limited to linear session types where each channel of communication has a unique provider and client. In this paper, we extend subtyping to shared session types where channels can now have multiple clients instead of a single client. We demonstrate that this generalization can statically capture protocol requirements that span multiple phases of interactions of a client with a shared service provider, something not possible in prior proposals. Moreover, the phases are manifest in the type of the client.

1 Introduction

Session types prescribe bidirectional communication protocols between concurrent processes [15,16]. Variations of this type system were later given logical correspondences with *intuitionistic* [4] and *classical* [22] linear logic where proofs correspond to programs and cut reduction to communication. This correspondence mainly provided an interpretation of *linear session types*, which denote sessions with exactly one client and one provider. *Shared session types*, which encode communication between multiple clients and one provider, were proposed with a *sharing semantics* interpretation in a prior work [2]. Clients communicating along a shared channel follow an *acquire-release* discipline where they must first *acquire* exclusive access to the provider, communicate linearly, and then finally *release* the exclusive access, allowing other clients to acquire.

However, not all protocols that follow this acquire-release paradigm are safe; if a client that successfully acquires some shared channel of type A releases it at an unrelated type B, other clients that are blocked while trying to acquire will still see the channel as type A while the provider will see the channel as type B. To resolve this, we require an additional constraint that clients must release at the same type at which it acquired. This was formally expressed in [2] as the *equi-synchronizing* constraint, which statically verifies that session types encode communication which does not release at the wrong type. Although shared session types serve an important role in making session typed process calculi theory

© IFIP International Federation for Information Processing 2021
Published by Springer Nature Switzerland AG 2021
F. Damiani and O. Dardha (Eds.): COORDINATION 2021, LNCS 12717, pp. 23–40, 2021.
https://doi.org/10.1007/978-3-030-78142-2_2

applicable to practical scenarios, we previously [19] showed that shared session types cannot express *phases*, or protocols across successive acquire-release cycles, due to the equi-synchronizing constraint being too restrictive (see Sect. 5).

We demonstrate that subtyping, first formalized in the session-typed process calculi setting by Gay and Hole [11], and its behavior across the two linear and shared modalities provide the groundwork for an elegant relaxation of the equi-synchronizing constraint, allowing for phases to be *manifest* in the session type. In message passing concurrency, subtyping allows a client and provider to safely maintain their own local views on the session type (or protocol) associated with a particular channel. Although previous papers [1,11] investigate subtyping in the purely linear session type setting, we found that extending these results to the linear and shared session type setting as in [2] yields very powerful results with both practical and theoretical significance.

In this paper, we build upon past results on subtyping and propose a formulation of subtyping compatible with shared session types. We in particular introduce the *subsynchronizing* constraint, a relaxation of the equi-synchronizing constraint.

The main contributions of this paper include:

- A full formalization of a subtyping relation for shared session types and their meta theory.
- The introduction of the subsynchronizing constraint, a relaxation of the equi-synchronizing constraint.
- Illustrations of practical examples in this richer type system, further bridging the gap between session-typed process calculi and practical programming languages.

The rest of the paper will proceed as follows: Sect. 2 provides a brief introduction to linear and shared session-typed message-passing concurrency. Section 3 demonstrates the inability for prior systems to express phasing and motivates our approach. Section 4 provides an introduction to linear subtyping along with an attempt to extend the relation to the shared setting. Section 5 introduces the notion of phasing and the subsynchronizing judgment. Section 6 presents a message passing concurrent system using our typesystem and the corresponding progress and preservation statements. Section 7 discusses related work. Section 8 concludes the paper with some points of discussion and future work.

An extended version of this paper is available as a technical report [20], containing detailed proofs, a complete formalization of the system, and more complex examples. This paper will focus on our advancements to the type system and key ideas while treating the syntax of the language and the operational interpretation informally.

2   Background

2.1   Linear Session Types

Based on the correspondence established between intuitionistic linear logic and the session-typed π-calculus [4, 21] we can interpret a intuitionistic *linear* sequent

$$A_1, A_2, \ldots, A_n \vdash B$$

as the typing judgment for a process P by annotating the linear propositions with channel names:

$$\underbrace{a_1 : A_1, a_2 : A_2, \ldots, a_n : A_n}_{\Delta} \vdash P :: (b : B)$$

Interpreted as a typing judgment, we say that process P *provides* a session of type B along channel b while *using* channels $a_1, \ldots, a_n$ with session types $A_1, \ldots, A_n$, respectively. Interpreted as a sequent, we say that P is a proof of some proposition B with hypotheses $A_1, \ldots, A_n$. Following linear logic, the context Δ is restricted and rejects contraction and weakening. Programatically, this means that linear channels cannot be aliased nor freely deleted – they must be fully consumed exactly once.

Since the session type associated with a channel denotes a bidirectional protocol, each connective has two operational interpretations – one from the perspective of the provider and one from the client. This operationally dual interpretation results in a schema where for any connective, either the client or provider will send while the other will receive as summarized in Table 1.

For example, a channel of type $A \otimes 1$ requires that the provider sends a channel of type A and proceeds as type 1 while the client receives a channel of type A and proceeds as 1. The multiplicative unit 1 denotes the end of the protocol – the provider must terminate and close its channel while a client must wait for the channel to be closed. A channel of type $\oplus\{\overline{l : A}\}$ (n-nary internal choice) requires the provider to choose and send a label i in $\overline{l}$ and proceed as A_i while the client must receive and branch on some label i and proceed as A_i. Similarly, a channel of type $\&\{\overline{l : A}\}$ requires the client to choose and send a label and the provider to receive and branch on a label. The *continuation type* of some session type refers to the type after a message exchange; for example, B would be the continuation type of $A \otimes B$ and similarly A_i of $\oplus\{\overline{l : A}\}$ for some i in $\overline{l}$. The unit 1 does not have a continuation type since it marks the end of communication.

We consider a session type denoting the interaction with a provider of a queue of integers, which we will develop throughout the paper:

$$\textbf{queue} = \&\{\,enqueue : \text{int} \supset \textbf{queue},$$
$$dequeue : \oplus\{\,some : \text{int} \land \textbf{queue}, \, none : \textbf{queue}\}\}$$

Table 1. A summary of the linear connectives and their operational interpretations

Type	Interpretation from provider	Interpretation from client	Continuation
1	Close channel (terminate)	Wait for channel to close	-
$A \otimes B$	Send channel of type A	Receive channel of type A	B
$A \multimap B$	Receive channel of type A	Send channel of type A	B
$\oplus\{\overline{l : A}\}$	Send a label $i \in \overline{l}$	Receive and branch on $i \in \overline{l}$	A_i
$\&\{\overline{l : A}\}$	Receive and branch on $i \in \overline{l}$	Send a label $i \in \overline{l}$	A_i

where we informally adopt value input and output $\supset$ and $\wedge$ [21] as value ana-
logues to channel input and output $\multimap$ and $\otimes$, respectively, which are orthogonal
to the advancements in this work. Following this protocol, a client must send a
label *enqueue* or *dequeue*. If it chooses *enqueue*, it must send an int and then
recur, and on the other hand, if it chooses *dequeue*, it will receive either some int
as indicated by the *some* branch of the internal choice or nothing as indicated
by the *none* branch. In either case, we let the queue recur[1]. Dually, a server
must first receive a label *enqueue* or *dequeue* from the client. If it receives an
enqueue, it will receive an int and then recur. If it receives a *dequeue* instead, it
must either send a *some* label followed by the appropriate int and then recur or
send a *none* label and then recur.

We adopt an *equi-recursive* [8] interpretation which requires that recursive
session types be *contractive* [11], guaranteeing that there are no messages associated with the unfolding of a recursive type. This in particular requires that we
reason about session types *coinductively*.

We now attempt to encode a protocol representing an auction based on [9].
An auction transitions between the bidding phase where clients are allowed to
place bids and the collecting phase where a winner is given the item while all
the losers are refunded their respective bids.

$$\textbf{bidding} = \&\{ bid : \oplus \{ ok : \text{id} \supset \text{money} \supset \textbf{bidding},$$
$$collecting : \textbf{collecting}\}\}$$
$$\textbf{collecting} = \&\{ collect : \text{id} \supset \oplus \{ prize : \text{item} \wedge \textbf{bidding},$$
$$refund : \text{money} \wedge \textbf{bidding},$$
$$bidding : \textbf{bidding}\}\}$$

In this example, we make the bidding phase and collecting phase explicit by
separating the protocol into **bidding** and **collecting**. Beginning with **bidding**,
a client must send a *bid* label[2]. The provider will either respond with an *ok*,
allowing the client to make a bid by sending its id, money, and then recursing
back to **bidding**, or a *collecting*, indicating that the auction is in the collecting
phase and thereby making the client transition to **collecting**.

---

[1] We do not consider termination to more easily align with later examples.

[2] The currently unnecessary unary choice will be useful later.

For **collecting**, the client must send a *collect* label. For ease of presentation, we require the client to also send its id immediately, giving enough information to the provider to know if the client should receive a *prize* or a *refund*, along with *bidding* if the client is in the wrong phase. The *prize* branch covers the case where the client won the previous bid, the *refund* branch covers the case where the client lost the bid, and the *bidding* branch informs the client that the auction is currently in the bidding phase.

Because linear channels have exactly one provider and one client, what we have described so far only encodes a single participant auction. One can assert that the provider is actually a broker to an auction of multiple participants, but that does not solve the fundamental problem, that is, encoding shared communication with multiple clients.

2.2 Shared Session Types

Although linear session types and their corresponding process calculi give a system with strong guarantees such as *session fidelity* (preservation) and *deadlock freedom* (progress), as we show in the previous section while attemping to encode an auction, they are not expressive enough to model systems with shared resources. Since multiple clients cannot simultaneously communicate to a single provider in an unrestricted manner, we adopt an *acquire-release* paradigm. The only action a client can perform on a shared channel is to send an acquire request, which the provider must accept. After successfully acquiring, the client is guaranteed to have exclusive access to the provider and therefore can communicate linearly until the client releases its exclusive access.

Instead of treating the acquire and release operations as mere operational primitives, in prior work [2] we extend the type system such that the acquire and release points are manifest in the type by stratifying session types into shared and linear types. Unlike linear channels, shared channels are unrestricted in that they can be freely aliased or deleted. In the remaining sections, we will make the distinction between linear and shared explicit by marking channel names and session type meta-variables with subscripts L and S respectively where appropriate. For example, a linear channel is marked a_L, while a shared channel is marked b_S.

Since shared channels represent unrestricted channels that must first be acquired, we introduce the modal upshift operator $\uparrow_L^S A_L$ for some A_L which requires clients to acquire and then proceed linearly as prescribed by A_L. Similarly, the modal downshift operator $\downarrow_L^S B_S$ for some B_S requires clients to release and proceed as a shared type. Type theoretically, these modal shifts mark transitions between shared to linear and vice versa. In summary, we have:

(Shared Layer) $A_S ::= \uparrow_L^S A_L$

(Linear Layer) $A_L, B_L ::= \downarrow_L^S A_S \mid 1 \mid A_L \otimes B_L \mid A_L \multimap B_L \mid \&\{\overline{l{:}A_L}\} \mid \oplus\{\overline{l{:}A_L}\}$

where we emphasize that the previously defined (linear) type operators such as $\otimes$ remain only at the linear layer – a shared session type can only be constructed by a modal upshift $\uparrow_L^S$ of some linear session type A_L.

As initially introduced, clients of shared channels follow an *acquire-release* pattern – they must first acquire exclusive access to the channel, proceed linearly, and then finally release the exclusive access that they had, allowing other clients of the same shared channel to potentially acquire exclusive access. The middle linear section can also be viewed as a *critical region* since the client is guaranteed unique access to a shared provider process. Therefore, this system naturally supports atomic operations on shared resources.

Using shared channels, we can encode a shared queue, where there can be multiple clients interacting with the same data:

$$
\begin{aligned}
\textbf{shared\_queue} = \uparrow_L^S \& \{ & enqueue : \text{int} \supset \downarrow_L^S \text{shared\_queue}, \\
& dequeue : \oplus \{ some : \text{int} \wedge \downarrow_L^S \text{shared\_queue}, \\
& \qquad\qquad none : \downarrow_L^S \text{shared\_queue} \} \}
\end{aligned}
$$

A client of such a channel must first send an **acquire** message, being blocked until the acquisition is successful. Upon acquisition, the client must then proceed linearly as in the previously defined linear queue. The only difference is that before recursing, the client must **release** its exclusive access, allowing other blocked clients to successfully acquire.

3   Equi-Synchronizing Rules Out Phasing

We can also attempt to salvage the previous attempt of encoding (multi-participant) auctions by "wrapping" the previous purely linear protocol between $\uparrow_L^S$ and $\downarrow_L^S$.

$$
\begin{aligned}
\textbf{bidding} = \uparrow_L^S \& \{ & bid : \oplus \{ ok : \text{id} \supset \text{money} \supset \downarrow_L^S \text{bidding}, \\
& \qquad\quad collecting : \downarrow_L^S \text{collecting} \} \} \\
\textbf{collecting} = \uparrow_L^S \& \{ & collect : \text{id} \supset \oplus \{ prize : \text{item} \wedge \downarrow_L^S \text{bidding}, \\
& \qquad\qquad\quad refund : \text{money} \wedge \downarrow_L^S \text{bidding}, \\
& \qquad\qquad\quad bidding : \downarrow_L^S \text{bidding} \} \}
\end{aligned}
$$

A client to **bidding** must first acquire exclusive access as indicated by $\uparrow_L^S$, proceed linearly, and then eventually release at either **bidding** (in the *ok* branch) or **collecting** (in the *collecting* branch). Similarly, a client to **collecting** must first acquire exclusive access, proceed linearly, and then eventually release at **bidding** since all branches lead to **bidding**.

Unfortunately, as formulated so far, this protocol is not sound. For example, consider two auction participants P and Q that are both in the collecting phase and blocked trying to acquire. Suppose P successfully acquires, in which case it follows the protocol linearly and eventually releases at **bidding**. Then, if Q successfully acquires, we have a situation where Q rightfully believes that it acquired at **collecting** but since P previously released at type **bidding**, the auctioneer believes that it currently accepted a connection from **bidding**. The subsequent label sent by the client, *collect* is not an available option for the provider; session fidelity has been violated.

Previous work [2] addresses this problem by introducing an additional requirement that if a channel was acquired at some type A_s, all possible future releases (by looking at the continuation types) must release at A_s. This is formulated as the *equi-synchronizing* constraint, defined coinductively on the structure of session types. In particular, neither **bidding** nor **collecting** are equi-synchronizing because they do not always release at the same type at which it was acquired. For **bidding**, the *collecting* branch causes a release at a different type, and for **collecting**, all branches lead to a release at a different type.

A solution to the auction scenario is to unify the two phases into one:

$$\mathbf{auction} = \uparrow_L^S \& \{bid : \oplus \{ok : \mathrm{id} \supset \mathrm{money} \supset \downarrow_L^S \mathbf{auction},$$
$$collecting : \downarrow_L^S \mathbf{auction}\},$$
$$collect : \mathrm{id} \supset \oplus \{prize : \mathrm{item} \wedge \downarrow_L^S \mathbf{auction},$$
$$refund : \mathrm{money} \wedge \downarrow_L^S \mathbf{auction},$$
$$bidding : \downarrow_L^S \mathbf{auction}\}\}$$

The type **auction** is indeed equi-synchronizing because all possible release points are at **auction**.

This presentation of the auction however loses the explicit denotation of the two phases; although the previous linear single participant version of the auction protocol can make explicit the bidding and collecting phases in the session type, the equi-synchronizing requirement forces the two phases to merge into one in the case of shared session types. In general, the requirement that all release points are equivalent prevents shared session types to encode protocols across multiple acquire-release cycles since information is necessarily "lost" after a particular acquire-release cycle.

4   Subtyping

So far, there is an implicit requirement that given a particular channel, both its provider and clients agree on its protocol or type. A relaxation of this requirement in the context of linear session types have been investigated by Gay and Hole [11], and in this section, we present subtyping in the context of both linear session types and shared session types.

If $A \leq B$, then a provider viewing its offering channel as type A can safely communicate with a client viewing the same channel as type B. This perspective reveals a notion of *substitutability*, where a process providing a channel of type A can be replaced by a process providing A' such that $A' \leq A$ and dually, a client to some channel of type B can be replaced by another process using the same channel as some type B' such that $B \leq B'$. The following subtyping rules, interpreted coinductively, formalize the subtyping relation between session types:

$$\frac{}{1 \leq 1} \leq_1 \qquad \frac{A_L \leq A'_L \quad B_L \leq B'_L}{A_L \otimes B_L \leq A'_L \otimes B'_L} \leq_\otimes \qquad \frac{A'_L \leq A_L \quad B_L \leq B'_L}{A_L \multimap B_L \leq A'_L \multimap B'_L} \leq_{\multimap}$$

$$\frac{\forall i \in \bar{l} \quad A_{iL} \leq A'_{iL}}{\oplus\{\overline{l{:}A_L}\} \leq \oplus\{\overline{l{:}A'_L}, \overline{m{:}B_L}\}} \leq_\oplus \qquad \frac{\forall i \in \bar{l} \quad A_{iL} \leq A'_{iL}}{\&\{\overline{l{:}A_L}, \overline{m{:}B_L}\} \leq \&\{\overline{l{:}A'_L}\}} \leq_\&$$

One of the notable consequences of adopting subtyping is that internal and external choices allow one side to have more labels or branches. For internal choice, since the provider sends some label, there is no harm in a client to be prepared to handle additional labels that it will never receive and vice versa for external choice. Another observation is that subtyping of session types is covariant in their continuations; following this paradigm, we can immediately define subtyping for the new type connectives $\uparrow^S_L$ and $\downarrow^S_L$:

$$\frac{A_L \leq B_L}{\uparrow^S_L A_L \leq \uparrow^S_L B_L} \leq_{\uparrow^S_L} \qquad \frac{A_S \leq B_S}{\downarrow^S_L A_S \leq \downarrow^S_L B_S} \leq_{\downarrow^S_L}$$

Remark 1. The subtyping relation $\leq$ is a partial order.

A key principle governing subtyping of session types is that *ignorance is bliss*; neither the client nor the provider need to know the precise protocol that the other party is following, as supported by our extended report [20] which proves the same progress and preservation theorems in an implementation of session typed process calculus with shared channels [2] in a system with subtyping.

Let us revisit the shared queue example:

$$\mathbf{shared\_queue} = \uparrow^S_L \&\{enqueue : \text{int} \supset \downarrow^S_L \mathbf{shared\_queue},$$
$$dequeue : \oplus \{some : \text{int} \wedge \downarrow^S_L \mathbf{shared\_queue},$$
$$none : \downarrow^S_L \mathbf{shared\_queue}\}\}$$

Instead of allowing all clients to freely enqueue and dequeue, suppose we only allow certain clients to enqueue and certain clients to dequeue. With subtyping, we first fix the provider's type to be **shared_queue**. Next, we restrict writer clients by removing the *dequeue* label and similarly restrict reader clients by removing the *enqueue* label:

$$\mathbf{producer} = \uparrow^S_L \&\{enqueue : \text{int} \supset \downarrow^S_L \mathbf{producer}\}$$
$$\mathbf{consumer} = \uparrow^S_L \&\{dequeue : \oplus\{some : \text{int} \wedge \downarrow^S_L \mathbf{consumer}, none : \downarrow^S_L \mathbf{consumer}\}\}$$

where it is indeed the case that **shared_queue** $\leq$ **producer** and **shared_queue** $\leq$ **consumer**, justifying both the writer and reader clients' views on the type of the channel.

We will defer the detailed discussion of the subtle interactions that occur between the notion of equi-synchronizing constraint and subtyping to Sect. 5.1. For this example however, the fact that all three types **shared_queue**, **producer**, and **consumer** are independently equi-synchronizing is a strong justification of its soundness.

5   Phasing

One of the most common patterns when encoding data structures and protocols via session types is to begin the linear type with an external choice. When these types recur, we are met with another external choice. A notion of *phasing* emerges from this pattern, where a single phase spans from the initial external choice to the recursion.

We introduced an auction protocol, which in its linear form can make explicit the two distinct phases, yet in its shared form cannot due to the equi-synchronizing constraint. With subtyping however, this seems to no longer be a problem; the auctioneer can view the protocol as auction whereas the clients can independently view the protocol as **bidding** or **collecting** depending on their current phase since **auction** $\leq$ **bidding** and **auction** $\leq$ **collecting**.

$$
\text{provider} \begin{cases}
\mathbf{auction} = \uparrow_L^S \& \{ bid : \oplus \{ ok : \mathrm{id} \supset \mathrm{money} \supset \downarrow_L^S \mathbf{auction}, \\
\qquad\qquad\qquad\quad collecting : \downarrow_L^S \mathbf{auction} \}, \\
\quad collect : \mathrm{id} \supset \oplus \{ prize : \mathrm{item} \wedge \downarrow_L^S \mathbf{auction}, \\
\qquad\qquad\qquad refund : \mathrm{money} \wedge \downarrow_L^S \mathbf{auction}, \\
\qquad\qquad\qquad bidding : \downarrow_L^S \mathbf{auction} \} \}
\end{cases}
$$

$$
\text{clients} \begin{cases}
\mathbf{bidding} = \uparrow_L^S \& \{ bid : \oplus \{ ok : \mathrm{id} \supset \mathrm{money} \supset \downarrow_L^S \mathbf{bidding}, \\
\qquad\qquad\qquad\qquad collecting : \downarrow_L^S \mathbf{collecting} \} \} \\
\mathbf{collecting} = \uparrow_L^S \& \{ collect : \mathrm{id} \supset \oplus \{ prize : \mathrm{item} \wedge \downarrow_L^S \mathbf{bidding}, \\
\qquad\qquad\qquad\qquad refund : \mathrm{money} \wedge \downarrow_L^S \mathbf{bidding}, \\
\qquad\qquad\qquad\qquad bidding : \downarrow_L^S \mathbf{bidding} \} \}
\end{cases}
$$

Unfortunately, there is a critical issue with this solution. Since shared channels can be aliased, a client in the collecting phase can alias the channel, follow the protocol, and then ignore the released type (bidding phase) – it can then use the previously aliased channel to communicate as if in the collecting phase. In general, the strategy of encoding phases in shared communication through a shared supertype allows malicious clients to re-enter previously encountered phases since they may internally store aliases. Thus, what we require is a subtyping relation across shared and linear modes since linear channels are restricted and in particular cannot be aliased.

We first add two new linear connectives $\uparrow_L^L$ and $\downarrow_L^L$ that, like $\uparrow_L^S$ and $\downarrow_L^S$, have operationally an acquire-release semantics but enforce a linear treatment of the associated channels. Prior work [14] has already explored such intra-layer shifts, albeit for the purpose of enforcing synchronization in an asynchronous message-passing system. Thus for example, the protocol denoted by $\uparrow_L^L A_L$ requires the client to "acquire" as in the shared case. If the provider happens to provide a linear channel $\uparrow_L^L A_L$, then this merely adds a synchronization point in the communication. The more interesting case is when the provider is actually providing a shared channel, some $\uparrow_L^S A_L$; a client should be able to view the session type as $\uparrow_L^L A_L$ without any trouble. We formalize this idea to the following additional subtyping relations:

$$\frac{A_L \leq B_L}{\uparrow_L^S A_L \leq \uparrow_L^L B_L} \leq_{\uparrow_L^S \uparrow_L^L} \quad \frac{A_S \leq B_L}{\downarrow_L^S A_S \leq \downarrow_L^L B_L} \leq_{\downarrow_L^S \downarrow_L^L} \quad \frac{A_L \leq B_L}{\uparrow_L^L A_L \leq \uparrow_L^L B_L} \leq_{\uparrow_L^L} \quad \frac{A_L \leq B_L}{\downarrow_L^L A_L \leq \downarrow_L^L B_L} \leq_{\downarrow_L^L}$$

Using the new connectives, we can complete the auction protocol where the two phases are manifest in the session type; a client must actually view the auction protocol linearly!

$$\mathbf{bidding} = \uparrow_L^L \& \{ bid : \oplus \{ ok : \mathrm{id} \supset \mathrm{money} \supset \downarrow_L^L \mathbf{bidding},$$
$$collecting : \downarrow_L^L \mathbf{collecting} \} \}$$
$$\mathbf{collecting} = \uparrow_L^L \& \{ collect : \mathrm{id} \supset \oplus \{ prize : \mathrm{item} \wedge \downarrow_L^L \mathbf{bidding},$$
$$refund : \mathrm{money} \wedge \downarrow_L^L \mathbf{bidding},$$
$$bidding : \downarrow_L^L \mathbf{bidding} \} \}$$

where **auction** $\leq$ **bidding** and **auction** $\leq$ **collecting**. Compared to the initially presented linear auction protocol, this version inserts the purely linear shifts $\uparrow_L^L$ and $\downarrow_L^L$ where appropriate such that the protocol is compatible with the shared auction protocol that the auctioneer provides. Therefore, the addition of $\uparrow_L^L$ and $\downarrow_L^L$ to our system allows a natural subtyping relation between shared session types and linear session types, where they serve as a means to safely bridge between shared and linear modalities.

Remark 2. A protocol spanning multiple phases can also be interpreted as a deterministic finite autonomata (DFA) where nodes represent the phase or the state of the protocol and edges represent choice branches. The previous auction protocol can be encoded as a two state DFA as shown in Fig. 1.

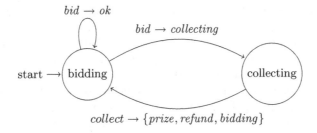

Fig. 1. A DFA representation of the two phases in the auction protocol. Multiple labels enclosed in brackets as in {*prize, refund, bidding*} mean that any of those labels can be selected.

5.1 Subsynchronizing Constraint

We note in Sect. 2.2 that in previous work [2], we require session types to be equi-synchronizing, which requires that processes following the protocol are released at the exact type at which it was acquired. This constraint guarantees that clients do not acquire at a type that they do not expect. With the introduction of subtyping however, there are two major relaxations that we propose on this constraint.

Releasing At a Subtype. A client P using some channel as some type $a_S:A_S$ can safely communicate with any (shared) process offering a channel of type $a_S:A_S'$ such that $A_S' \leq A_S$ due to subtyping. If another client acquires a_S and releases it at some A_S'' such that $A_S'' \leq A_S'$, then P can still safely communicate along a_S since $A_S'' \leq A_S$ by transitivity. Thus, one reasonable relaxation to the equi-synchronizing constraint is that processes do not need to be released at the same exact type but instead a subtype.

Branches That Never Occur. A major consequence of subtyping is that providers and clients can wait on some branches in the internal and external choices which in fact never will be sent by the other party. For example, suppose a provider P provides a channel of type $A_S = \uparrow_L^S \&\{a : \downarrow_L^S A_S, b : \downarrow_L^S B_S\}$. Assuming some unrelated B_S, we can see that A_S is not equi-synchronizing because the b branch can lead to releasing at a different type. However, suppose some client C views the channel as $\uparrow_L^S \&\{a : \downarrow_L^S A_S\}$ – in this case, P can only receive a, and the b branch can safely be ignored since C will never send the b label. This points to the necessity of using both the provider and client types to more finely verify the synchronizing constraint. Of course, if there is another client D that views the channel in a way that the b branch can be taken, then the entire setup is not synchronizing. Thus, we must verify the synchronization constraint for all pairs of providers and clients.

Following previous work [2], we formulate constraints by extending the shared types: $\hat{A} ::= \bot \mid A_S \mid \top$ where $\bot \leq A_S \leq \top$ for any A_S. Intuitively, $\top$ indicates a channel that has not been acquired yet (no constraints on a future release), A_S indicates the previous presentation of shared channels, and $\bot$ indicates a channel that will never be available (hence, any client attempting to acquire from this channel will never succeed and be blocked).

We are now ready to present the *subsynchronizing* judgment, interpreted coinductively, which is of the form $\vdash (A, B, \hat{D})$ ssync for some A and B such that $A \leq B$. It asserts that a provider providing a channel of type A and a client using that channel with type B is subsynchronizing with respect to some constraint $\hat{D}$. To verify a pair of types A and B to be subsynchronizing, we take $\top$ as its initial constraint (recall that $\top$ represents no constraint), that is, we say that A and B are subsynchronizing if $\vdash (A, B, \top)$ ssync.

$$\frac{}{\vdash (1, 1, \hat{D}) \text{ ssync}} \; S1$$

$$\frac{\vdash (B_L, B'_L, \hat{D}) \text{ ssync}}{\vdash (A_L \otimes B_L, A'_L \otimes B'_L, \hat{D}) \text{ ssync}} \; S\otimes \qquad \frac{\vdash (B_L, B'_L, \hat{D}) \text{ ssync}}{\vdash (A_L \multimap B_L, A'_L \multimap B'_L, \hat{D}) \text{ ssync}} \; S\multimap$$

$$\frac{\forall i \in \bar{l} \quad \vdash (A_{i_L}, A'_{i_L}, \hat{D}) \text{ ssync}}{\vdash (\oplus\{\overline{l{:}A_L}\}, \oplus\{\overline{l{:}A'_L}, \overline{m{:}B_L}\}, \hat{D}) \text{ ssync}} \; S\oplus \qquad \frac{\forall i \in \bar{l} \quad \vdash (A_{i_L}, A'_{i_L}, \hat{D}) \text{ ssync}}{\vdash (\&\{\overline{l{:}A_L}, \overline{m{:}B_L}\}, \&\{\overline{l{:}A'_L}\}, \hat{D}) \text{ ssync}} \; S\&$$

$$\frac{\vdash (A_L, A'_L, \hat{D}) \text{ ssync}}{\vdash (\uparrow^L_L A_L, \uparrow^L_L A'_L, \hat{D}) \text{ ssync}} \; S\uparrow^L_L \qquad \frac{\vdash (A_L, A'_L, \hat{D}) \text{ ssync}}{\vdash (\downarrow^L_L A_L, \downarrow^L_L A'_L, \hat{D}) \text{ ssync}} \; S\downarrow^L_L$$

$$\frac{\vdash (A_L, A'_L, \uparrow^S_L A_L) \text{ ssync}}{\vdash (\uparrow^S_L A_L, \uparrow^S_L A'_L, \top) \text{ ssync}} \; S\uparrow^S_L \qquad \frac{\vdash (A_S, A'_S, \top) \text{ ssync} \quad \downarrow^S_L A_S \leq \hat{D}}{\vdash (\downarrow^S_L A_S, \downarrow^S_L A'_S, \hat{D}) \text{ ssync}} \; S\downarrow^S_L$$

$$\frac{\vdash (A_L, A'_L, \uparrow^S_L A_L) \text{ ssync}}{\vdash (\uparrow^S_L A_L, \uparrow^L_L A'_L, \top) \text{ ssync}} \; S\uparrow^S_L\uparrow^L_L \qquad \frac{\vdash (A_S, A'_L, \top) \text{ ssync} \quad \downarrow^S_L A_S \leq \hat{D}}{\vdash (\downarrow^S_L A_S, \downarrow^L_L A'_L, \hat{D}) \text{ ssync}} \; S\downarrow^S_L\downarrow^L_L$$

The general progression of derivations to verify that two types are subsynchronizing is to first look for an upshift $\uparrow^S_L$ on the provider's type, involving either $S\uparrow^S_L$ or $S\uparrow^S_L\uparrow^L_L$. After encountering a $\uparrow^S_L$, it "records" the provider's type as the constraint and continues to look at the continuations of the types. When encountering internal and external choices, it only requires the continuations for the common branches to be subsynchronizing. When it encounters a downshift $\downarrow^S_L$ from the provider's side, it checks if the release point as denoted by the continuation of $\downarrow^S_L$ is a subtype of the recorded constraint, in which case it continues with the derivation with the $\top$ constraint.

Remark 3. Subsynchronizing is a strictly weaker constraint than equisynchronizing. In particular, if A is equi-synchronizing, then the pair A, A are subsynchronizing.

6   Metatheory

In this section we present the progress and preservation theorems in a synchronous message passing concurrent system implementing our type system. We defer many of the technical details of the system and the proofs to our extended report [20] which follows a similar style to the system in a previous work [2]. In particular, the two theorems are equally strong as the ones in [2], justifying our subtyping extension.

6.1   Process Typing

We take the typing judgment presented in Sect. 2.1 and extend it with shared channels as introduced in Sect. 2.2:

$$\Gamma \vdash P :: (a_S{:}A_S)$$
$$\Gamma; \Delta \vdash Q :: (a_L{:}A_L)$$

where $\Gamma = a_{1S}{:}\hat{A}_1, \ldots, a_{nS}{:}\hat{A}_n$ is a structural context of shared channels and constraints ($\perp$ and $\top$) which can appear at runtime.

The first judgment asserts that P provides a shared channel $a_S{:}A_S$ while using shared channels in Γ; the lack of dependence on any linear channels Δ is due to the *independence principle* presented in [2]. The second judgment asserts that Q provides a linear channel $a_L{:}A_L$ while using shared channels in Γ and linear channels in Δ.

Forwarding is a fundamental operation that allows a process to identify its offering channel with a channel it uses if the types match.

$$\frac{B_L \leq A_L}{\Gamma; y_L{:}B_L \vdash \mathsf{fwd}\ x_L\ y_L\ ::\ (x_L{:}A_L)}\ ID_L \qquad \frac{\hat{B} \leq A_S}{\Gamma, y_S{:}\hat{B} \vdash \mathsf{fwd}\ x_S\ y_S\ ::\ (x_S{:}A_S)}\ ID_S$$

$$\frac{\hat{B} \leq A_L}{\Gamma, y_S{:}\hat{B}; \cdot \vdash \mathsf{fwd}\ x_L\ y_S\ ::\ (x_L{:}A_L)}\ ID_{LS}$$

The rules ID_L and ID_S require the offering channel to be a supertype of the channel it is being identified with. Since we syntactically distinguish shared channels and linear channels, we require an additional rule ID_{LS} that allows linear channels to be forwarded with a shared channel provided the subtyping relation holds.

We also show the right rule of $\otimes$, which requires the provider to send a channel y_L alongside its offering channel x_L:

$$\frac{A'_L \leq A_L \quad \Gamma; \Delta \vdash P :: (x_L{:}B_L)}{\Gamma; \Delta, y_L{:}A'_L \vdash \mathsf{send}\ x_L\ y_L; P\ ::\ (x_L{:}A_L \otimes B_L)}\ \otimes R$$

Similar to the forwarding case, a shared channel can instead be sent if the appropriate subtyping relation holds:

$$\frac{\hat{A} \leq A_L \quad \Gamma, y_S{:}\hat{A}; \Delta \vdash P :: (x_L{:}B_L)}{\Gamma, y_S{:}\hat{A}; \Delta \vdash \mathsf{send}\ x_L\ y_S; P\ ::\ (x_L{:}A_L \otimes B_L)}\ \otimes R_S$$

One important observation is that typing judgments remain local in the presence of subtyping; the channels in Γ and Δ may be provided by processes at some subtype (maintained in the configuration; see Sect. 6.3) and need not match. We therefore do not adopt a general subsumption rule that allows arbitrary substitutions that preserve subtyping and instead precisely manage where subtyping occurs in the system.

6.2 Processes and Configuration

To reason about session types and process calculi, we must consider a collection of message passing processes, which is known as a *configuration*. In our system, we split the configuration into the shared fragment Λ and the linear fragment Θ, where Λ is a list of *process predicates* that offer shared channels and Θ is similarly a list of process predicates that offer linear channels.

The most fundamental process predicate denotes a process term P that provides some channel a and is of form $\text{proc}(a, P)$. We also introduce the predicate $\text{unavail}(a_S)$, which represents a shared process that is unavailable to be acquired, for example, due to it being acquired by another process, and $\text{connect}(a_L, b_S)$, which provides a linear reference a_L to a shared channel b_S, needed to express shared to linear subtyping.

We require the linear configuration Θ to obey an ordering that processes can only depend on processes that appear to its right; $\text{proc}(a_L, P), \text{proc}(b_L, Q)$ would be ill-formed if P depends on b_L. On the other hand, Λ has no ordering constraints. For the subsequent sections, we require that configurations are *well-formed*, which essentially requires that both shared and linear processes provide unique channel names thereby avoiding naming conflicts.

6.3 Configuration Typing

The configuration typing judgment asserts that a given configuration collectively provides a set of shared and linear channels; each fragment is checked separately as shown by the only typing rule for the combined configuration:

$$\frac{\Gamma \models \Lambda :: (\Gamma) \quad \Gamma \models \Theta :: (\Delta)}{\Gamma \models \Lambda; \Theta :: (\Gamma; \Delta)} \ \Omega$$

The shared context Γ appears on both sides due to circularity; the appearance on the left side allows any processes to depend on a particular shared channel in Γ while the appearance on the right side asserts that Λ collectively provides Γ. In most cases, $\hat{A}$ is some shared session type A_S, but the maximal and minimal types $\bot$ and $\top$ can appear at runtime.

For the shared fragment, we check each process predicate independently; in particular, a configuration typing rule for some $\text{proc}(a_S, P)$ is shown below.

$$\frac{\vdash (A'_S, A_S, \top) \text{ ssync} \quad \Gamma \vdash P :: (a_S{:}A'_S)}{\Gamma \models \text{proc}(a_S, P) :: (a_S{:}A_S)} \ \Lambda 3$$

An important point is that a_S is of type A_S in Γ and A'_S is only local to the process typing judgment; thus, the provider P views the channel a_S at type A'_S while all clients view the channel a_S at type A_S. The subtyping relation $A'_S \leq A_S$ is subsumed by the subsynchronizing judgment $\vdash (A'_S, A_S, \top)$ ssync which guarantees that the pair (A'_S, A_S) is subsynchronizing.

A configuration typing rule for some (linear) $\text{proc}(a_L, P), \Theta'$ is shown below.

$$\frac{a_S:\hat{A} \in \Gamma \quad \vdash (A'_L, A_L, \hat{A}) \text{ ssync} \quad \Gamma; \Delta_a \vdash P :: (a_L:A'_L) \quad \Gamma \models \Theta' :: (\Delta_a, \Delta')}{\Gamma \models \text{proc}(a_L, P), \Theta' :: (a : A_L, \Delta')} \; \Theta3$$

Since P may use some linear channels Δ_a, we split the offering channels of Θ' to Δ_a, Δ' and make explicit that P will consume Δ_a. Similar to the shared case, the process typing judgment (third premise) locally assumes a_L is of type A'_L such that $A'_L \leq A_L$ (again, subsumed by the subsynchronizing judgment), guaranteeing that a client of a_L view the channel as type A_L.

6.4   Dynamics

The operational semantics of the system is formulated through *multiset rewriting rules* [5], which is of form $S_1, \ldots, S_n \to T_1, \ldots, T_m$, where each S_i and T_j corresponds to a process predicate. Each rule captures a transition in a subset of the configuration; for example, the following is one of three rules that capture the semantics of forwarding:

$$\text{proc}(a_L, \text{fwd } a_L \; b_S) \to \text{connect}(a_L, b_S) \tag{D-FWDLS}$$

Connect predicates are consumed if a process acquires linearly on a channel that is provided by a shared process. We first show how a shared process providing some b_s can be acquired:

$$\begin{array}{l} \text{proc}(a_L, x_L \leftarrow \text{acq}_S \; b_S; P) \\ \text{proc}(b_S, x_L \leftarrow \text{acc}_S \; b_S; Q) \end{array} \to \begin{array}{l} \text{proc}(a_L, [b_L/x_L]P), \\ \text{proc}(b_L, [b_L/x_L]Q) \end{array}, \text{unavail}(b_S) \tag{D-$\uparrow^S_L$}$$

The rule says that a client can successfully acquire if there is a corresponding accept by the provider. In the following rule, a connect predicate "coordinates" the acquire/accept between different modes:

$$\begin{array}{l} \text{proc}(a_L, x_L \leftarrow \text{acq}_L \; b_L; P) \\ \text{proc}(c_S, x_L \leftarrow \text{acc}_S \; c_S; Q) \end{array}, \text{connect}(b_L, c_S) \to \begin{array}{l} \text{proc}(a_L, [c_L/x_L]P), \\ \text{proc}(c_L, [c_L/x_L]Q) \end{array}, \text{unavail}(c_S)$$
$$\tag{D-$\uparrow^S_L 2$}$$

6.5   Theorems

So far, we have incompletely introduced the statics [20, Appendix D] and the dynamics [20, Appendix E] of the system, focusing on the interesting cases that depart from the system presented in [2].

The preservation theorem, or session fidelity, guarantees that well-typed configurations remain well-typed. In particular, this means that processes will always adhere to the protocol denoted by the session type.

Theorem 1 (Preservation). *If $\Gamma \models \Lambda; \Theta :: (\Gamma; \Delta)$ for some $\Lambda, \Theta, \Gamma,$ and $\Delta,$ and $\Lambda; \Theta \to \Lambda'; \Theta'$ for some $\Lambda'; \Theta',$ then $\Gamma' \models \Lambda'; \Theta' :: (\Gamma'; \Delta)$ where $\Gamma' \preceq \Gamma$.*

Proof. By induction on the dynamics and constructing a well-typed configuration for each case. See [20, Appendix F] for the detailed proof, covering all cases.

The $\Gamma' \preceq \Gamma$ captures the idea that the configuration can gain additional shared processes and that the types of shared channels can become smaller. For example, if a process spawns an additional shared process, then the configuration will gain an additional channel in Γ and if a shared channel is released to a smaller type, the type of the shared channel in Γ can become smaller. Note that although it is indeed true that linear processes can be spawned, it will never appear in Δ since the linear channel that the newly spawned process offers must be consumed by the process that spawned the channel, meaning Δ is unchanged.

The progress theorem is as in [2], where we only allow configurations to be stuck due to failure of some client to acquire, for example, due to deadlock. A *poised* process [2,17] is one that is currently trying to communicate across its offering channel and is analogous to the role of *values* in typical functional languages. Both shared and linear configurations are poised if and only if all its processes are trying to communicate across its offering channel.

Theorem 2 (Progress). *If $\Gamma \models \Lambda; \Theta :: (\Gamma; \Delta)$ then either:*

1. *$\Lambda; \Theta \rightarrow \Lambda'; \Theta$ for some Λ' or*
2. *Λ is poised and one of:*
   (a) *$\Lambda; \Theta \rightarrow \Lambda'; \Theta'$ or*
   (b) *Θ is poised or*
   (c) *a linear process in Θ is unable stuck and therefore unable to acquire*

Proof. By induction on the typing of the configuration $\Lambda; \Theta$. We begin by induction on the typing of Λ to prove either (1) or Λ is poised. After, we prove (2) by induction on the typing of Θ while assuming Λ is poised. See [20, Appendix G] for the detailed proof.

Remark 4. Another paper [3] introduces additional static restrictions to allow a stronger and more common notion of progress, which are orthogonal to our results. Adopting this extension to the system we present here would give the usual notion of progress with deadlock freedom.

7   Related Work

Our paper serves as an extension to the manifest sharing system defined in [2] by introducing a notion of subtyping to the system which allows us to statically relax the equi-synchronizing constraint. Early glimpses of subtyping can be seen in the previous system with the introduction of $\perp$ and $\top$ as the minimal and maximal constraints, which happened to be compatible with our subtyping relation.

Subtyping for session types was first proposed by Gay and Hole [11], and a slightly modified style of session types guided from the correspondence with intuitionistic linear logic was given a subtyping extension [1]. Both these papers do not investigate the more recently discovered modal shifts, which is our contribution to the subtyping front.

There have also been many recent developments in subtyping in the context of multiparty session types [6,7,12,13], which are a different class of type systems that describe protocols between an arbitrary number of participants from a neutral global point of view. Understanding the relation of our subtyping system to these systems is an interesting item for future work.

8   Conclusion

We propose a subtyping extension to a message passing concurrency programming language introduced in previous work [2] and showed examples highlighting the expressiveness that this new system provides. Throughout the paper, we follow two important principles, *substitutability* and *ignorance is bliss*, which gave a rich type system that in particular allows *phases* (in a shared setting) to be manifest in the type.

One immediate application of shared subtyping is that combined with refinement types [9,10], it can encode finer specifications of protocols. For example in the auction scenario, we can statically show that each client that does not win a bid gets refunded precisely the exact amount of money it bid. Without shared to linear subtyping, specifications of shared communication across multiple acquire-release cycles were not possible.

A future work in a more theoretical platform is to extend the setting to adjoint logic [18], which provides a more general framework of reasoning about modal shifts in a message passing system. In particular, we found that affine session types, where contraction (aliasing) is rejected, have immediate applications.

Acknowledgements. We would like to thank the anonymous reviewers for feedback on the initially submitted version of this paper.

References

1. Acay, C., Pfenning, F.: Intersections and unions of session types. In: Kobayashi, N. (ed.) 8th Workshop on Intersection Types and Related Systems (ITRS 2016), EPTCS 242, Porto, Portugal, pp. 4–19, June 2016
2. Balzer, S., Pfenning, F.: Manifest sharing with session types. In: International Conference on Functional Programming (ICFP), pp. 37:1–37:29. ACM, September 2017. Extended version available as Technical Report CMU-CS-17-106R, June 2017
3. Balzer, S., Toninho, B., Pfenning, F.: Manifest deadlock-freedom for shared session types. In: Caires, L. (ed.) ESOP 2019. LNCS, vol. 11423, pp. 611–639. Springer, Cham (2019). https://doi.org/10.1007/978-3-030-17184-1_22
4. Caires, L., Pfenning, F.: Session types as intuitionistic linear propositions. In: Gastin, P., Laroussinie, F. (eds.) CONCUR 2010. LNCS, vol. 6269, pp. 222–236. Springer, Heidelberg (2010). https://doi.org/10.1007/978-3-642-15375-4_16
5. Cervesato, I., Scedrov, A.: Relating state-based and process-based concurrency through linear logic. Inf. Comput. **207**(10), 1044–1077 (2009)

6. Chen, T.c., Dezani-Ciancaglini, M., Scalas, A., Yoshida, N.: On the preciseness of subtyping in session types. Log. Methods Comput. Sci. **13**(2) (2017). https://doi.org/10.23638/LMCS-13(2:12)2017

7. Chen, T.C., Dezani-Ciancaglini, M., Yoshida, N.: On the preciseness of subtyping in session types. In: Proceedings of the Conference on Principles and Practice of Declarative Programming (PPDP 2014), Canterbury, UK. ACM, September 2014

8. Crary, K., Harper, R., Puri, S.: What is a recursive module? In: In SIGPLAN Conference on Programming Language Design and Implementation, pp. 50–63. ACM Press (1999)

9. Das, A., Balzer, S., Hoffmann, J., Pfenning, F., Santurkar, I.: Resource-aware session types for digital contracts. In: Küsters, R., Naumann, D. (eds.) 34th Computer Security Foundations Symposium (CSF 2021), Dubrovnik, Croatia. IEEE (June 2021, to appear)

10. Das, A., Pfenning, F.: Session types with arithmetic refinements. In: Konnov, I., Kovács, L. (eds.) 31st International Conference on Concurrency Theory (CONCUR 2020), LIPIcs, Vienna, Austria, vol. 171, pp. 13:1–13:18, September 2020

11. Gay, S.J., Hole, M.: Subtyping for session types in the π-calculus. Acta Informatica **42**(2–3), 191–225 (2005)

12. Ghilezan, S., Jakšić, S., Pantović, J., Scalas, A., Yoshida, N.: Precise subtyping for synchronous multiparty sessions. J. Log. Algebr. Methods Program. **104**, 127–173 (2019). https://doi.org/10.1016/j.jlamp.2018.12.002

13. Ghilezan, S., Pantović, J., Prokić, I., Scalas, A., Yoshida, N.: Precise subtyping for asynchronous multiparty sessions (2020)

14. Griffith, D.: Polarized substructural session types. Ph.D. thesis, University of Illinois at Urbana-Champaign (2015, in preparation)

15. Honda, K.: Types for dyadic interaction. In: Best, E. (ed.) CONCUR 1993. LNCS, vol. 715, pp. 509–523. Springer, Heidelberg (1993). https://doi.org/10.1007/3-540-57208-2_35

16. Honda, K., Vasconcelos, V.T., Kubo, M.: Language primitives and type discipline for structured communication-based programming. In: Hankin, C. (ed.) ESOP 1998. LNCS, vol. 1381, pp. 122–138. Springer, Heidelberg (1998). https://doi.org/10.1007/BFb0053567

17. Pfenning, F., Griffith, D.: Polarized substructural session types. In: Pitts, A. (ed.) FoSSaCS 2015. LNCS, vol. 9034, pp. 3–22. Springer, Heidelberg (2015). https://doi.org/10.1007/978-3-662-46678-0_1

18. Pruiksma, K., Pfenning, F.: A message-passing interpretation of adjoint logic. In: Martins, F., Orchard, D. (eds.) Workshop on Programming Language Approaches to Concurrency and Communication-Centric Software (PLACES), EPTCS 291, Prague, Czech Republic, pp. 60–79, April 2019

19. Sano, C.: On Session Typed Contracts for Imperative Languages. Masters thesis, Carnegie Mellon University, December 2019. Available as Technical Report CMU-CS-19-133, December 2019

20. Sano, C., Balzer, S., Pfenning, F.: Manifestly phased communication via shared session types. CoRR abs/2101.06249 (2021). https://arxiv.org/abs/2101.06249

21. Toninho, B.: A logical foundation for session-based concurrent computation. Ph.D. thesis, Carnegie Mellon University and Universidade Nova de Lisboa, May 2015. Available as Technical Report CMU-CS-15-109

22. Wadler, P.: Propositions as sessions. In: Proceedings of the 17th International Conference on Functional Programming (ICFP 2012), Copenhagen, Denmark, pp. 273–286. ACM Press, September 2012

Deconfined Global Types
for Asynchronous Sessions

Francesco Dagnino[1], Paola Giannini[2(✉)], and Mariangiola Dezani-Ciancaglini[3]

[1] DIBRIS, Università di Genova, Genoa, Italy
`paola.giannini@uniupo.it`
[2] DiSIT, Università del Piemonte Orientale, Alessandria, Italy
[3] Dipartimento di Informatica, Università di Torino, Turin, Italy

Abstract. Multiparty sessions with asynchronous communications and global types play an important role for the modelling of interaction protocols in distributed systems. In designing such calculi the aim is to enforce, by typing, good properties for all participants, maximising, at the same time, the behaviours accepted. The global types presented in this paper improve the state-of-the-art by extending the set of typeable asynchronous sessions and preserving decidability of type checking together with the key properties of Subject Reduction, Session Fidelity and Progress.

Keywords: Communication-based programming · Multiparty sessions · Global types

1 Introduction

Multiparty sessions [17,18] are at the core of communication-based programming, since they formalise message exchange protocols. A key choice in the modelling is synchronous versus asynchronous communications, giving rise to synchronous and asynchronous multiparty sessions. In the multiparty session approach *global types* play the fundamental role of describing the whole scenario, while the behaviour of participants is implemented by processes. A natural question is when a set of processes agrees with a global type. The straightforward answer is the design of type assignment systems relating processes and global types. Global types are *projected* onto participants to get the local behaviours prescribed by the protocol. In conceiving such systems one wants to permit all possible typings which guarantee desirable properties: the mandatory Subject Reduction, but also Session Fidelity and Progress. *Session Fidelity* [17,18] means that the content and the order of exchanged messages respect the prescriptions of the global type. *Progress* [9,12] requires that all participants willing to communicate will be able to do it and, in case of asynchronous communication, also that all sent messages (which usually are in a queue) will be received.

A standard way of getting more permissive typings is through *subtyping* [14]. Following the *substitution principle* [20], we can safely put a process of some type where a process of a bigger type is expected. For synchronous multiparty

© IFIP International Federation for Information Processing 2021
Published by Springer Nature Switzerland AG 2021
F. Damiani and O. Dardha (Eds.): COORDINATION 2021, LNCS 12717, pp. 41–60, 2021.
https://doi.org/10.1007/978-3-030-78142-2_3

sessions the natural subtyping allows less inputs and more outputs [11]. This subtyping is not only correct, but also *complete*, that is, any extension of this subtyping would be unsound [15]. A powerful subtyping for asynchronous sessions was proposed in [21] and recently proved to be complete [16]. The key idea of this subtyping is anticipating outputs before inputs to improve efficiency. The drawback of this subtyping is its undecidability [5,19]. To overcome this problem, some decidable restrictions of this subtyping were proposed [5,6,19] and a sound, but not complete, decision algorithm, is presented in [4].

Asynchronous communications better represent the exchange of messages between participants in different localities, and are more suitable for implementations. So it is interesting to find alternatives to subtyping which increase typability of asynchronous multiparty sessions. Recently a more permissive design of global types has been proposed [8]: it is based on the simple idea of splitting outputs and inputs in the syntax of global types. In this way outputs can anticipate inputs. Multiparty sessions are typed by *configuration types*, which are pairs of global types and queues. The freedom gained by this definition is rather confined in [8], whose main focus was to define an event structure semantics for asynchronous multiparty sessions. In particular global types must satisfy well-formedness conditions which strongly limit their use.

In the present paper we start from the syntax of global types in [8], significantly enlarging the set of allowed global types which are well formed. In this way we obtain a decidable type system in which we are able to type also an example requiring a subtyping which fails for the algorithm in [4]. On the negative side, we did not find a global configuration in our system for the running example of [4]. The well-formedness of global types must guarantee that participants in different branches of choices have coherent behaviours and that all sent messages found the corresponding readers. This last condition is particularly delicate for cyclic computations in which the number of unread messages may be unbounded. Our type system gains expressivity by:

- requiring to a participant the knowledge of the chosen branch only when her behaviour depends on that;
- allowing an unbound number of unread messages when all of them will be eventually read.

Our type system enjoys Subject Reduction, Session Fidelity and Progress.

We illustrate the proposed calculus with an example in which the number of unread messages is unbounded. We choose this example since typing this session in standard type systems for multiparty sessions requires a subtyping which is not derivable by the algorithm in [4]. In fact this session is Example 24 of that paper in our notation. In addition this example is not typeable in [8]. The process $P = \mathsf{q}?\{\lambda_1; P_1, \lambda_2; P_2\}$ waits from participant q either the label λ_1 or the label λ_2: in the first case it becomes P_1, in the second case it becomes P_2. Similarly the process $Q = \mathsf{p}!\{\lambda_1; Q_1, \lambda_2; Q_2\}$ sends to participant p either the label λ_1 becoming Q_1 or the label λ_2 becoming Q_2. So the multiparty session $\mathsf{p}[\![P]\!] \parallel \mathsf{q}[\![Q]\!] \parallel \emptyset$, where $\emptyset$ is the empty queue, can reduce as follows:

$$\mathsf{p}[\![P]\!] \parallel \mathsf{q}[\![Q]\!] \parallel \emptyset \xrightarrow{\mathsf{q}\,\mathsf{p}!\lambda_1} \mathsf{p}[\![P]\!] \parallel \mathsf{q}[\![Q_1]\!] \parallel \langle \mathsf{q}, \lambda_1, \mathsf{p}\rangle \xrightarrow{\mathsf{q}\,\mathsf{p}?\lambda_1} \mathsf{p}[\![P_1]\!] \parallel \mathsf{q}[\![Q_1]\!] \parallel \emptyset$$

decorating transition arrows with communications and denoting by $\langle q, \lambda_1, p \rangle$ the message exchanging label λ_1 from q to p. If $P_1 = q!\lambda; q!\lambda; q!\lambda; P$ and $Q_1 = p?\lambda; Q$ we get:

$$
\begin{aligned}
p[\![P_1]\!] \parallel q[\![Q_1]\!] \parallel \emptyset & \xrightarrow{pq!\lambda} p[\![q!\lambda; q!\lambda; P]\!] \parallel q[\![Q_1]\!] \parallel \langle p, \lambda, q \rangle \\
& \xrightarrow{pq!\lambda} p[\![q!\lambda; P]\!] \parallel q[\![Q_1]\!] \parallel \langle p, \lambda, q \rangle \cdot \langle p, \lambda, q \rangle \\
& \xrightarrow{pq!\lambda} p[\![P]\!] \parallel q[\![Q_1]\!] \parallel \langle p, \lambda, q \rangle \cdot \langle p, \lambda, q \rangle \cdot \langle p, \lambda, q \rangle \\
& \xrightarrow{pq?\lambda} p[\![P]\!] \parallel q[\![Q]\!] \parallel \langle p, \lambda, q \rangle \cdot \langle p, \lambda, q \rangle
\end{aligned}
$$

Then there is a loop in which for each cycle the number of messages $\langle p, \lambda, q \rangle$ on the queue increases by two. Assuming that $P_2 = q!\lambda; P_2$ and $Q_2 = p?\lambda; Q_2$, each of such messages is eventually read by q. This session can be typed by the configuration type whose queue is empty and whose global type is $G = q\,p!\{\lambda_1; q\,p?\lambda_1; G_1, \lambda_2; q\,p?\lambda_2; G_2\}$, where $G_1 = p\,q!\lambda; p\,q!\lambda; p\,q!\lambda; p\,q?\lambda; G$ and $G_2 = p\,q!\lambda; p\,q?\lambda; G_2$. The type G prescribes that q put on the queue either the label λ_1 or λ_2 for p who has to read the label from the queue. Then p and q must follow the protocols described by either G_1 or G_2. It should be intuitively clear why this global type is well formed. The formalisation of this intuition is given in the remainder of the paper and requires some ingenuity.

The effectiveness of our type system is demonstrated by the implementation described in the companion paper [3]. This tool (available at [2]) implements in co-logic programming the necessary predicates for the typing of sessions. *Outline* Our calculus of multiparty sessions is presented in Sect. 2, where the Progress property is defined. Section 3 introduces configuration types and their input/output matching, which will be completed by the algorithm given in Sect. 5. Global types are projected onto processes in Sect. 4, where we define the type system and state its properties.

2 A Core Calculus for Multiparty Sessions

Since our focus is on typing by means of global types we only consider one multiparty session instead of many interleaved multiparty sessions. This allows us to depart from the standard syntax of processes with channels [1,17] in favour of simpler processes with output and input operators and explicit participants as in [13,15,22].

We assume the following base sets: *participants* $p, q, r \in \mathsf{Part}$, and *labels* $\lambda \in \mathsf{Lab}$.

Definition 1 (Processes). Processes P are defined by:

$$ P ::=_\rho \mathbf{0} \mid p!\{\lambda_i; P_i\}_{i \in I} \mid p?\{\lambda_i; P_i\}_{i \in I} $$

where $I \neq \emptyset$ *and* $\lambda_j \neq \lambda_h$ *for* $j \neq h$.

The symbol $::=_\rho$, in the definition above and in other definitions, indicates that the productions should be interpreted *coinductively*. That is, they define possibly infinite processes. However, we assume such processes to be *regular*, that is, with finitely many distinct sub-processes. In this way, we only obtain processes which are solutions of finite sets of equations, see [10].

A process of shape $p!\{\lambda_i; P_i\}_{i \in I}$ (*internal choice*) chooses a label in the set $\{\lambda_i \mid i \in I\}$ to be sent to p, and then behaves differently depending on the sent label. A process of shape $p?\{\lambda_i; P_i\}_{i \in I}$ (*external choice*) waits for receiving one of the labels $\{\lambda_i \mid i \in I\}$ from p, and then behaves differently depending on the received label. Note that the set of indexes in choices is assumed to be non-empty, and the corresponding labels to be all different. An internal choice which is a singleton is simply written $p!\lambda; P$, and $p!\lambda; 0$ is abbreviated $p!\lambda$, analogously for an external choice.

In a full-fledged calculus, labels would carry values, namely they would be of shape $\lambda(v)$. For simplicity, here we consider pure labels.

Messages are triples $\langle p, \lambda, q \rangle$ denoting that participant p has sent label λ to participant q. Sent messages are stored in a queue, from which they are subsequently fetched by the receiver.

Message queues $\mathcal{M}$ are defined by:

$$\mathcal{M} ::= \emptyset \mid \langle p, \lambda, q \rangle \cdot \mathcal{M}$$

The order of messages in the queue is the order in which they will be read. Since order matters only between messages with the same sender and receiver, we always consider message queues modulo the following structural equivalence:

$$\mathcal{M} \cdot \langle p, \lambda, q \rangle \cdot \langle r, \lambda', s \rangle \cdot \mathcal{M}' \equiv \mathcal{M} \cdot \langle r, \lambda', s \rangle \cdot \langle p, \lambda, q \rangle \cdot \mathcal{M}' \quad \text{if} \quad p \neq r \ \text{or} \ q \neq s$$

Note, in particular, that $\langle p, \lambda, q \rangle \cdot \langle q, \lambda', p \rangle \equiv \langle q, \lambda', p \rangle \cdot \langle p, \lambda, q \rangle$. These two equivalent queues represent a situation in which both participants p and q have sent a message to the other one, and neither of them has read the message. This situation may happen in a multiparty session with asynchronous communication.

Multiparty sessions are comprised of pairs participant/process of shape $p[\![P]\!]$ composed in parallel, each with a different participant p, and a message queue.

Definition 2 (Multiparty sessions). *Multiparty sessions are defined by:*

$$\mathbb{N} \parallel \mathcal{M} \quad where \quad \mathbb{N} ::= p_1[\![P_1]\!] \parallel \cdots \parallel p_n[\![P_n]\!]$$

and $n > 0$ and $p_i \neq p_j$ for $i \neq j$ and $\mathcal{M}$ is a message queue.

In the following we use session as short for multiparty session.

We assume the standard structural congruence on sessions (denoted $\equiv$), that is, we consider sessions modulo permutation of components and adding/removing components of the shape $p[\![0]\!]$.

If $P \neq 0$ we write $p[\![P]\!] \in \mathbb{N}$ as short for $\mathbb{N} \equiv p[\![P]\!] \parallel \mathbb{N}'$ for some $\mathbb{N}'$. This abbreviation is justified by the associativity and commutativity of $\parallel$.

To define the *asynchronous operational semantics* of sessions, we use an LTS whose labels record the outputs and the inputs. To this end, *communications*

$$\mathsf{p}[\![\,\mathsf{q}!\{\lambda_i; P_i\}_{i \in I}\,]\!] \parallel \mathsf{N} \parallel \mathcal{M} \xrightarrow{\,\mathsf{p}\,\mathsf{q}!\lambda_h\,} \mathsf{p}[\![\,P_h\,]\!] \parallel \mathsf{N} \parallel \mathcal{M} \cdot \langle \mathsf{p}, \lambda_h, \mathsf{q}\rangle \quad \text{where } h \in I \qquad [\textsc{Send}]$$

$$\mathsf{q}[\![\,\mathsf{p}?\{\lambda_j; Q_j\}_{j \in J}\,]\!] \parallel \mathsf{N} \parallel \langle \mathsf{p}, \lambda_h, \mathsf{q}\rangle \cdot \mathcal{M} \xrightarrow{\,\mathsf{p}\,\mathsf{q}?\lambda_h\,} \mathsf{q}[\![\,Q_h\,]\!] \parallel \mathsf{N} \parallel \mathcal{M} \quad \text{where } h \in J \qquad [\textsc{Rcv}]$$

Fig. 1. LTS for asynchronous sessions.

(ranged over by β) are either the asynchronous emission of a label λ from participant p to participant q (notation $\mathsf{p}\,\mathsf{q}!\lambda$) or the actual reading by participant q of the label λ sent by participant p (notation $\mathsf{p}\,\mathsf{q}?\lambda$).

The LTS semantics of sessions is specified by the two rules [SEND] and [RCV] given in Fig. 1. Rule [SEND] allows a participant p with an internal choice (a sender) to send one of its possible labels λ_h, by adding the corresponding message to the queue. Symmetrically, rule [RCV] allows a participant q with an external choice (a receiver) to read the first message in the queue sent to her by a given participant p, if its label λ_h is one of those she is waiting for.

The semantic property we aim to ensure, usually called *progress* [9,12], is the conjunction of a safety property, *deadlock-freedom*, and two liveness properties: *input lock-freedom* and *orphan message-freedom*. Intuitively, a session is deadlock-free if, in every reachable state of computation, it is either terminated (i.e. of the shape $\mathsf{p}[\![\,\mathbf{0}\,]\!] \parallel \emptyset$) or it can move. It is input lock-free if every component wishing to do an input can eventually do so. Finally, it is orphan-message-free if every message stored in the queue is eventually read.

The following terminology and notational conventions are standard.

If $\mathsf{N} \parallel \mathcal{M} \xrightarrow{\beta_1} \cdots \xrightarrow{\beta_n} \mathsf{N}' \parallel \mathcal{M}'$ for some $n \geq 0$ (where by convention $\mathsf{N}' \parallel \mathcal{M}' = \mathsf{N} \parallel \mathcal{M}$ if $n = 0$), then we say that $\mathsf{N}' \parallel \mathcal{M}'$ is a *derivative* of $\mathsf{N} \parallel \mathcal{M}$. We write $\mathsf{N} \parallel \mathcal{M} \xrightarrow{\beta}$ if $\mathsf{N} \parallel \mathcal{M} \xrightarrow{\beta} \mathsf{N}' \parallel \mathcal{M}'$ for some $\mathsf{N}', \mathcal{M}'$.

Definition 3 (Live, terminated, deadlocked sessions). *A session* $\mathsf{N} \parallel \mathcal{M}$ *is said to be*

- live *if* $\mathsf{N} \parallel \mathcal{M} \xrightarrow{\beta}$ *for some* β;
- terminated *if* $\mathsf{N} \equiv \mathsf{p}[\![\,\mathbf{0}\,]\!]$ *and* $\mathcal{M} = \emptyset$;
- deadlocked *if it is neither live nor terminated.*

To formalise progress (Definition 6) we introduce another transition relation on sessions, which describes their lockstep execution: at each step, all components that are able to move execute exactly one asynchronous output or input.

We define the *player of a communication* as the sender in case of output and as the receiver in case of input:

$$\mathsf{play}(\mathsf{p}\,\mathsf{q}!\lambda) = \mathsf{p} \qquad \mathsf{play}(\mathsf{p}\,\mathsf{q}?\lambda) = \mathsf{q}$$

Let Δ denote a non empty set of communications. We say that Δ is *coherent* for a session $\mathsf{N} \parallel \mathcal{M}$ if

1. for all $\beta_1, \beta_2 \in \Delta$, $\mathsf{play}(\beta_1) = \mathsf{play}(\beta_2)$ implies $\beta_1 = \beta_2$, and
2. for all $\beta \in \Delta$, $\mathsf{N} \parallel \mathcal{M} \xrightarrow{\beta}$.

The *lockstep transition relation* $\mathsf{N} \parallel \mathcal{M} \overset{\Delta}{\Rightarrow} \mathsf{N}' \parallel \mathcal{M}'$ is defined by:

$\mathsf{N} \parallel \mathcal{M} \overset{\Delta}{\Rightarrow} \mathsf{N}' \parallel \mathcal{M}'$ if $\Delta = \{\beta_1, \ldots, \beta_n\}$ is a maximal coherent set for $\mathsf{N} \parallel \mathcal{M}$ and

$$\mathsf{N} \parallel \mathcal{M} \xrightarrow{\beta_1} \cdots \xrightarrow{\beta_n} \mathsf{N}' \parallel \mathcal{M}'$$

The notion of derivative can be reformulated for lockstep computations as follows.

If $\mathsf{N} \parallel \mathcal{M} \overset{\Delta_1}{\Rightarrow} \cdots \overset{\Delta_n}{\Rightarrow} \mathsf{N}' \parallel \mathcal{M}'$ for some $n \geq 0$ (where by convention $\mathsf{N}' \parallel \mathcal{M}' = \mathsf{N} \parallel \mathcal{M}$ if $n = 0$), then we say that $\mathsf{N}' \parallel \mathcal{M}'$ is a *lockstep derivative* of $\mathsf{N} \parallel \mathcal{M}$. Clearly each lockstep derivative is a derivative, but not vice versa.

A lockstep computation is an either finite or infinite sequence of lockstep transitions, and it is *maximal* if either it is finite and cannot be extended (because the last session is not live), or it is infinite. Let γ range over lockstep computations.

Formally, a lockstep computation γ can be denoted as follows, where $x \in \mathbf{N} \cup \{\omega\}$ is the length of γ:

$$\gamma = \{\mathsf{N}_k \parallel \mathcal{M}_k \overset{\Delta_k}{\Rightarrow}_k \mathsf{N}_{k+1} \parallel \mathcal{M}_{k+1}\}_{k<x}$$

That is, γ is represented as the set of its successive lockstep transitions, where the arrow subscript k is used to indicate that the transition occurs in the k-th step of the computation. This is needed in order to distinguish equal transitions occurring in different steps. For instance, in the session $\mathsf{N} \parallel \langle \mathsf{p}, \lambda, \mathsf{q} \rangle$, where $\mathsf{N} = \mathsf{p}\llbracket P \rrbracket \parallel \mathsf{q}\llbracket Q \rrbracket$ with $P = \mathsf{q}!\lambda; P$ and $Q = \mathsf{p}?\lambda; Q$, all lockstep transitions with $k \geq 1$ are of the form

$$\mathsf{N} \parallel \langle \mathsf{p}, \lambda, \mathsf{q} \rangle \xrightarrow{\{\mathsf{p}\,\mathsf{q}!\lambda, \mathsf{p}\,\mathsf{q}?\lambda\}}_k \mathsf{N} \parallel \langle \mathsf{p}, \lambda, \mathsf{q} \rangle$$

We can now formalise the progress property:

Definition 4 (Input-enabling session). *A session $\mathsf{N} \parallel \mathcal{M}$ is input-enabling if $\mathsf{p}\llbracket \mathsf{q}?\{\lambda_i; P_i\}_{i \in I} \rrbracket \in \mathsf{N}$ implies that, for all maximal*

$$\gamma = \{\mathsf{N}_k \parallel \mathcal{M}_k \overset{\Delta_k}{\Rightarrow}_k \mathsf{N}_{k+1} \parallel \mathcal{M}_{k+1}\}_{k<x}$$

with $\mathsf{N}_0 \parallel \mathcal{M}_0 = \mathsf{N} \parallel \mathcal{M}$, there exists $h < x$ such that $\mathsf{p}\,\mathsf{q}?\lambda_i \in \Delta_h$ for some $i \in I$.

Definition 5 (Queue-consuming session). *A session $\mathsf{N} \parallel \mathcal{M}$ is queue-consuming if $\mathcal{M} \equiv \langle \mathsf{p}, \lambda, \mathsf{q} \rangle \cdot \mathcal{M}'$ implies that, for all maximal*

$$\gamma = \{\mathsf{N}_k \parallel \mathcal{M}_k \overset{\Delta_k}{\Rightarrow}_k \mathsf{N}_{k+1} \parallel \mathcal{M}_{k+1}\}_{k<x}$$

with $\mathsf{N}_0 \parallel \mathcal{M}_0 = \mathsf{N} \parallel \mathcal{M}$, there exists $h < x$ such that $\mathsf{p}\,\mathsf{q}?\lambda \in \Delta_h$.

Definition 6 (Progress). *A session has the progress property if:*

1. *(Deadlock-freedom) None of its lockstep derivatives is deadlocked;*
2. *(No locked inputs) All its lockstep derivatives are input-enabling;*
3. *(No orphan messages) All its lockstep derivatives are queue-consuming.*

It is easy to see that deadlock-freedom implies no locked inputs and no orphan messages for finite computations.

Example 1. Let $\mathsf{N} = \mathsf{p}[\![\,P\,]\!] \parallel \mathsf{q}[\![\,Q\,]\!] \parallel \mathsf{r}[\![\,R\,]\!]$, where $P = \mathsf{q}!\lambda; P$, $Q = \mathsf{p}?\lambda; \mathsf{r}?\lambda'; Q$ and $R = \mathsf{q}!\lambda'; R$.

The unique maximal lockstep computation of $\mathsf{N} \parallel \emptyset$ is the following:

$$\mathsf{N} \parallel \emptyset \xrightarrow{\{\mathsf{p\,q!}\lambda, \mathsf{r\,q!}\lambda'\}} \mathsf{N} \parallel \langle \mathsf{p}, \lambda, \mathsf{q} \rangle \cdot \langle \mathsf{r}, \lambda', \mathsf{q} \rangle$$

$$\xrightarrow{\{\mathsf{p\,q!}\lambda, \mathsf{p\,q?}\lambda, \mathsf{r\,q!}\lambda'\}} \mathsf{p}[\![\,P\,]\!] \parallel \mathsf{q}[\![\,\mathsf{r}?\lambda'; Q\,]\!] \parallel \mathsf{r}[\![\,R\,]\!] \parallel \langle \mathsf{r}, \lambda', \mathsf{q} \rangle \cdot \langle \mathsf{p}, \lambda, \mathsf{q} \rangle \cdot \langle \mathsf{r}, \lambda', \mathsf{q} \rangle$$

$$\xrightarrow{\{\mathsf{p\,q!}\lambda, \mathsf{r\,q?}\lambda', \mathsf{r\,q!}\lambda'\}} \mathsf{N} \parallel \langle \mathsf{p}, \lambda, \mathsf{q} \rangle \cdot \langle \mathsf{r}, \lambda', \mathsf{q} \rangle \cdot \langle \mathsf{p}, \lambda, \mathsf{q} \rangle \cdot \langle \mathsf{r}, \lambda', \mathsf{q} \rangle$$

$$\cdots \qquad \cdots$$

It is easy to check that $\mathsf{N} \parallel \emptyset$ has the progress property. Indeed, every input communication in Q is eventually enabled, and, even though the queue grows at each step of the lockstep computation, every message in the queue is eventually read.

3   Configuration Types

As in [8], the key difference with respect to classical formulations of global types in literature is the splitting between output choices and inputs. Sessions are typed by configuration types, which are pairs of global types and queues.

Definition 7 (Global and configuration types).

1. Global types G *are defined by:*

$$\mathsf{G} ::=_\rho \mathsf{p\,q}!\{\lambda_i; \mathsf{G}_i\}_{i \in I} \mid \mathsf{p\,q}?\lambda; \mathsf{G} \mid \mathsf{End}$$

   where $I \neq \emptyset$ and $\mathsf{p} \neq \mathsf{q}$ and $\lambda_j \neq \lambda_h$ for $j \neq h$.
2. Configuration types *are pairs* $\mathsf{G} \parallel \mathcal{M}$, *where G is a global type and $\mathcal{M}$ is a message queue.*

As for processes, $::=_\rho$ indicates that global types are *regular*.

The global type $\mathsf{p\,q}!\{\lambda_i; \mathsf{G}_i\}_{i \in I}$ specifies that player p sends a label λ_k with $k \in I$ to participant q and then the interaction described by the global type G_k takes place. The global type $\mathsf{p\,q}?\lambda; \mathsf{G}$ specifies that player q receives label λ from participant p and then the interaction described by the global type G takes place. A choice between different inputs is useless, since only one label can be received in each branch of an output choice.

In configuration types, as specified by the previous definition, inputs and outputs may be unrelated both between them and with the messages in the

$$[\text{END}] \frac{}{\vdash_{\text{iom}} \text{End} \parallel \emptyset} \qquad [\text{IN}] \frac{\vdash_{\text{iom}} \text{G} \parallel \mathcal{M}}{\vdash_{\text{iom}} \text{p q}?\lambda; \text{G} \parallel \langle \text{p}, \lambda, \text{q} \rangle \cdot \mathcal{M}} \vdash_{\text{read}} (\text{G}, \mathcal{M})$$

$$[\text{OUT}] \frac{\vdash_{\text{iom}} \text{G}_i \parallel \mathcal{M} \cdot \langle \text{p}, \lambda_i, \text{q} \rangle \quad \forall i \in I}{\vdash_{\text{iom}} \text{p q}!\{\lambda_i; \text{G}_i\}_{i \in I} \parallel \mathcal{M}} \vdash_{\text{read}} (\text{G}_i, \mathcal{M} \cdot \langle \text{p}, \lambda_i, \text{q} \rangle) \; \forall i \in I$$

$$[\text{EMPTY-R}] \frac{}{\vdash_{\text{read}} (\text{G}, \emptyset)} \qquad [\text{OUT-R}] \frac{\vdash_{\text{read}} (\text{G}_i, \mathcal{M}) \quad (\forall i \in I)}{\vdash_{\text{read}} (\text{p q}!\{\lambda_i; \text{G}_i\}_{i \in I}, \mathcal{M})}$$

$$[\text{IN-R1}] \frac{\vdash_{\text{read}} (\text{G}, \mathcal{M})}{\vdash_{\text{read}} (\text{p q}?\lambda; \text{G}, \langle \text{p}, \lambda, \text{q} \rangle \cdot \mathcal{M})} \qquad [\text{IN-R2}] \frac{\vdash_{\text{read}} (\text{G}, \mathcal{M})}{\vdash_{\text{read}} (\text{p q}?\lambda; \text{G}, \mathcal{M})} \; \mathcal{M} \not\equiv \langle \text{p}, \lambda, \text{q} \rangle \cdot \mathcal{M}'$$

Fig. 2. Input/output matching of configuration types (Coinductive version).

queue. In order to get a type system which guarantees progress we need to single out suitable configuration types. Moreover, we want to do this without imposing unnecessary restrictions. In this section we introduce the first two conditions we impose on configuration types: input/output matching and boundedness. A third and last condition (projectability) will be discussed in Sect. 4, where we will relate configurations types to session computations.

To ensure correspondence between inputs and outputs, in Fig. 2 we define the input/output matching of configuration types. A configuration type $\text{G} \parallel \mathcal{M}$ is *input/output matching* if we can derive $\vdash_{\text{iom}} \text{G} \parallel \mathcal{M}$. The double dotted line indicates that the rules should be interpreted coinductively, i.e., we allow infinite proof trees. The intuition is that every input in the global type will find, when it is the first communication of a player, a corresponding message on the queue and every message put on the queue will be eventually read. To satisfy the first constraint rule [IN] requires that the message sent from p to q with the expected label be indeed the first message from p to q on the queue. To satisfy the second constraint if the global type is End, then there should be no messages on the queue, rule [END]. If the global type is a choice of outputs, rule [OUT] says that, after performing any output, the configurations (in which the queues have been augmented by the messages sent) should have matching inputs/outputs. Moreover rules [IN] and [OUT] require that all messages in the queue will be eventually read. This last restriction is enforced by the auxiliary judgment $\vdash_{\text{read}} (\text{G}, \mathcal{M})$, which means that (each path of) G *reads all the messages in* $\mathcal{M}$. The inductive definition of this judgment is given at the bottom of Fig. 2. If the queue is empty, rule [EMPTY-R], then the judgement holds. If G is a choice of outputs, rule [OUT-R], then in each branch of the choice all the messages in the queue must be read. For an input type $\text{p q}?\lambda; \text{G}$, if the message at the top of the queue (considered modulo $\equiv$) is $\langle \text{p}, \lambda, \text{q} \rangle$ we read it, rule [IN-R1], otherwise we do not to read messages, rule [IN-R2].

For example we can derive $\vdash_{\text{iom}} \text{G} \parallel \emptyset$, where G is the global type discussed in the Introduction. The proof has an infinite non-regular branch showing the judgments $\vdash_{\text{iom}} \text{G} \parallel \underbrace{\langle \text{p}, \lambda, \text{q} \rangle \cdots \langle \text{p}, \lambda, \text{q} \rangle}_{2n}$ for $n \geq 1$.

[END-I] $\dfrac{}{\mathcal{H} \vdash^{\mathcal{I}}_{\mathsf{iom}} \mathsf{End} \parallel \emptyset}$ [CYCLE] $\dfrac{\vdash_{\mathsf{ok}} (\mathsf{G}, \mathcal{M}, \mathcal{M}')}{\mathcal{H}, (\mathsf{G}, \mathcal{M}) \vdash^{\mathcal{I}}_{\mathsf{iom}} \mathsf{G} \parallel \mathcal{M}'}$

[OUT-I] $\dfrac{\mathcal{H}, (\mathsf{p\,q!}\{\lambda_i; \mathsf{G}_i\}_{i \in I}, \mathcal{M}) \vdash^{\mathcal{I}}_{\mathsf{iom}} \mathsf{G}_i \parallel \mathcal{M} \cdot \langle \mathsf{p}, \lambda_i, \mathsf{q}\rangle \quad \forall i \in I}{\mathcal{H} \vdash^{\mathcal{I}}_{\mathsf{iom}} \mathsf{p\,q!}\{\lambda_i; \mathsf{G}_i\}_{i \in I} \parallel \mathcal{M}}$

[IN-I] $\dfrac{\mathcal{H}, (\mathsf{p\,q?}\lambda; \mathsf{G}, \langle \mathsf{p}, \lambda, \mathsf{q}\rangle \cdot \mathcal{M}) \vdash^{\mathcal{I}}_{\mathsf{iom}} \mathsf{G} \parallel \mathcal{M}}{\mathcal{H} \vdash^{\mathcal{I}}_{\mathsf{iom}} \mathsf{p\,q?}\lambda; \mathsf{G} \parallel \langle \mathsf{p}, \lambda, \mathsf{q}\rangle \cdot \mathcal{M}}$

Fig. 3. Input/output matching of configuration types (Inductive version).

The coinductive formulation of input/output matching for configuration types is natural and elegant, but to get an effective type system we need an inductive formulation. Figure 3 gives such a formulation, which is parametric on the auxiliary judgment $\vdash_{\mathsf{ok}} (\mathsf{G}, \mathcal{M}, \mathcal{M}')$. This judgment will be detailed in Sect. 5, where the soundness proof of the inductive formulation w.r.t. the coinductive one is sketched. By $\mathcal{H}$ we denote a set of pairs $(\mathsf{G}, \mathcal{M})$ needed to detect when, starting from a configuration, we encounter a configuration with the same global type. Rules [END-I], [OUT-I] and [IN-I] are obtained from the corresponding rules in Fig. 2 by increasing the set of circular hypotheses as usual and by dropping the reading condition. The rule [CYCLE] can be applied when the global type already appeared in the derivation and it requires a condition involving the global type and the two queues associated with it, expressed by the judgment $\vdash_{\mathsf{ok}} (\mathsf{G}, \mathcal{M}, \mathcal{M}')$. This judgement must enforce the property that all messages in $\mathcal{M}'$ will be eventually read by G and moreover that every input in G should find, when it is enabled, a corresponding message in $\mathcal{M}'$. In [8] the trivial condition $\mathcal{M} = \mathcal{M}' = \emptyset$ is used. Requiring $\mathcal{M} \equiv \mathcal{M}'$ would mean to restrict the coinductive system to regular derivations. We will discuss more significant and expressive conditions in Sect. 5. Note that, to obtain an actual algorithm from the rules in Fig. 3, we have to force the application of [CYCLE] as soon as possible, and to fail if the judgement $\vdash_{\mathsf{ok}} (\mathsf{G}, \mathcal{M}, \mathcal{M}')$ does not hold.

Unfortunately input/output matching is not enough to avoid computations where some participant remains stuck forever. To enforce lock-freedom by typing, we need the boundedness condition (Definition 9) as shown in Example 4.

Let the *players* of a global type to be its active participants. The function players associates to global types their sets of *players*, which are the smallest sets such that:

$$\mathsf{players}(\mathsf{p\,q!}\{\lambda_i; \mathsf{G}_i\}_{i \in I}) = \{\mathsf{p}\} \cup \bigcup_{i \in I} \mathsf{players}(\mathsf{G}_i)$$
$$\mathsf{players}(\mathsf{p\,q?}\lambda; \mathsf{G}) = \{\mathsf{q}\} \cup \mathsf{players}(\mathsf{G}) \qquad \mathsf{players}(\mathsf{End}) = \emptyset$$

Note that the regularity assumption on global types ensures that the set of players of a global type is finite.

Global types can be naturally seen as trees. We use ξ to denote a *path* in global type trees, i.e., a possibly infinite sequence of communications $\mathsf{p\,q!}\lambda$ or $\mathsf{p\,q?}\lambda$. With ξ_n we represent the n-th communication in the path ξ, where $0 \leq n < x$ and $x \in \mathbf{N} \cup \{\omega\}$ is the length of ξ. With ϵ we denote the empty sequence and with · the concatenation of a finite sequence with a possibly infinite sequence. The function Paths gives the set of *paths* of global types, which are the greatest sets such that:

$$\text{Paths}(p\,q!\{\lambda_i; G_i\}_{i\in I}) = \bigcup_{i\in I}\{p\,q!\lambda_i \cdot \xi \mid \xi \in \text{Paths}(G_i)\}$$
$$\text{Paths}(p\,q?\lambda; G) = \{p\,q?\lambda \cdot \xi \mid \xi \in \text{Paths}(G)\} \qquad \text{Paths}(\text{End}) = \{\epsilon\}$$

We can now formalise the requirement that the first occurrences of players in a global type are at a bounded depth in all paths starting from the root. This is done by defining the *depth* of a player p in a global type G, depth(G, p).

Definition 8 (Depth of a player). *Let* G *be a global type. For* $\xi \in \text{Paths}(G)$ *set* depth$(\xi, p) = \inf\{n \mid \text{play}(\xi_n) = p\}$, *and define* depth(G, p), *the depth of* p *in* G, *as follows:*

$$\text{depth}(G, p) = \begin{cases} 1 + \sup\{\text{depth}(\xi, p) \mid \xi \in \text{Paths}(G)\} & p \in \text{players}(G) \\ 0 & \textit{otherwise} \end{cases}$$

Note that, if $p \neq \text{play}(\xi_n)$ for some path ξ and all $n \in \mathbf{N}$, then depth$(\xi, p) = \inf \emptyset = \infty$. Hence, if p is a player of a global type G, but it does not occur as a player in some path of G, then depth(G, p) = ∞.

Definition 9 (Boundedness). *A global type* G *is* bounded *if* depth(G', p) *is finite for all participants* $p \in \text{players}(G)$ *and all types* G' *which occur in* G.

Example 2. The following example shows the necessity of considering all types occurring in a global type for defining boundedness. Consider G = r q!λ; r q?λ; G', where

$$G' = p\,q!\{\lambda_1; p\,q?\lambda_1; q\,r!\lambda_3; q\,r?\lambda_3 , \lambda_2; p\,q?\lambda_2; G'\}$$

Then we have: depth(G, r) = 1   depth(G, p) = 3   depth(G, q) = 2 whereas

depth(G', r) = ∞ depth(G', p) = 1   depth(G', q) = 2

Since global types are regular the boundedness condition is decidable.

4   Type System

Usually in type assignment systems for multiparty sessions [17,18] global types are projected onto local types and local types are assigned to processes. The simplicity of our calculus allows us to project global types directly onto processes as in [8,22].

Figure 4 gives the rules defining the judgment $G\upharpoonright p \mapsto P$, saying that the global type G, projected onto participant p, gives the process P. The double dotted line indicates that such rules should be interpreted coinductively. Notice that proof trees are *regular*, that is, with finitely many distinct sub-trees.

The definition uses process contexts which can have an arbitrary number of holes indexed with natural numbers, where we assume that each hole has a

$$\mathcal{C} ::= [\,]_n \quad | \quad \mathsf{p}?\{\lambda_i; \mathcal{C}_i\}_{i \in I} \quad | \quad \mathsf{p}!\{\lambda_i; \mathcal{C}_i\}_{i \in I} \quad | \quad P \qquad \text{where } I \neq \emptyset,\ \lambda_j \neq \lambda_h \text{ for } j \neq h$$

$$[\text{Ext}] \ \frac{}{\mathsf{G} \upharpoonright \mathsf{p} \mapsto 0} \ \mathsf{p} \notin \text{players}(\mathsf{G}) \qquad [\text{Out-Snd}] \ \frac{\mathsf{G}_i \upharpoonright \mathsf{p} \mapsto P_i \quad \forall i \in I}{(\mathsf{p}\,\mathsf{q}!\{\lambda_i; \mathsf{G}_i\}_{i \in I}) \upharpoonright \mathsf{p} \mapsto \mathsf{q}!\{\lambda_i; P_i\}_{i \in I}}$$

$$[\text{Out-Rcv}] \ \frac{\mathsf{G}_i \upharpoonright \mathsf{q} \mapsto \mathcal{C}[\mathsf{p}?\lambda_i; P_{i,j}]_{j \in J} \quad \forall i \in I}{(\mathsf{p}\,\mathsf{q}!\{\lambda_i; \mathsf{G}_i\}_{i \in I}) \upharpoonright \mathsf{q} \mapsto \mathcal{C}[\mathsf{p}?\{\lambda_i; P_{i,j}\}_{i \in I}]_{j \in J}} \ \mathsf{q} \in \text{players}(\mathsf{p}\,\mathsf{q}!\{\lambda_i; \mathsf{G}_i\}_{i \in I})$$

$$[\text{Out-Ext}] \ \frac{\mathsf{G}_i \upharpoonright \mathsf{s} \mapsto \mathcal{C}[\mathsf{r}?\lambda_i'; R_{i,j}]_{j \in J} \quad \forall i \in I \qquad \mathsf{s} \notin \{\mathsf{p},\mathsf{q}\}}{(\mathsf{p}\,\mathsf{q}!\{\lambda_i; \mathsf{G}_i\}_{i \in I}) \upharpoonright \mathsf{s} \mapsto \mathcal{C}[\mathsf{r}?\{\lambda_i'; R_{i,j}\}_{i \in I}]_{j \in J}} \ \mathsf{s} \in \text{players}(\mathsf{G}_i) \ \forall i \in I$$

$$[\text{In-Rcv}] \ \frac{\mathsf{G} \upharpoonright \mathsf{q} \mapsto P}{(\mathsf{p}\,\mathsf{q}?\lambda; \mathsf{G}) \upharpoonright \mathsf{q} \mapsto \mathsf{p}?\lambda; P} \qquad [\text{In-Ext}] \ \frac{\mathsf{G} \upharpoonright \mathsf{s} \mapsto P \qquad \mathsf{s} \neq \mathsf{q}}{(\mathsf{p}\,\mathsf{q}?\lambda; \mathsf{G}) \upharpoonright \mathsf{s} \mapsto P} \ \mathsf{s} \in \text{players}(\mathsf{G})$$

Fig. 4. Projection of global types.

different index. Given a context $\mathcal{C}$ with holes indexed in J, we denote by $\mathcal{C}[P_j]_{j \in J}$ the process obtained by filling the hole indexed by j with P_j, for all $j \in J$.

Rule [Ext] states that projecting onto a participant which is not a player gives the inactive process. The following three rules describe the effect of projecting a global type which starts with the output of a label, chosen in a set, from player p to player q, and continues as G_i, if the label chosen was λ_i.

Rule [Out-Snd] projects the global type onto the sender p and, as expected, the resulting process is an output process sending the chosen label and continuing with the corresponding projections.

Rule [Out-Rcv] projects the output choice onto the receiver of the message and [Out-Ext] onto any other player of the global type. Such projections are well defined if the projections of the branches G_i, for $i \in I$, give processes which can be consistently combined to provide the resulting processes. More precisely, they have a common structure, modelled by a multi-hole context $\mathcal{C}$ with $j \in J$ holes, where the j-th holes in the projections of G_h and G_k for $h \neq k \in I$ can be filled with different processes. The processes filling the j-th holes of different branches must start with inputs from the same sender and labels identifying the branches. In this way, the processes in the j-th holes of all branches can be combined in an external choice, which is used to fill the same context in the resulting projection. If the context has no holes, i.e., it is a process, then the projections of all branches are just this process, which is also the resulting projection. For instance, if $\mathsf{G} = \mathsf{p}\,\mathsf{q}!\{\lambda_1; \mathsf{p}\,\mathsf{q}?\lambda_1; \mathsf{p}\,\mathsf{r}?\lambda, \lambda_2; \mathsf{p}\,\mathsf{q}?\lambda_2; \mathsf{p}\,\mathsf{r}?\lambda\}$, then $\mathsf{G} \upharpoonright \mathsf{r} = \mathsf{p}?\lambda$ since $(\mathsf{p}\,\mathsf{q}?\lambda_1; \mathsf{p}\,\mathsf{r}?\lambda) \upharpoonright \mathsf{r} = (\mathsf{p}\,\mathsf{q}?\lambda_2; \mathsf{p}\,\mathsf{r}?\lambda) \upharpoonright \mathsf{r} = \mathsf{p}?\lambda$.

The only difference between [Out-Rcv] and [Out-Ext] is that, in rule [Out-Rcv] the sender and the labels are those of the external choice to be projected, whereas in rule [Out-Ext] they are arbitrary. Note that, if the participant r sending the message to s in rule [Out-Ext] is not the participant p who chooses the branch, then also r before behaving differently, i.e., sending distinct messages to s in different branches, must receive distinct messages exposing the various branches. So in order to behave differently in various branches a player must know in which branch of the choice she is, by receiving a label from a player who knows in which branch of the choice she is.

The last two rules describe the effect of projecting a global type starting with player q reading label λ sent by participant p, and continuing as G. In rule [IN-RCV], projecting onto player q gives the process waiting for the input λ from p, and then continuing as the projection of G. In rule [IN-EXT], projecting onto any other player of G simply gives the projection of G. Note that the case where the participant is not a player in G is covered by rule [EXT].

Rules in Fig. 4 define a relation, while usually the projection of a global type is expected to be a function. We can prove that for bounded global types this is the case. We conjecture that the boundedness condition could be avoided. Assuming boundedness strongly simplifies the proof and it is anyway necessary to ensure progress, as shown in Example 4.

Proposition 1. *If* G *is a bounded global type and* $G \upharpoonright p \mapsto P$ *and* $G \upharpoonright p \mapsto Q$, *then* $P = Q$.

Thanks to the above proposition, for a bounded global type G, we denote by $G \upharpoonright p$ the unique P such that $G \upharpoonright p \mapsto P$, thus we have $G \upharpoonright p = P$. Since from now on we will only deal with bounded global types we will use this notation.

In the following example we consider a global type obtained by anticipating output choices and we show the need for multihole contexts in projecting a choice of outputs onto the receiver of the communication.

Example 3. Let $G = pq!\{\lambda_1; pq?\lambda_1; G', \lambda_2; pq?\lambda_2; G'\}$ where

$$G' = qp!\{\lambda_3; qp?\lambda_3, \lambda_4; qp?\lambda_4; G\}$$

We have the projection

$$G \upharpoonright q = p?\{\lambda_1; p!\{\lambda_3, \lambda_4; G \upharpoonright q\}, \lambda_2; p!\{\lambda_3, \lambda_4; G \upharpoonright q\}\}$$

by filling the empty context with the external choice obtained by combining the projections onto q of the branches $pq?\lambda_1; G'$ and $pq?\lambda_2; G'$.
Consider now $G'' = pq!\{\lambda_1; G_1, \lambda_2; G_2\}$ where

$$G_i = qp!\{\lambda_3; pq?\lambda_i; qp?\lambda_3, \lambda_4; pq?\lambda_i; qp?\lambda_4; G''\} \text{ for } i = 1, 2.$$

G'' is obtained from G by anticipating the output choice in G' before the inputs $pq?\lambda_1$ and $pq?\lambda_2$ in the two branches of G. To compute the projection of G'' onto q we find the context $\mathcal{C} = p!\{\lambda_3; [\ ]_1, \lambda_4; [\ ]_2\}$ to obtain

$$G'' \upharpoonright q = \mathcal{C}[\ p?\{\lambda_1, \lambda_2\}\ ]_1 [\ p?\{\lambda_1; G'' \upharpoonright q, \lambda_2; G'' \upharpoonright q\}\ ]_2$$
$$= p!\{\lambda_3; p?\{\lambda_1, \lambda_2\}, \lambda_4; p?\{\lambda_1; G'' \upharpoonright q, \lambda_2; G'' \upharpoonright q\}\}$$

Configuration types describing well behaved sessions must be input/output matching, with global types which are bounded and projectable onto all their players.

$$[\leq\text{-}0]\ \overline{0\leq 0} \qquad [\leq\text{-OUT}]\ \frac{P_i\leq Q_i \quad i\in I}{\mathsf{p}!\{\lambda_i;P_i\}_{i\in I}\leq \mathsf{p}!\{\lambda_i;Q_i\}_{i\in I\cup J}} \qquad [\leq\text{-IN}]\ \frac{P_i\leq Q_i \quad i\in I}{\mathsf{p}?\{\lambda_i;P_i\}_{i\in I\cup J}\leq \mathsf{p}?\{\lambda_i;Q_i\}_{i\in I}}$$

Fig. 5. Preorder on processes.

$$[\text{TYPE}]\ \frac{P_i\leq \mathsf{G}\!\restriction\!\mathsf{p}_i \quad i\in I \qquad \mathsf{players}(\mathsf{G})\subseteq\{\mathsf{p}_i\mid i\in I\}}{\vdash \Pi_{i\in I}\mathsf{p}_i[\![P_i]\!]\parallel \mathcal{M}:\mathsf{G}\parallel \mathcal{M}}$$

Fig. 6. Multiparty session typing rule.

Definition 10 (Well-formed configuration types). *We say that* $\mathsf{G}\parallel\mathcal{M}$ *is well formed if* $\vdash_{\mathsf{iom}}\mathsf{G}\parallel\mathcal{M}$ *holds and* G *is bounded and* $\mathsf{G}\!\restriction\!\mathsf{p}$ *is defined for all* $\mathsf{p}\in\mathsf{players}(\mathsf{G})$.

In our type assignment system we permit only well-formed configuration types. Processes and projections of global types are compared using the pre-order on processes defined in Fig. 5. To compare two processes they must be both internal choices or external choices or the inactive process. In the first case it is better the process doing less outputs and in the second case the one expecting more inputs and in both cases their continuations after the same label must be in the same relation. The only typing rule is given in Fig. 6. It requires that for each $\mathsf{p}_i[\![P_i]\!]$ in the session the process P_i be better than the projection of the global type onto p_i for all $i\in I$. The condition $\mathsf{players}(\mathsf{G})\subseteq\{\mathsf{p}_i\mid i\in I\}$ allows participants in the session paired with process $\mathbf{0}$: this is necessary to guarantee invariance of typing with respect to structural equivalence of sessions. Notice that we can compute the projections of global types, since the regularity assumption ensures that there is only a finite number of cases to examine. Moreover the contexts required in rules [OUT-RCV] and [OUT-EXT] can be determined by examining the projections of the branches in the output choices. The regularity of processes ensures that with a simple strategy based on cycle detection we can compare processes according to the preorder of Fig. 5. Therefore our type system is effective once we establish the decidability of $\vdash_{\mathsf{ok}}(\mathsf{G},\mathcal{M},\mathcal{M}')$ and that $\vdash_{\mathsf{iom}}^{\mathcal{I}}\mathsf{G}\parallel\mathcal{M}$ implies $\vdash_{\mathsf{iom}}\mathsf{G}\parallel\mathcal{M}$. We do not know if $\vdash_{\mathsf{iom}}\mathsf{G}\parallel\mathcal{M}$ implies $\vdash_{\mathsf{iom}}^{\mathcal{I}}\mathsf{G}\parallel\mathcal{M}$.

Example 4. Without the boundedness condition the configuration type $\mathsf{G}'\parallel\emptyset$ with G' defined in Example 2 could type the session $\mathsf{p}[\![P]\!]\parallel\mathsf{q}[\![Q]\!]\parallel\mathsf{r}[\![\mathsf{q}?\lambda_3]\!]\parallel\emptyset$, where $P=\mathsf{q}!\{\lambda_1,\lambda_2;P\}$ and $Q=\mathsf{p}?\{\lambda_1;\mathsf{r}!\lambda_3,\lambda_2;Q\}$. In this session participant r may wait forever.

In order to state the properties of our type system it is useful to introduce an LTS for configuration types as in [8], see Fig. 7. The first two rules show transitions of top level output choices and inputs. The other two rules deal with transitions performed inside output choices and inputs. For these to happen the player of the performed communication must be different from the player of the enclosing output choice or input. In the case of an output choice the same communication must be done in all branches. The relation between the

$$[\text{Top-Out}] \quad \mathsf{p}\,\mathsf{q}!\{\lambda_i; G_i\}_{i\in I} \parallel \mathcal{M} \xrightarrow{\;\mathsf{p}\,\mathsf{q}!\lambda_j\;} G_j \parallel \mathcal{M} \cdot \langle \mathsf{p}, \lambda_j, \mathsf{q}\rangle \quad j \in I$$

$$[\text{Top-In}] \quad \mathsf{p}\,\mathsf{q}?\lambda; G \parallel \langle \mathsf{p}, \lambda, \mathsf{q}\rangle \cdot \mathcal{M} \xrightarrow{\;\mathsf{p}\,\mathsf{q}?\lambda\;} G \parallel \mathcal{M}$$

$$[\text{Inside-Out}] \quad \frac{G_i \parallel \mathcal{M} \cdot \langle \mathsf{p}, \lambda_i, \mathsf{q}\rangle \xrightarrow{\beta} G_i' \parallel \mathcal{M}' \cdot \langle \mathsf{p}, \lambda_i, \mathsf{q}\rangle \quad i \in I}{\mathsf{p}\,\mathsf{q}!\{\lambda_i; G_i\}_{i\in I} \parallel \mathcal{M} \xrightarrow{\beta} \mathsf{p}\,\mathsf{q}!\{\lambda_i; G_i'\}_{i\in I} \parallel \mathcal{M}'} \quad \mathsf{p} \neq \mathsf{play}(\beta)$$

$$[\text{Inside-In}] \quad \frac{G \parallel \mathcal{M} \xrightarrow{\beta} G' \parallel \mathcal{M}'}{\mathsf{p}\,\mathsf{q}?\lambda; G \parallel \langle \mathsf{p}, \lambda, \mathsf{q}\rangle \cdot \mathcal{M} \xrightarrow{\beta} \mathsf{p}\,\mathsf{q}?\lambda; G' \parallel \langle \mathsf{p}, \lambda, \mathsf{q}\rangle \cdot \mathcal{M}'} \quad \mathsf{q} \neq \mathsf{play}(\beta)$$

Fig. 7. LTS for configuration types.

queues in the premises and in the conclusions of these rules mirror those of the rules for input/output matching, see Fig. 2, so that starting with well-formed types the LTS produces always well-formed types. The inside rules are needed to allow transitions of configuration types to mimic those of sessions. For example if $\mathsf{N} \equiv \mathsf{p}[\![\mathsf{q}?\lambda]\!] \parallel \mathsf{q}[\![\mathsf{p}?\lambda']\!]$, $\mathcal{M} \equiv \langle \mathsf{q}, \lambda', \mathsf{p}\rangle \cdot \langle \mathsf{p}, \lambda, \mathsf{q}\rangle$ and $G = \mathsf{p}\,\lambda?\mathsf{q}; \mathsf{q}\,\mathsf{p}?\lambda'$, then we get $\vdash \mathsf{N} \parallel \mathcal{M} : G \parallel \mathcal{M}$ and $\mathsf{N} \parallel \mathcal{M} \xrightarrow{\;\mathsf{q}\,\mathsf{p}?\lambda'\;} \mathsf{p}[\![\mathsf{q}?\lambda]\!] \parallel \langle \mathsf{p}, \lambda, \mathsf{q}\rangle$. We have $G \parallel \mathcal{M} \xrightarrow{\;\mathsf{q}\,\mathsf{p}?\lambda'\;} \mathsf{p}\,\lambda?\mathsf{q} \parallel \langle \mathsf{p}, \lambda, \mathsf{q}\rangle$ by rule [Inside-In].

As usual we start with Inversion and Canonical Form lemmas.

Lemma 1 (Inversion). *If* $\vdash \mathsf{N} \parallel \mathcal{M} : G \parallel \mathcal{M}$, *then for all* $\mathsf{p}[\![P]\!] \in \mathsf{N}$ *we have* $P \leq G{\restriction}\mathsf{p}$.

Lemma 2 (Canonical Form). *If* $\vdash \mathsf{N} \parallel \mathcal{M} : G \parallel \mathcal{M}$ *and* $\mathsf{p} \in \mathsf{players}(G)$, *then* $\mathsf{p}[\![P]\!] \in \mathsf{N}$ *and* $P \leq G{\restriction}\mathsf{p}$.

Subject Reduction ensures not only that the reduced session is typeable, but also that this session is typed by the configuration type obtained from the initial one by doing the same communication of the session transition.

Theorem 1 (Subject Reduction). *If* $\vdash \mathsf{N}\|\mathcal{M} : G\|\mathcal{M}$ *and* $\mathsf{N} \parallel \mathcal{M} \xrightarrow{\beta} \mathsf{N}' \parallel \mathcal{M}'$, *then* $G \parallel \mathcal{M} \xrightarrow{\beta} G' \parallel \mathcal{M}'$ *and* $\vdash \mathsf{N}' \parallel \mathcal{M}' : G' \parallel \mathcal{M}'$.

A transition of configuration types is mimicked by a transition of sessions with a communication which can differ for the label in case of output, while it is the same in case of input. The reason is that a process with less outputs is better than a process with more outputs. Therefore a global type in which a player chooses a label can have more outputs than the process implementing the player. To state Session Fidelity we define $\mathsf{p}\,\mathsf{q}!\lambda \cong \mathsf{p}\,\mathsf{q}!\lambda'$ and $\mathsf{p}\,\mathsf{q}?\lambda \cong \mathsf{p}\,\mathsf{q}?\lambda$ for all $\mathsf{p}, \mathsf{q}, \lambda, \lambda'$.

Theorem 2 (Session Fidelity). *If* $\vdash \mathsf{N} \parallel \mathcal{M} : G \parallel \mathcal{M}$ *and* $G \parallel \mathcal{M} \xrightarrow{\beta}$, *then* $\mathsf{N} \parallel \mathcal{M} \xrightarrow{\beta'}$ *with* $\beta \cong \beta'$.

The more interesting property of our type system is Progress. The proof of input enabling is based on the fact that all players have a finite depth in bounded global types and that this depth (when greater than 1) decreases by reducing global types at the top level. The proof of queue consuming uses input/output matching to ensure that messages in the queue will find suitable readers. In both cases we use Session Fidelity to get the transitions of sessions from the transitions of the configuration types typing them.

Theorem 3 (Progress). *If* $\vdash \mathbb{N} \parallel \mathcal{M} : G \parallel \mathcal{M}$, *then* $\mathbb{N} \parallel \mathcal{M}$ *has the progress property.*

5   An Algorithm for Input/Output Matching

In this section we show the effectiveness of our type system by completing the inductive definition of input/output matching, see Fig. 3. This amounts to specify the condition $\vdash_{ok} (G, \mathcal{M}, \mathcal{M}')$ of rule [CYCLE]. The coinductive definition of input/output matching, see Fig. 2, checks that all messages on the queue are read at each application of rules [IN] and [OUT], therefore rule [CYCLE] needs to do a similar check on the (final) queue $\mathcal{M}'$. Note that, if a message in $\mathcal{M}$ is not in $\mathcal{M}'$, then a coinductive derivation of the judgement $\vdash_{iom} G \parallel \mathcal{M}'$ would get stuck on rule [IN], i.e., the judgement would not be derivable. So we require that *all messages in* $\mathcal{M}$ *be in* $\mathcal{M}'$. Since we want to allow also derivations in which the queue between two occurrences of the same global type may increase we *allow* $\mathcal{M}' \equiv \mathcal{M} \cdot \mathcal{M}''$. In order to ensure that *the messages in the queue* $\mathcal{M}''$ do not interfere with the input/output matching of G we demand that they *can be moved after the outputs of* G. As a result the messages in $\mathcal{M}''$ will be accumulated at the end of the queue and must be read in all paths of G.

The following examples show the need for the above restrictions on the messages of $\mathcal{M}'$.

Example 5. 1. Let $G = p\,q!\lambda_1; p\,q?\lambda_1; G'$, where $G' = p\,q!\{\lambda_1; G, \lambda_2; p\,q?\lambda_2; G\}$. To derive $\vdash_{iom} G \parallel \emptyset$ we should have $\vdash_{iom} G \parallel \langle p, \lambda_1, q \rangle$ since the message $\langle p, \lambda_1, q \rangle$ is left on the queue in the branch of G' starting with $p\,q!\lambda_1$. The derivation of $\vdash_{iom} G \parallel \langle p, \lambda_1, q \rangle$ would require first $\vdash_{iom} G' \parallel \langle p, \lambda_1, q \rangle$ and then $\vdash_{iom} p\,q?\lambda_2; G \parallel \langle p, \lambda_1, q \rangle \cdot \langle p, \lambda_2, q \rangle$. But rule [IN] is not applicable to $\vdash_{iom} p\,q?\lambda_2; G \parallel \langle p, \lambda_1, q \rangle \cdot \langle p, \lambda_2, q \rangle$. Indeed the message $\langle p, \lambda_1, q \rangle$ prevents the message $\langle p, \lambda_2, q \rangle$ from being read by $p\,q?\lambda_2; G$.
2. Let $G = p\,q!\{\lambda_1; p\,q?\lambda_1; q\,p!\lambda_3; q\,p?\lambda_3; G', \lambda_2; p\,q?\lambda_2; q\,p!\lambda_3; q\,p!\lambda_3; q\,p?\lambda_3; G\}$, where
$G' = p\,q!\lambda_4; p\,q?\lambda_4; G'$. To get $\vdash_{read} (G, \langle q, \lambda_3, p \rangle)$ we need $\vdash_{read} (G', \langle q, \lambda_3, p \rangle)$, which does not hold. In fact the message $\langle q, \lambda_3, p \rangle$ may remain forever in the queue.

The first restriction is formalised by the judgement $\vdash_{agr} (G, \mathcal{M})$ in Fig. 8, to be read G *agrees with* $\mathcal{M}$. Rule [OUT-C] requires that the queue $\mathcal{M}$ either does not contain a message from p to q, or I is a singleton, let $I = \{1\}$, $\mathcal{M} \equiv \langle p, \lambda_1, q \rangle \cdot \mathcal{M}_1$

$$[\text{End-C}] \; \frac{}{\mathcal{H} \vdash_{\mathsf{agr}} (\mathsf{End}, \mathcal{M})} \qquad [\text{Cycle-C}] \; \frac{}{\mathcal{H}, (\mathsf{G}, \mathcal{M}) \vdash_{\mathsf{agr}} (\mathsf{G}, \mathcal{M})}$$

$$[\text{In-C}] \; \frac{\mathcal{H}, (\mathsf{p}\,\mathsf{q}?\lambda; \mathsf{G}, \mathcal{M}) \vdash_{\mathsf{agr}} (\mathsf{G}, \mathcal{M})}{\mathcal{H} \vdash_{\mathsf{agr}} (\mathsf{p}\,\mathsf{q}?\lambda; \mathsf{G}, \mathcal{M})}$$

$$[\text{Out-C}] \; \frac{\mathcal{H}, (\mathsf{p}\,\mathsf{q}!\{\lambda_i; \mathsf{G}_i\}_{i \in I}, \mathcal{M}) \vdash_{\mathsf{agr}} (\mathsf{G}_i, \mathcal{M}') \quad \forall i \in I}{\mathcal{H} \vdash_{\mathsf{agr}} (\mathsf{p}\,\mathsf{q}!\{\lambda_i; \mathsf{G}_i\}_{i \in I}, \mathcal{M})} \quad \mathcal{M} \cdot \langle \mathsf{p}, \lambda_i, \mathsf{q} \rangle \equiv \langle \mathsf{p}, \lambda_i, \mathsf{q} \rangle \cdot \mathcal{M}' \; \forall i \in I$$

$$[\text{Cycle-DR}] \; \frac{\vdash_{\mathsf{read}} (\mathsf{G}, \mathcal{M})}{\mathcal{G}, \mathsf{G} \vdash_{\mathsf{dread}} (\mathsf{G}, \mathcal{M})} \qquad [\text{End-DR}] \; \frac{}{\mathcal{G} \vdash_{\mathsf{dread}} (\mathsf{End}, \emptyset)}$$

$$[\text{In-DR}] \; \frac{\mathcal{G}, \mathsf{p}\,\mathsf{q}?\lambda; \mathsf{G}' \vdash_{\mathsf{dread}} (\mathsf{G}', \mathcal{M})}{\mathcal{G} \vdash_{\mathsf{dread}} (\mathsf{p}\,\mathsf{q}?\lambda; \mathsf{G}', \mathcal{M})} \qquad [\text{Out-DR}] \; \frac{\mathcal{G}, \mathsf{p}\,\mathsf{q}!\{\lambda_i; \mathsf{G}_i\}_{i \in I} \vdash_{\mathsf{dread}} (\mathsf{G}_i, \mathcal{M}) \quad (\forall i \in I)}{\mathcal{G} \vdash_{\mathsf{dread}} (\mathsf{p}\,\mathsf{q}!\{\lambda_i; \mathsf{G}_i\}_{i \in I}, \mathcal{M})}$$

Fig. 8. Agreement and deep read judgments.

and $\mathcal{M}' \equiv \mathcal{M}_1 \cdot \langle \mathsf{p}, \lambda_1, \mathsf{q} \rangle$ for some $\mathcal{M}_1$. We avoid non determinism asking to use rule [Cycle-C] whenever applicable. Considering Example 5(1) we can see that $\vdash_{\mathsf{agr}} (\mathsf{G}', \langle \mathsf{p}, \lambda_1, \mathsf{q} \rangle)$ does not hold, since $\langle \mathsf{p}, \lambda_1, \mathsf{q} \rangle \cdot \langle \mathsf{p}, \lambda_2, \mathsf{q} \rangle \not\equiv \langle \mathsf{p}, \lambda_2, \mathsf{q} \rangle \cdot \mathcal{M}_0$ for all $\mathcal{M}_0$.

The second restriction is formalised by the judgement $\vdash_{\mathsf{dread}} (\mathsf{G}, \mathcal{M})$, dubbed G *deeply reads* $\mathcal{M}$. If the global type is End, then the queue must be empty, as expected. In case the global type is a choice of outputs the messages in the queue must be consumed in all branches and likewise if it is an input. As soon as a cycle is reached we require that $\mathcal{M}$ be read with the standard judgment. The cycle is discovered by adding as premises the examined global types. With $\mathcal{G}$ we denote a set of global types. It is not difficult to show that $\vdash_{\mathsf{dread}} (\mathsf{G}, \emptyset)$ for any G. Looking at Example 5(2) we see that $\vdash_{\mathsf{read}} (\mathsf{G}', \langle \mathsf{q}, \lambda_3, \mathsf{p} \rangle)$ does not hold. Therefore $\vdash_{\mathsf{dread}} (\mathsf{G}, \langle \mathsf{q}, \lambda_3, \mathsf{p} \rangle)$ is not derivable, as expected.

To sum up $\vdash_{\mathsf{ok}} (\mathsf{G}, \mathcal{M}, \mathcal{M}')$ is defined by the following rule:

$$[\text{OK}] \; \frac{\vdash_{\mathsf{read}} (\mathsf{G}, \mathcal{M}) \quad \vdash_{\mathsf{agr}} (\mathsf{G}, \mathcal{M}'') \quad \vdash_{\mathsf{dread}} (\mathsf{G}, \mathcal{M}'')}{\vdash_{\mathsf{ok}} (\mathsf{G}, \mathcal{M}, \mathcal{M}')} \quad \mathcal{M}' \equiv \mathcal{M} \cdot \mathcal{M}''$$

The correctness of this definition is stated by the main result of this section, i.e. the Soundness Theorem (Theorem 4). The proof of this theorem is based on the fact that the agreements of two queues imply the agreement of their concatenation and the same holds for deep readability.

Lemma 3. *1. If $\vdash_{\mathsf{agr}} (\mathsf{G}, \mathcal{M}_1)$ and $\vdash_{\mathsf{agr}} (\mathsf{G}, \mathcal{M}_2)$, then $\vdash_{\mathsf{agr}} (\mathsf{G}, \mathcal{M}_1 \cdot \mathcal{M}_2)$.*
2. If $\vdash_{\mathsf{dread}} (\mathsf{G}, \mathcal{M}_1)$ and $\vdash_{\mathsf{dread}} (\mathsf{G}, \mathcal{M}_2)$, then $\vdash_{\mathsf{dread}} (\mathsf{G}, \mathcal{M}_1 \cdot \mathcal{M}_2)$.

Theorem 4 (Soundness). *If $\vdash_{\mathsf{iom}}^{\mathcal{I}} \mathsf{G} \parallel \mathcal{M}$, then $\vdash_{\mathsf{iom}} \mathsf{G} \parallel \mathcal{M}$.*

Proof (Sketch). First of all we observe that the definition of the judgement $\mathcal{H} \vdash_{\mathsf{iom}}^{\mathcal{I}} \mathsf{G} \parallel \mathcal{M}$ can be equivalently expressed assuming $\mathcal{H}$ to be a sequence rather than a set, the only difference is the rule [cycle] which will have the following shape

$$[\text{Cycle}']\ \frac{\vdash_{\mathsf{read}} (\mathsf{G}, \mathcal{M}) \quad \vdash_{\mathsf{agr}} (\mathsf{G}, \mathcal{M}'') \quad \vdash_{\mathsf{dread}} (\mathsf{G}, \mathcal{M}'')}{\mathcal{H}_1, (\mathsf{G}, \mathcal{M}), \mathcal{H}_2 \vdash^{\mathcal{I}}_{\mathsf{iom}} \mathsf{G} \parallel \mathcal{M}'} \quad \mathcal{M}' \equiv \mathcal{M} \cdot \mathcal{M}''$$

where we have used rule [OK].

We say that a sequence $\mathcal{H}$ is coherent if $\mathcal{H}_1 \vdash^{\mathcal{I}}_{\mathsf{iom}} \mathsf{G} \parallel \mathcal{M}$ holds for any decomposition $\mathcal{H} = \mathcal{H}_1, (\mathsf{G}, \mathcal{M}), \mathcal{H}_2$.

The proof is by coinduction on the definition of $\vdash_{\mathsf{iom}} \mathsf{G} \parallel \mathcal{M}$ (see Fig. 2). To this end, we define the set $\mathcal{A}$ as follows:

$$\widehat{\mathsf{G}} \parallel \widehat{\mathcal{M}} \in \mathcal{A} \text{ if } \widehat{\mathcal{M}} \equiv \mathcal{M}_1 \cdot \mathcal{M}_2,\ \vdash_{\mathsf{agr}} (\widehat{\mathsf{G}}, \mathcal{M}_2),\ \vdash_{\mathsf{dread}} (\widehat{\mathsf{G}}, \mathcal{M}_2) \text{ and } \mathcal{H} \vdash^{\mathcal{I}}_{\mathsf{iom}} \widehat{\mathsf{G}} \parallel \mathcal{M}_1$$

for some coherent $\mathcal{H}$.

From the hypothesis $\vdash^{\mathcal{I}}_{\mathsf{iom}} \mathsf{G} \parallel \mathcal{M}$, we have immediately that $\mathsf{G} \parallel \mathcal{M} \in \mathcal{A}$, since $\mathcal{M} \equiv \mathcal{M} \cdot \emptyset$, $\vdash_{\mathsf{agr}} (\mathsf{G}, \emptyset)$ and $\vdash_{\mathsf{dread}} (\mathsf{G}, \emptyset)$ always hold, and the empty sequence is coherent. Thus, to conclude the proof, we just have to show that $\mathcal{A}$ is consistent with respect to the rules in Fig. 2. We prove that for all $\mathcal{H}$ coherent, $\widehat{\mathsf{G}}$, $\mathcal{M}_1$ and $\mathcal{M}_2$, if $\mathcal{H} \vdash^{\mathcal{I}}_{\mathsf{iom}} \widehat{\mathsf{G}} \parallel \mathcal{M}_1$, $\vdash_{\mathsf{agr}} (\widehat{\mathsf{G}}, \mathcal{M}_2)$ and $\vdash_{\mathsf{dread}} (\widehat{\mathsf{G}}, \mathcal{M}_2)$, then $\vdash_{\mathsf{iom}} \widehat{\mathsf{G}} \parallel \mathcal{M}_1 \cdot \mathcal{M}_2$ is the conclusion of a rule in Fig. 2, whose premises are in $\mathcal{A}$.

The proof is by induction on the length of $\mathcal{H}$, splitting cases on the last rule used to derive $\mathcal{H} \vdash^{\mathcal{I}}_{\mathsf{iom}} \widehat{\mathsf{G}} \parallel \mathcal{M}_1$. Cases for rules [END-I], [IN-I] and [OUT-I] just use the corresponding rules in Fig. 2, relying on inversion lemmas for $\vdash_{\mathsf{agr}} (\widehat{\mathsf{G}}, \mathcal{M}_2)$ and $\vdash_{\mathsf{dread}} (\widehat{\mathsf{G}}, \mathcal{M}_2)$, on the fact that $\mathcal{H} \vdash^{\mathcal{I}}_{\mathsf{iom}} \widehat{\mathsf{G}} \parallel \mathcal{M}_1$ implies $\vdash_{\mathsf{read}} (\widehat{\mathsf{G}}, \mathcal{M}_1)$ and that this together with $\vdash_{\mathsf{dread}} (\widehat{\mathsf{G}}, \mathcal{M}_2)$ implies $\vdash_{\mathsf{read}} (\widehat{\mathsf{G}}, \mathcal{M}_1 \cdot \mathcal{M}_2)$. We only remark that, for the case [OUT-I], the commutativity requirement in the side condition of rule [OUT-C] is essential. In the case of rule [CYCLE'] we have $\mathcal{H} = \mathcal{H}_1, (\widehat{\mathsf{G}}, \mathcal{M}'), \mathcal{H}_2$, $\mathcal{M}_1 \equiv \mathcal{M}' \cdot \mathcal{M}''$, $\vdash_{\mathsf{agr}} (\widehat{\mathsf{G}}, \mathcal{M}'')$ and $\vdash_{\mathsf{dread}} (\widehat{\mathsf{G}}, \mathcal{M}'')$, and, since $\mathcal{H}$ is coherent, we have $\mathcal{H}_1 \vdash^{\mathcal{I}}_{\mathsf{iom}} \widehat{\mathsf{G}} \parallel \mathcal{M}'$ and $\mathcal{H}_1$ is coherent as well. Then, the thesis follows by induction hypothesis, applied to $\mathcal{H}_1 \vdash^{\mathcal{I}}_{\mathsf{iom}} \widehat{\mathsf{G}} \parallel \mathcal{M}'$ and $\mathcal{M}'' \cdot \mathcal{M}_2$, because $\mathcal{H}_1$ is shorter than $\mathcal{H}$ and $\vdash_{\mathsf{agr}} (\mathsf{G}, \mathcal{M}'' \cdot \mathcal{M}_2)$ and $\vdash_{\mathsf{dread}} (\widehat{\mathsf{G}}, \mathcal{M}'' \cdot \mathcal{M}_2)$ hold by Lemma 3.

Considering the global type G of the Introduction to prove the judgment $\vdash^{\mathcal{I}}_{\mathsf{iom}} \mathsf{G} \parallel \emptyset$ we have to show that the messages on the queue do not interfere with the outputs of the type G and they will be eventually read. This is done by deriving $\vdash_{\mathsf{agr}} (\mathsf{G}, \langle \mathsf{p}, \lambda, \mathsf{q} \rangle \cdot \langle \mathsf{p}, \lambda, \mathsf{q} \rangle)$ and $\vdash_{\mathsf{dread}} (\mathsf{G}, \langle \mathsf{p}, \lambda, \mathsf{q} \rangle \cdot \langle \mathsf{p}, \lambda, \mathsf{q} \rangle)$.

6 Conclusion and Future Work

In this paper we presented a new definition of well-formedness for global types specifying protocols for multiparty sessions. Using the proposal of [8], communications between participants are split into output choices and inputs and a queue is added to keep the messages sent but yet not received. The flexibility gained by this syntax must however be disciplined, since we do not want to loose the matching between outputs and inputs that is immediate in the standard formulations of global types. Moreover we require the progress property, that in this asynchronous setting means not only that participants willing to communicate will eventually do it, but also that no message will stay on the queue forever. To this aim already in [8] some well-formedness conditions were defined. We deconfine the global and configuration types by extending:

- the definition of input/output matching allowing the typing of multiparty sessions, such as our running example, in which the queue will contain an unbounded number of messages;
- the definition of projection allowing to anticipate output choices over inputs (see Example 3).

We give a coinductive definition of an input/output matching that shows explicitly the properties enforced, i.e., when the protocol gets to the point in which a participant is waiting for a message, the message is on the queue and at any point of the protocol the messages in the queue can be all consumed. The definition is not effective, so we formulate an inductive version, which we prove to be sound and still expressive enough to type our running example. An important advantage of the splitting of communications into outputs and inputs is that we can specify, at the type level, protocols in which outputs of a given participant may be anticipated before some of its inputs without the need for asynchronous subtyping. To take advantage of this feature we give a definition of projection which takes into account the tree-like shape of global types and generalises the one of [8].

As future work we plan to adapt the definition of projection to permit protocols in which a participant can send labels to different receivers in choices as in [7]. A problem left open is the completeness of the inductive definition of input/output matching with respect to the coinductive one. This is related to the proof of decidability/undecidability of the coinductive definition of input/output matching. We conjecture that completeness does not hold, but we did not find a counter-example.

Acknowledgment. We are grateful to Ilaria Castellani and Elena Zucca for enlightening discussions on the subject of this paper. We thank Elena Zucca also for her careful reading of the paper. Her suggestions led to many improvements. Last but not least we are indebted to the anonymous referees for their constructive remarks.

References

1. Bettini, L., Coppo, M., D'Antoni, L., De Luca, M., Dezani-Ciancaglini, M., Yoshida, N.: Global progress in dynamically interleaved multiparty sessions. In: van Breugel, F., Chechik, M. (eds.) CONCUR 2008. LNCS, vol. 5201, pp. 418–433. Springer, Heidelberg (2008). https://doi.org/10.1007/978-3-540-85361-9_33
2. Bianchini, R., Dagnino, F.: Asynchronous-global-types-implementation. https://github.com/RiccardoBianc/Asynchronous-global-types-implementation
3. Bianchini, R., Dagnino, F.: Asynchronous global types in co-logic programming. In: Damiani, F., Dardha, O. (eds.) COORDINATION 2021. LNCS, vol. 12717, pp. 134–146. Springer, Cham (2021)

4. Bravetti, M., Carbone, M., Lange, J., Yoshida, N., Zavattaro, G.: A sound algorithm for asynchronous session subtyping. In: Fokkink, W.J., van Glabbeek, R. (eds.) CONCUR. LIPIcs, vol. 140, pp. 38:1–38:16. Schloss Dagstuhl - Leibniz-Zentrum für Informatik (2019). https://doi.org/10.4230/LIPIcs.CONCUR.2019.38

5. Bravetti, M., Carbone, M., Zavattaro, G.: Undecidability of asynchronous session subtyping. Inf. Comput. **256**, 300–320 (2017). https://doi.org/10.1016/j.ic.2017.07.010

6. Bravetti, M., Carbone, M., Zavattaro, G.: On the boundary between decidability and undecidability of asynchronous session subtyping. Theoret. Comput. Sci. **722**, 19–51 (2018). https://doi.org/10.1016/j.tcs.2018.02.010

7. Castellani, I., Dezani-Ciancaglini, M., Giannini, P.: Reversible sessions with flexible choices. Acta Informatica, 553–583 (2019). https://doi.org/10.1007/s00236-019-00332-y

8. Castellani, I., Dezani-Ciancaglini, M., Giannini, P.: Global types and event structure semantics for asynchronous multiparty sessions. CoRR abs/2102.00865 (2021). https://arxiv.org/abs/2102.00865

9. Coppo, M., Dezani-Ciancaglini, M., Yoshida, N., Padovani, L.: Global progress for dynamically interleaved multiparty sessions. Math. Struct. Comput. Sci. **26**(2), 238–302 (2016). https://doi.org/10.1017/S0960129514000188

10. Courcelle, B.: Fundamental properties of infinite trees. Theoret. Comput. Sci. **25**, 95–169 (1983). https://doi.org/10.1016/0304-3975(83)90059-2

11. Demangeon, R., Honda, K.: Nested protocols in session types. In: Koutny, M., Ulidowski, I. (eds.) CONCUR 2012. LNCS, vol. 7454, pp. 272–286. Springer, Heidelberg (2012). https://doi.org/10.1007/978-3-642-32940-1_20

12. Deniélou, P.M., Yoshida, N.: Dynamic multirole session types. In: Thomas Ball, M.S. (ed.) POPL, pp. 435–446. ACM Press (2011). https://doi.org/10.1145/1926385.1926435

13. Dezani-Ciancaglini, M., Ghilezan, S., Jaksic, S., Pantovic, J., Yoshida, N.: Precise subtyping for synchronous multiparty sessions. In: Gay, S., Alglave, J. (eds.) PLACES. EPTCS, vol. 203, pp. 29–44. Open Publishing Association (2016). https://doi.org/10.4204/EPTCS.203.3

14. Gay, S., Hole, M.: Subtyping for session types in the pi calculus. Acta Informatica **42**(2/3), 191–225 (2005). https://doi.org/10.1007/s00236-005-0177-z

15. Ghilezan, S., Jaksic, S., Pantovic, J., Scalas, A., Yoshida, N.: Precise subtyping for synchronous multiparty sessions. J. Logic Algeb. Methods Program. **104**, 127–173 (2019). https://doi.org/10.1016/j.jlamp.2018.12.002

16. Ghilezan, S., Pantović, J., Prokić, I., Scalas, A., Yoshida, N.: Precise subtyping for asynchronous multiparty sessions. Proc. ACM Program. Lang. **5**(POPL), 1–28 (2021). https://doi.org/10.1145/3434297

17. Honda, K., Yoshida, N., Carbone, M.: Multiparty asynchronous session types. In: Necula, G.C., Wadler, P. (eds.) POPL, pp. 273–284. ACM Press (2008). https://doi.org/10.1145/1328897.1328472

18. Honda, K., Yoshida, N., Carbone, M.: Multiparty asynchronous session types. J. ACM **63**(1), 9:1–9:67 (2016). https://doi.org/10.1145/2827695

19. Lange, J., Yoshida, N.: On the undecidability of asynchronous session subtyping. In: Esparza, J., Murawski, A.S. (eds.) FoSSaCS 2017. LNCS, vol. 10203, pp. 441–457. Springer, Heidelberg (2017). https://doi.org/10.1007/978-3-662-54458-7_26

20. Liskov, B., Wing, J.M.: A behavioral notion of subtyping. ACM Trans. Program. Lang. Syst. **16**(6), 1811–1841 (1994). https://doi.org/10.1145/197320.197383

21. Mostrous, D., Yoshida, N., Honda, K.: Global principal typing in partially commutative asynchronous sessions. In: Castagna, G. (ed.) ESOP 2009. LNCS, vol. 5502, pp. 316–332. Springer, Heidelberg (2009). https://doi.org/10.1007/978-3-642-00590-9_23
22. Severi, P., Dezani-Ciancaglini, M.: Observational equivalence for multiparty sessions. Fundamenta Informaticae **167**, 267–305 (2019). https://doi.org/10.1007/s00236-019-00332-y

Relating Functional and Imperative Session Types

Hannes Saffrich[ID] and Peter Thiemann[(✉)][ID]

University of Freiburg, Freiburg im Breisgau, Germany
{saffrich,thiemann}@informatik.uni-freiburg.de

Abstract. Imperative session types provide an imperative interface to session-typed communication in a functional language. Compared to functional session type APIs, the program structure is simpler at the surface, but typestate is required to model the current state of communication throughout.

Most work on session types has neglected the imperative approach. We demonstrate that the functional approach subsumes previous work on imperative session types by exhibiting a typing and semantics preserving translation into a system of linear functional session types.

We further show that the untyped backwards translation from the functional to the imperative calculus is semantics preserving. We restrict the type system of the functional calculus such that the backwards translation becomes type preserving. Thus, we precisely capture the difference in expressiveness of the two calculi and conclude that the lack of expressiveness in the imperative calculus is solely due to its type system.

Keywords: Session types · Distributed programming · Translation

1   Introduction

Session types provide a type discipline for bidirectional communication protocols in concurrent programs. They originate with papers by Honda and others [9,25], who proposed them as an expressive type system for binary communication in pi-calculus. Later work considered embeddings in functional and object-oriented languages, both theoretically and practically oriented [7,10,15,22].

A typical incarnation of session types [7] supports a data type of channel ends described by a session type s governed by a grammar like this one:

$$s ::= \, !t.s \mid ?t.s \mid \oplus\{\ell_i : s_i\} \mid \&\{\ell_i : s_i\} \mid \mathsf{End} \qquad t ::= s \mid t \to t \mid t \otimes t \mid \ldots$$

Here, t ranges over all types in the language (functions, pairs, etc.) including session types s. The session type $!t.s$ describes a channel on which we can send a value of type t and then continue communicating according to s. Dually, we can receive a value of type t and continue according to s on a channel of type $?t.s$. The internal choice type $\oplus \ldots$ selects a choice ℓ_i and continues according to s_i. The external choice $\& \ldots$ continues with s_i if it receives ℓ_i. The session type End signifies the end of the conversation.

© IFIP International Federation for Information Processing 2021
Published by Springer Nature Switzerland AG 2021
F. Damiani and O. Dardha (Eds.): COORDINATION 2021, LNCS 12717, pp. 61–79, 2021.
https://doi.org/10.1007/978-3-030-78142-2_4

```
let server u =
   let (x, u) = receive u in     (* u: ?Int.?Int.!Int.s' *)
   let (y, u) = receive u in     (* u: ?Int.!Int.s' *)
   send (x+y, u)                 (* u: !Int.s' *)
```

Listing 1.1. Example server in functional style

```
fun server u =                    fun server' () =
   let x = receive u in              let x = receive u in
   let y = receive u in              let y = receive u in
   send x + y on u                   send x + y on u
```

Listing 1.2. Example server   **Listing 1.3.** Example server with capture

Functional vs Imperative Session Types. Most of the embedded session type systems rely on a functional treatment of channel ends. That is, the communication operations transform (the type of) a channel end as shown in this example where the receive operation consumes a channel of type $?t.s$ and returns a pair of the received value of type t and the continuation channel of type s:

$$\text{receive} : ?t.s \rightarrow (t \otimes s)$$

This design forces a programmer to explicitly thread the channel reference through the program. Moreover, the channel reference must be treated linearly because a repeated use at the same type would break the protocol. The typical programming pattern is to rebind a variable, say u, containing the channel end with a different type in every line as in Listing 1.1 (typings refer to the state *before* the operation in that line). Writing a program in this style feels like functional programming before the advent of monads, when programmers loudly complained about the need for "plumbing" as demonstrated with u. Moreover, this style is not safe for session types because most languages do not enforce the linearity needed to avoid aliasing of channel ends at compile time.

Embeddings in object-oriented languages make use of fluent interfaces, which favor the chaining of method calls [11], while embeddings in functional languages wrap a channel into a monad [17], which does not scale well to programs that process multiple channels. But much less work can be found that takes the alternative, imperative approach inspired by typestate-based programming [24].

Vasconcelos, Gay, and Ravara [27] proposed a session type calculus embedded in a multithreaded functional language, which we call VGR. It is a bit of a mystery why VGR was not called imperative[1] because it enables rewriting the program fragment in Listing 1.1 as shown in Listing 1.2. The parameter u of the server function is a reference to a communication channel. The operation receive takes a channel associated with session type $?Int.S$ and returns an integer[2]. Executing receive changes the type of the channel referred to by u to S, which

---

[1] The conference version of their paper [28] is called "Session Types for Functional Multithreading".

[2] Uppercase letters denote types in the VGR calculus.

indicates that the VGR calculus is a typestate-based system [24]. The function
send_on_ takes an integer to transmit and a channel associated with session type
!Int.S. It returns a unit value and updates the channel's type to S.

Taken together, the server function in Listing 1.2 expects that its argument u
refers to a channel of type ?Int.?Int.!Int.S' and leaves it in a state corresponding
to type S' on exit. This functionality is reflected in the shape of a function type
in VGR: $\Sigma_1; T_1 \rightarrow T_2; \Sigma_2$. In this type, T_1 and T_2 are argument and return type
of the function. The additional components Σ_1 and Σ_2 are environments that
reflect the state (session type) of the channels before (Σ_1) and after (Σ_2) calling
the function. The type of a channel, Chan α, serves as a pointer to the entry for
α in the current channel environment Σ. Channels in T_1 refer to entries in Σ_1
and channels in T_2 refer to entries in Σ_2, but both environments may refer to
further channels that describe channel references captured by the function (Σ_1)
or created by the function (Σ_2). In Listing 1.2, the type of server is

$$\{\alpha: ?\mathsf{Int}.?\mathsf{Int}.!\mathsf{Int}.S\}; \mathsf{Chan}\ \alpha \rightarrow \mathsf{Unit}; \{\alpha: S\}, \tag{1}$$

for some fixed channel name α and session type S.

Compared to other session type systems [6,7], VGR does **not** require linear
handling of channel references, as can be seen by the multiple uses of variable u
in Listing 1.2. Instead, it keeps track of the current state of every channel using
the environment Σ, which is threaded linearly through the typing rules.

In Sect. 2 we give deeper insights into VGR, the kind of programs that
it accepts, and the programs that fail to typecheck. To give a glimpse of its
peculiarities, we examine the type of server in Eq. (1) more closely.

First, the type refers to the *name* α. This name identifies a certain channel
so that the function cannot be invoked on other channels. Second, a function
of this type can be typechecked without knowledge of the channel names that
are currently in use and their state. This property enables the definition of the
server function in a library, say, but the typechecker does not allow us to call the
function on a channel named differently than α, even if its session type matches.
Hence, the library may end up defining a function that cannot be called.

A variation of the type in Eq. (1) replaces the argument type by Unit:

$$\{\alpha: ?\mathsf{Int}.?\mathsf{Int}.!\mathsf{Int}.S\}; \mathsf{Unit} \rightarrow \mathsf{Unit}; \{\alpha: S\}. \tag{2}$$

This type can be assigned to a function like server' in Listing 1.3 that is closed
over a reference to a channel of type Chan α. In this context, the fixation on a
certain channel name α is required for soundness: While we might want to apply
a function to different channels, it is not possible to replace a channel captured
in a closure. A function of type (2) may be called any time the channel α is in
a state matching the "before" session type of the function.

Subsequently, Gay and Vasconcelos created a functional session type calculus
based on a linear type system, which was later called LFST[3] [7]. While LFST
is still monomorphic, a function like server can be applied to several different

---

[3] Linear Functional Session Types.

channels with the same session type. In LFST, we can also close over a channel, but doing so turns a function like `server'` into a single-use function, whereas it can be called many times in VGR provided the channel α is available at the right type in the environment. Clearly, LFST lifts some restrictions of the VGR calculus, but it seems to impose other restrictions. In any case, the exact correspondence between the two calculi has never been studied.

There is another line of session-type research based on the Curry-Howard correspondence between fragments of linear logic and process calculi [4]. Programs/processes in these systems may also be regarded as handling channels "imperatively", perhaps even more so than VGR. We discuss these approaches in Sect. 7 along with other related work.

Contributions

- We show that LFST is at least as expressive as VGR by giving a typing-preserving translation which simulates VGR in LFST (Sect. 5).
- We show that untyped VGR is at least as expressive as LFST by giving a backwards translation which simulates LFST in VGR (Sect. 6).
- We exhibit a type system for LFST that characterizes the shortcomings of VGR exactly. The backwards translation becomes type preserving with respect to this system (Sect. 6.2).

In this paper we omit session type choice and recursion because these features are straightforward to add and our results extend seamlessly. An extended version of this paper with further proofs, the full rulesets of VGR and LFST, and full definitions of the translations is available at http://arxiv.org/abs/2010.08261.

2 Motivation

Channel Identities. Our discussion of VGR's function type $\Sigma_1; T_1 \to T_2; \Sigma_2$ in the introduction shows that a function that takes a channel as a parameter can only be applied to a single channel. A function like `server` (Listing 1.2) must be applied to the channel of type Chan α, for some fixed name α.

LFST sidesteps this issue by not encoding the identity of a channel in the type. It rather posits that session types are linear so that channel references cannot be duplicated. In consequence, the operations of the session API must consume a channel and return a (nother) channel to continue the protocol.

Data Transmission vs Channel Transmission. In VGR, it is possible to pass channels from one thread to another. The session type $!S'.S$ indicates a higher-order channel on which we can send a channel of type S'. The operation to send a channel has the following typing rule in VGR:

C-SENDS
$$\frac{\Gamma; v \mapsto \mathsf{Chan}\ \beta \qquad \Gamma; v' \mapsto \mathsf{Chan}\ \alpha}{\Gamma; \Sigma, \alpha : !S'.S, \beta : S'; \mathsf{send}\ v\ \mathsf{on}\ v' \mapsto \Sigma; \mathsf{Unit}; \alpha : S}$$

The premises are *value typings* that indicate that v and v' are references to different, fixed channels β and α under variable environment Γ. The conclusion is an *expression typing* of the form $\Gamma; \Sigma; e \mapsto \Sigma_1; T; \Sigma_2$ where Σ is the incoming channel environment, Σ_1 is the part of Σ that is passed through without change, and Σ_2 is the outgoing channel environment after the operation indicated by expression e which returns a result of type T. The rule states that channels β and α have session type S' and $!S'.S$, respectively. The channel β is consumed (it is sent to the other end of channel α) and α gets updated to session type S.

Compared to the function type, sending a channel is more flexible. Any channel of type S' can be passed because β is not part of channel α's session type. Alas, if the sender holds references to channel β (i.e., values of type Chan β), then these references can no longer be exercised as β has been removed from Σ. So one can say that rule C-SENDS passes ownership of channel β to the receiver.

Abstracting over the send operation is not useful because it would fix channel names in the function type.

However, there is another way to send a channel reference over a channel, namely if it is captured in a closure. To see what happens in this case, we look at VGR's typing rules for sending and receiving data of type D. Types of the form D comprise first-order types and function types, but not channels.

C-SENDD
$$\frac{\Gamma; v \mapsto D \qquad \Gamma; v' \mapsto \text{Chan } \alpha}{\Gamma; \Sigma, \alpha : !D.S; \text{send } v \text{ on } v' \mapsto \Sigma; \text{Unit}; \alpha : S}$$

C-RECEIVED
$$\frac{\Gamma; v \mapsto \text{Chan } \alpha}{\Gamma; \Sigma, \alpha : ?D.S; \text{receive } v \mapsto \Sigma; D; \alpha : S}$$

One possibility for type D is a function type like $D_1 = \{\beta : S'\}; \text{Unit} \to \text{Unit}; \{\beta : S''\}$. A function of this type captures a channel named β which may or may not occur in Σ. It is instructive to see what happens at the receiving end in rule C-RECEIVED. If we receive a function of type D_1 and Σ already contains channel β of appropriate session type, then we will be able to invoke the function.

If channel β is not yet present at the receiver, it turns out we cannot send it later, as the received channel gets assigned a fresh name d:

C-RECEIVES
$$\frac{\Gamma; v \mapsto \text{Chan } \alpha \qquad \text{fresh } d}{\Gamma; \Sigma, \alpha : ?S'.S; \text{receive } v \mapsto \Sigma; \text{Chan } d; d : S', \alpha : S}$$

For the same reason, it is impossible to send channel β first and then the closure that refers to it: β gets renamed to some fresh d while the closure still refers to β. Sending the channel effectively cuts all previous connections.

None of these issues arise in LFST because channels have no identity. Hence, any value whatsoever can be sent over a channel, higher-order session types are possible, and there is just one typing rule for sending and receiving, respectively.

Channel Aliasing. The VGR paper proposes the following function sendSend.

```
fun sendSend u v = send 1 on u; send 2 on v
```

```
fun sendSend u v sigma =              fun sendSend w sigma =
  let (cu, sigma) = sigma.u in          let (cw, sigma) = sigma.w in
  let cu' = send 1 on cu in             let cw' = send 1 on cw in
  let sigma = sigma * {u: cu'} in       let sigma = sigma * {w: cw'} in
  let (cv, sigma) = sigma.v in          let (cw, sigma) = sigma.w in
  let cv' = send 2 on cv in             let cw' = send 2 on cw in
  let sigma = sigma * {v: cv'} in       let sigma = sigma * {w: cw'} in
  ((), sigma)                           ((), sigma)
```

Listing 1.4. Without aliasing   **Listing 1.5.** With aliasing

It takes two channels and sends a number on each. This use is reflected in the following typing.

$$\mathsf{sendSend} : \Sigma_1; \mathsf{Chan}\ u \to (\Sigma_1; \mathsf{Chan}\ v \to \mathsf{Unit}; \Sigma_2); \Sigma_1 \qquad (3)$$

with $\Sigma_1 = \{u : !\mathsf{Int}.S_u, v : !\mathsf{Int}.S_v\}$ and $\Sigma_2 = \{u : S_u, v : S_v\}$.

Ignoring the types we observe that it would be semantically sound to pass a reference to the same channel `w`, say, of session type `!Int.!Int.End` for `u` and `v`. However, `sendSend w w` does not type check with type (3) because `w` would have to have identity u and v at the same time, but environment formation mandates they must be different.

Another typing of `sendSend` in VGR would be

$$\mathsf{sendSend}' : \Sigma_1; \mathsf{Chan}\ w \to (\Sigma_1; \mathsf{Chan}\ w \to \mathsf{Unit}; \Sigma_2); \Sigma_1 \qquad (4)$$

with $\Sigma_1 = \{w : !\mathsf{Int}.!\mathsf{Int}.S_w\}$ and $\Sigma_2 = \{w : S_w\}$. With this typing, `sendSend w w` type checks. Indeed, the typing forces the two arguments to be aliases!

In LFST, the invocation `sendSend w w` is not legal as it violates linearity. Indeed, to simulate the two differently typed flavors of `sendSend` requires two different expressions in LFST. As an illustration, we show LFST expressions as they are produced by our type-driven translation in Sect. 5. In the code fragment in Listing 1.4, `u` and `v` have unit type (translated from $\mathsf{Chan}\ u$ and $\mathsf{Chan}\ v$) and `sigma` is a linear record with fields `u` and `v` that contain the respective channels. The dot operator performs field selection and `*` is disjoint record concatenation. The notation for record literals is standard.

In the translation of `sendSend'` in Listing 1.5 record `sigma` only has one field `w` containing the channel.

Abstraction over Channel Creation. A server typically accepts many connections on the same access point and performs the same initialization (e.g., authentication) on each channel. Hence, it makes sense to abstract over the creation of a channel.

```
fun acceptAdd () =
  let c = accept addService in
  // authenticate client on c (omitted)
  c
```

$$C ::= \langle t \rangle \mid (C \| C) \mid (\nu x : [S])C \mid (\nu \gamma)C$$

$$t ::= v \mid \text{let } x = e \text{ in } t \mid \text{fork } t; t \qquad\qquad T ::= D \mid \text{Chan } \alpha$$

$$e ::= t \mid v\,v \mid \text{new } S \mid \text{accept } v \mid \text{request } v \qquad D ::= [S] \mid \Sigma; T \to T; \Sigma \mid \text{Unit}$$

$$\quad\mid \text{send } v \text{ on } v \mid \text{receive } v \mid \text{close } v \qquad S ::= ?D.S \mid !D.S \mid ?S.S \mid !S.S \mid \text{End}$$

$$v ::= \alpha \mid \lambda(\Sigma; x : T).e \mid () \qquad\qquad \Sigma ::= \varnothing \mid \Sigma, \alpha : S \qquad (\alpha \notin \Sigma)$$

$$\alpha ::= x \mid \gamma^p \qquad\qquad\qquad\qquad\qquad \Gamma ::= \varnothing \mid \Gamma, x : T \qquad (x \notin \Gamma)$$

$$p ::= + \mid -$$

Fig. 1. Syntax of VGR

$$E[(\lambda(\Sigma; y : T).e)v] \Rightarrow_e E[e[v/y]] \tag{5}$$

$$E[\text{let } x = v \text{ in } t] \Rightarrow_e E[t[v/x]] \tag{6}$$

$$E[\text{request } n] \overset{\text{request}\gamma}{\Rightarrow_e} E[\gamma^+] \qquad E[\text{accept } n] \overset{\text{accept}\gamma}{\Rightarrow_e} E[\gamma^-] \tag{7}$$

$$E[\text{receive } \gamma^p] \overset{\gamma^p ? v}{\Rightarrow_e} E[v] \qquad E[\text{send } v \text{ on } \gamma^p] \overset{\gamma^p ! v}{\Rightarrow_e} E[()] \tag{8}$$

$$\frac{t_1 \overset{\text{request}\gamma}{\Rightarrow_e} t_1' \qquad t_2 \overset{\text{accept}\gamma}{\Rightarrow_e} t_2'}{\langle t_1 \rangle \| \langle t_2 \rangle \overset{\text{accept}}{\Rightarrow_p} (\nu\gamma)\langle t_1' \rangle \| \langle t_2' \rangle} \qquad \frac{t_1 \overset{\gamma^p ? v}{\Rightarrow_e} t_1' \qquad t_2 \overset{\overline{\gamma^p} ! v}{\Rightarrow_e} t_2'}{\langle t_1 \rangle \| \langle t_2 \rangle \overset{\text{send}}{\Rightarrow_p} \langle t_1' \rangle \| \langle t_2' \rangle} \tag{9}$$

$$\langle E[\text{new } S] \rangle \overset{\text{new}}{\Rightarrow_p} (\nu n : [S])\langle E[n] \rangle \tag{10}$$

$$\langle E[\text{fork } t_1; t_2] \rangle \overset{\text{fork}}{\Rightarrow_p} \langle t_1 \rangle \| \langle E[t_2] \rangle \tag{11}$$

$$\frac{t \Rightarrow_e t'}{\langle t \rangle \Rightarrow_p \langle t' \rangle} \qquad \frac{C \overset{\ell}{\Rightarrow_p} C'}{(\nu\gamma)C \overset{\ell}{\Rightarrow_p} (\nu\gamma)C'} \qquad \frac{C \overset{\ell}{\Rightarrow_p} C'}{(\nu n : T)C \overset{\ell}{\Rightarrow_p} (\nu n : T)C'} \qquad \frac{C \overset{\ell}{\Rightarrow_p} C'}{C \| C'' \overset{\ell}{\Rightarrow_p} C' \| C''} \tag{12}$$

Fig. 2. Semantics of VGR

However, in VGR, the freshness condition on the channel created by accept only applies inside the function body. The actual VGR type of acceptAdd does not reflect freshness anymore as the name α, say, is fixed in the function type:

$$\{\}; \text{Unit} \to \text{Chan } \alpha; \{\alpha : ?\text{Int.?Int.!Int.}S'\}$$

In consequence, VGR cannot invoke acceptAdd twice in a row as the second invocation would result in an ill-formed environment that contains two specifications for channel α.

LFST elides this issue, again, by not tracking channel identities.

3   VGR: Imperative Session Types

Figure 1 defines the syntax of VGR [27]. Notably, expressions t are in A-normal form and types distinguish between data types D and channels because two different sets of typing rules govern sending and receiving of data vs. sending and receiving a channel. We already used this syntax informally in the examples.

C-CONST   C-CHAN   C-VAR $\begin{array}{l}\text{C-ABS}\\ \dfrac{\Gamma, x:T; \Sigma; e \mapsto \Sigma_1; U; \Sigma_2}{\Gamma; \lambda x.e \mapsto (\Sigma; T \to U; \Sigma_1, \Sigma_2)}\end{array}$

$\Gamma; () \mapsto \text{Unit}$ $\Gamma; \gamma^p \mapsto \text{Chan } \gamma^p$ $\Gamma, x:T; x \mapsto T$

Fig. 3. Value typing rules of VGR

$$\text{C-ACCEPT} \qquad \frac{\Gamma; v \mapsto [S] \qquad \text{fresh } c}{\Gamma; \Sigma; \text{accept } v \mapsto \Sigma; \text{Chan } c; \{c : S\}}$$

$$\text{C-REQUEST} \qquad \frac{\Gamma; v \mapsto [S] \qquad \text{fresh } c}{\Gamma; \Sigma; \text{request } v \mapsto \Sigma; \text{Chan } c; \{c : \overline{S}\}}$$

$$\text{C-VAL} \qquad \frac{\Gamma; v \mapsto T}{\Gamma; \Sigma; v \mapsto \Sigma; T; \varnothing}$$

$$\text{C-APP} \qquad \frac{\Gamma; v \mapsto (\Sigma; T \to U; \Sigma') \qquad \Gamma; v' \mapsto T}{\Gamma; \Sigma, \Sigma''; v\,v' \mapsto \Sigma''; U; \Sigma'}$$

$$\text{C-FORK} \qquad \frac{\Gamma; \Sigma; t_1 \mapsto \Sigma_1; T_1; \{\} \qquad \Gamma; \Sigma_1; t_2 \mapsto \Sigma_2; T_2; \{\}}{\Gamma; \Sigma; (\text{fork } t_1; t_2) \mapsto \Sigma_2; T_2; \{\}}$$

Fig. 4. Expression typing rules of VGR (excerpt)

We omit choices as they present no significant problem and as they can be simulated using channel passing. We also omit the standard congruence rules for processes and silently apply reduction rules up to congruence: parallel composition is a commutative monoid and the ν-binders admit scope extrusion.

Figure 2 defines the semantics of VGR. We use a slightly different, but equivalent definition than in the literature. We define evaluation contexts $E, F ::= \square \mid \text{let } x = E \text{ in } t$ that are used in many of the rules. This formulation avoids the commuting conversion rule R-LET in the literature and fixes an issue with the original reduction relation.[4] We distinguish between expression reduction $\overset{\ell}{\Rightarrow}_e$ and process reduction $\overset{\ell}{\Rightarrow}_p$, both of which are tagged with a label ℓ. This label indicates the effect of the reduction and it ranges over

$$\ell ::= \text{accept} \mid \text{send} \mid \text{new} \mid \text{fork} \mid \tau \qquad \text{processes}$$
$$\ell ::= \text{accept}\gamma \mid \text{request}\gamma \mid \gamma?v \mid \gamma!v \mid \tau \qquad \text{expressions}$$

where τ stands for effect freedom and can be omitted. Labeled expression reductions are paired with their counterpart at the process level as familiar from process calculi [13], that is, $\gamma?v$ ($\gamma!v$) stand for receiving (sending) v on γ which resolves to label send at the process level (9). Similarly, acceptγ (requestγ) stands for accepting (requesting) a connection on fresh channel γ and resolves to label accept at the process level.

Typing for VGR comes in three parts: value typing $\Gamma; v \mapsto T$ in Fig. 3, expression typing $\Gamma; \Sigma; e \mapsto \Sigma'; T; \Sigma''$ in Fig. 4, and configuration typing $\Gamma; \Sigma; C \mapsto \Sigma'$ (omitted). The value typing judgment relates an environment Γ and a value

---

[4] $\text{let } x = \text{fork } t; t' \text{ in } t''$ is stuck in the original work [27].

Constants	$k ::= \mathsf{fix} \mid \mathsf{fork} \mid \mathsf{send} \mid \mathsf{receive} \mid \mathsf{accept} \mid \mathsf{request} \mid \boxed{\mathsf{new}}$
Expressions	$e ::= x \mid \alpha \mid k \mid () \mid \lambda x.e \mid e\;e \mid (e,e) \mid \mathsf{let}\,(x,y) = e\,\mathsf{in}\,e$
	$\mid\; \{\} \mid \{\alpha = e\} \mid e \cdot e \mid e.\alpha \mid \mathsf{split}^*\,e, \alpha^*$
Configurations	$C ::= \langle e \rangle \mid C\Vert C \mid (\nu\gamma\delta)C \mid \boxed{(\nu n)C}$
Types	$t ::= s \mid [s] \mid \mathsf{Unit} \mid t \to t \mid t \multimap t \mid t \otimes t \mid \{r\}$
SessionTypes	$s ::= ?t.s \mid !t.s \mid \mathsf{End}$
Rows	$r ::= \varnothing \mid r, \alpha : t$
Environments	$\Gamma ::= \varnothing \mid \Gamma, \alpha : t \mid \Gamma, x : t$

Fig. 5. Syntax of LFST

v to a type T. The expression typing judgment is very similar to a type state system. It relates a typing environment Γ, an incoming channel environment Σ, and an expression to an environment $\Sigma' \subseteq \Sigma$ which contains the channels not used by e, the type T, and the outgoing channel environment Σ''. Σ'' contains typings for channels that have been used by e or created by e. The configuration typing relates Γ, incoming Σ, and configuration C with $\Sigma' \subseteq \Sigma$ which contains the channels not used by C.

4   Linear Functional Session Types

On the functional side, we consider an extension of a synchronous variant of the LFST calculus [7] by linear records with disjoint concatenation. Figure 5 gives its syntax. The constants k and the first line of the expression grammar are taken from the literature. The second line of the expression grammar is new and defines operations on linear records. The empty record is $\{\}$, $\{\alpha = e\}$ constructs a singleton record with field α given by e, $e_1 \cdot e_2$ is the disjoint concatenation of records e_1 and e_2, $e.\alpha$ projects field α out of the record e and returns a pair of the contents of the field and the remaining record, $\mathsf{split}^*\,e, \alpha^*$ generalizes splitting to a list of names α^* and returns a pair of two records, one with the fields α^* and the other with the remaining fields.

A configuration C can be a single thread, two configurations running in parallel, a channel abstraction binding the two ends to γ and δ, or an access point abstraction $(\nu n)C$. The latter is a straightforward addition to LFST, which assumes the existence of globally known access points.

Metavariable t ranges over types, s ranges over session types, and r ranges over rows, which are lists of bindings of names to types.

$$\text{unr End}\quad \text{unr}\,([s])\quad \text{unr Unit}\quad \frac{\text{unr}\,t_1 \qquad \text{unr}\,t_2}{\text{unr}\,(t_1 \otimes t_2)}\quad \text{unr}\,(t_1 \to t_2)\quad \frac{(\forall \alpha : t \in r)\,\text{unr}\,t}{\text{unr}\,\{r\}}$$

T-FORK
$$\frac{\Gamma \vdash e : \text{Unit}}{\Gamma \vdash \text{fork}\,e : \text{Unit}}$$

T-SEND
$$\frac{\Gamma = \Gamma_1 + \Gamma_2 \qquad \Gamma_1 \vdash e_1 : t \qquad \Gamma_2 \vdash e_2 : !t.s}{\Gamma \vdash \text{send}\,e_1\,\text{on}\,e_2 : s}$$

T-RECV
$$\frac{\Gamma \vdash e : ?t.s}{\Gamma \vdash \text{receive}\,e : t \otimes s}$$

T-NEW
$$\frac{\text{unr}\,\Gamma}{\Gamma \vdash \text{new}\,s : [s]}$$

T-ACCEPT
$$\frac{\Gamma \vdash e : [s]}{\Gamma \vdash \text{accept}\,e : s}$$

T-REQUEST
$$\frac{\Gamma \vdash e : [s]}{\Gamma \vdash \text{request}\,e : \bar{s}}$$

T-EMP
$$\frac{\text{unr}\,\Gamma}{\Gamma \vdash \{\} : \{\}}$$

T-SINGLE
$$\frac{\Gamma \vdash e : t}{\Gamma \vdash \{\alpha = e\} : \{\alpha : t\}}$$

T-SPLITRECORD
$$\frac{\Gamma \vdash e : \{r_1 + r_2\} \qquad \text{dom}(r_1) = \alpha^*}{\Gamma \vdash \text{split}^*\,e, \alpha^* : \{r_1\} \otimes \{r_2\}}$$

T-CONCAT
$$\frac{\Gamma = \Gamma_1 + \Gamma_2 \qquad \Gamma_1 \vdash e_1 : \{r_1\} \qquad \Gamma_2 \vdash e_2 : \{r_2\} \qquad r_1 \,\|\, r_2}{\Gamma \vdash e_1 \cdot e_2 : \{r_1, r_2\}}$$

T-FIELD
$$\frac{\Gamma \vdash e : \{r, \alpha : t\}}{\Gamma \vdash e.\alpha : t \otimes \{r\}}$$

Fig. 6. Typing rules for communication primitives and record operations in LFST

Figure 6 recalls the definition of the predicate $\text{unr}\,t$ for unrestricted types, which we lift pointwise to typing environments. It also contains the well-known typing rules for the communication primitives as well as for the record fragment of LFST. The rule T-EMP typechecks the empty record with the premise $\text{unr}\,\Gamma$ which states that Γ only contains unrestricted types. The rule T-SINGLE is unsurprising. Premise $\Gamma = \Gamma_1 + \Gamma_2$ of rule T-CONCAT splits the incoming environment Γ so that bindings to a linear type end up either in Γ_1 or in Γ_2. Premise $r_1 \,\|\, r_2$ states that rows r_1 and r_2 are disjoint, which means they bind different field names. Under these assumptions the (disjoint) concatenation of records e_1 and e_2 is accepted.

The rules for field access and splitting of the record generalize the elimination rule for linear pairs. Rule T-FIELD shows that fields access singles out the field named α. Its content is paired up with a record comprising the remaining fields. Linearity of the record's content is preserved as the pair is also linear. Rule T-SPLITRECORD is similar, but splits its subject e according to a list α^* of names which must be present in e. The result is a linear pair of two records. We consider an empty record to be unrestricted so that we can drop it if needed.

The remaining typing rules are taken from the original paper [7] (cf. also Fig. 10). We modified the operational semantics to perform synchronous communication and to fit with the labeled transition style used for VGR in Sect. 3. Its formalization is omitted because of its similarity to VGR.

C-APP
$$\Big\langle\!\!\Big\langle \frac{\Gamma; v \mapsto (\Sigma; T \to U; \Sigma') \quad \Gamma; v' \mapsto T}{\Gamma; \Sigma, \Sigma''; v\,v' \mapsto \Sigma''; U; \Sigma'} \Big\rangle\!\!\Big\rangle_\sigma = \langle\!\langle v \rangle\!\rangle \, \langle\!\langle v' \rangle\!\rangle \, \sigma$$

C-SENDS
$$\Big\langle\!\!\Big\langle \frac{\Gamma; v \mapsto \mathsf{Chan}\ \beta \quad \Gamma; v' \mapsto \mathsf{Chan}\ \alpha}{\Gamma; \Sigma, \alpha:\,!S'.S, \beta:S'; \mathsf{send}\ v\ \mathsf{on}\ v' \mapsto \Sigma; \mathsf{Unit}; \alpha:S} \Big\rangle\!\!\Big\rangle_\sigma =
\begin{aligned}
&\mathsf{let}\ (c,\sigma) = \sigma.\alpha\ \mathsf{in} \\
&\mathsf{let}\ (p,\sigma) = \sigma.\beta\ \mathsf{in} \\
&\mathsf{let}\ c = \mathsf{send}\ p\ \mathsf{on}\ c\ \mathsf{in} \\
&((),\sigma\cdot\{\alpha=c\})
\end{aligned}$$

C-FORK
$$\Big\langle\!\!\Big\langle \frac{\Gamma; \Sigma; t_1 \mapsto \Sigma_1; T_1; \{\} \quad \Gamma; \Sigma_1; t_2 \mapsto \Sigma_2; T_2; \{\}}{\Gamma; \Sigma; (\mathsf{fork}\ t_1; t_2) \mapsto \Sigma_2; T_2; \{\}} \Big\rangle\!\!\Big\rangle_\sigma =
\begin{aligned}
&\mathsf{let}\ (\sigma_1,\sigma_2) = \mathsf{split}^*\ \sigma, \mathrm{dom}(\Sigma_1 \setminus \Sigma_2)\ \mathsf{in} \\
&\mathsf{let}\ \_ = \mathsf{fork}\ \langle\!\langle t_1 \rangle\!\rangle_{\sigma_1}\ \mathsf{in} \\
&\langle\!\langle t_2 \rangle\!\rangle_{\sigma_2}
\end{aligned}$$

C-NEW
$$\langle\!\langle \Gamma; \Sigma; \mathsf{new}\ S \mapsto \Sigma; [S]; \varnothing \rangle\!\rangle_\sigma = (\mathsf{new}\ \langle\!\langle S \rangle\!\rangle, \sigma)$$

Fig. 7. Translation of expressions and threads (excerpt)

C-THREAD
$$\Big\langle\!\!\Big\langle \frac{\vec{x}:[\vec{S}]; \Sigma; t \mapsto \Sigma'; T; \{\}}{\vec{x}:[\vec{S}]; \Sigma; \langle t \rangle \mapsto \Sigma'} \Big\rangle\!\!\Big\rangle = \langle \mathsf{let}\ \sigma = \{\vec{\gamma} = \vec{\gamma}\}\ \mathsf{in}\ \langle\!\langle t \rangle\!\rangle_\sigma \rangle \\ \textit{where}\ \vec{\gamma} = \mathrm{dom}(\Sigma' \setminus \Sigma)$$

Fig. 8. Translation of configurations (excerpt)

5   Translation: Imperative to Functional

As a first step, we discuss the translation of the imperative session type calculus VGR into the linear functional session type calculus LFST-rec. The extension with record types is not essential, but it makes stating the translation more accessible. All records could be elided by replacing them with suitably nested pairs and mapping record labels to indices.

The translation from VGR to LFST-rec is type driven, i.e., it is a translation of typing derivations. The gist of the approach is to translate VGR expressions into a parameterized linear state transformer monad. It is parameterized in the sense of Atkey [2] because the type of the state changes during the computation.

In particular, we map derivations for VGR value typing, VGR expression typing, and VGR configuration typing such that the following typing preservation results hold. For brevity, we indicate the translation with $\langle\!\langle e \rangle\!\rangle$ and $\langle\!\langle C \rangle\!\rangle$ where the arguments are really the typing derivations for e and C, respectively. The translations on types $\langle\!\langle T \rangle\!\rangle$, environments $\langle\!\langle \Gamma \rangle\!\rangle$, $\langle\!\langle \Sigma \rangle\!\rangle$, and values $\langle\!\langle v \rangle\!\rangle$ are homomorphic by induction on the syntax (see extended version), except for

$$\langle\!\langle \mathsf{Chan}\ \alpha \rangle\!\rangle = \mathsf{Unit} \qquad\qquad\qquad \langle\!\langle \gamma^\pm \rangle\!\rangle = ()$$
$$\langle\!\langle \Sigma_1; T_1 \to T_2; \Sigma_2 \rangle\!\rangle = \langle\!\langle T_1 \rangle\!\rangle \to \{\langle\!\langle \Sigma_1 \rangle\!\rangle\} \to (\langle\!\langle T_2 \rangle\!\rangle \times \{\langle\!\langle \Sigma_2 \rangle\!\rangle\}) \quad \langle\!\langle \lambda x.e \rangle\!\rangle = \lambda x.\lambda\sigma.\langle\!\langle e \rangle\!\rangle_\sigma$$

Translation of types

$$\langle\!\langle !T.S \rangle\!\rangle = !\langle\!\langle T \rangle\!\rangle.\langle\!\langle S \rangle\!\rangle$$
$$\langle\!\langle ?T.S \rangle\!\rangle = ?\langle\!\langle T \rangle\!\rangle.\langle\!\langle S \rangle\!\rangle$$
$$\langle\!\langle \mathsf{End} \rangle\!\rangle = \mathsf{End}$$
$$\langle\!\langle \mathsf{Unit} \rangle\!\rangle = \mathsf{Unit}$$
$$\langle\!\langle [S] \rangle\!\rangle = [\langle\!\langle S \rangle\!\rangle]$$
$$\langle\!\langle \mathsf{Chan}\ \alpha \rangle\!\rangle = \mathsf{Unit}$$
$$\langle\!\langle \Sigma_1; T_1 \to T_2; \Sigma_2 \rangle\!\rangle = \langle\!\langle T_1 \rangle\!\rangle \to \{\langle\!\langle \Sigma_1 \rangle\!\rangle\} \to (\langle\!\langle T_2 \rangle\!\rangle \times \{\langle\!\langle \Sigma_2 \rangle\!\rangle\})$$

Translation of values

$$\langle\!\langle () \rangle\!\rangle = ()$$
$$\langle\!\langle \gamma^{\pm} \rangle\!\rangle = ()$$
$$\langle\!\langle x \rangle\!\rangle = x$$
$$\langle\!\langle \lambda x.e \rangle\!\rangle = \lambda x.\lambda \sigma.\langle\!\langle e \rangle\!\rangle_\sigma$$

Fig. 9. Type translation

Proposition 1 (Typing Preserving Translation).

PRESERVE-VALUE
$$\frac{\Gamma; v \mapsto T}{\langle\!\langle \Gamma \rangle\!\rangle \vdash \langle\!\langle v \rangle\!\rangle : \langle\!\langle T \rangle\!\rangle}$$

PRESERVE-EXPRESSION
$$\frac{\Gamma; \Sigma; e \mapsto \Sigma_1; T; \Sigma_2}{\langle\!\langle \Gamma \rangle\!\rangle, \sigma : \{\langle\!\langle \Sigma \setminus \Sigma_1 \rangle\!\rangle\} \vdash \langle\!\langle e \rangle\!\rangle_\sigma : \langle\!\langle T \rangle\!\rangle \times \{\langle\!\langle \Sigma_2 \rangle\!\rangle\}}$$

PRESERVE-CONFIG
$$\frac{\Gamma; \Sigma; C \mapsto \Sigma_1}{\langle\!\langle \Gamma \rangle\!\rangle, \langle\!\langle \Sigma \setminus \Sigma_1 \rangle\!\rangle \vdash \langle\!\langle C \rangle\!\rangle}$$

These statements are proved by mutual induction on the derivations of the VGR judgments in the premises. The VGR typing judgments for expressions and configurations pass through unused channels (in Σ_1) in the style of leftover typings [1]. While this style is convenient for some proofs, it cannot be used for the translation as it fails when trying to translate the term $\mathsf{fork}\,t_1; t_2$. The first premise of its typing rule C-FORK is $\Gamma; \Sigma; t_1 \mapsto \Sigma_1; T_1; \{\}$, which says that executing t_1 consumes some of the incoming channels Σ and does not touch the ones in Σ_1. The second premise $\Gamma; \Sigma_1; t_2 \mapsto \Sigma_2; T_2; \{\}$ picks up Σ_1 and demands that t_2 consumes all its channels. This pattern does not work for the translation, which is based on explicit channel passing: if we would pass all channels in Σ to t_1, which is forked as a new thread, there would be no way to obtain the leftover channels Σ_1 after thread t_1 has finished. Moreover, these channels have to be available for t_2 even before t_1 has finished! The same issue arises with translating the parallel composition of two configurations. For that reason, in LFST-rec the translated expressions and configurations are supplied with exactly the channels needed. Hence the necessity to compute the needed channels as the difference $\Sigma \setminus \Sigma_1$.

Figure 9 contains the details of the type translation, the translation of environments, and the translation of values. The only interesting case of the type translation is the one for function types, which maps a function to a Kleisli arrow in a linear, parameterized state monad. The incoming and outgoing channel environments are mapped to the incoming and outgoing state record types. The other observation is that any channel type is mapped to the unit type.

The translation of values has two interesting cases. A channel value is mapped to unit because channels are handled on the type level and channel references are resolved by accessing the corresponding field of the state record. Lambdas obtain an extra argument σ for the incoming state. The body of a lambda is translated by the expression translation which is indexed by the incoming state record σ and returns a pair of the result and the outgoing state record.

Figure 7 shows select cases from the translation of expressions that demonstrate the role of the record operations. The conclusion of PRESERVE-EXPRESSION shows that an expression is translated to a linear state transformer as in the translation of the function type.

Figure 8 contains the translation of the C-THREAD configuration rule, which is the only interesting case. Its reifies the channels that are used in the thread by collecting them in a record σ and injecting that record as the initial state of the state monad. This record is transformed by the expression translation which returns a pair of the return value of type $\langle\!\langle T \rangle\!\rangle$ and the final record of type $\{\langle\!\langle \varnothing \rangle\!\rangle\}$. It is easy to see that this pair is unrestricted because the translation of a type T is generally an unrestricted type and the empty record is also unrestricted.

We would like the translation to induce a simulation in that each step of a typed VGR configuration C gives rise to one or more steps in its translation $\langle\!\langle C \rangle\!\rangle$ in LFST-rec. Unfortunately, the situation is not that simple because administrative reductions involving the state get in the way.

Proposition 2 (Simulation). *If* $\Gamma; \Sigma; C \mapsto \Sigma'$ *and* $C \Rightarrow_p^{\ell} C'$ *in VGR, then there is a configuration* $\overline{C}$ *in LFST-rec such that* $\langle\!\langle C \rangle\!\rangle \rightarrow_p^{\ell}{}^+ \overline{C}$ *and* $\langle\!\langle C' \rangle\!\rangle \rightarrow_p^{\tau}{}^+ \overline{C}$.

6 Translation: Functional to Imperative

For the backwards translation we consider LFST programs without records and we informally extend the expression language of VGR with pairs—analogous to LFST, but unrestricted.

We first consider an untyped translation that demonstrates that the calculi are equally expressive. Then we restrict the type system of LFST to identify a subset on which the translation preserves typing.

6.1 Untyped Translation

In a first approximation, the backwards translation might map the send and receive operations naively as follows.

$$(\!|\text{send } e_1 \text{ on } e_2|\!) = \text{let } x = (\!|e_1|\!) \text{ in let } y = (\!|e_2|\!) \text{ in let } z = \text{send } x \text{ on } y \text{ in } y \qquad (13)$$

$$(\!|\text{receive } e|\!) = \text{let } y = (\!|e|\!) \text{ in let } x = \text{receive } y \text{ in } (\ x, y) \qquad (14)$$

This mapping, extended to the rest of LFST, yields a program in A-normal form to fit with VGR's syntactic restrictions. The functional send operation returns the updated channel, so we have to duplicate the channel reference y in its image in VGR. Similarly, the functional receive operation returns a pair of the received value and the updated channel, so the translation needs to construct a pair from the received value and the updated channel y.

However, to prove a tight relation between reduction in LFST and VGR, we need to be more careful to avoid administrative reductions. For example, if e in (14) is already a value, then the inserted $\mathsf{let}\, y = (\!|e|\!)$ in ... is gratuitous and results in an extra (administrative) reduction in VGR.

This phenomenon is known since Plotkin's treatise of the CPS translation [16]. Hence, we factor the backwards translation in two steps. The first step transforms the LFST program to A-normal form using an approach due to Sabry and Felleisen [19]. This transformation is known to give rise to a strong operational correspondence (a reduction correspondence [20]), it is typing preserving, and it is applicable to LFST because it preserves linearity. The definition for this translation $\|e\|$ may be found in the extended version.

This refined ANF translation is compatible with evaluation because it is compatible with values, evaluation contexts, and substitution.

Proposition 3 (ANF Simulation).

1. If $e \to_e e'$, then $\|e\| \to_e^+ \|e'\|$.   2. If $C \xrightarrow{\ell}_p C'$, then $\|C\| \xrightarrow{\ell}_p^+ \|C'\|$.

The second step is the expression translation $(\!|e|\!)$ from LFST-ANF to VGR. This translation is very simple because the source calculus is already in A-normal form. The idea of the translation as stated at the beginning of this section is clearly reflected in the first two lines of the expression translation $(\!|e|\!)$. The remaining cases work homomorphically (see extended version).

$$(\!|\mathsf{send}\, v\, \mathsf{on}\, w|\!) = \mathsf{let}\, z = \mathsf{send}\, (\!|v|\!)\, \mathsf{on}\, (\!|w|\!)\, \mathsf{in}\, (\!|w|\!)$$
$$(\!|\mathsf{receive}\, v|\!) = \mathsf{let}\, x = \mathsf{receive}\, (\!|v|\!)\, \mathsf{in}\, (\, x, (\!|v|\!)\,)$$
$$(\!|\mathsf{fork}\, e|\!) = \mathsf{fork}\, (\!|e|\!);\, (\,)$$

This setup establishes a tight connection between LFST-ANF and VGR, because the translation preserves values, evaluation contexts, and substitution.

Proposition 4 (Backwards simulation). *Let e, e' and C, C' be expressions and configurations in LFST-ANF.*

1. If $e \to_e e'$, then $(\!|e|\!) \Rightarrow_e (\!|e'|\!)$.   2. If $C \xrightarrow{\ell}_p C'$, then $(\!|C|\!) \Rightarrow_p^{\ell\,+} (\!|C'|\!)$.

Putting the results for the two steps together, we obtain the desired tight simulation result by composing Propositions 3 and 4.

Proposition 5 (Full Backwards Simulation). *Suppose that e, e' and C, C' are expressions and configurations in LFST.*

1. If $e \to_e e'$, then $(\!|\|e\||\!) \Rightarrow_e^+ (\!|\|e'\||\!)$.   2. If $C \xrightarrow{\ell}_p C'$, then $(\!|\|C\||\!) \Rightarrow_p^{\ell\,+} (\!|\|C'\||\!)$.

$$\text{T-LamU'}$$
$$\frac{\text{unr } \Gamma \qquad \Gamma, x : t_2 \vdash' e : t_1 / \Sigma_0 \mapsto \Sigma_1}{\Gamma \vdash' \lambda x.e : t_2 \rightarrow^{\Sigma_0 \mapsto \Sigma_1} t_1 / \Sigma \mapsto \Sigma}$$

$$\text{T-App'}$$
$$\frac{\Gamma = \Gamma_1 + \Gamma_2 \qquad \Gamma_1 \vdash' e_1 : t_2 \twoheadrightarrow^{\Sigma_2 \mapsto \Sigma_3} t_1 / \Sigma_0 \mapsto \Sigma_1 \qquad \Gamma_2 \vdash' e_2 : t_2 / \Sigma_1 \mapsto \Sigma_2, \Sigma_2'}{\Gamma \vdash' e_1 e_2 : t_1 / \Sigma_0 \mapsto \Sigma_3, \Sigma_2'}$$

$$\text{T-Send''}$$
$$\frac{\Gamma = \Gamma_1 + \Gamma_2 \qquad \Gamma_1 \vdash' e_1 : s'_\beta / \Sigma \mapsto \Sigma' \qquad \Gamma_2 \vdash' e_2 : (!s'.s)_\alpha / \Sigma' \mapsto \Sigma'', \alpha : !t.s, \beta : s'}{\Gamma \vdash' \text{send } e_1 \text{ on } e_2 : s_\alpha / \Sigma \mapsto \Sigma'', \alpha : s}$$

$$\text{T-Recv''}$$
$$\frac{\Gamma \vdash' e : (?s'.s)_\alpha / \Sigma \mapsto \Sigma', \alpha : ?s'.s}{\Gamma \vdash' \text{receive } e : s'_\beta \otimes s_\alpha / \Sigma \mapsto \Sigma', \alpha : s, \beta : s'}$$

$$\text{T-New'}$$
$$\frac{\text{unr } \Gamma}{\Gamma \vdash' \text{new } s : [s] / \Sigma \mapsto \Sigma}$$

Fig. 10. Typing rules for LFST-EFF (excerpt)

6.2 Typed Backwards Translation

One can add the necessary information for a typed backwards translation to the type system of LFST, at the price of making it more restrictive. We start with an informal review of the requirements.

As VGR tracks channel identities, they have to be reflected in the LFST type systems. Following Padovani [14], we tag session types as in s_α consisting of a session type s tagged with an identity α.

The function type in VGR specifies a transformation on the channels that are implicitly or explicitly affected by the function. Hence, we must augment the LFST type system with tracking the identities of channels, on which the program performs an effect. To this end, we equip LFST with a suitable sequential effect system [8]. It distinguishes between incoming and outgoing channels, Σ_i and Σ_o, which are also reflected in the latent effect on the function arrow.

$$\Gamma \vdash' e : t / \Sigma_i \mapsto \Sigma_o$$

We define tagged session types by adding an identity tag α to all session types and augmenting function types with a set of uniquely tagged sessions. We carve out a set of data types d, which can be transmitted in VGR programs. Hence, session types proper (denoted by s) are a subset of LFST's session types.

Types	$t ::= s_\alpha \mid [s] \mid \text{Unit} \mid t \rightarrow^{\Sigma \mapsto \Sigma} t \mid t \twoheadrightarrow^{\Sigma \mapsto \Sigma} t \mid t \otimes t$
Data	$d ::= [s] \mid \text{Unit} \mid t \rightarrow^{\Sigma \mapsto \Sigma} t \mid t \twoheadrightarrow^{\Sigma \mapsto \Sigma} t$
Sessions	$s ::= ?d.s \mid !d.s \mid ?s.s \mid !s.s \mid \text{End}$

Using mostly standard effect typing rules (see Fig. 10), we show that effect typing is a proper restriction of LFST typing.

$$(\! |!t.s| \!) = !(\! |t| \!).(\! |s| \!) \qquad (\! |[s]| \!) = [(\! |s| \!)] \qquad (\! |t_1 \to^{\Sigma_1 \mapsto \Sigma_2} t_2| \!) = \Sigma_1; (\! |t_1| \!) \to (\! |t_2| \!); \Sigma_2$$

$$(\! |?t.s| \!) = ?(\! |t| \!).(\! |s| \!) \qquad (\! |s_\alpha| \!) = \mathsf{Chan}\ \alpha \qquad (\! |t_1 \to\!\!\!*^{\Sigma_1 \mapsto \Sigma_2} t_2| \!) = \Sigma_1; (\! |t_1| \!) \to (\! |t_2| \!); \Sigma_2$$

$$(\! |\mathsf{End}| \!) = \mathsf{End} \qquad (\! |\mathsf{Unit}| \!) = \mathsf{Unit} \qquad (\! |t_1 \otimes t_2| \!) = (\! |t_1| \!) \times (\! |t_2| \!)$$

Fig. 11. Type translation from LFST-EFF to VGR

Lemma 1 (Conservative Extension). $\Gamma \vdash' e : t/\Sigma \mapsto \Sigma'$ *implies* $|\Gamma| \vdash e : |t|$.

The translation to ANF does not affect LFST typing with effects.

Lemma 2 (ANF Compatible). *Suppose that* $\Gamma \vdash' e : t/\Sigma \mapsto \Sigma'$.
  Then $\Gamma \vdash' \lfloor\!\lfloor e \rfloor\!\rfloor : t/\Sigma \mapsto \Sigma'$.

Figure 11 contains the backwards translation for types. An α-tagged session type turns into the channel type $\mathsf{Chan}\ \alpha$ and the effect annotation on function types gets mapped to the before and after environments in VGR function types.

Proposition 6 (Typing Preservation (Backwards)).
Suppose that $\Gamma \vdash' e : t/\Sigma_1 \mapsto \Sigma_2$ *for some expression* e *in LFST-ANF. Then for all* Σ *such that* $\Sigma \# \Sigma_1$ *and* $\Sigma \# \Sigma_2$, $(\! |\Gamma| \!); \Sigma, \Sigma_1; (\! |e| \!) \mapsto (\! |t| \!); \Sigma; \Sigma_2$.

7 Related Work

Pucella and Tov [17] give an embedding of a session type calculus in Haskell. Like our translation, their embedding relies on a parameterized monad, which is layered on top of the IO monad using phantom types. Linearity is enforced by the monad abstraction. Multiple channels are implemented by stacking so that channel names are de Bruijn indices. Stacking only happens at the (phantom) type level, so that stack rearrangement has no operational consequences. The paper comes with a formalization and a soundness proof of the implementation. Sackman and Eisenbach [21] also encode session types for a single channel in Haskell using an indexed (parameterized) monad.

Imai and coworkers [12] propose an encoding of binary session-based communication as a library in OCaml. This library is based on an indexed state monad that maintains the current state of a set of channels in a tuple. Channel names are encoded by lenses operating on this state and operations an a channel change the index type at the position indicated by the lens. The programming style resembles VGR, but it is explicitly monadic. The monad and its type indexing are closely related to our encoding, which is linear by typing.

Another line of work on session types is based on process calculi obtained through the Curry-Howard correspondence applied to fragments of linear logic [3–5]. The resulting programs have an imperative flavor as they are based on process calculus. The correspondence structures communication as a string of interactions on a channel name. This channel name "changes type" by rebinding at each communication operation. There is a monadic embedding of this approach into a pure functional language [26]. In this stratified language, processes are snippets of imperative code encapsulated as first-class monadic values into the functional language. These values can be plugged into a process term by a suitable version of the monadic bind operation. Processes may transmit channel names or values from the functional stratum. Processes have the imperative flavor as already mentioned. It would be interesting future work to relate this line of work with the correspondence developed in the present paper.

Alias types [23] presents a type system for a low-level language where the type of a function expresses the shape of the store on which the function operates. Function types can abstract over store locations α and the shape of the store is described by *aliasing constraints* of the form $\{\alpha \mapsto T\}$. Constraint composition resembles separating conjunction [18] and ensures that locations are unique. Analogous to our channel types, pointers in the alias types system can be duplicated and have a singleton type indicating their store location. Alias types also include non-linear constraints, which are not required in our system.

8   Conclusion

Disregarding types, the imperative and functional session calculi are equally powerful. But typing is the essence of a session calculus so that the imperative calculus is strictly less expressive. Two issues are responsible for the limitations.

1. Identity tracking for channels restricts the usability of functional abstraction. With explicit identity, functions are fixed to specific channels.
2. Having different typing rules for sending channels and sending (other) data gives rise to lack of abstraction and hinders modularity. Higher-order channel passing has subtle problems that render a transmitted channel useless.

Our results suggest that the type system severely restricts VGR's expressiveness. Hence, it is an interesting future work to extend VGR's type system such that there are type and semantics preserving translations in both directions.

References

1. Allais, G.: Typing with leftovers - a mechanization of intuitionistic multiplicative-additive linear logic. In: 23rd International Conference on Types for Proofs and Programs, TYPES 2017. LIPIcs, Budapest, Hungary, May 29–June 1, 2017, vol. 104, pp. 1:1–1:22. Schloss Dagstuhl - Leibniz-Zentrum für Informatik (2017). https://doi.org/10.4230/LIPIcs.TYPES.2017.1
2. Atkey, R.: Parameterised notions of computation. J. Funct. Program. **19**(3–4), 335–376 (2009). https://doi.org/10.1017/S095679680900728X
3. Balzer, S., Toninho, B., Pfenning, F.: Manifest Deadlock-freedom for shared session types. In: Caires, L. (ed.) ESOP 2019. LNCS, vol. 11423, pp. 611–639. Springer, Cham (2019). https://doi.org/10.1007/978-3-030-17184-1_22

4. Caires, L., Pfenning, F.: Session types as intuitionistic linear propositions. In: Gastin, P., Laroussinie, F. (eds.) CONCUR 2010. LNCS, vol. 6269, pp. 222–236. Springer, Heidelberg (2010). https://doi.org/10.1007/978-3-642-15375-4_16

5. Das, A., Pfenning, F.: Session types with arithmetic refinements. In: Konnov, I., Kovács, L. (eds.) 31st International Conference on Concurrency Theory, CONCUR 2020 (Virtual Conference). LIPIcs, Vienna, Austria, 1–4 September 2020, vol. 171, pp. 13:1–13:18. Schloss Dagstuhl - Leibniz-Zentrum für Informatik (2020). https://doi.org/10.4230/LIPIcs.CONCUR.2020.13

6. Fowler, S., Lindley, S., Morris, J.G., Decova, S.: Exceptional asynchronous session types: session types without tiers. Proc. ACM Program. Lang. 3(POPL), 28:1–28:29 (2019). https://doi.org/10.1145/3290341

7. Gay, S.J., Vasconcelos, V.T.: Linear type theory for asynchronous session types. J. Funct. Program. 20(1), 19–50 (2010). https://doi.org/10.1017/S0956796809990268

8. Gordon, C.S.: A generic approach to flow-sensitive polymorphic effects. In: 31st European Conference on Object-Oriented Programming, ECOOP 2017. LIPIcs, Barcelona, Spain, 19–23 June 2017, vol. 74, pp. 13:1–13:31. Schloss Dagstuhl - Leibniz-Zentrum für Informatik (2017). https://doi.org/10.4230/LIPIcs.ECOOP.2017.13

9. Honda, K.: Types for dyadic interaction. In: Best, E. (ed.) CONCUR 1993. LNCS, vol. 715, pp. 509–523. Springer, Heidelberg (1993). https://doi.org/10.1007/3-540-57208-2_35

10. Hu, R., Kouzapas, D., Pernet, O., Yoshida, N., Honda, K.: Type-safe eventful sessions in Java. In: D'Hondt, T. (ed.) ECOOP 2010. LNCS, vol. 6183, pp. 329–353. Springer, Heidelberg (2010). https://doi.org/10.1007/978-3-642-14107-2_16

11. Hu, R., Yoshida, N.: Hybrid session verification through endpoint API generation. In: Stevens, P., Wąsowski, A. (eds.) FASE 2016. LNCS, vol. 9633, pp. 401–418. Springer, Heidelberg (2016). https://doi.org/10.1007/978-3-662-49665-7_24

12. Imai, K., Yoshida, N., Yuen, S.: Session-OCaml: a session-based library with polarities and lenses. Sci. Comput. Program. 172, 135–159 (2019). https://doi.org/10.1016/j.scico.2018.08.005

13. Milner, R.: Communicating and Mobile Systems - The Pi-Calculus. Cambridge University Press, New York (1999)

14. Padovani, L.: Context-free session type inference. In: Yang, H. (ed.) ESOP 2017. LNCS, vol. 10201, pp. 804–830. Springer, Heidelberg (2017). https://doi.org/10.1007/978-3-662-54434-1_30

15. Padovani, L.: A simple library implementation of binary sessions. J. Funct. Program. 27, e4 (2017). https://doi.org/10.1017/S0956796816000289

16. Plotkin, G.D.: Call-by-name, call-by-value and the lambda-calculus. Theor. Comput. Sci. 1(2), 125–159 (1975). https://doi.org/10.1016/0304-3975(75)90017-1

17. Pucella, R., Tov, J.A.: Haskell session types with (almost) no class. In: Proceedings of the 1st ACM SIGPLAN Symposium on Haskell, Haskell 2008, Victoria, BC, Canada, 25 September 2008, pp. 25–36. ACM (2008). https://doi.org/10.1145/1411286.1411290

18. Reynolds, J.C.: Separation logic: a logic for shared mutable data structures. In: 17th IEEE Symposium on Logic in Computer Science (LICS 2002), Copenhagen, Denmark, 22–25 July 2002, Proceedings, pp. 55–74. IEEE Computer Society (2002). https://doi.org/10.1109/LICS.2002.1029817

19. Sabry, A., Felleisen, M.: Reasoning about programs in continuation-passing style. LISP Symb. Comput. 6(3–4), 289–360 (1993)

20. Sabry, A., Wadler, P.: A reflection on call-by-value. ACM Trans. Program. Lang. Syst. 19(6), 916–941 (1997). https://doi.org/10.1145/267959.269968

21. Sackman, M., Eisenbach, S.: Session types in Haskell updating message passing for the 21st century (2008). https://spiral.imperial.ac.uk:8443/handle/10044/1/5918

22. Scalas, A., Yoshida, N.: Lightweight session programming in Scala. In: 30th European Conference on Object-Oriented Programming, ECOOP 2016. LIPIcs, Rome, Italy, 18–22 July 2016, vol. 56, pp. 21:1–21:28. Schloss Dagstuhl - Leibniz-Zentrum für Informatik (2016). https://doi.org/10.4230/LIPIcs.ECOOP.2016.21

23. Smith, F., Walker, D., Morrisett, G.: Alias types. In: Smolka, G. (ed.) ESOP 2000. LNCS, vol. 1782, pp. 366–381. Springer, Heidelberg (2000). https://doi.org/10.1007/3-540-46425-5_24

24. Strom, R.E., Yemini, S.: Typestate: a programming language concept for enhancing software reliability. IEEE Trans. Software Eng. **12**(1), 157–171 (1986). https://doi.org/10.1109/TSE.1986.6312929

25. Takeuchi, K., Honda, K., Kubo, M.: An interaction-based language and its typing system. In: Halatsis, C., Maritsas, D., Philokyprou, G., Theodoridis, S. (eds.) PARLE 1994. LNCS, vol. 817, pp. 398–413. Springer, Heidelberg (1994). https://doi.org/10.1007/3-540-58184-7_118

26. Toninho, B., Caires, L., Pfenning, F.: Higher-order processes, functions, and sessions: a monadic integration. In: Felleisen, M., Gardner, P. (eds.) ESOP 2013. LNCS, vol. 7792, pp. 350–369. Springer, Heidelberg (2013). https://doi.org/10.1007/978-3-642-37036-6_20

27. Vasconcelos, V.T., Gay, S.J., Ravara, A.: Type checking a multithreaded functional language with session types. Theor. Comput. Sci. **368**(1–2), 64–87 (2006). https://doi.org/10.1016/j.tcs.2006.06.028

28. Vasconcelos, V., Ravara, A., Gay, S.: Session types for functional multithreading. In: Gardner, P., Yoshida, N. (eds.) CONCUR 2004. LNCS, vol. 3170, pp. 497–511. Springer, Heidelberg (2004). https://doi.org/10.1007/978-3-540-28644-8_32

Safe Session-Based Asynchronous Coordination in Rust

Zak Cutner$^{(\boxtimes)}$ and Nobuko Yoshida

Imperial College London, London, UK
zachary.cutner17@imperial.ac.uk, n.yoshida@imperial.ac.uk

Abstract. Rust is a popular systems language focused on performance and reliability, with an emphasis on providing "fearless concurrency". *Message passing* has become a widely-used pattern by Rust developers although the potential for communication errors leaves developing safe and concurrent applications an unsolved challenge. In this ongoing work, we use *multiparty session types* to provide safety guarantees such as deadlock-freedom by coordinating message-passing processes. In contrast to previous contributions [20–22], our implementation targets *asynchronous* applications using `async/await` code in Rust. Specifically, we incorporate *asynchronous subtyping* theory, which allows program optimisation through reordering input and output actions. We evaluate our ideas by developing several representative use cases from the literature and by taking microbenchmarks. We discuss our plans to support full API generation integrating asynchronous optimisations.

Keywords: Rust · Asynchronous communication · Deadlock-freedom · Session types

1 Introduction

Rust is a statically typed language designed for systems software development. It is rapidly growing in popularity and has been voted "most loved language" over five years of surveys by Stack Overflow [12]. Rust aims to offer the safety of a high-level language without compromising on the performance enjoyed by low-level languages. *Message passing* over *typed channels* is widely used in concurrent Rust applications, whereby (low-level) threads or (high-level) actors communicate efficiently and safely by sending each other messages containing data.

This paper proposes a new implementation framework (RUMPSTEAK) for efficiently coordinating concurrent processes using *asynchronous* message-passing communication in Rust based on *multiparty session types* (MPST) [16,17,31]. MPST coordinate interactions through *linearly typed channels*, where each channel must be used exactly once, ensuring *protocol compliance* without deadlocks or communication mismatches. Rust's affine type system is particularly well-suited to MPST by statically guaranteeing a linear usage of session channels.

Previous implementations based on session types for Rust [20–22] operate under a *synchronous model*—that is upon attempting to receive a message,

© IFIP International Federation for Information Processing 2021
Published by Springer Nature Switzerland AG 2021
F. Damiani and O. Dardha (Eds.): COORDINATION 2021, LNCS 12717, pp. 80–89, 2021.
https://doi.org/10.1007/978-3-030-78142-2_5

a thread is *blocked* until the operation has completed. Although simple, this model can cause significant computational resources to be wasted while a thread is blocked and, moreover, many systems are inherently not synchronous. An *asynchronous model* instead makes no assumptions about how long an operation will take. After beginning to receive a message, a process can continue with its execution and be notified when the operation is complete. In practice, Rust supports the monadic `async`/`await` syntax to perform asynchronous operations. Functions that are asynchronous are annotated with `async`, causing them to return *futures*; and `await` is attached to futures, denoting that execution should continue elsewhere until the future is completed. Unfortunately, as shown in the Rust Survey 2020 [29], "async" and "concurrency" are ranked as the 5th and 7th most "tricky" or "very difficult" features among Rust programmers.

To improve both the safety and efficiency of communications in Rust, our work provides a Rust MPST toolchain (RUMPSTEAK), which supports asynchronous execution. We focus on two key challenges: **(C1)** how to correctly integrate MPST with Rust's `async`/`await` syntax, preserving safety and deadlock-freedom; and **(C2)** how to improve performance by using asynchronous execution. For **(C1)**, we develop a set of `async`/`await` primitives to build up MPST (see Sect. 2); and, for **(C2)**, we evaluate the efficiency of our primitives using microbenchmarks and develop several representative examples from the literature [10,24] with asynchronous communication optimisations (see Sect. 3). Finally, we discuss design choices for integration with advanced MPST theories, such as *asynchronous subtyping* [14] and *asynchronous multiparty compatibility* [24] to maximise communication speed-up, while still preserving safety between asynchronous components in Rust (see Sect. 4). We include further examples, source code and benchmarks in our repository [2] and the full version [11].

2   Overview

Workflow. RUMPSTEAK uses the *top-down* approach to ensure *correctness by design*. In **[Step 1]** we write a *global type G* to describe the interactions between all roles, and project it onto each role to obtain an endpoint finite state machine (EFSM) M_i; in **[Step 2]** we optimise each M_i to obtain M_i'; in **[Step 3]** we generate an API A_i from each M_i'; and in **[Step 4]** we use each A_i to create an asynchronous Rust process P_i. The group of processes $P_1...P_n$ created in this way are free from communication errors such as deadlocks.

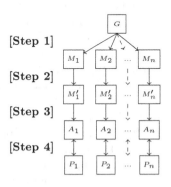

Projection. For **[Step 1]**, RUMPSTEAK uses νSCR [3]: a new lightweight and extensible Scribble toolchain implemented in OCaml. The Scribble language [27,32] is widely used to describe multiparty protocols, agnostic to target

$$G = \mu t.\mathbf{A} \rightarrow \mathbf{B} : \left\{ add(\mathtt{i32}).\mathbf{B} \rightarrow \mathbf{C} : \left\{ \begin{array}{l} add(\mathtt{i32}).\mathbf{C} \rightarrow \mathbf{A} : \{add(\mathtt{i32}).\mathtt{t}\} \\ sub(\mathtt{i32}).\mathbf{C} \rightarrow \mathbf{A} : \{sub(\mathtt{i32}).\mathtt{t}\} \end{array} \right\} \right\}$$

Fig. 1. Global type for the `ring-choice` protocol

languages. For illustration, we use a ring protocol extended with choice (`ring-choice` [11]), whose global type G is given in Fig. 1. Role **B** chooses between sending an *add* and *sub* message to role **C**, which must in turn send the same label to role **A**.

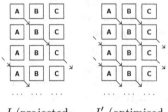

I (projected interactions)   *I'* (optimised interactions)

Asynchronous Optimisation. Since G is *synchronous*, naïvely projecting it onto **B** produces an overly synchronised EFSM $M_\mathbf{B}$[1]. If **A** is slow to send its value to **B** then the entire interaction is blocked (as shown in *I*). Instead, assuming each process begins with its own initial value, **B** could send its value to **C** in the meantime, allowing **C** to begin its next iteration (as shown in *I'*).

Therefore, in **[Step 2]**, we transform $M_\mathbf{B}$ into the more optimal $M'_\mathbf{B}$. Importantly, we ensure that **(1)** no data dependencies exist between interactions, allowing their order to be changed; and **(2)** $M'_\mathbf{B}$ is an *asynchronous subtype* [14] of $M_\mathbf{B}$, allowing it to *safely* be used as a substitution while preserving deadlock-freedom. Presently, these steps are performed manually (see Sect. 4).

Code Generation. RUMPSTEAK includes a code generator to produce an API in **[Step 3]**. Listing 1 shows the API $A_\mathbf{B}$ corresponding to the EFSM $M'_\mathbf{B}$, from which we have elided other participants. To ensure that our API remains readable by developers and to eliminate extensive boilerplate code, we make use of Rust procedural macros [28]. By decorating types with #[...], these macros perform additional compile-time code generation. For each role, we generate a struct storing its communication channels with other roles. For example, **B** (line 3) contains unidirectional channels from **A** and to **C** as per the protocol. We use #[derive(Role)] to retrieve channels from the struct.

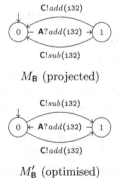

$M_\mathbf{B}$ (projected)

$M'_\mathbf{B}$ (optimised)

Following the approach of [22], we build a set of *generic primitives* to construct a simple API—reducing the amount of generated code and avoiding arbitrarily named types. For instance, the `Receive` primitive (line 22) takes a role, label and continuation as generic parameters. For readability, we elide two additional parameters used to store channels at runtime with #[session].

---

[1] We use session type syntax [31] where ! and ? denote send and receive respectively.

```
1   #[derive(Role)]
2   #[message(Label)]
3   struct B {
4       #[route(A)] a: Receiver,
5       #[route(C)] c: Sender,
6   }
7
8   #[derive(Message)]
9   enum Label {
10      Add(Add),
11      Sub(Sub),
12  }
13
14  struct Add(i32);
15  struct Sub(i32);
16
17  #[session]
18  type RingB = Select<C, RingBChoice>;
19
20  #[session]
21  enum RingBChoice {
22      Add(Add, Receive<A, Add, RingB>),
23      Sub(Sub, Receive<A, Add, RingB>),
24  }
```

```
1   async fn ring_b(
2       role: &mut B,
3       mut input: i32,
4   ) -> Result<Infallible> {
5       try_session(
6           role,
7           |mut s: RingB<'_, _>| async {
8               loop {
9                   let x = input * 2;
10                  s = if x > 0 {
11                      let s = s.select(Add(x)).await?;
12                      let (Add(y), s) = s.receive().await?;
13                      input = y + x;
14                      s
15                  } else {
16                      let s = s.select(Sub(x)).await?;
17                      let (Add(y), s) = s.receive().await?;
18                      input = y - x;
19                      s
20                  };
21              }
22          },
23      ).await
24  }
```

Listing 1. Rust session type API for M'_B (A_B)

Listing 2. Possible Rust implementation for process **B** (P_B) using A_B

Each choice generates an enum, as seen in `RingBChoice` (line 21), allowing processes to pattern match when branching to determine which label was received. Methods allowing the enum to be used with `Branch` or `Select` primitives are also generated with `#[session]`. An enum is required since Rust's lack of variadic generics means choice cannot be easily implemented as a primitive. We show how the `RingBChoice` type can be used with selection in the `Ring` type (line 18).

Our API requires only one session type for each role, internally sending a `Label` enum (line 9) over reusable channels. We create a type for each label (lines 14 and 15) and use `#[derive(Message)]` to generate methods for converting to and from the `Label` enum. In contrast, [22] requires a tuple of binary sessions for each role and communicates using typed, one-shot channels. Our approach is simpler, requiring fewer definitions, and also more performant (see Sect. 3).

Process Implementation. Using the API A_B, we suggest a possible implementation of the process P_B, shown in Listing 2, for **[Step 4]**. Linear usage of channels is checked by Rust's *affine type system* to prevent channels from being used multiple times. When a primitive is executed, it consumes itself, preventing reuse, and returns its continuation. While [21] and [22] use compiler hints to warn the programmer when a session is discarded without use, we ensure this *statically* by harnessing the type checker. Developers are prevented from constructing primitives directly using visibility modifiers and must instead use `try_session` (line 5). Its closure argument accepts the input session type and returns the terminal type `End`. If a session is discarded, breaking linearity, then the developer will have no `End` to return and the type checker will complain. Even so, we can implement processes with infinitely recursive types (containing no `End`) such as `RingB`. We use an infinite loop (line 8) which is assigned

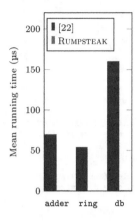

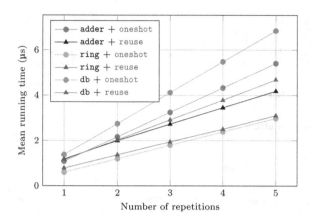

Fig. 2. Comparison of RUMPSTEAK and [22]

Fig. 3. Comparison of **oneshot** and **reuse** under asynchronous execution

Infallible: Rust's never (or bottom) type. **Infallible** can be implicitly cast to any other type, including **End**, allowing the closure to pass the type checker as before.

We allow roles to be reused across sessions since the channels they contain can be expensive to create. Crucially, to prevent communication mismatches between different sessions, **try_session** takes a *mutable* reference to the role. The same role, therefore, cannot be used multiple times at once because Rust's borrow checker enforces this requirement for mutable references.

3   Evaluation

Microbenchmarks. We investigate RUMPSTEAK's performance, comparing it with the most recent related work [22]. We introduce three protocols from [11]:

- (**adder**) an adder protocol between three participants;

$$G = \mathbf{A} \to \mathbf{B} : \{add(i32).\mathbf{B} \to \mathbf{A} : \{add(i32).\mathbf{A} \to \mathbf{C} : \{add(i32).$$
$$\mathbf{B} \to \mathbf{C} : \{add(i32).\mathbf{C} \to \mathbf{A} : \{sum(i32).\mathbf{C} \to \mathbf{B} : \{sum(i32).\mathbf{end}\}\}\}\}\}\}$$

- (**ring**) a simpler version of **ring-choice**; and

$$G = \mathbf{A} \to \mathbf{B} : \{value(i32).\mathbf{B} \to \mathbf{C} : \{value(i32).\mathbf{C} \to \mathbf{A} : \{value(i32).\mathbf{end}\}\}\}$$

- (**db**) a double buffering protocol [19] between source **S**, kernel **K** and sink **T**.

$$G = \mathbf{K} \to \mathbf{S} : \{ready.\mathbf{S} \to \mathbf{K} : \{copy(i32).\mathbf{T} \to \mathbf{K} : \{ready.$$
$$\mathbf{K} \to \mathbf{T} : \{copy(i32).\mathbf{K} \to \mathbf{S} : \{ready.\mathbf{S} \to \mathbf{K} : \{copy(i32).$$
$$\mathbf{T} \to \mathbf{K} : \{ready.\mathbf{K} \to \mathbf{T} : \{copy(i32).\mathbf{end}\}\}\}\}\}\}\}\}$$

Only terminating protocols are used so that we can practically measure their running times. Most previous session type implementations in Rust [20,21] support only *binary* protocols. Our contribution and benchmarks instead target *multiparty* protocols, therefore we compare RUMPSTEAK only against [22] which has a similar scope. Since [22] is built upon [21], we expect both to have similar performance for binary protocols. We execute all benchmarks using an 8-core Intel® Core™ i7-7700K CPU @ 4.20 GHz with hyperthreading, 16GB RAM, Ubuntu 20.04.2 LTS and Rust 1.51.0. We use version 0.3.4 of the Criterion.rs library [15] to perform microbenchmarking and a *single-threaded* asynchronous runtime from version 1.5.0 of the Tokio library [30].

Our first benchmark (Fig. 2) performs a direct comparison between RUMPSTEAK and [22] for all three protocols. It shows that RUMPSTEAK can run these protocols around 50–150 times faster. We attribute this to our approach of using asynchronous execution. Asynchronous tasks are significantly more lightweight than kernel threads and so incur much lower overheads. We note that blocking operations do not contribute to weaker synchronous performance as we benchmark with significantly more cores than the number of roles.

As discussed previously (see Sect. 2), RUMPSTEAK uses reusable channels in contrast to one-shot channels used by [22]. To compare both approaches fairly, Fig. 3 benchmarks RUMPSTEAK (**reuse**) against a subset of [22] ported to use asynchronous execution (**oneshot**). We simulate a longer protocol by reusing the same channels for a parameterised number of repetitions, although one-shot channels, by design, cannot be reused. In **adder** and **ring**, **oneshot** performs better than **reuse** for a single iteration. However, as the number of repetitions increases, constructing a growing number of one-shot channels quickly outweighs the one-time instantiation penalty of reusable channels. By the second iteration, **reuse** overtakes the performance of **oneshot** in **adder** and **db**. Only for **ring** (which contains the least number of exchanges) is **oneshot** still faster after five iterations, although the gradients suggest that **reuse** will eventually overtake. We conclude that **reuse** is more efficient than **oneshot** in all but the shortest protocols.

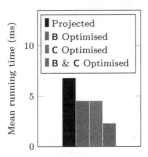

Fig. 4. Comparison of **ring** optimisations

We explore an asynchronous optimisation to **ring** in Fig. 4 by swapping **B/C**'s input and output actions. We also insert artificial 1ms communication delays to simulate a more realistic scenario. We observe a significant performance improvement by applying the optimisation to either **B** or **C**. Moreover, the effect is compounded by optimising both participants at once, resulting in a $^2/_3$ speed-up.

Figure 5 shows an asynchronous optimisation to **db** whereby **K** sends **S** both *ready* messages at once, further discussed in the full version [11]. We insert similar artificial communication delays between **S** and **K** for our experimental setup. Interestingly, this optimisation causes duality between **S** and **K** to break. Since [22] uses a tuple of binary session types for each role, it is crucially unable to express this optimisation. Therefore, we further propose a weaker optimisation for [22] by sending the second *ready* message only after **K** has received the first *copy* message to preserve duality. Figure 5 shows that while this weaker optimisation has little effect on performance, the original and stronger optimisation which is expressable by RUMPSTEAK results in around a 25% improvement.

Expressiveness. We further illustrate the expressiveness of RUMPSTEAK compared with [22] in Fig. 6. We implement several examples of protocols from the literature using RUMPSTEAK. For each example, we detail its key features, particularly if it makes use of asynchronous optimisations, and whether we can also express the protocol using [22].

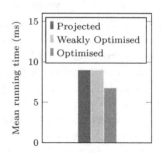

Fig. 5. Comparison of db optimisations

Our results demonstrate that [22] is less expressive than RUMPSTEAK for asynchronously-optimised protocols since its workflow does not include an optimisation step. Some optimisations, which are marked with ◀, can nevertheless be expressed in [22] by implementing them directly using its endpoint API. However, this method does not benefit from using the workflow in [22]. Even then, as discussed for db, [22] uses a tuple of binary session types for each role and therefore any optimisation must not break duality between each pair of participants. Unfortunately, this prohibits it from performing most asynchronous optimisations, even in this more limited way. In contrast, RUMPSTEAK enjoys complete flexibility to perform more complex optimisations in a wide-ranging number of examples from the literature.

Conclusion. By using asynchronous execution, RUMPSTEAK is around two orders of magnitude faster than [22], and this benefit is even greater in longer-running protocols due to our use of reusable channels. We observe the need for asynchronous optimisation by demonstrating several significant performance improvements and show that, in several cases, RUMPSTEAK can express stronger and more valuable optimisations than are expressable in [22].

4   Related and Future Work

There are a vast number of studies on session types, some of which are implemented in programming languages [4] and tools [13]. A code generation toolchain takes a protocol description and produces well-typed APIs, conforming to that protocol. Several implementations use an EFSM-based approach to generate APIs from Scribble [3,27,32] for target programming languages such as Java [18], F# [26], Go [9], F⋆ [33] and TypeScript [25]. We closely compared with previous work on API generation in Rust from MPST protocols [22] (see detailed comparisons with [21] and [20] in [22]). We justify our work is **(1)** robust, using affine typing, while providing a simpler API (see Sect. 2) and **(2)** faster and more expressive by using `async`/`await` and reusable channels (see Sect. 3). Here, our aim is ensuring *correctness/safety by construction*, maximising *asynchrony* for gaining *efficiency* of message passing in Rust applications.

Protocol	Features				Expressable	
	C	R	IR	AO	[22]	Rumpsteak
Two Adder [3]	●	●			●	●
adder [11]					●	●
ring [10,11]		●[a]	●[a]		●	●
Optimised ring [10,11]		●[a]	●[a]	●	◀	●
ring-choice [10,11]	●	●	●		●	●
Optimised ring-choice [10,11]	●	●	●	●	◀	●
db [10,11]		●[a]	●[a]		●	●
Optimised db [10,19,11]		●[a]	●[a]	●		●
Alternating Bit [24,1]	●	●	●		◀	●
Elevator[b] [24,5]	●	●	●	●		●
FFT [10]					●	●

C Contains choice R Recursive IR Infinitely recursive AO Uses asynchronous optimisations

[a] Although non-recursive, we can easily extend the protocol to make it recursive.

[b] We use the communicating session automata variation from [24].

Fig. 6. Expressiveness of [22] and Rumpsteak

Our main remaining challenge is how to validate the well-formedness of a set of optimised EFSMs, i.e. $\{M_i'\}_{i \in I}$ generated in [**Step 2**] of the workflow presented in Sect. 2. One possible approach is the use of *multiparty asynchronous subtyping* [14] to validate $M_i' \leqslant M_i$ for each participant. Asynchronous session subtyping was shown to be undecidable, even for binary sessions [8,23], hence, in general, checking $M_i' \leqslant M_i$ is undecidable. Various limited classes of session types for which $M_i' \leqslant M_i$ is decidable [6,7,10,23] are proposed but not applicable to our use cases since (**1**) the relations in [6,8,23] are *binary* and the same limitations do not work for multiparty; and (**2**) the relation in [10, Def. 6.1] does not handle subtyping across unrolling recursions, e.g. the relation is inapplicable to the double buffering algorithm [19] (see [10, Remark 8.1]). Hence, we need to find non-trivial decidable approximations of our multiparty asynchronous subtyping relation. The second approach is to use *k-multiparty compatibility* developed in [24] to analyse a whole set of $\{M_i'\}_{i \in I}$. We investigate both options and report our findings at the conference presentation.

Acknowledgements. We thank Nicolas Lagaillardie and Fangyi Zhou for their helpful comments and suggestions. The work is supported by EPSRC, grants EP/T006544/1, EP/K011715/1, EP/K034413/1, EP/L00058X/1, EP/N027833/1, EP/N028201/1, EP/T014709/1, and EP/V000462/1 and by NCSS/EPSRC VeTSS.

References

1. Introduction to Protocol Engineering. http://cs.uccs.edu/~cs522/pe/pe.htm. Accessed 19 Feb 2021
2. Rumpsteak. https://github.com/zakcutner/rumpsteak
3. νScr. https://github.com/nuscr/nuscr
4. Ancona, D., et al.: Behavioral types in programming languages. Found. Trends Program. Lang. 3(2–3), 95–230 (2016)
5. Bouajjani, A., Enea, C., Ji, K., Qadeer, S.: On the completeness of verifying message passing programs under bounded asynchrony. In: Chockler, H., Weissenbacher, G. (eds.) CAV 2018. LNCS, vol. 10982, pp. 372–391. Springer, Cham (2018). https://doi.org/10.1007/978-3-319-96142-2_23
6. Bravetti, M., Carbone, M., Lange, J., Yoshida, N., Zavattaro, G.: A sound algorithm for asynchronous session subtyping. Leibniz Int. Proc. Inform. 140, 38:1–38:16 (2019)
7. Bravetti, M., Carbone, M., Zavattaro, G.: Undecidability of asynchronous session subtyping. Inf. Comput. 256, 300–320 (2017)
8. Bravetti, M., Carbone, M., Zavattaro, G.: On the boundary between decidability and undecidability of asynchronous session subtyping. Theoret. Comput. Sci. 722, 19–51 (2018)
9. Castro, D., Hu, R., Jongmans, S.S., Ng, N., Yoshida, N.: Distributed Programming Using Role-parametric Session Types in Go: Statically-typed Endpoint APIs for Dynamically-instantiated Communication Structures. Proceedings of the ACM on Programming Languages 3(POPL), 29:1–29:30 (2019)
10. Castro-Perez, D., Yoshida, N.: CAMP: cost-aware multiparty session protocol. Proc. ACM Program. Lang. 4(OOPSLA), 1–30 (2020)
11. Cutner, Z., Yoshida, N.: Safe session-based asynchronous coordination in rust. https://github.com/zakcutner/coordination-2021
12. Donovan, R.: Why the developers who use rust love it so much (2020). https://stackoverflow.blog/2020/06/05/why-the-developers-who-use-rust-love-it-so-much/. Accessed 31 Jan 2021
13. Gay, S., Ravara, A.: Behavioural Types: From Theory to Tools. River Publisher (2017)
14. Ghilezan, S., Pantovic, J., Prokic, I., Scalas, A., Yoshida, N.: Precise subtyping for asynchronous multiparty sessions. In: Proceedings of the ACM on Programming Languages, POPL, vol. 5, pp. 16:1–16:28. ACM (2021)
15. Heisler, B.: Criterion.rs. https://github.com/bheisler/criterion.rs
16. Honda, K., Yoshida, N., Carbone, M.: Multiparty asynchronous session types. In: Proceedings of the ACM on Programming Languages, POPL, pp. 273–284. ACM (2008)
17. Honda, K., Yoshida, N., Carbone, M.: Multiparty asynchronous session types. JACM 63, 1–67 (2016)
18. Hu, R., Yoshida, N.: Hybrid session verification through endpoint API generation. In: Stevens, P., Wąsowski, A. (eds.) FASE 2016. LNCS, vol. 9633, pp. 401–418. Springer, Heidelberg (2016). https://doi.org/10.1007/978-3-662-49665-7_24
19. Huang, H., Pillai, P., Shin, K.G.: Improving wait-free algorithms for interprocess communication in embedded real-time systems. In: 2002 USENIX Annual Technical Conference (USENIX ATC 02). USENIX Association (2002)
20. Jespersen, T.B.L., Munksgaard, P., Larsen, K.F.: Session types for rust. In: Proceedings of the 11th ACM SIGPLAN Workshop on Generic Programming, WGP, pp. 13–22. ACM (2015)

21. Kokke, W.: Rusty variation: deadlock-free sessions with failure in rust. Electron. Proc. Theoret. Comput. Sci. **304**, 48–60 (2019)

22. Lagaillardie, N., Neykova, R., Yoshida, N.: Implementing multiparty session types in rust. In: Bliudze, S., Bocchi, L. (eds.) COORDINATION 2020. LNCS, vol. 12134, pp. 127–136. Springer, Cham (2020). https://doi.org/10.1007/978-3-030-50029-0_8

23. Lange, J., Yoshida, N.: On the undecidability of asynchronous session subtyping. In: Esparza, J., Murawski, A.S. (eds.) FoSSaCS 2017. LNCS, vol. 10203, pp. 441–457. Springer, Heidelberg (2017). https://doi.org/10.1007/978-3-662-54458-7_26

24. Lange, J., Yoshida, N.: Verifying asynchronous interactions via communicating session automata. In: Dillig, I., Tasiran, S. (eds.) CAV 2019. LNCS, vol. 11561, pp. 97–117. Springer, Cham (2019). https://doi.org/10.1007/978-3-030-25540-4_6

25. Miu, A., Ferreira, F., Yoshida, N., Zhou, F.: Communication-safe web programming in typescript with routed multiparty session types. In: Proceedings of the 30th ACM SIGPLAN International Conference on Compiler Construction, CC, pp. 94–106. ACM (2021)

26. Neykova, R., Hu, R., Yoshida, N., Abdeljallal, F.: A session type provider: compile-time API generation of distributed protocols with refinements in F#. In: 27th International Conference on Compiler Construction, CC, pp. 128–138. ACM (2018)

27. Scribble Authors: Scribble: Describing Multi Party Protocols (2015). http://www.scribble.org/

28. The Rust Project Developers: Procedural Macros. https://doc.rust-lang.org/reference/procedural-macros.html

29. The Rust Survey Team: Rust Survey 2020 Results (2020). https://blog.rust-lang.org/2020/12/16/rust-survey-2020.html. Accessed 31 Jan 2021

30. Tokio Contributors: Tokio. https://github.com/tokio-rs/tokio

31. Yoshida, N., Gheri, L.: A very gentle introduction to multiparty session types. In: Hung, D.V., D'Souza, M. (eds.) ICDCIT 2020. LNCS, vol. 11969, pp. 73–93. Springer, Cham (2020). https://doi.org/10.1007/978-3-030-36987-3_5

32. Yoshida, N., Hu, R., Neykova, R., Ng, N.: The scribble protocol language. In: Abadi, M., Lluch Lafuente, A. (eds.) TGC 2013. LNCS, vol. 8358, pp. 22–41. Springer, Cham (2014). https://doi.org/10.1007/978-3-319-05119-2_3

33. Zhou, F., Ferreira, F., Hu, R., Neykova, R., Yoshida, N.: Statically verified refinements for multiparty protocols. Proc. ACM Program. Lang. 4(OOPSLA) (2020)

A Session Subtyping Tool

Lorenzo Bacchiani[1]([✉]), Mario Bravetti[1,2], Julien Lange[3],
and Gianluigi Zavattaro[1,2]

[1] University of Bologna, Bologna, Italy
lorenzo.bacchiani2@unibo.it
[2] Focus Team, Inria, Sophia Antipolis, France
[3] Royal Holloway, University of London, Egham, UK

Abstract. Session types are becoming popular and have been integrated in several mainstream programming languages. Nevertheless, while many programming languages consider asynchronous FIFO channel communication, the notion of subtyping used in session type implementations is the one defined by Gay and Hole for synchronous communication. This might be because there are several notions of asynchronous session subtyping, these notions are usually undecidable, and only recently sound (but not complete) algorithmic characterizations for these subtypings have been proposed. But the fact that the definition of asynchronous session subtyping and the theory behind related algorithms are not easily accessible to non-experts may also prevent further integration. The aim of this paper, and of the tool presented therein, is to make the growing body of knowledge about asynchronous session subtyping more accessible, thus promoting its integration in practical applications of session types.

1 Introduction

In recent years, session types have been integrated into several mainstream programming languages (see, e.g., [1,15,19,23–26]) where they specify the pattern of interactions that each endpoint must follow, i.e., a communication protocol. All of these practical applications show a good level of maturity of the session type theory, but there are still some limitations. In particular, the notion of subtyping considered in such tools usually assumes synchronous communication channels, while, in many cases, communication takes place over asynchronous point-to-point FIFO channels (where outputs are non-blocking). In this setting, the emitted messages are stored inside channels, and there may be an arbitrary delay between an output (on an endpoint) and the corresponding input (on the opposite endpoint). The impact on session subtyping of these aspects related with asynchronous communication has been initially studied in [12,20,21], but the notions of subtyping proposed therein were subsequently proved to be undecidable [6,18]. Only recently, sound (but not complete) algorithms for asynchronous session subtyping have been proposed [5,7,9]. However, the theory behind asynchronous session types (see [11] for a gentle introduction) and related algorithms

© IFIP International Federation for Information Processing 2021
Published by Springer Nature Switzerland AG 2021
F. Damiani and O. Dardha (Eds.): COORDINATION 2021, LNCS 12717, pp. 90–105, 2021.
https://doi.org/10.1007/978-3-030-78142-2_6

is rather intricate and this could limit their dissemination in the research community, as well as their adoption in practical applications.

The aim of this paper, and of the tool that we introduce, is to make the growing body of knowledge about asynchronous session subtyping more accessible. More precisely, we present in an uniform and intuitive way various notions of (a)synchronous session subtyping that were presented in the literature following different formalisms, e.g., types in [9] or communicating finite-state machines in [5]. Our tool integrates several algorithms for checking subtyping that can be invoked from an easy-to-use Python GUI. This interface allows the user to input, using standard session type syntax, two types: the candidate subtype and supertype. The tool automatically generates the graphical representation of these session types as communicating finite-state machines [3]. It is also possible to execute on them the desired subtyping algorithm(s). The tool has been implemented in a modular way, and it is possible to easily include several subtyping algorithms, simply by customizing a JSON configuration file. In the current version, we consider: two algorithms from [17] for synchronous session subtyping (based on Gay and Hole's [14] and Kozen et al.'s [16] algorithms), a sound algorithm for checking (orphan message free) asynchronous session subtyping [5], and a sound algorithm for checking fair asynchronous session subtyping [9]. The implementations of these algorithms, besides returning a verdict about subtyping of the two types, also return a graphical representation of the so-called *subtyping simulation game*: i.e., the procedure to check that each relevant input/output action that can be performed by the candidate subtype has a corresponding matching action in the candidate supertype. This graphical representation is helpful to understand the reason behind the given verdict. The original command line Haskell implementations of the algorithms in [5,9,17] have been adapted and integrated by: (*i*) uniformizing their graphical notation/colors (e.g., *inner/outer* states represented as rectangles, with the initial one being thicker, error ones being red, content of outer ones being blue, etc...), (*ii*) reimplementing the synchronous algorithm so to also generate the simulation graph, (*iii*) completely rewriting, in the fair asynchronous algorithm, the controllability check (existance of a compliant peer, see Sect. 2.1) and (*iv*) error detection with generation of red states for all algorithms, (*v*) pre-transforming inputted types with a Python ANTLR4 parser that produces a common raw syntax.

Synopsis. Section 2 recalls basic notions about session subtyping using tool-simulated examples and Sect. 3 describes the functionalities of the tool. Finally, in Sect. 4 we conclude the paper.

The tool sources/binaries are available at [2].

2   Session Subtyping

We first recall the syntax of session types and their automata representation in the style of communicating finite-state machines (CFSM) [3]. We then show how our tool can generate simulation graphs for supported session subtyping relations: synchronous [17], asynchronous [5] and fair asynchronous subtyping [9].

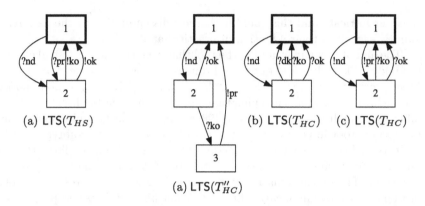

(a) LTS(T_{HS})   (b) LTS(T'_{HC})   (c) LTS(T_{HC})

(a) LTS(T''_{HC})

Fig. 1. Hospital server.   **Fig. 2.** Hospital clients.

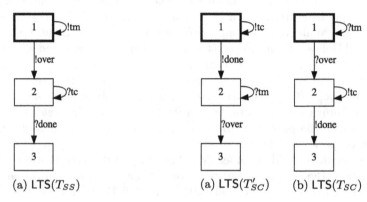

(a) LTS(T_{SS})   (a) LTS(T'_{SC})   (b) LTS(T_{SC})

Fig. 3. Satellite protocol server.   **Fig. 4.** Satellite protocol clients.

In the asynchronous cases automata are assumed to communicate over unbounded FIFO channels as for CFSMs.

2.1 Session Types and Their Automata Representation

The formal syntax of two-party session types is given below. Notice that we follow the simplified notation used in, e.g., [6,9,13], which abstracts away from data carried by messages (payloads). This is done in order to focus on the key aspects of the session subtyping problem (as we will see co/contra-variance of output/input and output anticipation): passing data or channels (delegation) are features that we deem orthogonal to such a problem.

Definition 1 (Session Types). *Given a set of label names $\mathcal{L}$, ranged over by l, the syntax of two-party session types is given by the following grammar:*

$$T ::= \oplus\{l_i; T_i\}_{i\in I} \quad | \quad \&\{l_i; T_i\}_{i\in I} \quad | \quad \mu X.T \quad | \quad X \quad | \quad \mathbf{end}$$

where $I \neq \emptyset$ and $\forall i \neq j \in I. \; l_i \neq l_j$.

Type $\oplus\{l_i; T_i\}_{i \in I}$ represents an internal choice among *outputs*, specifying that the chosen label name $l_i \in \mathcal{L}$ is sent and, then, continuation T_i is executed. $\&\{l_i; T_i\}_{i \in I}$ represents, instead, an external choice among *inputs*, specifying that, once a label name $l_i \in \mathcal{L}$ is received, continuation T_i takes place. Types $\mu\mathbf{X}.T$ and $\mathbf{X}$ denote standard recursion constructs. We assume recursion to be guarded, i.e., in $\mu\mathbf{X}.T$ the recursion variable $\mathbf{X}$ occurs only after receiving or sending a label. Type **end** denotes the end of the interaction. Session types are closed, i.e., all recursion variables $\mathbf{X}$ occur under the scope of a corresponding binder $\mu\mathbf{X}.T$.

In the tool we graphically represent the behaviour of a session type T as a Labeled Transition System (LTS), see, e.g., Figs. 1, 2, 3 and 4. Following the notation of CFSMs, we denote a LTS by $(Q, q_0, \rightarrow)$, with Q being a set of states, q_0 the initial state and $\rightarrow$ a transition relation over $Q \times (\{!,?\} \times \mathcal{L}) \times Q$, with label "$! \, l$" representing output on l and label "$? \, l$" representing input on l.

We use $\mathsf{LTS}(T)$ to denote the LTS of type T. Let $\mathcal{T}$ be the set of all session types T. We define transition relation $\longrightarrow \subseteq \mathcal{T} \times (\{!,?\} \times \mathcal{L}) \times \mathcal{T}$, as the least transition set satisfying the following rules

$$\oplus\{l_i; T_i\}_{i \in I} \xrightarrow{! \, l_i} T_i \quad i \in I \qquad \&\{l_i; T_i\}_{i \in I} \xrightarrow{? \, l_i} T_i \quad i \in I \qquad \frac{T\{\mu\mathbf{X}.T/\mathbf{X}\} \xrightarrow{\ell} T'}{\mu\mathbf{X}.T \xrightarrow{\ell} T'}$$

with label ℓ ranging over $\{!,?\} \times \mathcal{L}$. Notice that a state **end**, called *termination state*, has no outgoing transitions. Given a session type T we define $\mathsf{LTS}(T)$ as being $(Q_T, T, \rightarrow_T)$, where: Q_T is the set of terms T' which are reachable from T according to $\longrightarrow$ relation and $\rightarrow_T$ is defined as the restriction of $\longrightarrow$ to $Q_T \times (\{!,?\} \times \mathcal{L}) \times Q_T$.

Notice that in general an LTS may express more behaviours than the ones described by session types: it can include non-deterministic and mixed choices, i.e. choices including both inputs and outputs. Here we only consider LTSs $(Q, q_0, \rightarrow)$ such that $\exists T \in \mathcal{T}. \mathsf{LTS}(T) = (Q, q_0, \rightarrow)$.

Example 1. As an example of session types we consider the Hospital server from [5]:

$$T_{HS} = \mu\mathbf{X}. \&\{nd; \oplus\{ko; \mathbf{X}, \ ok; \mathbf{X}\}, \ pr; \oplus\{ko; \mathbf{X}, \ ok; \mathbf{X}\}\}$$

Figure 1 shows $\mathsf{LTS}(T_{HS})$ as produced by our tool. The server T_{HS} expects to receive two types of messages: nd (next patient data) or pr (patient report). Then it may send either ok or ko, indicating whether the evaluation of received data was successful or not, and it loops.

We now define the *dual* of a session type T, written $\overline{T}$. $\overline{T}$ is inductively obtained from T as follows: $\overline{\oplus\{l_i; T_i\}_{i \in I}} = \&\{l_i; \overline{T}_i\}_{i \in I}$, $\overline{\&\{l_i; T_i\}_{i \in I}} = \oplus\{l_i; \overline{T}_i\}_{i \in I}$, $\overline{\mathbf{end}} = \mathbf{end}$, $\overline{\mathbf{X}} = \mathbf{X}$, and $\overline{\mu\mathbf{X}.T} = \mu\mathbf{X}.\overline{T}$. For example, the dual of the Hospital server T_{HS} is:

$$\overline{T_{HS}} = \mu\mathbf{X}. \oplus\{nd; \&\{ko; \mathbf{X}, \ ok; \mathbf{X}\}, \ pr; \&\{ko; \mathbf{X}, \ ok; \mathbf{X}\}\}$$

Example 2. We now consider examples of session types that are clients of the Hospital service: an "ideal" client T_{HC} and two specific ones T'_{HC} and T''_{HC}, respectively.

$$T_{HC} = \overline{T_{HS}} = \mu\mathbf{X}. \oplus\{nd; \&\{ko; \mathbf{X}, \ ok; \mathbf{X}\}, \ pr; \&\{ko; \mathbf{X}, \ ok; \mathbf{X}\}\}$$
$$T'_{HC} = \mu\mathbf{X}. \oplus\{nd; \&\{ko; \mathbf{X}, \ ok; \mathbf{X}, \ dk; \mathbf{X}\}\}$$
$$T''_{HC} = \mu\mathbf{X}. \oplus\{nd; \&\{ko; \mathbf{X}, \ ok; \oplus\{pr; \mathbf{X}\}\}\}$$

Figure 2 shows $\mathsf{LTS}(T''_{HC})$, $\mathsf{LTS}(T'_{HC})$ and $\mathsf{LTS}(T_{HC})$,[1] as produced by our tool.

The "ideal" client T_{HC} is simply the dual of the Hospital server: first it may send two types of messages nd or pr, then it expects to receive either ok or ko. In general, a client that is *compliant* with the Hospital server is a type such that: (i) each message sent by the client (resp. server) can be received by the server (resp. client), and (ii) neither the server nor the client blocks in a receive. For example, the client T'_{HC}, a slightly modified version of T_{HC} that may send nd only and expects to receive also dk (don't know) besides ok and ko (i.e., it applies covariance of outputs and contravariance of inputs, see [17]) is still compliant with the Hospital server. Hence we say that T'_{HC} is a subtype of T_{HC}.

Under asynchronous communication client compliance is relaxed by requiring that all messages that are sent are *eventually* received. For example, in this setting, client T''_{HC} (that may anticipate output nd w.r.t. inputs) is also a compliant client, see [5], hence T''_{HC} is an asynchronous subtype of T_{HC}.

Notice that, both for synchronous and asynchronous communication (see [7]), it holds, for any session type T, T': T' subtype of T implies $\overline{T}$ subtype of $\overline{T'}$ (closure under duality). As we will see, our tool automatically handles the generation of the *dual subtyping problem* ($\overline{T}$ subtype of $\overline{T'}$) from T' subtype of T by exchanging and dualizing inputted types.

Example 3. As another example, we consider clients of the Satellite protocol from [9]: an "ideal" client (the dual of the Satellite protocol server T_{SS} whose LTS is depicted in Fig. 3) and a specific one; here denoted with T_{SC} and T'_{SC}, respectively.

$$T_{SC} = \overline{T_{SS}} = \mu\mathbf{X}. \&\{tm; \mathbf{X}, \ over; \mu\mathbf{Y}. \oplus \{tc; \mathbf{Y}, \ done; \mathbf{end}\}\}$$
$$T'_{SC} = \mu\mathbf{X}. \oplus \{tc; \mathbf{X}, \ done; \mu\mathbf{Y}. \&\{tm; \mathbf{Y}, \ over; \mathbf{end}\}\}$$

Figure 4 shows $\mathsf{LTS}(T'_{SC})$ and $\mathsf{LTS}(T_{SC})$, as produced by our tool. The "ideal" client T_{SC} may receive a number of telemetries (tm), followed by a message $over$. In the second phase, the client sends a number of telecommands (tc), followed by a message $done$. Under *fair* asynchronous communication client T'_{SC} (with phases exchanged) is also compliant with the server, i.e. T'_{SC} a fair asynchronous subtype of T_{SC}, see [9]. Compared to asynchronous communication considered in Example 2, here client compliance entails that, under *fairness assumption* (i.e.

---

[1] As we will see, the order in which the LTSs are presented reflects the subtyping relation (we will show that T''_{HC} and T'_{HC} are subtypes of T_{HC}) and the positions in which types are inputed in the tool.

communication loops with some exit are assumed to be eventually escaped), both the client and the server must reach successfull termination with no messages left to be consumed in the FIFO channels.

2.2 Synchronous Session Subtyping

In order to establish whether type T' is a synchronous subtype of a type T [17] we can perform synchronous simulation of the (ordered) pair of LTSs $\mathsf{LTS}(T') = (Q', q'_0, \rightarrow')$ and $\mathsf{LTS}(T) = (Q, q_0, \rightarrow)$. Simulation states are pairs (q', q), with $q' \in Q'$ and $q \in Q$. The simulation proceeds by starting from state (q'_0, q_0) and by synchronously matching transitions of $\mathsf{LTS}(T')$ and $\mathsf{LTS}(T)$ having the *same* labels (both "$!\,l$" or both "$?\,l$"). For each reached simulation state (q', q) we must have: (i) the set of outputs (resp. inputs) fireable by q' is subset (resp. superset) or equal to the set of outputs (resp. inputs) fireable by q; this enacts covariance (resp. contravariance) of outputs (resp. inputs), (ii) if (q', q) performs no transitions then both q' and q must perform no transitions (successfully terminate).

On the contrary, simulation states (q', q) for which the above constraints are not satisfied are called *failure simulation states* (depicted in red in our tool) and cause synchronous subtyping not to hold.

Example 4. Figure 6 shows the synchronous simulation graph, as produced from our tool, for the pair $\mathsf{LTS}(T'_{HC})$ and $\mathsf{LTS}(T_{HC})$. Notice that our tool builds the simulation graph as a tree: when a pair (q', q) is reached, which was previously traversed (as e.g. for the $(1, 1)$ pair), simulation does not proceed further in that branch and a dashed line is depicted connecting the two copies of (q', q). Notice that, if in T'_{HC} we turn $?ko$ into $?ko1$ (creating a mismatch with the server), T'_{HC} is no longer a synchronous subtype of T_{HC}. This can be seen in Fig. 7 where the originated failure simulation state is depicted in red.

We now give the formal definition of synchronous subtyping. We first define set of inputs and set of outputs fireable by a state q as follows: $\mathsf{in}(q) = \{l \mid \exists q'.q \xrightarrow{?\,l} q'\}$ and $\mathsf{out}(q) = \{l \mid \exists q'.q \xrightarrow{!\,l} q'\}$.

Example 5. Consider $\mathsf{LTS}(T_{HC})$ (Fig. 2), we have the following:

$$\begin{aligned} \mathsf{in}(1) &= \emptyset & \mathsf{in}(2) &= \{ko, ok\} \\ \mathsf{out}(1) &= \{nd, nd\} & \mathsf{out}(2) &= \emptyset \end{aligned}$$

Definition 2 (Synchronous Simulation). *Given set of label names $\mathcal{L}$ and two LTSs $(P, p_0, \rightarrow_1)$ and $(Q, q_0, \rightarrow_2)$, synchronous simulation is defined as a labeled transition system over states of $P \times Q$, i.e. pairs denoted by $p \preccurlyeq q$, with $p \in P$ and $q \in Q$. In particular, the initial state is $p_0 \preccurlyeq q_0$ and the transition relation $\hookrightarrow$, labeled over $\{!,?\} \times \mathcal{L}$, is defined as the minimal relation satisfying rules:*

$$\frac{p \xrightarrow{?\,l}_1 p' \quad q \xrightarrow{?\,l}_2 q' \quad \mathsf{in}(p) \supseteq \mathsf{in}(q)}{p \preccurlyeq q \xrightarrow{?\,l} p' \preccurlyeq q'} \;(\mathsf{In}) \qquad \frac{p \xrightarrow{!\,l}_1 p' \quad q \xrightarrow{!\,l}_2 q' \quad \mathsf{out}(p) \subseteq \mathsf{out}(q)}{p \preccurlyeq q \xrightarrow{!\,l} p' \preccurlyeq q'} \;(\mathsf{Out})$$

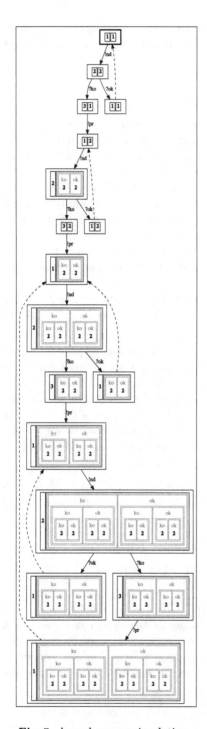

Fig. 5. Asynchronous simulation.

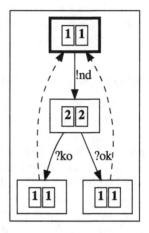

Fig. 6. Synchronous simulation.

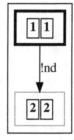

Fig. 7. Failed synchronous simulation.

Formally, a type T' is a synchronous subtype of a type T if the LTS obtained as the synchronous simulation of the pair $\mathsf{LTS}(T')$ and $\mathsf{LTS}(T)$ is such that, for every state $q' \preccurlyeq q$ reachable from the initial simulation state, we have: if $q' \preccurlyeq q$ performs no transitions then both q' and q perform no transitions.

2.3 Asynchronous Session Subtyping

In contrast to synchronous simulation, the asynchronous one gives the possibility of "anticipating", in the right-hand LTS, output transitions w.r.t. input transitions that precede them. This can be shown, using our tool, via an example.

Example 6. Figure 5 shows the asynchronous simulation tree, as produced from our tool, for the pair $\mathsf{LTS}(T''_{HC})$ and $\mathsf{LTS}(T_{HC})$. Simulation of Fig. 5 proceeds as follows. For instance, after transitions $!nd$, $?ko$ and $!pr$ (i.e. path "$!nd\,?ko\,!pr$") are synchronously performed by $\mathsf{LTS}(T''_{HC})$ and $\mathsf{LTS}(T_{HC})$, they reach states 1 and 2, respectively. Now, $\mathsf{LTS}(T''_{HC})$ in state 1 can only do output $!nd$, while $\mathsf{LTS}(T_{HC})$ in state 2 can only do inputs. Being asynchronous, the simulation can proceed by calculating the so-called state 2 *input tree* $\mathsf{inTree}(2) = \langle ko : 1,\ ok : 1 \rangle$, i.e. the spanning tree from state 2 (constructed considering input transitions only), which has two leaves, both being state 1. Provided that all leaves of $\mathsf{inTree}(2)$ can perform $!nd$, the simulation can proceed by considering $\langle ko : [],\ ok : [] \rangle$ as an "accumulated" input for the right-hand LTS and by making all states in its leaves evolve by performing the $!nd$ transition. Therefore, after simulation performs $!nd$, $\mathsf{LTS}(T''_{HC})$ and $\mathsf{LTS}(T_{HC})$ reach states 2 and $\langle ko : 2,\ ok : 2 \rangle$, respectively (the state reached by the right-hand LTS is actually an input tree).

In general, input trees (e.g. $\langle ko : 2,\ ok : 2 \rangle$ in the example above) are defined in [5] as *input contexts* $\mathcal{A}$ (representing "accumulated" input, e.g. $\langle ko : [],\ ok : [] \rangle$ in the example above with *holes* "$[]$" replaced by LTS states. Their syntax is:

$$\mathcal{A} ::= \quad [] \quad | \quad \langle l_i : \mathcal{A}_i \rangle_{i \in I}$$

In the tool we represent input trees by nested boxes. For instance the input tree $\langle ko : \langle ko : 1,\ ok : 1 \rangle,\ ok : \langle ko : 1,\ ok : 1 \rangle \rangle$ is represented as:

In general, due to input accumulation, represented by an input tree, even if two types are in an asynchronous subtyping relation, the simulation could proceed infinitely without meeting failure simulation states (as it would happen for the pair $\mathsf{LTS}(T''_{HC})$ and $\mathsf{LTS}(T_{HC})$ of Example 6). In our tool we use the algorithm of [5] for checking asynchronous subtyping, which is sound but not complete (in some cases it terminates without returning a decisive verdict). In a nutshell, such an algorithm proceeds as follows. The subtyping simulation terminates when we encounter a failure state (depicted in red in our tool), meaning that the two types are not in the subtyping relation, or when we detect a repetitive behaviour in the simulation (which, we show, can always be found, in case of infinite simulation). In the latter case, we check whether this repetitive behaviour satisfies sufficient conditions (see [5] for details) that guarantee that the subtyping simulation will never encounter failures. If the conditions are satisfied the algorithm concludes that the two types are in the subtyping relation, otherwise a *maybe* verdict is returned.

Therefore, the tool always produces a finite simulation tree: for types that are detected to be subtypes, simulation can stop in a state that is identified (via a dashed transition in our tool) to a previously encountered state, even if they are not identical; see bottommost state of Fig. 5 (outgoing dashed transition). The sufficient conditions checked by the algorithm guarantees that the behaviour beyond such a simulation state is a repetition of the behaviour already observed.

We now give the formal definition of asynchronous subtyping. Given a LTS $(Q, q_0, \rightarrow)$, we write $q_0 \xrightarrow{\ell_1 \cdots \ell_k} q_k$ iff there are $q_1, \ldots, q_{k-1} \in Q$ such that $q_{i-1} \xrightarrow{\ell_i} q_i$ for $1 \leq i \leq k$. Given a list of messages $\omega = l_1 \cdots l_k$ ($k \geq 0$), we write $?\omega$ for the list $?l_1 \cdots ?l_k$ and $!\omega$ for $!l_1 \cdots !l_k$.

Definition 3 (Input Context). *An input context is a term of the grammar*

$$\mathcal{A} ::= []_j \mid \langle l_i : \mathcal{A}_i \rangle_{i \in I}$$

where: All indices j, denoted by $I(\mathcal{A})$, are distinct and are associated to holes. Moreover, $I \neq \emptyset$ and $\forall i \neq j \in I.\ l_i \neq l_j$.

Holes are, thus, actually indexed so to make it possible to individually replace them. In this way $\mathcal{A}[q_i]^{i \in I(\mathcal{A})}$ denotes the *input tree* obtained by syntactically replacing each hole $[]_i$ in $\mathcal{A}$ by a specific state $q_i \in Q$. In the sequel, we use $\mathcal{IT}_Q$ to denote the set of input trees over states $q \in Q$.

Auxiliary Functions. Given a CSFM $(Q, q_0, \rightarrow)$ and a state $q \in Q$, we define:

- $\mathsf{cycle}(\star, q) \iff \exists \omega \in \mathcal{L}^*, \omega' \in \mathcal{L}^+, q' \in Q.\ q \xrightarrow{\star\omega} q' \xrightarrow{\star\omega'} q'$ (with $\star \in \{!, ?\}$),
- the *partial* function $\mathsf{inTree}(\cdot)$ as

$$\mathsf{inTree}(q) = \begin{cases} \bot & \text{if } \mathsf{cycle}(?, q) \\ q & \text{if } \mathsf{in}(q) = \emptyset \\ \langle l_i : \mathsf{inTree}(q_i') \rangle_{i \in I} & \text{if } \mathsf{in}(q) = \{l_i \mid i \in I\} \neq \emptyset \end{cases}$$

with q_i' being the state such that $q \xrightarrow{?l_i} q_i'$.

Predicate $\mathsf{cycle}(\star, q)$ says that, from q, we can reach a cycle with only sends (resp. receives), depending on whether $\star =!$ or $\star =?$. The partial function $\mathsf{inTree}(q)$, when defined, returns the tree containing all sequences of messages which can be received from q until a final or sending state is reached. Intuitively, $\mathsf{inTree}(q)$ is undefined when $\mathsf{cycle}(?, q)$ as it would return an infinite tree.

Example 7. Consider $\mathsf{LTS}(T_{HC})$ (Fig. 2), we have the following:

$$\mathsf{inTree}(1) = 1 \quad \mathsf{inTree}(2) = \langle ko : 1, \, ok : 1 \rangle$$

ko	ok
1	**1**

inTree(2) tool
representation

Example 8. Consider the LTS of Fig. 8. From state 1 we can reach state 2 with an output. The latter can loop with an output into itself. Hence, we have both cycle$(!, 1)$ and cycle$(!, 2)$.

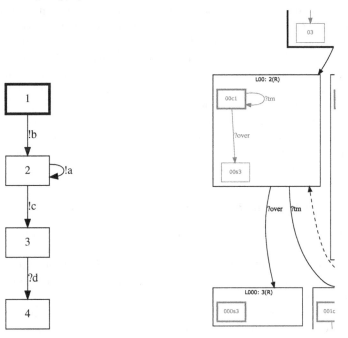

Fig. 8. Output cycle example.   **Fig. 9.** Fair asynchronous simulation fragment.

Definition 4 (Asynchronous Simulation). *Given set of label names $\mathcal{L}$ and two LTSs: $LTS_1 = (P, p_0, \rightarrow_1)$ and $LTS_2 = (Q, q_0, \rightarrow_2)$, asynchronous simulation is defined as a labeled transition system over states of $P \times \mathcal{IT}_Q$, i.e. pairs denoted by $p \preccurlyeq \mathcal{A}[q_j]^{j \in J}$, with $p \in P$ and $\mathcal{A}[q_j]^{j \in J} \in \mathcal{IT}_Q$. In particular, the initial state is $p_0 \preccurlyeq q_0$ and the transition relation $\hookrightarrow$, labeled over $\{!, ?\} \times \mathcal{L}$, is defined as the minimal relation satisfying rules in Definition 2, plus the following ones:*

$$\frac{p \xrightarrow{?l_k}_1 p' \quad k \in I \quad \mathsf{in}(p) \supseteq \{l_i \mid i \in I\}}{p \preccurlyeq \langle l_i : \mathcal{A}_i[q_{i,j}]^{j \in J_i}\rangle_{i \in I} \xrightarrow{?l_k} p' \preccurlyeq \mathcal{A}_k[q_{k,j}]^{j \in J_k}} \text{(InCtx)}$$

$$\frac{p \xrightarrow{!l}_1 p' \qquad \neg\mathsf{cycle}(!,p)}{\forall j \in J.\left(\mathsf{in Tree}(q_j) = \mathcal{A}_j[q_{j,h}]^{h \in H_j} \wedge \forall h \in H_j.(\mathsf{out}(p) \subseteq \mathsf{out}(q_{j,h}) \wedge q_{j,h} \xrightarrow{!l}_2 q'_{j,h}))}{p \preccurlyeq \mathcal{A}[q_j]^{j \in J} \xrightarrow{!l} p' \preccurlyeq \mathcal{A}[\mathcal{A}_j[q'_{j,h}]^{h \in H_j}]^{j \in J}} \text{(OutA)}$$

The two additional rules express how inputs are accumulated and consumed by means of input trees in the LTS_2. The first one is applicable when the input tree state of the LTS_2 is non-empty and the state p of the LTS_1 is able to perform a receive action corresponding to any message located at the root of the input tree (contra-variance of receive actions). The second rule allows the LTS_1 to execute some send actions by matching them with send actions that, in the LTS_2, occur after receives. Intuitively, each send action outgoing from state p of the LTS_1 must also be executable from each of the states $q_{j,h}$ of $\mathsf{in Tree}(q_j) = \mathcal{A}_j[q_{j,h}]^{h \in H_j}$, with q_j being a leaf of the input tree state $\mathcal{A}[q_j]^{j \in J}$ of the LTS_2 (covariance of send actions). The constraint $\neg\mathsf{cycle}(!,p)$ guarantees that accumulated receive actions will be eventually executed.

2.4   Fair Asynchronous Session Subtyping

Consider again the satellite protocol of Example 3. The asynchronous subtyping of previous Sect. 2.3 rejects T'_{SC} as a subtype of T_{SC}. Indeed that notion of subtyping allows for anticipation of outputs only when they are preceded by a *bounded* number of inputs. However the outputs of T_{SC} occur after an arbitrary number of inputs. That notion of subtyping requires that all sent messages are consumed along *all* possible computations of the receiver. While in T'_{SC} there is a degenerate execution where the candidate subtype sends an infinite number of tc messages and thus never performs the required inputs.

In contrast, *fair* asynchronous session subtyping [9] relies on the assumption that such degenerate executions cannot occur under the natural assumption the loop of outputs eventually terminates, i.e., only a finite (but unspecified) amount of messages can be emitted.

Concretely, the fair subtyping uses a more expressive notion of input contexts $\mathcal{A}$ that also include recursive constructs. Their syntax becomes:

$$\mathcal{A} ::= [] \mid \langle l_i : \mathcal{A}_i\rangle_{i \in I} \mid \mu\mathbf{X}.\mathcal{A} \mid \mathbf{X}$$

These input context can encode the recursive reception of messages in the satellite example and thus identify T'_{SC} as a fair asynchronous subtype of T_{SC}.

Figure 9 shows a fragment of the resulting fair asynchronous simulation tree, as produced from our tool: due to the more complex syntax of input contexts, states now contain a (possibly looping) automaton instead of an input tree.

3   Main Functionalities of the Tool

Besides the classic operations that a text editor allows (e.g. edit, load, save), users can compute the dual of: either a single session type or the entire subtyping problem. To facilitate understanding of session types, the tool offers the possibility to view/save the graphical representation of a given type by means of "Show Image" and "Save Image" respectively. In our tool types are inputted by means of *two text areas*: the leftmost one is used for the candidate subtype and the rightmost one for the candidate supertype. Input types must be expressed with the syntax presented in Definition 1, with "+" standing for "$\oplus$" and "*rec*" standing for "μ". In addition the tool accepts: (i) the alternative "raw" syntax $[!\,a\,;T,!\,b\,;T',\dots]$ standing for $\oplus\{a\,;T,b\,;T',\dots\}$ and $[?\,a\,;T,?\,b\,;T',\dots]$ for $\&\{a\,;T,b\,;T',\dots\}$ (ii) the abbreviations $!\,a\,;T$ and $?\,a\,;T$ standing for $\oplus\{a\,;T\}$ and $\&\{a\,;T\}$. A Python parser checks that the inputted types fit the above syntax using the following *EBNF* syntax:

$$
\begin{aligned}
S \quad &::= \; OP\,\{\,id\,;S\,(,\;id\,;S\,)^*\} \quad | \quad \mathbf{rec}\,id.\; S \quad | \quad id \quad | \quad \mathbf{end} \\
&\quad !\,id\,;S \quad | \quad [\,!\,id\,;S\,(,\,!\,id\,;S\,)^*] \quad | \quad ?\,id\,;S \quad | \quad [\,?\,id\,;S\,(,\,?\,id\,;S\,)^*] \\
OP &::= +\;\; | \;\; \&
\end{aligned}
$$

where *id* is a non-empty sequence of uppercase and lowercase letters possibly followed by trailing numbers.

The core of the tool is the algorithm menu. Users can choose between different subtyping algorithms and possibly set a maximum number of execution steps. The algorithm response can be: "true", "false" or "maybe" (for asynchronous algorithms, due to undecidability, or when the specified number of steps is not enough to determine the subtyping relation), along with the time needed. In addition, it is possible to run all the algorithms to have an overview of the types of relationship that hold. Finally, the "Simulation Result" menu, which is initially disabled, makes it possible to show or save the graphical output of the last performed algorithm.

3.1   Extensibility of the Tool

Our tool (and its GUI) is automatically extensible with new subtyping algorithms by simply modifying its json configuration file that we will detail in the next section. Such a file can also be modified, directly from the GUI, by using the "Algorithm configuration" menu under "Settings". Configuration of a new algorithm is done by providing: its displayed name and the path and calling pattern of its execution command, in the form

```
ExecutableName [flag] [t1] [t2] [steps]
```

The tool will replace [flag][t1][t2][steps] with: the user-selected flags, the pair of session types the user wants to check and the number of steps the algorithm is requested to do. The above order of bracketed elements ([steps] is optional) may change according to the algorithm. The json file also maps algorithm-dependent flag names into tool functionalities by categorizing them. For instance, the default *flag* category includes flags that simply modify the behaviour of algorithms: e.g. the asynchronous one has the --nofallback flag that prevents the algorithm from trying to fall back to the dual subtyping problem in case of an initial maybe verdict. Moreover, the *execution flag* category is useful when an executable encloses different (alternative) algorithms, e.g. Gay and Hole (--gayhole) and Kozen et al.'s (--kozen) algorithms for synchronous subtyping (with one indicated as being the default). Moreover, the *visual flag* category includes just the name of the flag causing the algorithm to produce the graphical simulation.

When adding an algorithm to the tool, the following requirements have to be satisfied: they have to support command line execution (with the possibility of taking .txt files as input) and have to fit the "raw" syntax described above. Regarding the algorithm response, the only requirement is that it is printed on the standard output. Finally, to generate the graphical output, it is mandatory that the algorithm creates a .dot file no matter what its name is (since it is specified in dedicated section of the json configuration). It is important to observe that our tool is agnostic to the implementation language of algorithms, since it makes use of their executable version.

3.2 Configuration of Tool Algorithms

The json file presented below is an example of the "algorithms_config.json" currently used by the tool. The *standard_exec* field specifies the default execution flag, e.g. Gay and Hole or Kozen. Moreover, the *simulation_file* field indicates the relative path to the algorithm generated *Graphviz* ".dot" simulation file. Similarly *win, osx* and *linux* point at the folder in which the tool looks for the algorithm binaries for that specific os.

```
 1  [{
 2    "alg_name": "Async Subtyping",
 3    "flag": "--nofallback",
 4    "execution_flag": "",
 5    "standard_exec": "",
 6    "visual_flag": "--pics",
 7    "simulation_file": "tmp/simulation_tree",
 8    "win": "asynchronous-subtyping\\win\\",
 9    "osx": "asynchronous-subtyping/osx/",
10    "linux": "asynchronous-subtyping/linux/",
11    "exec_comm": "Checker [flags] [t1] [t2]"
12  },
13  {
14    "alg_name": "Fair Async Subtyping",
15    "flag": "",
16    "execution_flag": "",
17    "standard_exec": "",
18    "visual_flag": "--debug",
```

```
19        "simulation_file": "tmp/simulation_tree",
20        "win": "fair-asynchronous-subtyping\\win\\",
21        "osx": "fair-asynchronous-subtyping/osx/",
22        "linux": "fair-asynchronous-subtyping/linux/",
23        "exec_comm": "Checker [flags] [t1] [t2] [steps]"
24    },
25    {
26        "alg_name": "Sync Subtyping",
27        "flag": "",
28        "execution_flag": "--gayhole,--kozen",
29        "standard_exec": "--gayhole",
30        "visual_flag": "--pics",
31        "simulation_file": "tmp/simulation_tree",
32        "osx": "sync_subtyping/osx/",
33        "win": "sync_subtyping\\win\\",
34        "linux": "sync_subtyping/linux/",
35        "exec_comm": "Checker [flags] [t1] [t2]"
36    }]
```

4   Conclusion

In this paper we introduced an integrated extensible GUI-based tool which: applies algorithms for synchronous and (fair) asynchronous session subtyping, and generates graphical simulations showing how underlying algorithms work.

Concerning future work, we plan to use our synchronous subtyping simulation algorithm (with error detection) in the context of type checking for object oriented programming languages where classes are endowed with usage protocols [8]. Indeed, extending the theory of [8] with protocol subtyping, would make it possible to verify correctness also for class inheritance. In particular, we have started integrating our algorithm into the Java checker [22], which is based on [8]. Finally, we plan to extend the syntax of session types managed by our tool, e.g. by including passing of data/channels and, possibly, by also encompassing preemption mechanisms [4,10], which are often used in communication protocols.

References

1. Ancona, D., et al.: Behavioral types in programming languages. Found. Trends Program. Lang. **3**(2–3), 95–230 (2016)
2. Bacchiani, L., Bravetti, M., Lange, J., Zavattaro, G.: Tool source files for Linux, Windows and OSx (and binaries for Windows and OSx). https://github.com/LBacchiani/session-subtyping-tool
3. Brand, D., Zafiropulo, P.: On communicating finite-state machines. J. ACM **30**(2), 323–342 (1983)
4. Bravetti, M.: Axiomatizing maximal progress and discrete time. Log. Methods Comput. Sci. **17**(1), 1:1–1:44 (2021)

5. Bravetti, M., Carbone, M., Lange, J., Yoshida, N., Zavattaro, G.: A sound algorithm for asynchronous session subtyping and its implementation. Log. Methods Comput. Sci. **17**(1), 20:1–20:35 (2021)

6. Bravetti, M., Carbone, M., Zavattaro, G.: Undecidability of asynchronous session subtyping. Inf. Comput. **256**, 300–320 (2017)

7. Bravetti, M., Carbone, M., Zavattaro, G.: On the boundary between decidability and undecidability of asynchronous session subtyping. Theor. Comput. Sci. **722**, 19–51 (2018)

8. Bravetti, M., et al.: Behavioural types for memory and method safety in a core object-oriented language. In: Oliveira, B.C.S. (ed.) APLAS 2020. LNCS, vol. 12470, pp. 105–124. Springer, Cham (2020). https://doi.org/10.1007/978-3-030-64437-6_6

9. Bravetti, M., Lange, J., Zavattaro, G.: Fair refinement for asynchronous session types. In: Kiefer, S., Tasson, C. (eds.) FOSSACS 2021. LNCS, vol. 12650, pp. 144–163. Springer, Cham (2021). https://doi.org/10.1007/978-3-030-71995-1_8

10. Bravetti, M., Zavattaro, G.: On the expressive power of process interruption and compensation. Math. Struct. Comput. Sci. **19**(3), 565–599 (2009)

11. Bravetti, M., Zavattaro, G.: Asynchronous session subtyping as communicating automata refinement. Softw. Syst. Model. **20**(2), 311–333 (2020). https://doi.org/10.1007/s10270-020-00838-x

12. Chen, T., Dezani-Ciancaglini, M., Scalas, A., Yoshida, N.: On the preciseness of subtyping in session types. Log. Methods Comput. Sci. **13**(2), 1–61 (2017)

13. Deniélou, P.-M., Yoshida, N.: Multiparty compatibility in communicating automata: characterisation and synthesis of global session types. In: Fomin, F.V., Freivalds, R., Kwiatkowska, M., Peleg, D. (eds.) ICALP 2013. LNCS, vol. 7966, pp. 174–186. Springer, Heidelberg (2013). https://doi.org/10.1007/978-3-642-39212-2_18

14. Gay, S.J., Hole, M.: Subtyping for session types in the pi calculus. Acta Inf. **42**(2–3), 191–225 (2005)

15. Hu, R., Yoshida, N.: Hybrid session verification through endpoint API generation. In: Stevens, P., Wąsowski, A. (eds.) FASE 2016. LNCS, vol. 9633, pp. 401–418. Springer, Heidelberg (2016). https://doi.org/10.1007/978-3-662-49665-7_24

16. Kozen, D., Palsberg, J., Schwartzbach, M.I.: Efficient recursive subtyping. Math. Struct. Comput. Sci. **5**(1), 113–125 (1995)

17. Lange, J., Yoshida, N.: Characteristic formulae for session types. In: Chechik, M., Raskin, J.-F. (eds.) TACAS 2016. LNCS, vol. 9636, pp. 833–850. Springer, Heidelberg (2016). https://doi.org/10.1007/978-3-662-49674-9_52

18. Lange, J., Yoshida, N.: On the undecidability of asynchronous session subtyping. In: Esparza, J., Murawski, A.S. (eds.) FoSSaCS 2017. LNCS, vol. 10203, pp. 441–457. Springer, Heidelberg (2017). https://doi.org/10.1007/978-3-662-54458-7_26

19. Lindley, S., Morris, J.G.: Embedding session types in Haskell. In: Haskell 2016, pp. 133–145 (2016)

20. Mostrous, D., Yoshida, N.: Session typing and asynchronous subtyping for the higher-order π-calculus. Inf. Comput. **241**, 227–263 (2015)

21. Mostrous, D., Yoshida, N., Honda, K.: Global principal typing in partially commutative asynchronous sessions. In: Castagna, G. (ed.) ESOP 2009. LNCS, vol. 5502, pp. 316–332. Springer, Heidelberg (2009). https://doi.org/10.1007/978-3-642-00590-9_23

22. Mota, J., Giunti, M., Ravara, A.: Java typestate checker. In: Damiani, F., Dardha, O. (eds.) COORDINATION 2021. LNCS, vol. 12717, pp. 121–133. Springer, Cham (2021)

23. Neykova, R., Hu, R., Yoshida, N., Abdeljallal, F.: A session type provider: compile-time API generation for distributed protocols with interaction refinements in F♯. In: CC 2018. ACM (2018)
24. Orchard, D.A., Yoshida, N.: Effects as sessions, sessions as effects. In: Principles of Programming Languages (POPL 2016), pp. 568–581 (2016)
25. Padovani, L.: A simple library implementation of binary sessions. J. Funct. Program. **27**, e4 (2017)
26. Scalas, A., Yoshida, N.: Lightweight session programming in scala. In: European Conference on Object-Oriented Programming (ECOOP 2016), pp. 21:1–21:28 (2016)

Towards Probabilistic Session-Type Monitoring

Christian Bartolo Burlò[1]([✉]) [iD], Adrian Francalanza[2] [iD], Alceste Scalas[3] [iD], Catia Trubiani[1] [iD], and Emilio Tuosto[1] [iD]

[1] Gran Sasso Science Institute, L'Aquila, Italy
christian.bartolo@gssi.it
[2] Department of Computer Science, University of Malta, Msida, Malta
[3] DTU Compute, Technical University of Denmark, Kongens Lyngby, Denmark

Abstract. We present a tool-based approach for the runtime analysis of communicating processes grounded on probabilistic binary session types. We synthesise a monitor out of a probabilistic session type where each choice point is augmented with a probability distribution. The monitor observes the execution of a process, infers its probabilistic behaviour and issues warnings when the observed behaviour deviates from the one specified by the probabilistic session type.

Keywords: Runtime Verification · Probabilistic session types · Monitor Synthesis

1 Introduction

Communication is central to present day computation. The expected communication protocol between two parties can be formalised as a *(binary) session type*, typically describing qualitative aspects such as the order and choice of service invocations at their corresponding payloads. In recent work, *quantitative* aspects of the communication protocol are also layered over a session type [8,19].

Example 1. Consider a server hosting a guessing game by selecting an integer n between 1 and 100. A client can repeatedly *(i)* try to guess, *(ii)* ask for a hint, or *(iii)* quit the game. The expected interaction sequence of the guessing game server can be specified with the session type S_{game} below:

$$S_{game} = \text{rec } X.\& \left\{ \begin{array}{l} \text{?Guess(Int)}[0.75].\oplus \left\{ \begin{array}{l} \text{!Correct}[0.01].X, \\ \text{!Incorrect}[0.99].X \end{array} \right\}, \\ \text{?Help}[0.2].\text{!Hint(Str)}[1].X, \\ \text{?Quit}[0.05].\text{end} \end{array} \right\}$$

The work has been partly supported by: the project MoVeMnt (No: 217987-051) under the Icelandic Research Fund; the BehAPI project funded by the EU H2020 RISE under the Marie Skłodowska-Curie action (No: 778233); the MIUR projects PRIN 2017FTXR7S IT MATTERS and 2017TWRCNB SEDUCE; the EU Horizon 2020 project 830929 *CyberSec4Europe*; the Danish Industriens Fonds Cyberprogram 2020-0489 *Security-by-Design in Digital Denmark*.

F. Damiani and O. Dardha (Eds.): COORDINATION 2021, LNCS 12717, pp. 106–120, 2021.
https://doi.org/10.1007/978-3-030-78142-2_7

The server waits for the client's choice (at the external branching point $\&$) to either Guess a number, ask for Help, or Quit. If the client asks for help then the server replies with a Hint message including a string and the session loops. After the outcome of a guess, (described by the internal choice $\oplus$) is communicated to the client, the protocol recurs. The type for the client is *dual* and denoted by $\overline{S_{game}}$: each '$\oplus$' is swapped with '$\&$' and each '!' is swapped with '?'.

Besides enforcing that parties follow a certain communication pattern, our (augmented) session types also specify some quantitative aspects of the protocol. For instance, S_{game} above specifies that the server should give the client a realistic chance of guessing correctly (*i.e.*, 1%), while $\overline{S_{game}}$ specifies that the client should request for help 20% of the time. According to this augmented specification with quantitative requirements, a burst of client Help requests without any attempts to guess the correct answer (that far exceeds 20% of total requests) would constitute a violation of the protocol. More specifically, a substantial deviation from the expected behaviour could be seen as an indicator of abnormal behaviours such as an attempted denial-of-service attack. $\diamond$

Session types (and their probabilistic variants) are usually checked statically, by type checking the code of the interacting parties (*e.g.*, the clients and the server in this case). However, in an open network, it is common for one or more interacting parties *not* to be available for analysis in a classical pre-deployment fashion. There are even cases where, although we have full access to the participants, it is hard to statically verify their behaviour (*e.g.*, when a client is a human being, or generated via machine-learning techniques). This forces the verifier to carry out certain correctness checks in a post-deployment phase of software production. Recent work has shown that detections and enforcements of qualitative process properties expressed in terms of automata-like formalisms can be carried out effectively, at runtime, using monitors [1,4–6,16]. There are however limits to a monitoring approach for verification [2,14]. At runtime, a monitor *(i)* cannot observe more than one execution, *(ii)* can only observe finite prefixes of a (possibly infinite) complete execution, and *(iii)* cannot detect execution branches that could never have been taken (*i.e.*, the analysis is evidence-based). These constraints make it unclear whether quantitative behavioural aspects such as the observation of branching probabilities, defined over complete (*i.e.*, potentially infinite) sequences of interactions, can be adequately monitored at runtime. Note that, in order to determine (with absolute certainty) whether the client-server interactions will observe the probabilities prescribed in S_{game} above at runtime, one needs access to the code for *both* the server *and* the client. Having access to just the source code of the server—as it is reasonable to expect when the specification is dictated by the party providing the service—does not help us in determining whether the probabilities at the external branching point $\&$ will be observed, since these depend on the choices made by the client (which is often determined at runtime).

In this paper, we develop a tool-supported methodology for the runtime monitoring of quantitative behaviour for two interacting components. In particular, given a Probabilistic Session Type (PST) such as S_{game} above, we synthesise a monitor that, at runtime, *(i)* observes the messages exchanged within the protocol to ensure that they follow the protocol prescribed by the session type, *(ii)* estimates the probabilistic behaviour of the interacting parties from the interactions observed at runtime, and *(iii)* determines whether to issue a warning for behavioural deviations from the branching probabilities prescribed in the PST, up to a pre-specified level of confidence. For generality, we target the scenario with the weakest level of assumptions, namely where the monitor and its instrumentation are oblivious to the actual implementation of *both* interacting parties participating in the session. Nevertheless, our solution still applies to cases where we have access to the source of the interacting parties.

The rest of the paper is structured as follows. Section 2 explains our methodology in detail. This lays the necessary foundations for the construction of our monitoring tool, described in Sect. 3. Comparisons to related work and discussions about possible future work are given in Sect. 4. To the best of our knowledge, the work we present here is the first attempt at verifying PSTs via runtime monitoring.

2   Methodology

Our proposed methodology operates post-deployment, where *both* participants in the session are analysed *at runtime*. As mentioned earlier, to maximise its applicability and generality, our methodology does not require any part of the participants' behaviour to be analysed pre-deployment, effectively treating them as *black boxes*. The definite verdict of whether an execution exhibited by a system abides by some probabilistic specification can only be given once it terminates (if at all). Nonetheless, our methodology is able to issue probabilistic judgements from incomplete executions, based on the interactions observed up to that point.

Our runtime analysis employs *online* passive monitors [13,23]. These are computational entities that run live and observe the *incremental* behaviour of two communicating parties (as the execution proceeds) without affecting their interactions. Although our monitors have no prior information about the actual behaviour of the two parties, they are nevertheless able to:

(a) approximate on-the-fly the probabilistic behaviour of the interacting parties, iteratively revising the approximation when a new interaction is observed, and

(b) make (revocable) judgements that are based on the *probability distribution* described by our PSTs, for a preset *confidence level*.

Our methodology is supported by a tool, discussed in Sect. 3, that automatically synthesises a monitor from a PST S. At run-time, the monitor estimates the probabilities for each choice point of S (by observing the messages being sent and received), and determines whether such estimates respect the desired probabilities specified in S. This way, the monitor can apportion blame to the interacting party that has control at the choice point where a potential violation is detected. In the sequel, we present the technical details of our methodology; in Sect. 4 we discuss possible alternatives.

2.1 Probabilistic Session Types (PSTs)

In order to formalise probabilistic protocols, we adopt session types augmented with probability distributions over the choice points ($\&$ and $\oplus$): they allow us to specify the probability of a particular choice being taken by one of the components interacting in a session. The syntax of our PSTs (from which S_{game} in Sect. 1 is derived) is:

$$
\begin{aligned}
S \;::=\;\; & \&\big\{?\mathtt{l}_i(\mathtt{s}_i)[p_i].S_i\big\}_{i \in I} && \textit{(external choice)} \\
\mid\;\; & \oplus\big\{!\mathtt{l}_i(\mathtt{s}_i)[p_i].S_i\big\}_{i \in I} && \textit{(internal choice)} \\
\mid\;\; & \mathsf{rec}\ X.S && \textit{(recursion)} \\
\mid\;\; & X && \textit{(recursion variable)} \\
\mid\;\; & \mathsf{end} && \textit{(termination)}
\end{aligned}
$$

In choice points ($\&$ and $\oplus$) the indexing set I is finite and non-empty, the *choice labels* $\mathtt{l}_i$ are pairwise distinct, and the *sorts* $\mathtt{s}_i$ range over basic data types (Int, Str, Bool, *etc.*). Every choice point S_j is given a *multinomial distribution* interpretation. We assume that $\sum_{i \in I} p_i = 1$ where every p_i is positive, and represents the probability of selecting the branch labelled by $\mathtt{l}_i$, over *every* choice point of interest S_j. The probabilities prescribed at a choice point impose a behavioural obligation on the interacting party who has control over the selection at that choice point. For instance, at the external choice in Example 1, it is the client that is required to adhere to the probabilities prescribed. As usual, we assume that recursion is guarded, *i.e.*, a recursion variable X can only appear under an external or internal prefix.

2.2 Monitoring Sessions

For the sake of the presentation, we assume that choice points of a PST S are indexed by a finite set of indices $j \in J$, which allows us to uniquely identify each choice point as S_j. Accordingly, we let I_j be a set indexing the labels $\mathtt{l}_{i,j}$ of the choice point S_j, and denote the probability assigned at S_j to the branch labelled by $\mathtt{l}_{i,j}$ as $p_{i,j}$. Our runtime analysis maintains the following counters:

- c_j: number of times the choice point S_j is observed at run-time;
- $c_{i,j}$: number of times the label $\mathtt{l}_{i,j}$ ($i \in I_j$) of choice S_j is taken.

For each $j \in J$, these counters yield the *estimated probability*:

$$
\widehat{p_{i,j}} \;=\; \frac{c_{i,j}}{c_j} \qquad j \in J,\ i \in I_j \tag{1}
$$

Namely, $\widehat{p_{i,j}}$ is the frequency with which the i-th branch $\mathtt{l}_{i,j}$ of choice point S_j has been taken *so far*. The monitor continuously updates the estimated probabilities as it observes the interactions taking place while the execution unfolds.

The monitor cannot base its decision to issue a warning only on these estimated probabilities. These could potentially be very inaccurate if either of the components briefly exhibits sporadic behaviour at any point in time of execution. To assess whether the monitored sequence of interactions has *substantially* deviated from the probabilistic behaviour specified in a session type, the runtime analysis needs to consider how accurate these estimated probabilities are in conveying the observed behaviour of the components. We relate this problem to *statistical inference*, where the sequence of interactions observed up to the current point of execution is a *sample* of the larger population, being the entire (possibly infinite) execution.

There are various established paradigms for statistical inference. Our proposed methodology takes a *frequentist* approach. In particular, we calculate *confidence intervals* (CIs) [20] around each desired probability $p_{i,j}$ in a session type to give an approximation of the expected probabilistic behaviour based on the sample size and a *confidence level* $0 \leq \ell < 1$. For any S-abiding execution that iterates through choice point S_j for c_j times, the interval would contain the acceptable range of values for the estimated probabilities with confidence ℓ. To calculate the CI for a choice point S_j, we first calculate the *standard error SE* on the specified probabilities $p_{i,j}$, which depends on the number of times that choice point c_j has iterated (*i.e.,* the sample size). This is then used to calculate the *maximum acceptable error E* (2) based on the given confidence level ℓ, where the multiplier $Z(\ell)$ is the number of standard deviations of a normal distribution representing the particular branch, covering $(\ell \times 100)\%$ of its values [20].

$$E_{i,j} = Z(\ell) \cdot SE_{i,j} \quad \text{where } SE_{i,j} = \sqrt{\frac{p_{i,j}(1 - p_{i,j})}{c_j}} \quad \text{for } j \in J, \ i \in I_j \ (2)$$

Having calculated the error $E_{i,j}$, the runtime analysis calculates the confidence interval around $p_{i,j}$ as:

$$[p_{i,j} - E_{i,j}, \ p_{i,j} + E_{i,j}] \tag{3}$$

If and when an estimated probability $\widehat{p_{i,j}}$ (1) falls *outside* this interval, the proposed runtime analysis for our methodology issues a *warning* implying that:

> The estimated probability $\widehat{p_{i,j}}$ has deviated enough from the specified probability $p_{i,j}$ to conclude, with confidence ℓ, that the interacting party responsible for the choice point S_j violates the prescribed probability.

The higher the confidence level ℓ specified, the longer it takes for the maximum error $E_{i,j}$ in (2) to converge [20]. Consequently:

- when a higher confidence ℓ is required, the monitor will have *wider* confidence intervals, hence it needs to collect more evidence (*i.e.,* a larger sample size) in order to issue a warning;
- when a lower confidence ℓ is required, the monitor will have *narrower* confidence intervals, hence it might deem an observed session to deviate substantially from the probabilities specified in S at an earlier point in execution. This means that the monitor may potentially issue spurious warnings.

Importantly, after a warning is issued, the subsequent behaviour of the monitored components might cause the (updated) estimated probabilities to fall back within the confidence intervals. As a result, the monitor may *retract* the warning. The warnings issued by the monitor become irrevocable verdicts only when the session terminates (if at all).

Example 2. Recall S_{game} from Example 1. Assume that a monitor for S_{game} is instantiated with confidence level $\ell = 99.999\%$, and that in the running session, the client's choice $(\&)$ has iterated nine times, with the client choosing Help five times. Thus, the runtime analysis counters are:

$$c_{\&} = 9 \qquad c_{\text{Help},\&} = 5$$

The monitor calculates the estimated probability $\widehat{p_{\text{Help},\&}} = 0.56$ from these counter values using (1). It then calculates the error $E_{\text{Help},\&} = 0.59$ from (2) (with $Z(\ell) = 4.4172$) for the Help branch in S. Using the specified probability $p_{\text{Help},\&} = 0.2$ and $E_{\text{Help},\&}$, it calculates the confidence interval from (3) 0.2 ± 0.59, that is $[-0.39, 0.79]$. Since the estimated probability $\widehat{p_{\text{Help},\&}} = 0.56$ falls within this confidence interval, the monitor does *not* issue a warning.

Now, assume that the session continues, the external choice point $\&$ is iterated, and the client chooses Help eight consecutive times more. This means that the counters of our runtime analysis become:

$$c_{\&} = 17 \qquad c_{\text{Help},\&} = 13$$

From (1), the estimated probability is updated to $\widehat{p_{\text{Help},\&}} = 0.76$. From (2), the monitor also updates the confidence interval. Since $c_{\&}$ is now larger, it yields $E_{\text{Help},\&} = 0.43$ which results in the narrower confidence interval $[-0.23, 0.63]$. At this point, our runtime analysis detects that the estimated $\widehat{p_{\text{Help},\&}}$ falls outside this confidence interval and the corresponding warning is issued.

Note that a monitor for S_{game} with lower confidence level $\ell = 95\%$ (*i.e.*, $Z(\ell) = 1.9599$) would issue a warning earlier, *e.g.*, when $c_{\&} = 9$ and $c_{\text{Help},\&} = 5$. In fact, the lower confidence level would yield $E_{\text{Help},\&} = 0.26$ giving the tighter confidence interval $[-0.06, 0.46]$ which does not include $\widehat{p_{\text{Help},\&}} = 0.56$.   ◇

3   The Tool

We extend the monitoring framework in [5] to implement our probabilistic session type monitors. The implementation is available at:

https://github.com/chrisbartoloburlo/stmonitor

The overall approach is depicted in Fig. 1: our tool synth generates a passive monitor mon (written in Scala) from a probabilistic session type S that behaves as a partial-identity [17]. In addition to carrying out the runtime analysis, such monitors are also tasked with forwarding the messages analysed, offering higher degrees of control for stopping execution once a violation is detected.   Accord-

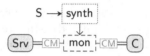

Fig. 1. Outline of monitor synthesis and instrumentation

ingly, the synthesised executable analysis mon, is instrumented to act as an inter-
mediary proxy between two interacting components participating in the session,
e.g., between a client (C) and a server (Srv) for our PST S_{game} from Example 2. Internally, the synthesised monitor mon uses the `lchannels` library [22] to
represent the session type within Scala. To interact with the components, the
monitor makes use of user-supplied *connection managers* (CM) that sit between
the monitor and the components.[1] The connection managers act as *translators*
and *gatekeepers* by transforming messages from the transport protocols supported by C and Srv to the session type representation used by mon, and *vice
versa*. These allow the monitor synthesis to abstract over the communication
protocols in use: *i.e.,* the synthesis is agnostic to the message transportation
being used.

The quantitative analysis of the communicated messages applies only if the
qualitative aspects of the type are being respected. Similarly to the monitors
produced in [5], the code synthesised by our tool can be seen as communicating
finite-state machines [7] where states correspond to choice points in a session
type. Upon receiving a message, the actual direction of the choice point triggers
the analysis of a state's transition modelling such a choice, potentially producing
a warning (or a warning retraction) as a side-effect. Algorithm 1 outlines the logic
inside a single state representing a choice point S_j. The synthesis in [5] generates
the code that conducts the dynamic typechecking on the messages received, and
issues violation verdicts committed to S (line 12). In this work, we augment the
synthesis to equip the monitor logic with the ability to conduct the quantitative
analysis (lines 3 to 8) as discussed in Sect. 2.

---

[1] This design is conveniently inherited from [4,5] but is orthogonal to our approach.

Algorithm 1: Synthesised state of a monitor

---

1 **receive** choice i at choice point S_j
2   **if** $i \in$ *choices* I_j **then**
3   increment counters c_j and $c_{i,j}$
4   **forall** *choices* $i \in I_j$ **calculate**
5   **if not** *checkInterval(*c_i, $c_{i,j}$, $p_{i,j}$*)* **then**
6   issue a warning blaming the sender
7   **else**
8   retract warning
9   **forward** choice i to the other side
10   proceed according to the continuation of choice i in choice point j of S
11   **else**
12   issue a violation verdict

The monitors generated by our tool include message counters along with the logic necessary to estimate the probabilities of the choices in a running session. This logic is used to issue warnings whenever the observed (partial) execution deviates from the probabilities in each state S_j. If the message received by the monitor respects the choice point S_j (line 2 in Algorithm 1), it increments the counters of the current choice point, c_j, and that of the choice taken $c_{i,j}$. For every choice within the choice point, the monitor invokes the function *checkInterval* (described in Algorithm 2) to *calculate* and *test* whether the estimated probability falls within the respective confidence interval (line 5). If the estimated probability is not within the interval, the monitor issues a warning and assigns blame to the sender of the current message (line 6). Otherwise, if the probability lies within the interval, the monitor retracts a previously issued warning (line 8). In an effort to minimise unnecessary (repeated) notifications, the monitors generated by our tool only issue (resp. retract) a warning the *first time* an estimated probability transitions outside (resp. inside) the calculated confidence interval. All subsequent notifications are suppressed in case of estimated probabilities that *remain* outside (resp. inside) the interval.

Algorithm 2 is the function implementing the methodology outlined in Algorithm 2. It calculates the estimated probability and confidence interval around the probability specified in the type, based on the counters maintained by the monitor itself. We note that this function can be adapted to other techniques that test whether the behaviour is being respected without affecting the main synthesis of the monitor; see Sect. 4 for further discussions on this point.

Algorithm 2: Function to calculate intervals

---

1 **def** *checkInterval(c_i, $c_{i,j}$, $p_{i,j}$):*

2   **calculate** the estimated probability $\widehat{p_{i,j}}$ (1) using c_i and $c_{i,j}$

3   **calculate** the error $E_{i,j}$ (2) using c_j and $p_{i,j}$

4   **return** $(\widehat{p_{i,j}}$ in $[p_{i,j} - E_{i,j}, p_{i,j} + E_{i,j}])$

Example 3. Recall the PST S_{game} from Example 1 and assume that the monitor synthesised from S_{game} is instantiated with the confidence level $\ell = 99.999\%$. Consider the extended case from Example 2 whereby, after guessing incorrectly 4 times, the client asks for Help 13 times; it then guesses correctly 2 consecutive times, which brings the monitor counters of the respective internal choice point ($\oplus$) to:

$$c_{\oplus} = 6 \qquad c_{\mathsf{Correct},\oplus} = 2 \qquad c_{\mathsf{Incorrect},\oplus} = 4$$

Following the logic in Algorithm 1, after having incremented the counters (line 3), the monitor checks the confidence intervals for *every* choice present in the choice point (line 4). It invokes the function *checkInterval* with the arguments $c_{\oplus}$, $c_{\mathsf{Correct},\oplus}$, $p_{\mathsf{Correct},\oplus}$ where $p_{\mathsf{Correct},\oplus} = 0.01$ for the choice Correct in S_{game}. The monitor calculates:

$$\widehat{p_{\mathsf{Correct},\oplus}} = 0.33 \qquad E_{\mathsf{Correct},\oplus} = 0.18 \qquad p_{\mathsf{Correct},\oplus} \pm E_{\mathsf{Correct},\oplus} = [-0.17, 0.19]$$

Since $\widehat{p_{\mathsf{Correct},\oplus}}$ is not included in the interval, the function returns False. Consequently, the monitor issues a warning blaming the server for sending Correct with a probability higher than that specified in S_{game}. Next, the monitor invokes *checkInterval* for the choice Incorrect with the arguments $c_{\oplus}$, $c_{\mathsf{Incorrect},\oplus}$, $p_{\mathsf{Incorrect},\oplus}$ where $p_{\mathsf{Incorrect},\oplus} = 0.99$. Similarly, the monitor calculates:

$$\widehat{p_{\mathsf{Incorrect},\oplus}} = 0.67 \quad E_{\mathsf{Incorrect},\oplus} = 0.18 \quad p_{\mathsf{Incorrect},\oplus} \pm E_{\mathsf{Incorrect},\oplus} = [0.81, 1.17]$$

and since $\widehat{p_{\mathsf{Incorrect},\oplus}}$ does not lie within the interval, the monitor issues another warning, again blaming the server for this choice.

Consider now the case where the client sends 6 further guesses, to which the server replies with Incorrect for all. Therefore, the monitor counters for this choice point are now updated as follows:

$$c_{\oplus} = 12 \qquad c_{\mathsf{Correct},\oplus} = 2 \qquad c_{\mathsf{Incorrect},\oplus} = 10$$

Similarly, the monitor calculates the intervals for both choices:

$$\widehat{p_{\mathsf{Correct},\oplus}} = 0.17 \qquad E_{\mathsf{Correct},\oplus} = 0.13 \qquad p_{\mathsf{Correct},\oplus} \pm E_{\mathsf{Correct},\oplus} = [-0.12, 0.14]$$

$$\widehat{p_{\mathsf{Incorrect},\oplus}} = 0.67 \quad E_{\mathsf{Incorrect},\oplus} = 0.13 \quad p_{\mathsf{Incorrect},\oplus} \pm E_{\mathsf{Incorrect},\oplus} = [0.86, 1.12]$$

Note that after the monitor observes more messages for this choice point, the intervals shrink for both choices, gradually converging to the specified probabilities. Nonetheless, the estimated probabilities from the observed behaviour still do not fall within the confidence intervals in both cases. Accordingly, the monitor does not issue any warnings since it had already issued one previously when the potential violation was originally detected.

In fact, the monitor only *retracts* the warnings when the estimated probabilities fall within the interval. Concretely, the client would have to guess incorrectly 6 more times, setting the counters to:

$$c_\oplus = 18 \qquad c_{\text{Correct},\oplus} = 2 \qquad c_{\text{Incorrect},\oplus} = 16$$

These counters result in the intervals:

$$\widetilde{p_{\text{Correct},\oplus}} = 0.11 \qquad E_{\text{Correct},\oplus} = 0.1 \qquad p_{\text{Correct},\oplus} \pm E_{\text{Correct},\oplus} = [-0.09, 0.11]$$

$$\widetilde{p_{\text{Incorrect},\oplus}} = 0.89 \qquad E_{\text{Incorrect},\oplus} = 0.1 \qquad p_{\text{Incorrect},\oplus} \pm E_{\text{Incorrect},\oplus} = [0.89, 1.09]$$

that both include the estimated probability, causing the monitor to retract the warnings.   ◇

It is often the case that warnings for certain branches have little significance. For instance, in Example 3 above, the monitor also issues a warning for the choice Incorrect in addition to that for Correct. In practice, one might only be interested in knowing that the server replied Correct with a *higher* probability than that specified. To enable such specifications, we enrich the syntax of the probabilistic session types in Sect. 2 with the possibility of using $*$ which specifies to the monitor to not issue warnings for the respective branch or interval boundary.

Example 4. The PST S_{game} from Example 1 can be modified to the type description S'_{game} below:

$$S'_{game} = \text{rec } X.\&\left\{\begin{array}{l} ?\text{Guess}(\text{Int})[0.75, *].\oplus\left\{\begin{array}{l} !\text{Correct}[0.01].X, \\ !\text{Incorrect}[*].X \end{array}\right\}, \\ ?\text{Help}[*, 0.2].!\text{Hint}(\text{Str})[*].X, \\ ?\text{Quit}[*].\text{end} \end{array}\right\}$$

The new type indicates to the monitor *exactly* which choices it should issue warnings for. For the external choice, the monitor should only issue a warning when the estimated probability of the client sending Guess is *lower* than 0.75 and that of sending Help is *higher* than 0.2, completely ignoring the probability of the choice Quit. Similarly, for the internal choice, the monitor should only issue a warning for the choice Correct, and suppress those for Incorrect.   ◇

With this minor extension to the probabilistic session types we reduce the number of warnings issued and retracted by the monitor. Moreover, we also decrease the amount of computation performed by the monitor at runtime to only those choices that are deemed important. Effectively, this improves the overheads induced by the monitor.

4   Conclusions and Discussion

We have presented a tool-based methodology to analyse specifications augmented with quantitative requirements *at runtime*. More specifically, we extend existing work to implement the synthesis of monitors from probabilistic session types that conduct analysis of the interaction between two parties at runtime. The synthesised monitors issue warnings based only on evidence observed up to the current point of execution while taking into account its accuracy. Notably, the proposed methodology can serve as the basis for other runtime analysis techniques in which the specifications describe any quantitative behaviour.

We conjecture that our approach can be used for systems where protocol-based interactions are replicated in large numbers, and where human intervention is required to ensure their correct execution (*e.g.*, healthcare and fraud detection in e-payments or online gambling). In such applications, our monitors would direct human operation (*i.e.*, the scarce resource) to the cases that have the highest likelihood of exhibiting anomalous behaviour. Another potential application is that of control software that is derived using AI learning techniques. Although effective, such software is often not fully understood and notorious for sudden unexpected behaviour. With our approach, we can automate the monitoring of its interactions and shut off communication whenever the approximated runtime behaviour deviates considerably from that projected.

4.1   Related Work

Our methodology uses PSTs akin to those introduced in [19]. The authors use a type system to *statically* estimate the probability of well-typed processes *reaching successful states*. Notably, types are dynamically checked in our approach and we do not guarantee probabilistic properties; the proposed runtime analysis only issues warnings when the observed behaviour at runtime substantially deviates from the specification. Moreover, our PSTs can also specify behaviour of deterministic systems and are not restricted to probabilistic systems.

Several works apply probabilistic monitoring to minimise the number of runs to be monitored, based on predefined confidence levels [18,21,26]. In [24], probability is estimated to check whether the system's behaviour modelled as a hidden Markov model satisfies a temporal property in cases where gaps are present in the execution trace. Unlike these approaches, we use probabilities to specify quantitative aspects of communication protocols which we then check whether they are being respected at runtime.

On the runtime verification of probabilistic systems, the work in [11] models systems as discrete-time Markov chains and expresses requirements using Probabilistic Computation Tree Logic. Their aim is to adapt the behaviour of the underlying system to satisfy non-functional requirements, such as reliability or energy consumption. The work in [10] also monitors Markov Chains whereby monitors are able to verify if a property is satisfied by executing the system and steer it to take certain paths. Similarly to [11], Markov decision processes are used in [12] to model probabilistic systems and optimise the performance of their verification with the aim of using the results obtained to steer the system. In [10,11] and [12], the authors adopt incremental verification techniques that exploit the results of previous analyses of the system, whereas our runtime analysis only considers the *current* execution without any prior knowledge on the system. Moreover, we employ monitors that are passive and do not alter nor control the behaviour of the monitored system in any way.

4.2 Future Work

Improving Confidence Interval Estimation. The proposed approach using on confidence intervals described in Sect. 2 serves the goal of instantiating our interpretation of probabilistic session types (Sect. 2.1) on a concrete mechanism for monitors to emit judgements on the probabilistic behaviour of components at runtime. Our approach is not limited, nor bound, to the current statistical inference technique. For instance, we can improve our CI estimation by utilising the Wilson score interval [25], which is more costly but also more reliable than normal approximation when the sample size (observed messages up to the current point of execution) is small or the specified probability is close to 0 or 1. With an easy extension, we can additionally support different confidence levels per choice points. We also plan to study alternative statistical inference paradigms apart from the frequentist approach considered here, such as the Bayesian intervals [3] which would potentially give different interpretations to the PSTs. In turn, this would enable monitors to issue warnings based on the *aggregate recommendations* of the different estimators.

Alternative Interpretations of Probabilistic Session Types. In the proposed approach we opted for an interpretation of probabilistic session types that only considers probabilities at each individual choice point rather than the *global probabilistic behaviour.* We plan to study different interpretations that consider the *dependencies* among choice points in a session type, and also probabilities that are data (payload) dependent.

An intricate aspect of our approach is that it may lead to a potential trade-off between two extremes: taking longer to issue a warning with high confidence, or issue warnings earlier with low confidence. The first extreme corresponds to an increased risk of false negatives: a monitored application could substantially diverge from the observed session type, without being flagged. The second extreme corresponds to an increased risk of false positives: a statistically well-behaving monitored application could be flagged after a minor divergence from the expected frequency of choices. Finding the right value for the confidence level requires careful calibration since it depends on the application and on the relative cost of false negatives when compared to that of false positives.

Application-dependent heuristics together with more advanced interpretations of probabilistic session types can be used to overcome these difficulties. For instance, we could consider the introduction of an observation window of length w, and the probabilities in the session type could refer to a limited number of observed communications regulated by w. Accordingly, the monitor could keep track of the number of communications observed in the desired window, and use this information to issue warnings in case deviations persist. Concretely, with the interpretation of probabilities described in Sect. 2.1, a client in Example 1 is allowed to send any number of consecutive requests for help, as long as their frequency is not far from 20%, calculated by considering the *entire history* of the session. By introducing a small observation window, we can ensure that two consecutive requests of help would be flagged at any point during the session, regardless of their frequency.

Other Extensions and Improvements. We are in the process of conducting empirical evaluations to assess the effectiveness of our methodology. There are a number of extensions that can be realised relatively easily to improve the tool's flexibility and applicability. For instance, our methodology can be extended so that the probabilities within the session type are (machine-)learnt from a series of observed interactions of different parties. Moreover, monitor (verdict) *explainability* [9,15] is rapidly gaining importance: our tool can be readily extended to provide useful explanations to support the warnings raised. We are also considering the adaptation of our methodology to the pre-deployment phase of development, thus turning monitors into test drivers that can steer-and-verify implementations.

References

1. Aceto, L., Achilleos, A., Francalanza, A., Ingólfsdóttir, A., Lehtinen, K.: Adventures in monitorability: from branching to linear time and back again. Proc. ACM Program. Lang. **3**(POPL), 52:1–52:29 (2019). https://doi.org/10.1145/3290365
2. Aceto, L., Achilleos, A., Francalanza, A., Ingólfsdóttir, A., Lehtinen, K.: An operational guide to monitorability with applications to regular properties. Softw. Syst. Model. **20**(2), 335–361 (2021). https://doi.org/10.1007/s10270-020-00860-z
3. Agresti, A., Hitchcock, D.B.: Bayesian inference for categorical data analysis. Stat. Methods Appl. **14**(3), 297–330 (2005). https://doi.org/10.1007/s10260-005-0121-y
4. Bartolo Burlò, C., Francalanza, A., Scalas, A.: On the monitorability of session types, in theory and practice. In: 35th European Conference on Object-Oriented Programming, ECOOP 2021, 12–17 July 2021 (2021, to appear)
5. Bartolo Burlò, C., Francalanza, A., Scalas, A.: Towards a hybrid verification methodology for communication protocols (short paper). In: Gotsman, A., Sokolova, A. (eds.) FORTE 2020. LNCS, vol. 12136, pp. 227–235. Springer, Cham (2020). https://doi.org/10.1007/978-3-030-50086-3_13
6. Bocchi, L., Chen, T., Demangeon, R., Honda, K., Yoshida, N.: Monitoring networks through multiparty session types. Theor. Comput. Sci. **669**, 33–58 (2017). https://doi.org/10.1016/j.tcs.2017.02.009
7. Brand, D., Zafiropulo, P.: On communicating finite-state machines. J. ACM **30**(2), 323–342 (1983). https://doi.org/10.1145/322374.322380
8. Das, A., Wang, D., Hoffmann, J.: Probabilistic resource-aware session types. CoRR abs/2011.09037 (2020). https://arxiv.org/abs/2011.09037
9. Dawes, J.H., Reger, G.: Explaining violations of properties in control-flow temporal logic. In: Finkbeiner, B., Mariani, L. (eds.) RV 2019. LNCS, vol. 11757, pp. 202–220. Springer, Cham (2019). https://doi.org/10.1007/978-3-030-32079-9_12

10. Esparza, J., Kiefer, S., Kretínský, J., Weininger, M.: Online monitoring ω-regular properties in unknown Markov chains. CoRR abs/2010.08347 (2020). https://arxiv.org/abs/2010.08347
11. Filieri, A., Tamburrelli, G., Ghezzi, C.: Supporting self-adaptation via quantitative verification and sensitivity analysis at run time. IEEE Trans. Softw. Eng. **42**(1), 75–99 (2016). https://doi.org/10.1109/TSE.2015.2421318
12. Forejt, V., Kwiatkowska, M., Parker, D., Qu, H., Ujma, M.: Incremental runtime verification of probabilistic systems. In: Qadeer, S., Tasiran, S. (eds.) RV 2012. LNCS, vol. 7687, pp. 314–319. Springer, Heidelberg (2013). https://doi.org/10.1007/978-3-642-35632-2_30
13. Francalanza, A.: A theory of monitors. Inf. Computa. 104704 (2021, to appear). https://doi.org/10.1016/j.ic.2021.104704
14. Francalanza, A., Aceto, L., Ingólfsdóttir, A.: Monitorability for the Hennessy-Milner logic with recursion. Formal Methods Syst. Des. **51**(1), 87–116 (2017). https://doi.org/10.1007/s10703-017-0273-z
15. Francalanza, A., Cini, C.: Computer says no: verdict explainability for runtime monitors using a local proof system. J. Log. Algebraic Methods Program. **119**, 100636 (2021). https://doi.org/10.1016/j.jlamp.2020.100636
16. Francalanza, A., Mezzina, C.A., Tuosto, E.: Towards choreographic-based monitoring. In: Ulidowski, I., Lanese, I., Schultz, U.P., Ferreira, C. (eds.) RC 2020. LNCS, vol. 12070, pp. 128–150. Springer, Cham (2020). https://doi.org/10.1007/978-3-030-47361-7_6
17. Gommerstadt, H., Jia, L., Pfenning, F.: Session-typed concurrent contracts. In: Ahmed, A. (ed.) ESOP 2018. LNCS, vol. 10801, pp. 771–798. Springer, Cham (2018). https://doi.org/10.1007/978-3-319-89884-1_27
18. Grunske, L.: An effective sequential statistical test for probabilistic monitoring. Inf. Softw. Technol. **53**(3), 190–199 (2011). https://doi.org/10.1016/j.infsof.2010.10.003
19. Inverso, O., Melgratti, H.C., Padovani, L., Trubiani, C., Tuosto, E.: Probabilistic analysis of binary sessions. In: CONCUR. LIPIcs, vol. 171, pp. 14:1–14:21. Schloss Dagstuhl - Leibniz-Zentrum für Informatik (2020). https://doi.org/10.4230/LIPIcs.CONCUR.2020.14
20. Newcombe, R.G.: Confidence Intervals for Proportions and Related Measures of Effect Size. CRC Biostatistics Series. CRC Press, Chapman & Hall, Boca Raton (2012)
21. Ruchkin, I., Sokolsky, O., Weimer, J., Hedaoo, T., Lee, I.: Compositional probabilistic analysis of temporal properties over stochastic detectors. IEEE Trans. Comput. Aided Des. Integr. Circ. Syst. **39**(11), 3288–3299 (2020). https://doi.org/10.1109/TCAD.2020.3012643
22. Scalas, A., Yoshida, N.: Lightweight session programming in scala. In: ECOOP. LIPIcs, vol. 56, pp. 21:1–21:28. Schloss Dagstuhl - Leibniz-Zentrum für Informatik (2016). https://doi.org/10.4230/LIPIcs.ECOOP.2016.21
23. Schneider, F.B.: Enforceable security policies. ACM Trans. Inf. Syst. Secur. **3**(1), 30–50 (2000). https://doi.org/10.1145/353323.353382
24. Stoller, S.D., et al.: Runtime verification with state estimation. In: Khurshid, S., Sen, K. (eds.) RV 2011. LNCS, vol. 7186, pp. 193–207. Springer, Heidelberg (2012). https://doi.org/10.1007/978-3-642-29860-8_15

25. Wilson, E.B.: Probable inference, the law of succession, and statistical inference. J. Am. Stat. Assoc. **22**(158), 209–212 (1927). https://www.tandfonline.com/doi/abs/10.1080/01621459.1927.10502953
26. Zhu, Y., Xu, M., Zhang, P., Li, W., Leung, H.: Bayesian probabilistic monitor: a new and efficient probabilistic monitoring approach based on Bayesian statistics. In: QSIC, pp. 45–54. IEEE (2013). https://doi.org/10.1109/QSIC.2013.55

Java Typestate Checker

João Mota[(✉)][iD], Marco Giunti[iD], and António Ravara[iD]

NOVA LINCS and NOVA School of Science and Technology, Caparica, Portugal
jd.mota@campus.fct.unl.pt, marco.giunti@gmail.com, aravara@fct.unl.pt

Abstract. Detecting programming errors and vulnerabilities in software is increasingly important, and building tools that help developers with this task is a crucial area of investigation on which the industry depends. In object-oriented languages, one naturally defines stateful objects where the safe use of methods depends on their internal state; the correct use of objects according to their protocols is then enforced at compile-time by an analysis based on behavioral types.

We present Java Typestate Checker (JATYC), a tool based on the Checker Framework that verifies Java programs with respect to typestates. These define the object's states, the methods that can be called in each state, and the states resulting from the calls. The tool offers the following strong guarantees: sequences of method calls obey to object's protocols; completion of objects' protocols; detection of null-pointer exceptions; and control of the sharing of resources through access permissions.

To the best of our knowledge, there are no research or industrial tools that offer all these features. In particular, the implementation of sharing control in a typestate-based tool seems to be novel, and has an important impact on programming flexibility, since, for most programs, the linear discipline imposed by behavioral types is too strict.

Sharing of objects is enabled by means of an assertion language incorporating fractional permissions; to lift from programmers the burden of writing the assertions, JATYC infers all of these by building a constraint system and solving it with Z3, producing general assertions sufficient to accept the code, if these exist.

Keywords: Behavioral types · object-oriented programming · typestates · access permissions · inference

1 Introduction

Programming errors such as de-referencing null pointers, or using resources wrongly, e.g., reading from a closed file, just to name a few, result in programs that might malfunction in many ways, producing unexpected behaviors or even crashing. It is, therefore, crucial to develop tools that assist the software development process by detecting mistakes as early as possible since these bugs occur more often than one might think [31].

© IFIP International Federation for Information Processing 2021
Published by Springer Nature Switzerland AG 2021
F. Damiani and O. Dardha (Eds.): COORDINATION 2021, LNCS 12717, pp. 121–133, 2021.
https://doi.org/10.1007/978-3-030-78142-2_8

In programming languages, some common errors are detected thanks to type systems implemented in type checkers [8]. Unfortunately, the subset of errors detected in present mainstream languages is still limited. For instance, most *OOP* languages, including Java, do not statically ensure that methods are called according to a specified protocol, like calling *hasNext* before calling *next* in an iterator. Usually, the protocol is specified in natural language in the documentation, but not statically enforced: this is a source of many errors, like accessing a variable that was not initialized [4]. More subtle undetected errors include concurrent threads reading and eventually closing a shared resource unexpectedly. While some language frameworks support a refined analysis, they require expert users to provide complex specifications, for example, in separation logic [20,21,29].

In this paper, we provide a tool to help filling this gap and introduce *Java Typestate Checker (JATYC)*, which type-checks a Java program where objects are associated with typestates. Java classes are annotated with typestates defining the behavior of class instances in terms of available methods and state transitions. With *JATYC*, well-typed programs have the following properties: objects are used according to their protocols (typestates); protocols reach the *end* state; null-pointer exceptions are not raised; data-races at the level of variables/fields and interference between method calls on the same object do not occur. Ensuring these properties is crucial to avoid protocol bugs like one found in [33], where an app tracing COVID-19 failed to perform a crucial step in the protocol: notify users if they were in close contact with potentially infectious patients, leaving the protocol uncompleted.

JATYC is a new implementation of Mungo [24] that adds critical features and fixes known issues, like assuming that a *continue* statement jumps to the beginning of the loop's body, thus skipping the condition expression [25], which may produce false negatives. *JATYC* was implemented in Kotlin [22] as a plugin for the Checker Framework [28].

Originally, Mungo was implemented with JastAdd [13], an extension to Java that supports a specification formalism called Rewritable Circular Reference Attributed Grammars [12], enabling the modular implementation of compiler tools and languages [13]. Unfortunately, JastAdd does not seem to be actively maintained[1] and editor support is lacking (except for syntax highlighting)[2]. The Checker Framework [28] is a tool that supports adding type systems to the Java language. With a plugin written in Java or any other Java interoperable language, one defines the type qualifiers and enforces the semantics of the type system. Programmers can then write the type qualifiers in their programs, with Java annotations[3], and use the plugin to detect errors [28]. The Checker Framework is actively maintained, well-integrated with the Java language and toolset,

---

[1] The second to last release was on 2019: https://jastadd.cs.lth.se/releases/jastadd2/2.3.4/release-notes.php.

[2] https://jastadd.cs.lth.se/web/tool-support/.

[3] https://www.oracle.com/technical-resources/articles/java/ma14-architect-annotations.html.

and has being used to detect bugs in popular projects, like null-pointer errors in *Google Collections* [11], with their *Nullness Checker* plugin[4]. Together with Kotlin, it allowed us to be more productive in the development of the tool.

JATYC was developed in the context of the first author's master's dissertation [25]. The document and the code are freely distributed[5]. The major contributions with respect to the current version of Mungo are:

- checking the **absence of null pointer errors**, which is critical to avoid the "The Billion Dollar Mistake" [18];
- checking that the **protocols of objects are completed**, i.e. protocols reach the *end* state;
- support for the **static control of sharing** of objects, allowing safe aliasing and concurrency, while preventing data-races, patterns which are very common in object-oriented programming languages, thus increasing expressiveness and programming flexibility.

2   Related Work

We are interested in object-oriented languages where well-typed programs follow these properties: objects follow their specified protocols; protocols reach the *end* state; null-pointer exceptions are not raised; and data-races do not occur. We now present a review of relevant works we know on the topics. A more complete overview of existing works is also available in the first author's master's dissertation [25].

Behavioral Types are type disciplines that describe properties associated with the behavior of programs [19]. Type systems that include this notion, allow for the static verification of interactions and protocol compliance, like ensuring that the *hasNext* method is called before *next* in an iterator object.

If multiple references to the same object exist (i.e. aliasing), type information can get outdated if the object changes state via another reference. In solutions that implement **behavioral types**, it is common to force the **linear use of objects**, meaning that there is only one reference for each object [2]. Unfortunately, this restricts what a programmer can do, since sharing references is common practice in imperative and object-oriented programming languages.

One solution to statically verify code with shared data is the use of **access permissions** [5,6]: abstract capabilities that characterize the way a shared resource can be accessed by multiple references [30]. This notion is built on Linear Logic [16], which treats permissions as linear resources, and Separation Logic [27,29], which reasons about program behavior against specifications. Access permissions are used to ensure that only a reference can write on a particular location at any given time, and to ensure that if a location is read by a thread, all other threads only have read permission for that location, thus avoiding interference in concurrent programs [30].

---

[4] https://checkerframework.org/manual/#nullness-checker.

[5] https://github.com/jdmota/java-typestate-checker.

Fractional permissions [6] are concrete fractional numbers, ranged over 0 and 1, representing the permission for a shared resource: absence of permission is represented by 0; full permission (to read and write) is represented by 1; and shared read-only access is represented by a value strictly between 0 and 1. Fractional permissions can be split into a number of fractions and distributed among multiple references. For example, a permission s can be split into s_1 and s_2 such that $s = s_1 + s_2$, allowing two references to have read access to the same resource. Permissions that were split may also be joined again [6,30].

Mungo [24] is a tool that extends Java with typestate definitions [15] which are associated with Java classes and define the behavior of instances of those classes, specifying the sequences of method calls allowed in terms of a state machine. Mungo then statically checks that method calls happen in order, following the specified behavior, and ensures that protocols reach the *end* state. Mungo does not allow aliasing of objects associated with typestates [24].

Fugue [10] integrates typestates [15] with an object-oriented programming language, allowing the programmer to add declarative specifications on interfaces, providing preconditions and postconditions, and marking methods that are used for allocating or releasing resources, thus limiting the order in which object's methods are called. Fugue then ensures that methods are called in correct order, preconditions are met before a method is called, and resources are not used before allocated or after being released. Fugue allows aliasing through its guarded types (*NotAliased* and *MayBeAliased*), which track the lifetime but not the number of references to an object [10].

Plaid [17,26,32] is a typestate-oriented programming language [15] designed for concurrency. In Plaid, the class of an object represents its current state, and that class can change dynamically during runtime. Not only the interface (i.e. available methods) depends on the state, the behavior (i.e. implementation) also depends on the current state. Plaid also incorporates access permissions, which are associated with each type to express the aliasing and the mutability of the corresponding object, using keywords such as *unique*, *shared* and *immutable*. Unfortunately, Plaid does not seem to be maintained any longer [17,30]. As far as we know, Plaid as no notion of protocol completion.

To statically ensure the absence of **null-pointer exceptions**, there are tools such as the *Nullness Checker* of the Checker Framework. This tool enhances the Java's type system so that types are non-nullable by default, which means that *null* values cannot be assigned to them. To declare a variable or field with a nullable type (i.e. a variable or field where the *null* value can be assigned to), one can use the *Nullable* annotation[6]. Some modern languages, such as Kotlin, also distinguish non-null types from nullable types, thus avoiding these exceptions[7]. Nonetheless, these may produce false positives that might force the programmer to provide additional checks, following a style known as *defensive programming*, that a value is not *null*, even when it is provable that the code is safe[8].

---

[6] https://checkerframework.org/manual/#nullness-checker.

[7] https://kotlinlang.org/docs/null-safety.html.

[8] An example is available at https://tinyurl.com/2hmwx7vk.

3   Motivating Example

To motivate the need for *JATYC*, consider a *LineReader* Java class that is responsible for both opening a file and reading it line by line[9]. Listing 1.1 presents an implementation.

Listing 1.1. *LineReader* class

```
 1  import java.io.*;
 2  public class LineReader {
 3    private FileReader file = null;
 4    private int curr;
 5
 6    public Status open(String f) {
 7      try {
 8        file = new FileReader(f);
 9        curr = file.read();
10        return Status.OK;
11      } catch (IOException exp) {
12        return Status.ERROR;
13      }
14    }
15
16    public String read()
17      throws IOException {
18      StringBuilder str =
19        new StringBuilder();
20      while (
21        curr != 10 && curr != -1
22      ) {
23        str.append((char) curr);
24        curr = file.read();
25      }
26      if (curr == 10)
27        curr = file.read();
28      return str.toString();
29    }
30
31    public boolean eof() {
32      return curr == -1;
33    }
34
35    public void close()
36      throws IOException {
37      file.close();
38    }
39
40    public enum Status { OK, ERROR }
41  }
```

The intended protocol is defined implicitly by the sequences of method calls that are supported, and by the "states" reached via those calls. To use the *LineReader*, one must invoke the *open* method passing the path of the file. If the call returns *ERROR*, then the file could not be opened. If it returns *OK*, then one can proceed to read the file. Before calling the *read* method, one must call the *eof* method to ensure that the end of the file was not reached. Each *read* call returns a string with a new line. After reading the file, the *close* method must be called to free the resources and close the underlying stream.

If this contract is not followed, errors may occur or wrong results may be produced. If one attempts to *read* before calling *open*, a *NullPointException* will

---

[9] The class could be a subclass of the abstract class java.io.Reader.

be thrown since the *file* field has a null reference (line 24). Additionally, if one calls the *read* method after calling *close*, an *IOException* will occur since the stream is closed (line 37). Finally, if one keeps reading the file after *eof* returns *true*, then *read* will return empty strings, giving a false impression that the file being read contains empty lines[10]. While the Java compiler accepts most of the wrong behaviors described above, in the next section we will show how to enrich Java programs with *typestate annotations* that allow rejecting programs containing these kinds of behavioral errors at compile-time.

4   What Is the Tool Good For?

Protocols. All instances of a Java class having a typestate are checked in order to enforce the prescribed behavior. The typestate specifications are written in *.protocol* files, with the form *typestate* $T\{S_1 \ldots S_n\}$, where each state S_i is a list of *method transitions* $\{M_1 \ldots M_j\}$, and the general form of M_i is: T m(T1,...,Tk) : <v1: S1, ..., vm: Sm>, with $T, T_1, \ldots, T_k$ Java types: when *method* m is executed and returns value v_i, the typestate switches to state S_i[11].

Listing 1.2 presents the protocol for the *LineReader* (cf. Listing 1.1). It specifies four states, *Init*, *Open*, *Read* and *Close*, and implicitly includes the *end* state, which is the final state. In the initial state *Init*, only the *open* method is available to be called (line 3). If the method returns *OK*, the state changes to *Open*; otherwise, the state changes to *end*, where no operations are allowed. After opening the file, the *close* method may be called anytime, except if the file was already closed (lines 7, 11, and 14). In the *Open* state, one may call the *eof* method (line 6). If it returns *true*, the state changes to *Close*; otherwise, the state changes to *Read*. In the *Read* state one may call the *read* method, which then changes the state to *Open* (line 10).

Listing 1.2. *LineReader* protocol

```
1   typestate LineReaderProtocol {
2      Init = {
3         Status open(String): <OK: Open, ERROR: end>
4      }
5      Open = {
6         boolean eof(): <true: Close, false: Read>,
7         void close(): end
8      }
9      Read = {
10        String read(): Open,
11        void close(): end
12     }
13     Close = {
14        void close(): end
15     }
16  }
```

To associate a protocol with a Java class, one must include a *Typestate* annotation containing the (relative) path of the protocol file. For backwards-

---

[10] Code examples are available online at https://git.io/JtR7E.
[11] The complete grammar is available at https://git.io/JtMu3.

compatibility with Mungo, we support the *Typestate* annotation from the *mungo.lib* package (Listing 1.3).

Listing 1.3. *LineReader* class with *Typestate* annotation

```
1   import mungo.lib.Typestate;
2   @Typestate("LineReader.protocol")
3   public class LineReader { /* ... */ }
```

Protocol Compliance and Completion. *JATYC* ensures that instances of Java classes associated with a typestate not only obey to the corresponding protocol, but are also consumed (that is, they reach the *end* state): as a consequence, potentially important method calls are not forgotten and resources are freed. To add more flexibility, it is also possible to declare states in which an object may stop to be used. These *droppable states* [25] are declared by including the following special transition *drop: end*[12].

To see an example of incorrect use of *LineReader*, consider Listing 1.4, where errors are indicated in the comments. According to the protocol (Listing 1.2), the reader object is in the *Close* state (line 5); thus, the only available method is *close*, that is, *read* is not available. Negating the loop condition fixes the error. Moreover, the *close* method is called nowhere: therefore the protocol does not reach the *end* state.

Listing 1.4. *LineReader* use

```
1   LineReader reader = new LineReader();
2   switch (reader.open()) {
3     case OK:
4       while (reader.eof()) {
5         System.out.println(reader.read());
6         // Error: cannot call "read" on state Close
7       }
8       break;
9     case ERROR:
10        System.err.println("Could not open file");
11        break;
12  }
13  // Error: object did not complete its protocol
```

Nullness Checking. Null pointer errors are the cause of most runtime exceptions in Java programs [4,31]: being able to detect these errors at compile-time is therefore crucial. Towards that direction, *JATYC* offers the following guarantees: (1) types are non-null by default (contrary to Java's default type system[13]), method calls and field accesses are only performed on non-null types; (2) false positives (in classes associated to protocols) are ruled out by taking into account that methods are only called in a specific order. To allow a type to be nullable, one can use the *Nullable* annotation. The analysis is based on the formal work done in [7] for a language that served as basis for Mungo.

To exemplify guarantee (1), Listing 1.5 presents two scenarios where methods are potentially called on null values. In line 5, *JATYC* reports an error since a

---

[12] Example of *droppable states* at https://git.io/JOqfc.

[13] The fact that null is a value of any type is the source of Java not being type safe [1].

method call could be performed on null. In line 9, no error is reported since the code checks for null first (line 8).

Listing 1.5. Nullness checking example (1)

```
1  import org.checkerframework.checker.jtc.lib.Nullable;
2  import java.io.FileReader;
3  public class Main {
4    void use1(@Nullable FileReader file) {
5      int c = file.read(); // Error: cannot call "read" on null
6    }
7    void use2(@Nullable FileReader file) {
8      if (file != null)
9        int c = file.read(); // Safe operation
10   }
11 }
```

To see how guarantee (2) works, consider Listing 1.6: if one calls the *read* method before *open*, a null pointer error will occur. But since *open* must be called first (according to the protocol), we know that the *file* field is non-null when *read* is called; thus, the operation is safe. Notice the absence of *defensive programming*, required by many static analysis tools, namely by the *Nullness Checker* of the Checker Framework.

Listing 1.6. Nullness checking example (2)

```
1  import org.checkerframework.checker.jtc.lib.Nullable;
2  // ...
3  public class LineReader {
4    private @Nullable FileReader file = null;
5    // ...
6    public String read() {
7      // ...
8      curr = file.read(); // Safe operation
9      // ...
10   }
11 }
```

Sharing. In imperative languages, it is common to have multiple references to the same object. Aliasing makes it more difficult to track the state of each object, since it may change via another reference. The whole challenge becomes even harder in the presence of concurrent computations and accesses. Consider the example in Listing 1.7 where a reference is stored in a field (line 1) and passed to a method call (line 5). Depending on the body of the *use* method, the program in Listing 1.7 can be safe or unsafe: if the method modifies the state of the reader object (by calling methods on it), then the assumptions the *wrapper* made about the state of the stored reference are wrong, and in turn the program must be rejected, otherwise the program could be accepted. *JATYC* is able to track the potential state changes in the *use* method, thus allowing for a more liberal and sound management of resources.

Listing 1.7. Aliasing example (1)

```
1   class Wrapper { public LineReader reader = new LineReader(); }
2   class Main {
3     void main() {
4       Wrapper wrapper = new Wrapper();
5       use(wrapper.reader);
6     }
7     // ...
8   }
```

Table 1. Assertions' grammar

Assertion := Term | Term "∧" Assertion
Term := Access | Equality | TypeOf | Packed | Unpacked

Access := "access" "(" AccessLocation "," f ")"
Equality := "eq" "(" Location "," Location ")"
TypeOf := "typeof" "(" Location "," t ")"
Packed := "packed" "(" Location ")"
Unpacked := "unpacked" "(" Location ")"

Location := id | id "." Location
AccessLocation := id | id "." "0" | id "." AccessLocation

To track aliasing and control the operations that can be allowed, we integrate **behavioral types** [19] with **fractional permissions** [6] in an **assertion language**, obtaining an original (and promising) combination. Table 1 shows the grammar of assertions. Each assertion is a conjunction of five types of predicates: *access* (specifies the fractional permissions for *access locations*); *typeof* (asserts the current state of an object); *packed* (asserts that the object's fields are hidden behind the abstract typestate view); *unpacked* (asserts that the object's fields are exposed); *eq* (asserts that two locations point to the same object). *Access locations* refer to variables, fields, or the objects pointed by those, for example: x refers to the local variable x; $x.y$ refers to the field y of the object pointed by x; $x.0$ refers to the object pointed by variable x. The $x.0$ notion allows us to distinguish the permissions to call methods on objects from the permissions to read from or write to the variables or fields themselves.

Listing 1.8. Aliasing example (2)

```
1   LineReader r1 = new LineReader(), r2 = r1;
2   // access(r1, 1) ∧ access(r1.0, 1/2) ∧ typeof(r1, State "Init") ∧
3   // access(r2, 1) ∧ access(r2.0, 1/2) ∧ typeof(r2, State "Init") ∧
4   // packed(r1) ∧ packed(r2) ∧ eq(r1, r2)
```

Listing 1.8 shows an assertion example for two variables with the same reference. The predicate *access(r1, 1)* indicates there is read and write access permission to the variable; *access(r1.0, 1/2)* indicates that there is only read permission to the object pointed by the variable (thus, only methods that keep the object in the same state may be called); *typeof(r1, State "Init")* asserts that the object is in the *Init* state; and *packed(r1)* indicates that the object's fields are hidden behind the abstract typestate view. The same meanings apply to *r2*. Finally, *eq(r1, r2)* asserts that both variables hold the same reference.

To relieve the programmer from writing the assertions, *JATYC* embeds a prototypal **algorithm that infers all the assertions**. The **inference algorithm** is inspired by the work done in [14]. It has four steps: variables and fields are collected; assertions over symbolic fractions, types and equalities are constructed and associated with each expression in the code (before and after); each expression is analyzed and constraints over the symbols are produced; and finally, the constraint system is given to the Z3 Solver [9]. A satisfiable system ensures: objects obey each other's protocols, even in the presence of aliasing; no data-races occur at the level of variables and fields; method calls that change the state of an object do not interfere with each other.

Listing 1.9 shows a file being read in a separate thread (line 5), while in the main thread, the reader is closed before waiting for the thread to finish (line 9). This will result in an *IOException* when trying to read the closed file (line 5). The algorithm infers that full permission to the reader object is required in the thread (to read from it), and in the main thread (to close it). When *t.start* is called, full permission is acquired, leaving the main thread with no permission to the reader. When *r.close* is called, full permission is necessary, but not available. This contradiction will result in no solution being found, showing that there is a problem in the code. If *r.close()* is moved after *t.join()*, a solution will be found, and the code accepted, since *t.join()* gives back the permissions acquired when the thread started.

Listing 1.9. Concurrent *LineReader* use

```
1    LineReader r = new LineReader ();
2    if (r.open() == Status.OK) {
3      Thread t = new Thread(() -> {
4        while (!r.eof()) {
5          println(r.read());
6        }
7      });
8      t.start();
9      r.close();
10     t.join();
11   }
```

Limitations. First, subtyping and dynamic method dispatch in Java are currently ignored. This means that the programmer currently needs to avoid using these Java features to still benefit from the guarantees that the tool provides. Secondly, the inference algorithm has some issues: all objects are considered to be unpacked, what causes problems if for example we want to work with recursive data structures; the analysis of threads only works if the thread is started and waited upon in the context in which it was created; and if the algorithm reports that it found no solution, no further information is given about the possible root problem. Thirdly, although the tool is fast at inferring the fractional permissions, it is slow at inferring the types. Finally, only concurrent scenarios with either a single reader and writer or multiple readers are allowed. For example, the scenario in Listing 1.10 is not currently possible.

Listing 1.10. One writer and one reader

```
1  new Thread (() -> {
2    while (!r.eof())
3      println(r.read());
4  });
5
6  new Thread (() -> {
7    while (!r.eof()) {}
8  });
```

5 Future Work

To lift the restrictions leading to the rejection of the code in Listing 1.10, allowing more permissible yet safe concurrent accesses to data, we will incorporate standard approaches like Rely-Guarantee [23], locks and monitors. We also plan to fix limitations previously mentioned by taking into account subtyping and dynamic method dispatching. We are aware of the work done in [3], and it would be interesting to integrate the notion of synchronous session subtyping in *JATYC*. Subtyping support is crucial and it should be our first next step. Additionally, we plan to implement the inference of packing and unpacking, and pinpoint the code locations that caused the constraint system to be unsatisfiable, allowing the programmer to find out where the problem is. Furthermore, we would like to support generics and collections. Finally, we plan to improve the performance of the inference algorithm by only using Z3 to infer the fractional permissions and using a different technique to infer the types.

Acknowledgements. We warmly acknowledge the anonymous reviewers whose comments and suggestions pushed us to present a more complete and well-rounded discussion of the topics.

This work was partially supported by the EU H2020 RISE programme under the Marie Skłodowska-Curie grant agreement No. 778233 (BehAPI) and by NOVA LINCS (UIDB/04516/2020) via the Portuguese Fundação para a Ciência e a Tecnologia.

References

1. Amin, N., Tate, R.: Java and Scala's type systems are unsound: the existential crisis of null pointers. ACM SIGPLAN Notices **51**(10), 838–848 (2016). https://doi.org/10.1145/3022671.2984004
2. Ancona, D., et al.: Behavioral types in programming languages. Found. Trends Program. Lang. **3**(2–3), 95–230 (2016). https://doi.org/10.1561/2500000031
3. Bacchiani, L., Bravetti, M., Lange, J., Zavattaro, G.: A session subtyping tool, to appear. In: 23rd International Conference on Coordination Models and Languages (2021)
4. Beckman, N.E., Kim, D., Aldrich, J.: An empirical study of object protocols in the wild. In: Mezini, M. (ed.) ECOOP 2011. LNCS, vol. 6813, pp. 2–26. Springer, Heidelberg (2011). https://doi.org/10.1007/978-3-642-22655-7_2

5. Bornat, R., Calcagno, C., O'Hearn, P., Parkinson, M.: Permission accounting in separation logic. In: The 32nd ACM SIGPLAN-SIGACT Symposium on Principles of Programming Languages, pp. 259–270 (2005). https://doi.org/10.1145/1040305. 1040327

6. Boyland, J.: Checking interference with fractional permissions. In: Cousot, R. (ed.) SAS 2003. LNCS, vol. 2694, pp. 55–72. Springer, Heidelberg (2003). https://doi. org/10.1007/3-540-44898-5_4

7. Bravetti, M., et al.: Behavioural types for memory and method safety in a core object-oriented language. In: Oliveira, B.C.S. (ed.) APLAS 2020. LNCS, vol. 12470, pp. 105–124. Springer, Cham (2020). https://doi.org/10.1007/978-3-030-64437-6_6

8. Cardelli, L.: Type systems. ACM Comput. Surv. **28**(1), 263–264 (1996). https:// doi.org/10.1145/234313.234418

9. de Moura, L., Bjørner, N.: Z3: an efficient SMT solver. In: Ramakrishnan, C.R., Rehof, J. (eds.) TACAS 2008. LNCS, vol. 4963, pp. 337–340. Springer, Heidelberg (2008). https://doi.org/10.1007/978-3-540-78800-3_24

10. DeLine, R., Fähndrich, M.: The fugue protocol checker: Is your software baroque. Technical Report, Technical Report MSR-TR-2004-07, Microsoft Research (2004)

11. Dietl, W., Dietzel, S., Ernst, M.D., Muşlu, K., Schiller, T.W.: Building and using pluggable type-checkers. In: The 33rd International Conference on Software Engineering, pp. 681–690 (2011). https://doi.org/10.1145/1985793.1985889

12. Ekman, T., Hedin, G.: Rewritable reference attributed grammars. In: Odersky, M. (ed.) ECOOP 2004. LNCS, vol. 3086, pp. 147–171. Springer, Heidelberg (2004). https://doi.org/10.1007/978-3-540-24851-4_7

13. Ekman, T., Hedin, G.: The jastadd extensible java compiler. In: The 22nd Annual ACM SIGPLAN Conference on Object-oriented Programming Systems and Applications, pp. 1–18 (2007). https://doi.org/10.1145/1297105.1297029

14. Ferrara, P., Müller, P.: Automatic inference of access permissions. In: Kuncak, V., Rybalchenko, A. (eds.) VMCAI 2012. LNCS, vol. 7148, pp. 202–218. Springer, Heidelberg (2012). https://doi.org/10.1007/978-3-642-27940-9_14

15. Garcia, R., Tanter, É., Wolff, R., Aldrich, J.: Foundations of typestate-oriented programming. ACM Trans. Program. Lang. Syst. (TOPLAS) **36**(4), 12 (2014). https://doi.org/10.1145/2629609

16. Girard, J.Y.: Linear logic. Theoretical Comput. Sci. **50**(1), 1–101 (1987). https:// doi.org/10.1016/0304-3975(87)90045-4

17. Group, T.P.: The plaid programming language - introduction. https://www.cs. cmu.edu/aldrich/plaid/plaid-intro.pdf. Accessed 10 Apr 2021

18. Hoare, T.: Null references: The billion dollar mistake, Presentation at QCon London (2009). https://tinyurl.com/eyipowm4

19. Hüttel, H., et al.: Foundations of session types and behavioural contracts. ACM Comput. Surv. (CSUR) **49**(1), 1–36 (2016). https://doi.org/10.1145/2873052

20. Ishtiaq, S.S., O'hearn, P.W.: Bi as an assertion language for mutable data structures. In: The 28th ACM SIGPLAN-SIGACT Symposium on Principles of Programming Languages, pp. 14–26 (2001). https://doi.org/10.1145/1988042.1988050

21. Jacobs, B., Smans, J., Philippaerts, P., Vogels, F., Penninckx, W., Piessens, F.: VeriFast: a powerful, sound, predictable, fast verifier for C and Java. In: Bobaru, M., Havelund, K., Holzmann, G.J., Joshi, R. (eds.) NFM 2011. LNCS, vol. 6617, pp. 41–55. Springer, Heidelberg (2011). https://doi.org/10.1007/978-3-642-20398-5_4

22. Jemerov, D., Isakova, S.: Kotlin in Action. Manning Publications Company, New York (2017)

23. Jones, C.B.: Specification and design of (parallel) programs. In: Mason, R.E.A. (ed.) The IFIP 9th World Computer Congress Information Processing, Paris, vol. 83, pp. 321–332 (1983). North-Holland/IFIP (1983)

24. Kouzapas, D., Dardha, O., Perera, R., Gay, S.J.: Typechecking protocols with mungo and stmungo. In: The 18th International Symposium on Principles and Practice of Declarative Programming, pp. 146–159. ACM (2016). https://doi.org/10.1145/2967973.2968595

25. Mota, J.: Coping with the reality: adding crucial features to a typestate-oriented language. Master's thesis, NOVA School of Science and Technology (2021). https://github.com/jdmota/java-typestate-checker/blob/master/docs/msc-thesis.pdf

26. Naden, K., Bocchino, R., Aldrich, J., Bierhoff, K.: A type system for borrowing permissions. ACM SIGPLAN Notices **47**(1), 557–570 (2012). https://doi.org/10.1145/2103621.2103722

27. O'Hearn, P., Reynolds, J., Yang, H.: Local reasoning about programs that alter data structures. In: Fribourg, L. (ed.) CSL 2001. LNCS, vol. 2142, pp. 1–19. Springer, Heidelberg (2001). https://doi.org/10.1007/3-540-44802-0_1

28. Papi, M.M., Ali, M., Correa Jr, T.L., Perkins, J.H., Ernst, M.D.: Practical pluggable types for java. In: The 2008 International Symposium on Software Testing and Analysis, pp. 201–212 (2008). https://doi.org/10.1145/1390630.1390656

29. Reynolds, J.C.: Separation logic: a logic for shared mutable data structures. In: Proceedings 17th Annual IEEE Symposium on Logic in Computer Science, pp. 55–74. IEEE (2002). https://doi.org/10.1109/lics.2002.1029817

30. Sadiq, A., Li, Y.F., Ling, S.: A survey on the use of access permission-based specifications for program verification. J. Syst. Softw. **159**, 110150 (2020). https://doi.org/10.1016/j.jss.2019.110450

31. Sunshine, J.: Protocol programmability. Ph.D. thesis, Carnegie Mellon University, Pittsburgh (2013)

32. Sunshine, J., Naden, K., Stork, S., Aldrich, J., Tanter, É.: First-class state change in plaid. ACM SIGPLAN Notices **46**(10), 713–732 (2011). https://doi.org/10.1145/2076021.2048122

33. Wetsman, N.: Contact tracing app for England and wales failed to flag people exposed to Covid-19. The Verge (2020). https://www.theverge.com/2020/11/2/21546618/uk-coronavirus-contact-tracing-app-error-alert-isolation

Asynchronous Global Types in Co-logic Programming

Riccardo Bianchini and Francesco Dagnino(✉)

DIBRIS, Università di Genova, Genoa, Italy
francesco.dagnino@dibris.unige.it

Abstract. Global types are at the core of communication based programming. They allow a high level specification of protocols involving many participants and enforce good safety and liveness properties, such as absence of deadlock, locked participants and orphan messages. In this paper, we describe an implementation of a novel formalism of global types for sessions with asynchronous communications in co-logic programming, where we use coinduction to properly handle the coinductive syntax of global types and processes. We also define a simple query language to write sessions and global types, providing primitives for type checking.

Keywords: Global types · Prolog · Coinduction

1 Introduction

We describe an implementation in *co-logic programming* [1,9,11] of a novel formulation of global types for asynchronous sessions, described in a companion paper [4]. Co-logic programming is an extension of logic programming where predicates can be marked as coinductive. In this case, resolution relies on a mechanism of cycle detection which gives (successful) termination when the same goal is encountered twice.

The benefits of this work are twofold: on one hand, to provide an implementation of the type system described in [4], and a simple user interface for making related queries. On the other hand, global types and related judgments provide a very interesting and challenging case study for co-logic programming, since their encoding forces to clearly understand and express the either inductive or coinductive nature of definitions, and the related termination issues. Notably, sometimes inductive predicates are adequate, sometimes they need to be implemented, rather than directly, as the negation of a predicate defined coinductively, in other cases it is necessary to use the coinductive extension of SWI-Prolog. Finally, in some cases, a by-hand cycle detection mechanism is needed, since neither a standard inductive definition, nor a coinductive definition using built-in cycle detection are enough to ensure termination. These issues are discussed in detail in Sect. 5. We used SWI-Prolog [12] version 8.2.2 for x64-win64.

© IFIP International Federation for Information Processing 2021
Published by Springer Nature Switzerland AG 2021
F. Damiani and O. Dardha (Eds.): COORDINATION 2021, LNCS 12717, pp. 134–146, 2021.
https://doi.org/10.1007/978-3-030-78142-2_9

The tool is composed of two components:

- the core part, that is, the Prolog implementation of definitions in [4], such as sessions, global types, projections, and typing judgments
- the query language, which provides a more user-friendly syntax, and a simple typechecking phase to avoid inconsistencies in the user's code.

Section 2 reports the definitions from [4] implemented in the tool. Section 3 is a brief presentation of co-logic programming. Section 4 describes the query language, and Sect. 5 the Prolog implementation, discussing termination issues. Finally, in Sect. 6 we summarize the contribution and discuss future developments. The complete code, and instructions for using the prototype, can be found at https://github.com/RiccardoBianc/Asynchronous-global-types-implementation.

2 Global Types for Asynchronous Sessions

We briefly summarize the formulation of global types for asynchronous sessions introduced in [3], and subsequently extended in [4], reporting the formal definitions implemented in the tool. The key idea in [3] is to directly handle asynchrony at the level of global types, in the sense that an output and the corresponding input operation are modeled by distinct type constructors. In this way, we can directly assign a global type to an asynchronous session without the need of asynchronous subtyping, but this comes at the cost that not all global types ensure the desired properties, hence a notion of *well-formedness* becomes crucial in our setting.

Another novelty with respect to classical presentations [2,5] of global types is that a *coinductive approach* is adopted. Namely, processes and types with an infinite behaviour are expressed as infinite regular terms, rather than by an explicit fixed-point operator, and, correspondingly, functions handling them, e.g., the projection, are also defined coinductively. This feature makes the implementation in co-logic programming very natural, as shown in the following.

Processes and Sessions. We assume base sets of *participants* $\mathsf{p}, \mathsf{q}, \mathsf{r} \in \mathsf{Part}$, and *labels* $\lambda \in \mathsf{Lab}$. The syntax of *processes* is as follows:

$$P ::=_\rho \mathsf{p}!\{\lambda_i.P_i\}_{i \in I} \mid \mathsf{p}?\{\lambda_i.P_i\}_{i \in I} \mid 0 \qquad I \neq \emptyset, \lambda_j \neq \lambda_h \text{ for } j \neq h$$

The symbol $::=_\rho$ indicates that the productions should be interpreted *coinductively*, rather than inductively as in the standard case. That is, they define possibly infinite terms. However, we assume such infinite terms to be *regular*, that is, with finitely many distinct sub-terms.

A process of shape $\mathsf{p}!\{\lambda_i.P_i\}_{i \in I}$ (*internal choice*) sends to p one of the labels in a set, and then behaves differently depending on the sent label. A process of shape $\mathsf{p}?\{\lambda_i.P_i\}_{i \in I}$ (*external choice*) waits for receiving from p one of the labels in a set, and then behaves differently depending on the received label. An internal choice which is a singleton is simply written $p!\lambda.P$, and $p!\lambda.\mathbf{0}$ is abbreviated $p!\lambda$, and analogously for an external choice.

$Queues$ are sequences of $messages$, which are triples consisting of a sender, a label, and a receiver, as shown below:

$$\mathcal{M} ::= \emptyset \mid \langle p, \lambda, q \rangle \cdot \mathcal{M}$$

$(Multiparty)$ $sessions$ consist of pairs participant/process composed in parallel, each with a different participant, and a queue. That is, a session has shape $N \parallel \mathcal{M}$, where

$$N ::= p_1 \llbracket P_1 \rrbracket \parallel \cdots \parallel p_n \llbracket P_n \rrbracket \qquad p_i \neq p_j \text{ for } i \neq j$$

For example consider the session:

$$p \llbracket q!\lambda.q?\lambda' \rrbracket \parallel q \llbracket p!\lambda'.p?\lambda \rrbracket \parallel \emptyset \tag{1}$$

where each of the participants p and q wishes to first send a message to and then receive a message from the other one. In a synchronous setting, this session would be stuck, because a communication arises from the synchronisation of an output with a matching input, and here the output $q!\lambda$ of p cannot synchronise with the input $p?\lambda$ of q, since the latter is guarded by the output $p!\lambda'$. Symmetrically, the output $p!\lambda'$ of q cannot synchronise with the input $q?\lambda'$ of p. Instead, in an asynchronous setting, p could put its message for q on the queue and q could read it after putting its message for p on the queue and viceversa.

$Type$ $System.$ Classical global types describe the interaction in a session with communications specifying the sender of the message, its receiver, and the sent message. So a communication embeds both the sending and the receiving of the message. Hence, it is not possible to assign a global type, e.g., to the session above, since this type should specify that either the communication in which p sends λ to q or the one in which q sends λ' to p takes place first. In the global types of [3], instead, communications are split into outputs and inputs, as follows:

$$G ::=_\rho pq!\{\lambda_i.G_i\}_{i \in I} \mid pq?\lambda.G \mid \text{End} \qquad p \neq q, I \neq \emptyset, \lambda_j \neq \lambda_h \text{ for } j \neq h$$

A global type of shape $pq!\{\lambda_i.G_i\}_{i \in I}$ specifies that p sends to q one of the labels in a set, and then an interaction takes place which depends on the sent label. A global type of shape $pq?\lambda.G$ specifies that q receives from p the label λ, and then the interaction described by G takes place. As processes, global types are defined coinductively, so that infinite global types are allowed, but only of regular shape. The $players$ of a global type are those p occurring as senders in outputs $(pq!\{\lambda_i.G_i\}_{i \in I})$ or receivers in inputs $(qp?\lambda.G)$.

With these types, it is possible to describe the asynchronous session (1) with the type

$pq!\lambda.qp!\lambda'.pq?\lambda.qp?\lambda'.\text{End}$

or with the others obtained by swapping the order of outputs or inputs, that is,

qp!λ'.pq!λ.pq?λ.qp?λ'.End
pq!λ.qp!λ'.qp?λ'.pq?λ.End
qp!λ'.pq!λ'.qp?λ'.pq?λ.End

Configuration types are pairs $G\|\mathcal{M}$ where G is a global type and $\mathcal{M}$ is a queue. A configuration type describes a session in which some participant sent a message that is not yet read from its receiver. *Well-formedness* of $G\|\mathcal{M}$ is defined as the conjunction of the following properties:

- $G\|\mathcal{M}$ is *input/output matching*, that is, every message put on the queue will be eventually read and every enabled input should find a corresponding message in the queue.
- G is *bounded*, that is, the first occurrence as player of a participant, if any, is at a bounded depth in all paths, ensuring that no player remains stuck forever.
- The projection of G on each player is well-defined (explained below).

The tool implements these properties as described in [4], which significantly enlarge the class of typable sessions with respect to [3].

The notion of projection is a key one in type systems for multiparty sessions. Usually [5,6], global types are projected onto *local types* and local types are assigned to processes. In the simple calculus in [4], global types can be directly projected onto processes, as in [3,8]. Projection computes, starting from a global type G, the (most general) process P associated with a single participant p. This is modeled by the judgment $G \upharpoonright p \mapsto P$, which is defined coinductively.

Example 1. For instance, the previously considered global type

$$G = pq!\lambda.qp!\lambda'.pq?\lambda.qp?\lambda'.End$$

is projected to processes $P = q!\lambda.q?\lambda'.\mathbf{0}$ for participant p and $Q = p!\lambda'.p?\lambda.\mathbf{0}$ for participant q.

As already mentioned, the notion of well-formedness is crucial in this setting as not all global types ensure desirable properties of asynchronous sessions. We show below some examples of such global types explaining why they are not well-formed.

Example 2. The following global type describes a deadlocked session, as q is blocked waiting for the message λ_2:

$$G = pq!\lambda_1.qp!\lambda_2.pq?\lambda_2.qp?\lambda_2.G$$

This type is not input/output matching, as the input $pq?\lambda_2$ does not match any previous output, hence G is not well-formed.

Example 3. The following global type describes a session where the participant r can wait forever, because p and q can exchange the message λ_1 forever:

$$G = p\,q!\{\lambda_1.pq?\lambda_1.G,\ \lambda_2.pq?\lambda_2.qr!\lambda.qr?\lambda.G\}$$

This type is not well-formed as it is not bounded precisely because of the infinite path $pq!\lambda_1.pq?\lambda_1.pq!\lambda_1\ldots$, which does not involve r.

Example 4. The following global type describes a session where the first message is never read:

$$G = qp!\lambda_1.G_1 \qquad G_1 = pq!\lambda.pq?\lambda.G_1$$

This type is not input/output matching, as the output $qp!\lambda_1$ is not matched by any subsequent input, hence it is not well-formed.

Boundedness and projection, together with their Prolog implementation, will be described in more detail in Sect. 5.

The typing judgment $N\|\mathcal{M} : G\|\mathcal{M}$ checks that the session $N\|\mathcal{M}$ is consistent with the global protocol represented by the configuration type $G\|\mathcal{M}$. The judgment is derived from the following conditions, for $N = p_1[\![P_1]\!] \| \cdots \| p_n[\![P_n]\!]$:

- For each participant p_i, the associated P_i should be *consistent* with that obtained as projection of the global type. That is, the protocol specified through the global type can be more general than the process in the session, as formalized by a preorder on processes.
- The players of the global type are a subset of the participants $p_1, \ldots, p_n$ of the session. The converse is not required, so that, if a session is well-typed, then the session obtained adding participants with inactive processes is well-typed as well.

Whereas the tool is devoted to the implementation of the type system, hence of the syntactic definitions and judgments described so far, [4] also provides an *asynchronous operational semantics* for multiparty sessions, by means of a labelled transition system, and proves that the type system ensures the following properties of computations: deadlock-freedom (in every reachable state of computation, the session is either terminated or it can move); input lock-freedom (every component wishing to do an input will eventually do so); orphan-message-freedom (every message stored in the queue is eventually read).

3   Co-logic Programming

A limit of standard logic programming is that we cannot define predicates on non-well-founded structures, such as infinite lists. To overcome this, logic programming has been extended to support coinduction by *coinductive logic programming* [1,9,11], where terms are coinductively defined, that is, can be infinite, and predicates are coinductively defined as well. Possibly infinite terms are represented by finite sets of equations between finite terms. For instance, the equation $L = [1,2|L]$ represents the infinite list $[1,2,1,2,\ldots]$. On the other hand, the infinite list of odd numbers *cannot* be represented by a finite set of equations.

Moreover, standard SLD resolution is replaced by co-SLD resolution [1,11], which, roughly speaking, keeps trace of already encountered goals, called *coinductive hypotheses*, so that, when a goal is found the second time, it is considered successful.

A drawback of coinductive logic programming is that *all* predicates are interpreted coinductively, whereas in applications it is often the case that predicates to be interpreted inductively and coinductively should coexist. To overcome this issue, *co-logic programming* [10] marks predicates as either inductive or coinductive; however, no mutual recursion is allowed between an inductive and a coinductive predicate, that is, stratification is needed. Hence each layer can be interpreted as the least or greatest fixed point, respectively, of an inference system where the lower levels are assumed as axioms. This approach of marking predicates is supported by SWI-Prolog, the Prolog environment used for the implementation.

4   Query Language

Together with the implementation, we provide a high-level query language which can be used to easily check the judgments described in Sect. 2. A program in this language consists of *groups*, each one consisting of many *tests*. Both groups and tests have names. For instance, the program below consists in a single group, composed of two tests. In the first test, the global type and the processes are those of Example 1, hence all queries succeed. In the second test, the global type is that of Example 3, and the query not bounded G succeeds, indeed the global type is not bounded.

```
Test_Group[
Example_1{
Process P = q!L; q?L1; 0
Process Q = p!L1; p?L; 0
GlobalType G = p>q!L; q>p!L1; p>q?L; q>p?L1; End
Session S = p[P] | q[Q] | Empty
io-match G|Empty
bounded G
proj(G,q) ==   Q
wf G|Empty
S has type G|Empty
}

Example_3{
GlobalType G = p>q!
    {
    L1; p>q?L1; G,
    L2; p>q?L2; q>r!L; q>r?L; G
    }
not bounded G
}

]
```

Each test consists of a list of declarations, followed by a list of queries.

Declarations begin with a keyword for the kind of declared entity: `Process` for processes, `GlobalType` for global types, `Queue` for queues, and `Session` for sessions. The syntax for such entities closely follows that of Sect. 2, apart that we use the separator > to suggest the direction of the communication. The empty queue is represented by the constant `Empty`. The declarations can be mutually recursive. The tool performs a rudimentary typechecking, e.g., rejecting a program where a declared process is used as a queue.

Queries correspond to judgments described in Sect. 2. In particular:

- `io-match` G|M checks that the configuration type G|M is input/output matching
- `bounded` G checks that the global type G is bounded
- `proj(G,p) == P` checks that the projection of the global type G on p is P
- `exists-proj(G,p)` checks that the projection of the global type G on p is well-defined
- `exist-all-proj` G checks that all the projections of the global type G are well-defined
- `wf` G|M checks that the configuration type G|M is well-formed.
- `S has type` G|M checks that S is well-typed with respect to the configuration type G|M
- for each query, it is also possible to check that its negation holds by prepending `not`.

Again, the tool checks that entities are used in the queries accordingly to their declaration. For instance, in the typing query it is checked that the first argument is a session and the second argument is a configuration type.

The query language is parsed using ANTLR [7], generating a parsing tree which is used to obtain the Prolog code. Then, the tool executes the Prolog file directly using the Java `Runtime` standard library and its method `exec` to execute string commands in separate processes and, finally, the results are shown.

5   Prolog Implementation

We illustrate some fragments of Prolog code, chosen simple for space limits, yet providing the flavour of the kind of issues to be faced in the implementation. First of all we mention that global types, being coinductively defined, are implemented by (equations between) terms G of shape either `output_type(A,B,[L-G|LGs]))`, or `input_type(A,B,L,G))`, or **end**, where A, B are participants, L are labels, and L-G and LGs are pairs ⟨label, global type⟩ and lists of such pairs, respectively.

The first two are examples of cases where, to implement a coinductively defined judgment, it is not adequate to just use a coinductive predicate, but other strategies need to be used.

Consider the definition of `player(G,A)`, checking whether the participant `A` occurs as player in `G`. On an infinite (regular) global type, an inductive definition of `player` would not terminate in the negative case, while a coinductive definition would be not correct, since it would be successful, when finding a cycle (that is, the same global type), for an arbitrary argument. The solution is to define `player` as the negation of a predicate `not_player`.

```
player(G,A) :-
    \+not_player(G,A).

not_player(output_type(A,_,LGs), B):-
        B \= A,
        not_player_list(LGs, B).

not_player(input_type(_,B,_,G), A) :-
        A \= B,
        not_player(G,A).

not_player(end,_).
```

The predicate visits the global type and checks that at each node the participant argument is not a player. This predicate being coinductive, when a cycle is found the call succeeds, hence the predicate `player` fails, correctly, in the negative case. On the other hand, in the positive case (an argument which is a player) the predicate `not_player` finitely fails, hence the predicate `player` succeeds.

In other cases, a by-hand cycle detection mechanism is needed. An example is the definition of `players(G,As)`, computing the set of players `As` of `G`. On an infinite (regular) global type, again an inductive definition would not terminate. On the other hand, a coinductive definition would accept *all the supersets* of the players, implementing a slightly different concept. The solution is to define `players` using an additional parameter, the list `Gs` of already encountered global types, initially empty.

```
players(Gs,G,[]) :-
    member(G,Gs).

players(Gs,output_type(A,B,LGs),As) :-
    \+member(output_type(A,B,LGs),Gs),
    players_list([output_type(A,B,LGs)|Gs],LGs,Bs),
    union(A,Bs,As).

players(Gs,input_type(A,B,L,G),As) :-
    \+member(input_type(A,B,L,G),Gs),
    players([input_type(A,B,L,G)|Gs],G,Bs),
    union(B,Bs,As).

players(_,end,[]).
```

The predicate visits the global type, and, at each node, the current global type is added to the list if not present yet, otherwise a cycle is detected and the result is the empty set. At each step, the result is the union of the players of the subterms and of the current node; since, when a cycle is found, the result is only the empty set, the only solution is exactly the set of players, rather than all the supersets as in the coinductive case.

As more significant and involved examples, we describe the implementation of the boundedness check and of the projection judgment. This is interesting since it is not trivial to design a concrete algorithm from these abstract definitions.

Boundedness. Global types can be naturally seen as trees. We use ξ to denote a *path* in global type trees, that is, a possibly infinite sequence of communications $\mathsf{p\,q!}\lambda$ or $\mathsf{p\,q?}\lambda$. With ξ_n we represent the n-th communication in the path ξ, where $0 \leq n < x$ and $x \in \mathbf{N} \cup \{\omega\}$ is the length of ξ. With ϵ we denote the empty sequence and with $\cdot$ the concatenation of a finite sequence with a possibly infinite sequence. The function Paths gives the set of *paths* of global types, which are the greatest sets such that:

$$\mathsf{Paths}(\mathsf{pq!}\{\lambda_i.G_i\}_{i\in I}) = \bigcup_{i\in I}\{\mathsf{pq!}\lambda_i \cdot \xi \mid \xi \in \mathsf{Paths}(G_i)\}$$
$$\mathsf{Paths}(\mathsf{pq?}\lambda.G) = \{\mathsf{pq?}\lambda \cdot \xi \mid \xi \in \mathsf{Paths}(G)\}$$
$$\mathsf{Paths}(\mathsf{End}) = \{\epsilon\}$$

The definition of boundedness is based on the concept of *depth* of a player. Let G be a global type. For $\xi \in \mathsf{Paths}(G)$, set $\mathsf{depth}(\xi, \mathsf{p}) = \inf\{n \mid \mathsf{play}(\xi_n) = \mathsf{p}\}$, and define $\mathsf{depth}(G, \mathsf{p})$, the *depth* of p in G, as follows:

$$\mathsf{depth}(G, \mathsf{p}) = \begin{cases} 1 + \sup\{\mathsf{depth}(\xi, \mathsf{p}) \mid \xi \in G\} & \mathsf{p} \in \mathsf{players}(G) \\ 0 & \text{otherwise} \end{cases}$$

Note that, if p is a player of G, but it does not occur as player in some path ξ of G (that is, $\mathsf{p} \neq \mathsf{play}(\xi_n)$ for all $n \in \mathbf{N}$), then $\mathsf{depth}(\xi, \mathsf{p}) = \inf \emptyset = \infty$, modelling the fact that p may wait forever.

A global type G is *bounded* if $\mathsf{depth}(G', \mathsf{p})$ is finite for all $\mathsf{p} \in \mathsf{players}(G)$ and all types G' which occur in G.

This check is implemented by the predicate **bounded** below.

```
bounded(G) :-
    players(G,As),
    bounded_list(G,As).

bounded_list(G,[A]) :-
        all_finite_depth(G,A).

bounded_list(G,[A|As]) :-
        all_finite_depth(G,A),
        bounded_list(G,As).
```

The set of players of the global type is computed, and then, for each player, it is checked that its depth in each subterm of the global type is finite, by the predicate `all_finite_depth`, described below.

In the abstract definition given above, the depth of a player in G is obtained by computing its depth in each of the paths of G. To enforce boundedness in an algorithmic way, in the implementation we take a different approach, by defining the predicate `finite_depth` which holds if a participant has finite depth in a global type. That is, if the participant is a player, then it occurs as player in each path of the given global type. Then, we define the predicate `all_finite_depth` which checks that `finite_depth` holds for each subterm of the given type.

```
finite_depth(G,A,_) :-
        not_player(G,A).

finite_depth(output_type(A,_,_),A,_).

finite_depth(input_type(_,A,_,_),A,_).

finite_depth(output_type(A,B,LGs),C,G_found) :-
        \+member(output_type(A,B,LGs),G_found),
        finite_depth_list(LGs,C,[output_type(A,B,LGs)|G_found]).

finite_depth(input_type(A,B,_,G),C,G_found) :-
        \+member(input_type(A,B,_,G),G_found),
        finite_depth(G,C,[input_type(A,B,_,G)|G_found]).
```

In the first clause, if the participant is not a player of the global type, then the depth is 0, so it is finite.

In the second and third clause, if the participant is a player in the root node, then the depth is 1, so it is finite. Otherwise, we have to check that the participant is a player for all the paths starting from the children nodes. To avoid non-termination in this check, we use a by-hand cycle detection mechanism, implemented with the argument `G_found`. This argument is the list of already encountered global types, which grows at each recursive call. When the same global type is encountered twice, that is, is already in `G_found`, the goal is rejected, because it means that following that path the participant has not been found as a player, so its depth is infinite.

Note the difference between `player(G,A)`, holding if A occurs as player in some path, and `finite_depth(G,A,[])`, holding if A occurs as player in each path (or is not a player at all). The negation of the former is a universal property (A never occurs as a player), which can be defined by a coinductive predicate, namely, `not_player(G,A)`, so to rely on the built-in cycle detection mechanism offered by SWI-Prolog. The negation of the latter is an existential property (A is a player, and it does not occur in some path) which cannot be defined by a coinductive predicate. The solution is to use a by-hand cycle detection mechanism as described above.

The predicate `finite_depth_list`, not reported, is the lifting to lists of pairs label-global type of the predicate.

Finally, note that there is no clause for the inactive process because this case is covered by the first clause.

The above predicate is applied to all the sub-terms of a global type by the predicate `all_finite_depth`.

```
all_finite_depth(output_type(A,B,LGs),C) :-
            finite_depth(output_type(A,B,LGs),C,[]),
            all_finite_depth_list(LGs,C).

all_finite_depth(input_type(A,B,Lambda,G),C) :-
            finite_depth(input_type(A,B,Lambda,G),C,[]),
            all_finite_depth(G,C).

all_finite_depth(end,_).
```

This predicate is declared coinductive, because in this case when the goal is encountered twice it must be accepted. The predicate `all_finite_depth_list`, not reported, is the lifting to lists of pairs label-global type of the predicate.

$$\mathcal{C} ::= []_n \quad | \quad \mathsf{p}?\{\lambda_i.\mathcal{C}_i\}_{i\in I} \quad | \quad \mathsf{p}!\{\lambda_i.\mathcal{C}_i\}_{i\in I} \quad | \quad \mathsf{P} \qquad \text{where } I \neq \emptyset,\ \lambda_j \neq \lambda_h \text{ for } j \neq h$$

$$[\text{Out-Rcv}] \quad \frac{\mathsf{G}_i \lceil \mathsf{q} \mapsto \mathcal{C}[\mathsf{p}?\lambda_i.\mathsf{P}_{i,j}]_{j\in J} \ \forall i \in I}{(\mathsf{pq}!\{\lambda_i.\mathsf{G}_i\}_{i\in I}) \lceil \mathsf{q} \mapsto \mathcal{C}[\mathsf{p}?\{\lambda_i.\mathsf{P}_{i,j}\}_{i\in I}]_{j\in J}} \quad \mathsf{q} \in \mathsf{play}(\mathsf{G}_i)\ i \in I$$

Fig. 1. Projection: contexts and example of rule

Projection. The definition of projection $\mathsf{G} \lceil \mathsf{q} \mapsto \mathsf{P}$ uses process contexts with an arbitrary number of holes indexed with natural numbers, where each hole has a different index. Given a context $\mathcal{C}$ with holes indexed in J, we denote by $\mathcal{C}[\mathsf{P}_j]_{j\in J}$ the process obtained by filling the hole indexed by j in P_j, for all $j \in J$. In Fig. 1 we report the definition of contexts and one rule, namely, the one defining the projection of an output choice on the receiver q, in the case it is a player in the global type (the projection on a non-player is always the inactive process).

The rule states that the projection is well-defined if the projections on q of the branches G_i, for $i \in I$, give processes which can be consistently combined to provide the resulting projection. More precisely, they have a common structure, modelled by a multi-hole context $\mathcal{C}$, where, for each hole $j \in J$, this is filled by a different process subterm in the projection of each branch. The process filling the j-th hole of the projection of branch i must start with an input from p and label λ_i. In this way, the processes in the j-th holes of all branches can be combined in an external choice, which is used to fill the context in the resulting projection.

Note that the rule just assumes the *existence* of context $\mathcal{C}$, whereas in the implementation this context, if any, should be *constructed*. We show below how this is achieved, in a simplified version, yet illustrating all the key features of real code:

```
projection(output_type(A,B,[L1-G1,L2-G2|LGs]),B,P) :-
      player(output_type(A,B,[L1-G1,L2-G2|LGs]),B),
      projection_list([L1-G1,L2-G2|LGs],B,[P1,P2|Ps]),
      build_context(P1,P2,A,L1,L2,Context),
      pairs_keys(LGs,Ls),
      check_each_process(Context,A,[L1,L2|Ls],
                         [P1,P2|Ps],Fillings),
      build_process_result(Context,Fillings,A,P).
```

This clause models the case when the output choice has two or more branches; the case of only one branch is handled by an ad-hoc clause that does not build any context, because this is not necessary. After checking that the participant B is a player in the global type, the predicate projection_list computes the projections on B of all the subterms. Then, the predicate build_context, declared as coinductive, is used to build the context $\mathcal{C}$. This predicate visits at the same time the processes P1 and P2 obtained as projection of the first two branches, checking that they are equal node by node, and reporting this common structure in Context, until one among these three conditions occurs:

- Both processes are inactive.
- Both are an input node receiving from A the corresponding label (L1 and L2, respectively), as explained above.
- Both are encountered for a second time.

In the first case the resulting context is the inactive process. In the second case the result is a hole context, since holes model the different process subterms after the input. In the third case, the query is successful, as it happens in a coinductive predicate, hence the context result turns out to be cyclic as well. After building the context, the predicate pairs_keys obtains the list of the branch labels. Then, the predicate check_each_process checks that all the processes computed as projections of the subterms can be obtained by filling the holes in the context, producing Fillings, a list with an element for each branch $i \in I$, which is in turn a list with an element $\lambda_i.P_{i,j}$ for each hole $j \in J$. Finally, the predicate build_process_result builds the final process result, filling the context as explained above.

6   Conclusion

The work described in this paper is an implementation in co-logic programming of a novel formulation of global types for asynchronous session, where asynchrony is expressed at the level of the type system. The tool has been developed in parallel with the theoretical investigation, thus it has been very useful to check the proposed definitions, finding in some cases subtle bugs. The main challenge has been to solve termination problems, naturally arising since we had to deal with infinite, yet regular, structures. Our solutions, only illustrated on simple examples in this short paper, are based on coinductive techniques mixed with inductive ones, also employing in some cases user-defined cycle detection mechanisms.

The tool could be improved in many directions. First of all, the current implementation is a prototype, which should be refined and equipped with a suitable user interface to become more usable. Currently, we only allow in the user language queries with a yes/no answer. Queries computing a result, e.g., the projection of a global type on a participant, can be easily performed at the Prolog level, but the tool still lacks a reverse translation to show the user language version of the Prolog answer. Finally, another direction could be a more efficient implementation, for example using a language such as C++.

Acknowledgements. We thank all the anonymous referees for their careful reading and useful comments, which helped us improve the paper. We are also grateful to Paola Giannini and Elena Zucca for their many suggestions to make the presentation clearer.

References

1. Ancona, D., Dovier, A.: A theoretical perspective of coinductive logic programming. Fund. Inform. **140**(3–4), 221–246 (2015). https://doi.org/10.3233/FI-2015-1252
2. Bettini, L., Coppo, M., D'Antoni, L., De Luca, M., Dezani-Ciancaglini, M., Yoshida, N.: Global progress in dynamically interleaved multiparty sessions. In: van Breugel, F., Chechik, M. (eds.) CONCUR 2008. LNCS, vol. 5201, pp. 418–433. Springer, Heidelberg (2008). https://doi.org/10.1007/978-3-540-85361-9_33
3. Castellani, I., Dezani-Ciancaglini, M., Giannini, P.: Global types and event structure semantics for asynchronous multiparty sessions. CoRR abs/2102.00865 (2021). https://arxiv.org/abs/2102.00865
4. Dagnino, F., Giannini, P., Dezani-Ciancaglini, M.: Deconfined global types for asynchronous sessions. In: Damiani, F., Dardha, O. (eds.) COORDINATION 2021. LNCS, vol. 12717, pp. 41–60. Springer, Cham (2021)
5. Honda, K., Yoshida, N., Carbone, M.: Multiparty asynchronous session types. In: Necula, G.C., Wadler, P. (eds.) ACM Symposium on Principles of Programming Languages, POPL 2006, pp. 273–284. ACM Press (2008). https://doi.org/10.1145/1328438.1328472
6. Honda, K., Yoshida, N., Carbone, M.: Multiparty asynchronous session types. J. ACM **63**(1), 9:1–9:67 (2016). https://doi.org/10.1145/2827695
7. Parr, T.: The Definitive ANTLR 4 Reference. Pragmatic Bookshelf (2013)
8. Severi, P., Dezani-Ciancaglini, M.: Observational equivalence for multiparty sessions. Fund. Inform. **170**(1–3), 267–305 (2019). https://doi.org/10.3233/FI-2019-1863
9. Simon, L.: Extending logic programming with coinduction. Ph.D. thesis, University of Texas at Dallas (2006)
10. Simon, L., Bansal, A., Mallya, A., Gupta, G.: Co-logic programming: extending logic programming with coinduction. In: Arge, L., Cachin, C., Jurdziński, T., Tarlecki, A. (eds.) ICALP 2007. LNCS, vol. 4596, pp. 472–483. Springer, Heidelberg (2007). https://doi.org/10.1007/978-3-540-73420-8_42
11. Simon, L., Mallya, A., Bansal, A., Gupta, G.: Coinductive logic programming. In: Etalle, S., Truszczyński, M. (eds.) ICLP 2006. LNCS, vol. 4079, pp. 330–345. Springer, Heidelberg (2006). https://doi.org/10.1007/11799573_25
12. Wielemaker, J., Schrijvers, T., Triska, M., Lager, T.: SWI-prolog. Theory Pract. Logic Program. **12**(1–2), 67–96 (2012)

Large-Scale Decentalised Systems

Tuple-Based Coordination in Large-Scale Situated Systems

Roberto Casadei[1]([✉])(ID), Mirko Viroli[1](ID), Alessandro Ricci[1](ID),
and Giorgio Audrito[2](ID)

[1] Alma Mater Studiorum–Università di Bologna, Cesena, Italy
{roby.casadei,mirko.viroli,a.ricci}@unibo.it
[2] Università di Torino, Turin, Italy
giorgio.audrito@unibo.it

Abstract. *Space* and *time* are key elements for many computer-based systems and often elevated to first-class abstractions. In tuple-based coordination, Linda primitives have been independently extended with space (with tuples and queries spanning spatial regions) or time information (mostly for tuple scoping). However, recent works in collective adaptive systems and aggregate computing show that space and time can naturally be considered as two intertwined facets of a common coordination abstraction for situated distributed systems. Accordingly, we introduce the *Spatiotemporal Tuples* model, a natural adaptation of Linda model for physically deployed large-scale networks. Unlike prior research, spatiotemporal properties – expressing where and when a tuple should range and has to be deposited/retrieved – naturally turn into specifications of collective adaptive processes, to be carried on in cooperation by the devices filling the computational environment, and sustaining tuple operations in a resilient way, possibly even in mobile and faulty environments. Additionally, the model promotes decentralised implementations where tuples actually reside where they are issued, which is good for supporting peer-to-peer and mobile ad-hoc networks as well as privacy. In this paper, we *(i)* present and formalise the Spatiotemporal Tuples model, based on the unifying notion of computational space-time structure, *(ii)* provide an implementation in the ScaFi aggregate computing framework, turning tuple operations into aggregate processes, and finally *(iii)* provide evaluation through simulation and a rescue case study.

Keywords: tuple-based coordination · spatial tuples ·
self-organisation · aggregate computing · SCAFI

1 Introduction

Space and time are fundamental aspects of our reality. *Space*, logical or physical, plays a fundamental role for many computer-based systems. This has been recognised, e.g., in the Dagstuhl seminar on space-oriented computation [20], where

© IFIP International Federation for Information Processing 2021
Published by Springer Nature Switzerland AG 2021
F. Damiani and O. Dardha (Eds.): COORDINATION 2021, LNCS 12717, pp. 149–167, 2021.
https://doi.org/10.1007/978-3-030-78142-2_10

(i) coping with space for computational efficiency, *(ii) embedding in space*, and *(iii) representing space* are shown to be dimensions characterising a wide range of computing applications. Accordingly, several research fields have elevated space to a first-class abstraction [7]. A notable example in the coordination field, and specifically in tuple-space coordination [21], is the *Spatial Tuples* model [30], where tuples are situated in regions of space and Linda coordination primitives also depend on the spatial situation of the coordinating agents. Dually, *time* has also been investigated as an explicit abstraction, leading to notions of time for tuple-based systems [25,26]. However, recent works in collective adaptive systems and field-based coordination/aggregate computing [6,8,32] show that space and time can naturally be considered as intertwined facets of a common coordination abstraction for situated distributed systems.

Therefore, in this paper we introduce a tuple-based coordination model that considers space and time in combined form. Differently from prior research, spatiotemporal properties – expressing where and when a tuple should range and has to be deposited/retrieved – naturally turn into specifications of collective adaptive processes, to be carried on in cooperation by the devices filling the computational environment, and sustaining tuple operations in a resilient way even in mobile and faulty environments. Most specifically, an out creates a tuple that spreads in a dynamically changing region of space, rd similarly spreads a query that unblocks the initiator if a match is found in the intersection of a tuple region, and finally in performs like rd but additionally disables/removes the tuple, making it inaccessible to other queries. Therefore, our contribution is threefold[1]:

1. we present the *Spatiotemporal Tuples model*, in terms of a declarative semantics of coherent tuple space evolution, and a compliant protocol solution by a set of processes running on a computational space-time structure;
2. we describe an implementation in the ScaFi *aggregate computing* toolkit [13,14], where tuple operations and spatiotemporal properties are expressed as aggregate processes [15] creating so-called *computational fields*; and
3. we evaluate model and implementation by means of simulation.

A major merit of the overall approach is that it fosters implementations that are inherently suitable to different kinds of system deployments, ranging from fully peer-to-peer systems to centralised, cloud-based architectures.

The paper is organised as follows. Section 2 provides background and related work in the area of tuple-based and space-based coordination. Section 3 describes the Spatiotemporal Tuple model. Section 4 describes an implementation of the model in terms of aggregate processes in SCAFI. Section 5 provides evaluation. Finally, Sect. 6 provides conclusion and future work.

---

[1] This work extends the workshop paper in [17] with formalisation, full implementation, and evaluation.

2   Background and Related Work

Tuple-based coordination is a coordination paradigm where a collection of *processes* coordinate by reading and writing *tuples* (ordered groups of values) on a *shared tuple space* [21]. Tuple-based coordination logic can be expressed in a language, such as the progenitor *Linda* [21], specifying process evolution in terms of operations on tuples (e.g., write, read, removal). Tuple-based coordination has been subject of extensive research, giving rise to several variants, extensions, and implementations. In particular, in distributed and pervasive computing scenarios, issues with the notion of a centralised tuple space tend to promote alternative models with several local tuple spaces [22]. In the following literature review, we survey the main contributions focussing on spatiotemporally situated systems.

2.1   Tuple-Based Coordination in Pervasive Systems and Space(-Time)

Works have been proposed in the literature implementing tuple-based coordination for peer-to-peer (P2P) and mobile ad-hoc networks (MANETs) [23]. In these scenarios, challenges and opportunities include mobility, dynamicity, locality, openness. Such features are often found in nature-inspired systems (cf. *SwarmLinda* [31]) and can be exploited to build scalable systems exhibiting *collective intelligence* [16]. These challenges require proper middleware support and, sometimes, model and language extensions to deal with specific aspects including situatedness and mobility. When a device is physically situated, it also acts as a representative of a space-time region, providing a means for representing, measuring, computing space—as exploited by *spatial computing* approaches [7].

$\sigma\tau$-*Linda* [33] is an approach where Linda operations can be combined with time- and network-oriented operations. Example constructs include *neigh* (to spread an operation to the neighbourhood), *next* (to post-pone an operation to the next program evaluation), and *finally* (to run an operation after a barrier of other operations). A further extension proposed by $\sigma\tau$-Linda is spatiotemporally limited tuple operations, which this paper develops in a principled way.

LIME [27] provides a support for Linda in MANETs. It distinguishes between *logical* and *physical* mobility of agents and hosts, to model both component situation as well as topology change. Agents own a tuple space locally, and group with other co-located and neighbour-host agents to consolidate tuple spaces, supporting access to the overall tuple space of the entire group by a *transient sharing* mechanism. In this paper, we also leverage a notion of "group", to mean the set of devices cooperating to support a space-time tuple operation.

The *TOTA* approach [24] views tuples as dynamic elements, which can be copied and change both their location and shape. Specifically, *scope*, *transformation*, and *maintenance* rules can be specified to define and control how tuples are to be propagated in a network, and how these must evolve and react to environmental events along the path. In this paper, we leverage similar ideas to propagate tuple *operations* (rather than tuples). The idea in TOTA that tuples automatically propagate to neighbours is also at the basis of the approach of this paper, where aggregate processes deal with propagation control (cf. Sect. 4.1).

In *GeoLinda* [28], tuples spaces are distributed and *geometry-aware*: both tuples and reading operations have a *volume* (spatial extension). They call the volume of a tuple its *shape*, and the volume of a reading operation its *addressing shape*. Shapes can take various geometric forms (spheres, cones, etc.) and are expressed relatively to a device's location and orientation. In this paper, we leverage the same idea of giving tuple operations a space-time extension, and also define a way to express them in spatiotemporally situated networks of devices.

2.2 Spatial Tuples

Spatial Tuples [30] is a coordination model combining tuple-based with space-based coordination. Its idea is to decorate tuples with spatial information, in order to situate them to some *point in space* or some *spatial region* (in which case, the tuple is said to have a *spatial extension*). The Spatial Tuples approach comprises multiple *languages* for working with spatial tuples: a *communication language* is used to express tuples and tuple templates (for matching), a *space description language* is used to express spatial information, and a *coordination language* is used for process interaction and evolution. The latter consists of the following main spatial primitives [30]:

- out(t @ r)—for situating a tuple t to a spatial location or region r.
- rd(tt @ r)—for blocking until a tuple t matching template tt and intersecting region r is read (with non-deterministic choice).
- in(tt @ r)—for blocking until a tuple t matching template tt and intersecting region r is removed (with non-deterministic choice).

The space description language is application- or domain-specific and may allow expressing geographic locations and regions. The situation of a tuple, however, does not need to be constant. For instance, a tuple can be attached to another situated component, and hence its position would be defined *indirectly*. Given a component id, t @ id would express that tuple t is *bound* to id. Such a notion of *binding* is especially relevant in scenarios with *mobility*. Locations and bindings could also be specified implicitly:

- t @ here: situates tuple t at the current position of the running component;
- t @ me: the location of tuple t is bound to that of the running component.

The Spatial Tuples approach fosters space-oriented coordination through mechanisms for *situated/stigmergic communication*, where processes deposit and sense data at specific locations, and *spatial synchronisation*, where the actions multiple interacting processes are ordered depending on their spatial situation.

In Spatial Tuples, the key idea is to use spatial information to annotate and retrieve tuples. There are parallelisms with *attribute-based* coordination [1], whereby attributes are used to form and let ensembles interact. In this work, however, we consider spatial information not just as a mere annotation to tuples or components but as a specification driving and evolving spatiotemporally situated computational processes.

3   A Model for Spatiotemporal Tuple-Based Coordination

3.1   Requirements

The Spatiotemporal Tuples model is designed to address the following concerns:

- **Space.** The model should capture situations in space, and provide suitable spatial abstractions to capture diverse situations. Namely, we mean to provide a *computational* notion of space, where space locations are associated with computational nodes, and proximity of locations matches the ability of a device to directly perceive its context, there including message reception.
- **Time.** The model should dually capture temporal situations, while abstracting over the notion of time, and hence of system evolution. Also, since we expressly target fully distributed systems, for which no general notion of global time exists [19], the model should provide the expressiveness to specify what/how notions of local time can be used and propagated. Menezes et al. [25] discuss the issues with using external notions of time in Linda-based systems, and propose to measure time locally to observers of fadeable tuples.
- **Consistency.** The model should adhere to the general Linda semantics, namely, ensuring safe interaction of primitives out/rd/in as formalised in [11]. Unfortunately, in distributed settings, the *CAP theorem* [10] enters the picture, asserting that you may pick only two among the three properties: consistency, availability, and partition tolerance. This is an issue when implementing atomic consumption of tuples (for in operation). However, designers can leverage the many nuances in these properties and combinations.
- **Heterogeneous deployments.** The model should provide for a direct implementation for different kinds of underlying platforms, such as MANETs, P2P networks, client/server, and cloud-based architectures. Namely, it should be sufficiently *general* to capture diverse settings, also considering the architectures and constraints of modern distributed systems.

3.2   Computational Space-Time Model

Defining a spatiotemporal model for Linda primitives requires a suitable underlying notion of computability, since there is need of tracking information propagation in space and time. Thus, we base our model on the notion of *space-time computability* of [2], which in turn founds on the *event structure* framework [34]. In this section, we recall this framework, tailored for the needs of this paper.

Definition 1 (Augmented Event Structure [2]). *An augmented event structure is a quadruple* $\mathbf{E} = \langle E, \leadsto, d, s \rangle$ *where E is a countable set of events, $\leadsto \subseteq E \times E$ is a messaging relation, $d : E \to \Delta$ is a mapping from events to the devices where they happened, $s : E \to S$ is a mapping from events to sensors status (for any choice of a representation of sensors status $\sigma \in S$), such that:*

- *for any $\delta \in \Delta$, the set of events $E_\delta = \{\epsilon \in E \mid d(\epsilon) = \delta\}$ forms a sequence of chains, i.e., there are no distinct $\epsilon, \epsilon_1, \epsilon_2 \in E_\delta$ such that either $\epsilon \leadsto \epsilon_i$ for $i = 1, 2$ or $\epsilon_i \leadsto \epsilon$ for $i = 1, 2$,*

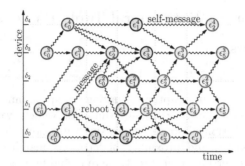

Fig. 1. An augmented event structure **E**. It depicts events (circle nodes), messaging relations (curly arrows), devices $\delta_0, ..., \delta_4$ (y-axis) and each circle node is labelled with the depicted event of **E**. Colours denote the causal relation w.r.t. the reference event ϵ_1^2 (doubly-circled, blue), partitioning events into causal past (red), causal future (green) and concurrent (non-ordered, in black). (Color figure online)

- *the transitive closure of* $\rightsquigarrow$ *forms an irreflexive partial order* $< \subseteq E \times E$, *called* causality relation,
- *the set* $X_\epsilon = \{\epsilon' \in E \mid \epsilon' < \epsilon\} \cup \{\epsilon' \in E \mid \epsilon \rightsquigarrow \epsilon'\}$ *is finite for all* ϵ *(i.e.,* $\rightsquigarrow$ *and* $<$ *are locally finite).*

We say that event ϵ' *is a* supplier *of event* ϵ *iff* $\epsilon' \rightsquigarrow \epsilon$.

The intuition of this definition is that the messaging relation between events on the same device represents one-step passage of time, while the messaging relation between events on different devices represents proximity in space (and ability to directly interact). Figure 1 depicts a sample augmented event structure $\mathbf{E} = \langle E, \rightsquigarrow, d, s \rangle$ where $\mathbf{E} = \{\epsilon_0^0, ..., \epsilon_4^0, \epsilon_0^1, ..., \epsilon_5^1, \epsilon_0^2, ..., \epsilon_4^2, \epsilon_0^3, ..., \epsilon_3^3, \epsilon_0^4, ..., \epsilon_5^4\}$ consists of 24 events such that $d(\epsilon_j^i) = \delta_i$.

In this model, spatio-temporal tuple *regions* are definable subsets of the augmented event structure with a unique originating event.

Definition 2 (Spatio-temporal Region). *Let* $\mathbf{E} = \langle E, \rightsquigarrow, d, s \rangle$ *be an augmented event structure. A* spatio-temporal region $\mathbf{r}$ *is a definable[2] predicate associating a Boolean value* $\mathbf{r}(\epsilon, \epsilon') \in \{\top, \bot\}$ *to every pair of events* $\epsilon, \epsilon' \in \mathbf{E}$, *such that* $\mathbf{r}(\epsilon, \epsilon') = \top$ *implies that* $\epsilon \leq \epsilon'$.

We write $\mathbf{r}_\epsilon = \{\epsilon' \mid \mathbf{r}(\epsilon, \epsilon') = \top\} \subseteq E$ *for the set of events that belong to the spatio-temporal region described by* $\mathbf{r}$ *and originating from* ϵ. *We say such a set is* connected *if for every* $\epsilon' \in \mathbf{r}_\epsilon$ *with* $\epsilon' \neq \epsilon$, *there exists an* $\epsilon'' \in \mathbf{r}_\epsilon$ *such that* $\epsilon'' \rightsquigarrow \epsilon'$. *We say predicate* $\mathbf{r}$ *is* connected *if* $\mathbf{r}_\epsilon$ *is connected for every* $\epsilon \in E$.

---

[2] We do not give an explicit syntax for spatio-temporal regions, in order to cover applications with any such syntax. *Definable* corresponds to space-time computable [2], thus requiring the existence of a computational procedure deciding whether the predicate $\mathbf{r}(\epsilon, \epsilon')$ holds in some event ϵ' using only information in the past of ϵ'.

In the definition above, ϵ can be understood as the event originating the region, and ϵ' as another event which is being checked for belonging to the region. Connected regions can be used to guide the local propagation of a spatial process, which can expand from the originating event to neighbours filtering out those outside of the region, and reach every event in the region this way. Propagation in non-connected regions $\mathbf{r}'$ needs to be handled by providing a connected region $\mathbf{r}$ to guide the propagation of the spatial process, such that $\mathbf{r}'_\epsilon \subset \mathbf{r}_\epsilon$, making the process inactive in events outside of $\mathbf{r}'$. As a paradigmatic example, consider the following two region predicates:

– $\mathtt{me}_k$, which holds on future events within k hops of the originating device:
  $\mathtt{me}_k(\epsilon, \epsilon') \Leftrightarrow \exists \epsilon_0 \ldots \epsilon_k \in E.\; d(\epsilon) = d(\epsilon_0) \;\wedge\; \epsilon \leq \epsilon_0 \rightsquigarrow \ldots \rightsquigarrow \epsilon_k = \epsilon';$
– $\mathtt{here}_k$, which holds on future events within k hops of the originating *location*:
  $\mathtt{here}_k(\epsilon, \epsilon') \Leftrightarrow \exists \epsilon_0 \ldots \epsilon_k \in E.\; \ell(\epsilon) = \ell(\epsilon_0) \;\wedge\; \epsilon \leq \epsilon_0 \rightsquigarrow \ldots \rightsquigarrow \epsilon_k = \epsilon'$, where $\ell : E \rightarrow \mathcal{L}$ is a given map associating a location (from a finite set of locations $\mathcal{L}$) to each event. Notice that multiple devices may be simultaneously in the same location (unlike the $\mathtt{me}$ region).

We remark that the given theory can be applied to any other definable regions.

3.3 Specifications for Spatio-Temporal Tuple Operators

To provide a formalisation of spatio-temporal tuple operations, we specify what an acceptable behaviour is for them, by mirroring the traditional non-deterministic semantics of Linda in a distributed "event structures" setting. This effectively constitutes a declarative semantics of the spatio-temporal tuples language: a semantics at a denotational level is outlined in Sect. 3.4, while a concrete operational implementation is given in Sect. 4.2. To state the specification, we first need to define a notion of *tuple space evolution*, which is ultimately built from the following grammar of processes.

Definition 3 (Extended Spatio-temporal Process). *We define spatio-temporal processes P and extended spatio-temporal processes Q according to the following grammar:*

$$P ::= \mathtt{out}^\tau(\mathtt{t} \;@\; \mathtt{r}) \mid \mathtt{in}^\tau(\mathtt{tt} \;@\; \mathtt{r}).P \mid \mathtt{rd}^\tau(\mathtt{tt} \;@\; \mathtt{r}).P$$
$$Q ::= P \mid \mathtt{got}^{\tau_o, \tau_i}$$

where $\mathtt{t}$ *are tuples,* $\mathtt{tt}$ *tuple templates,* $\mathtt{r}$ *regions,* τ *unique identifiers.*

In this grammar, we avoided an explicit mention to classic process operators (parallel and non-deterministic composition, replication, etc.), as their treatment is orthogonal to the scope of this paper. This grammar follows closely that in Sect. 2.2, with few notable differences. First, every $\mathtt{out}$, $\mathtt{in}$ and $\mathtt{rd}$ construct is marked with a unique identifier τ, discriminating every process from every other. Second, inert $\mathtt{got}$ processes are introduced in Q to mark the accesses of tuples from the distributed space, issued in the events when agreement is first reached about the matching of the out tuple with a corresponding in or rd process. As we shall see in the following definition, these agreement events must necessarily follow matching events (belonging to the intersection of the regions of the corresponding out and in/rd processes) and precede the continuation of the in/rd processes. These inert processes are of the form got^{τ_o,τ_i} where τ_o is the unique identifier of the out process introducing the tuple, and τ_i is the unique identifier of the in or rd process accessing (and possibly removing) that tuple. Notice that the got processes are necessary for the formal definition of which matches are occurring in a computation. This information cannot be uniquely reconstructed from the continuations alone: indeed, the same continuation P may arise from reading/accessing (possibly) different tuples by different parent processes.

In the remainder of this paper, we write $name(P)$ for the τ first occurring in P and write $name(got^{\tau_o,\tau_i}) = (\tau_o, \tau_i)$. We also write $kind(P)$ for the construct first occurring in P (out, in or rd).

Definition 4 (Tuple Space Evolution). *Let* $\mathbf{E} = \langle E, \rightsquigarrow, d, s \rangle$ *be an augmented event structure, and let* Q *be the set of extended spatio-temporal processes according to Definition 3. A tuple space evolution is a function* $TS : E \to Q^*$ *associating a finite set of processes* $TS(\epsilon) = \{Q_1, \ldots, Q_n\}$ *to each event* ϵ.

The following definition of a consistent tuple space evolution thus provides a specification of acceptable behaviours for spatio-temporal tuple processes.

Definition 5 (Coherent Tuple Space Evolution). *Let* $TS : E \to Q^*$ *be a tuple space evolution on* $\mathbf{E} = \langle E, \rightsquigarrow, d, s \rangle$ *and* Q. *We say that* TS *is coherent if it respects the following properties for any* $\epsilon_x \in E$ *where* $x = 1, 2, 3, g, i, o$.

1. **Identifier uniqueness:** *given* $Q_1 \in TS(\epsilon_1)$ *and* $Q_2 \in TS(\epsilon_2)$, *if* $name(Q_1) = name(Q_2)$, *then* $\epsilon_1 = \epsilon_2$ *and* $Q_1 = Q_2$. *Given an identifier* τ, *we write* $proc(\tau)$ *for the unique* P *appearing in* TS *such that* $name(P) = \tau$.
2. **Continuation markers:** *given* $Q_1 = op^{\tau_i}(\text{tt } @ \text{ r}).P \in TS(\epsilon_1)$ *and* $Q_2 \in TS(\epsilon_3)$ *such that* $name(P) = name(Q_2)$, *then there is* τ_o *such that* $got^{\tau_o,\tau_i} \in TS(\epsilon_2)$ *where* $\epsilon_1 \leq \epsilon_2 \leq \epsilon_3$.
3. **Consistency:** *if* $got^{\tau_o,\tau_i} \in TS(\epsilon_g)$, *then:*
   - *there exist* $P_x = proc(\tau_x) \in TS(\epsilon_x)$ *for* $x \in i, o$;
   - $P_i = op^{\tau_i}(\text{tt } @ \text{ r}_i).P'$ *with* $op \in \{in, rd\}$ *and* $P_o = out^{\tau_o}(\text{t } @ \text{ r}_o)$;
   - *there is* $\epsilon' \leq \epsilon_g$ *in* E *such that* $\mathbf{r}_i(\epsilon_i, \epsilon')$ *and* $\mathbf{r}_o(\epsilon_o, \epsilon')$ *both hold;*
   - *there exists a substitution* σ *such that* $\text{tt}[\sigma] = \text{t}$;
   - *for every* $got^{\tau_o,\tau'} \in TS(\epsilon')$ *with any* $\epsilon' \leq \epsilon_g$ *in* E, $kind(proc(\tau')) = rd$.
4. **Atomicity:** *if* got^{τ_o,τ_i} *and* got^{τ_o,τ'_i} *both appear in* TS *and* $kind(proc(\tau_i)) = kind(proc(\tau'_i)) = in$, *then* $\tau_i = \tau'_i$.

The above properties state that (1) operation identifiers are globally unique; (2) a got process always exists between a rd/in request and it is unblocking; (3) a rd/in unblocks if there is a properly intersecting (in space-time and by tuple match) tuple (region); and finally (4) no pair of in can consume the same tuple.

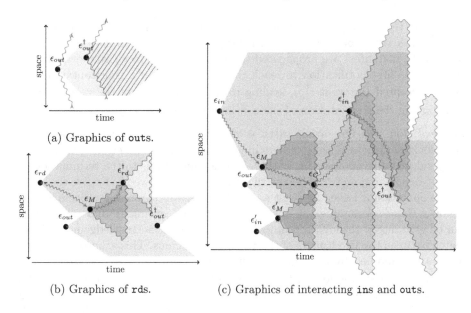

(a) Graphics of outs.

(b) Graphics of rds.

(c) Graphics of interacting ins and outs.

Fig. 2. Graphics illustrating the spatiotemporal tuple operations. (Color figure online)

3.4   Spatiotemporal Tuple-Based Coordination

Note that the declarative specification of coherent tuple space evolutions just introduced does not hint at which underlying protocol may be used to respect it. Here, we propose a sample such protocol, via a high-level denotational description (i.e., at a global event structure level instead of a local interaction level) of the spatial processes that are created and propagated by each P, and how they interact together. This protocol assumes that every region r is equipped with *leader* predicate $lead^r(\epsilon, \epsilon')$ which is satisfied for a set of events which is a subset of the region $lead^r_\epsilon \subseteq r_\epsilon$ and consists of a single chain of events: $lead^r_\epsilon = \{\epsilon, \epsilon_1, \ldots, \epsilon_n\}$ where $\epsilon \rightsquigarrow \epsilon_1 \rightsquigarrow \ldots \rightsquigarrow \epsilon_n$.

Write (Fig. 2a). Operation out(t @ r) in an event ϵ_{out} emits tuple t to spatiotemporal region r, corresponding to the set of events $r_{\epsilon_{out}}$. The spatio-temporal extension of the emitted tuple is bounded to region r (light and dark areas together), which is a subset of the future event cone of ϵ_{out} (marked by the wiggled lines coming out from it). The actual region where a tuple is available may be smaller if a matching in operation occurs: tuple removal in event $\epsilon^\dagger_{out}$ results in removing the future event cone of $\epsilon^\dagger_{out}$ (darker area) from the availability region (lighter area). This behaviour can be implemented through a simple broadcasting process bounded to region r.

Read (Fig. 2b). Operation rd(tt @ r).P reads, non-deterministically and in a blocking fashion, a tuple t matching template tt, situated in some spatiotemporal region r' intersecting with r. The operation is issued at event ϵ_{rd}, and propagates through a process within region r (blue). When the process enters the region r' (red) of an out operation with a tuple t matching template tt, notifications of the match(es) are propagated through broadcast in r (from events such as ϵ_M). The first notification to reach the leader chain of r (horizontal dashed line) is accepted (in event $\epsilon_{rd}^\dagger$), leading to the termination of the *read* process, and starting the computation of the continuation process P in $\epsilon_{rd}^\dagger$.

Removal (Fig. 2c). Operation in(tt @ r).P fetches, non-deterministically and in a blocking fashion, a tuple t matching template tt, situated in some spatio-temporal region r' intersecting with r. This fetching leads to the termination of the out region, and no two different in operations are allowed to receive the same t. The operation is issued at event ϵ_{in}, and propagates through a process within region r (blue). Assuming the absence of partitions, atomicity and consistency can be guaranteed through a protocol involving a joint acknowledgement of the match between the two leaders of the in and out regions. This acknowledgement process is embodied by a chain of events of the form $\epsilon_{in} \leq \epsilon_M \leq \epsilon_C \leq \epsilon_{in}^\dagger \leq \epsilon_{out}^\dagger$. In ϵ_M a match is found: this is notified within region r' to reach for the leader chain (dashed lines) of the out operation in ϵ_C, which commits to the first arriving request (if any). The commitment is then broadcast through both regions r' and r until it reaches the leader chain of the in operation. This leader chain also commits to the first arriving request (in event $\epsilon_{in}^\dagger$) leading to the immediate termination of the in region and notifying the out region, which is reached in event $\epsilon_{out}^\dagger$ and terminates afterwards. It is possible that after the leader chain of an out operation commits to an incoming request (event ϵ_C), the leader chain of the accepted request does not accept the commitment, since it has already received another one. This can be detected by the out, given absence of partitions (cf. Sect. 6), in this case, the leader chain of the out operation erases its commitment, opening to new incoming requests. Notice that as multiple acknowledgements are necessary, concurrency of multiple in and out operations may lead to none of them being served.

4   Spatiotemporal Tuples as Aggregate Processes

The model in Sect. 3 founds on the idea that tuple operations are tasks that are *collective, adaptive* and *situated*, namely on-going, collaborative computations run by devices interacting in some spatial environment. In field calculi [32], the notion of *aggregate process* [15] has been recently proposed to capture dynamic, concurrent field computations and hence providing a programming abstraction for collective adaptive processes. In this section, we provide a brief recap of aggregate processes and their implementation in SCAFI (Sect. 4.1), then we describe an implementation of Spatiotemporal Tuples (Sect. 4.2) conforming to the model of Sect. 3—whereas its correctness and usability will be empirically evaluated in Sect. 5.

4.1 Aggregate Processes

In the field calculus (FC) [6], the formal model backing *aggregate comput-ing* [8,32], dynamic collective behaviour is modelled as a functional manipu-lation of *computational fields* (i.e., maps from devices to values). A FC program encodes both computation and data exchange, and must be repeatedly evaluated by each device against its local context (sensor values, state, and received mes-sages). The output of evaluation is a message to be broadcast to neighbours for coordination. So, when a device locally evaluates a FC expression, it can use data from its neighbours that also evaluated that very expression—a notion known as *alignment* [5]. In order to evaluate a dynamic number of expression, a mech-anism is needed to properly deal with alignment. Also, whereas a FC program is generally run by every device in the system, and branching mechanisms exist to scope an expression on a partition of the system, dynamically controlling the evolution of the scope of an expression tends to be tricky. A recent proposal is to use a dedicated construct, called spawn , for generating and running dynamic field computations [15]. Also called *aggregate processes*, their idea is to align on a *process identifier* (like a *pid* in operating systems) and to let devices opt in/out their execution and control the spreading of the process to neighbours.

Aggregate processes can be programmed in SCAFI as follows.

```
// 1. Define an aggregate process function, fixing types for pids, arguments, return values
val process: Pid => Args => (Return, Boolean) = ???
// 2. Define a field of pids for processes to be locally instantiated
val pids: Set[Pid] = ??? // e.g., reading a sensor for user commands, or via a FC expression
// 3. A field of arguments for the active process instances
val args: A = ???
// 3. A spawn expression is like a VM for processes of some kind
val map: Map[Pid,Return] = spawn[Pid,Args,Return](process _, keys, args)
```

The program is evaluated by every device repeatedly in *execution rounds* inter-valled by sleeping periods where *coordination messages* are also exchanged between neighbours, asynchronously. The execution and interaction protocol is "fixed", and dynamically gives rise to an augmented event structure (cf. Fig. 1); what changes is the payload of messages, determined by local evaluation of the program—namely, the program itself defines both local behaviour and data to be exchanged for coordination. As evaluation proceeds, aggregate processes will be generated and managed through spawn, and variable map will contain, at any device, the map of the locally active processes (their IDs and local outputs).

Suppose the goal is to let the devices of the system emit messages within some distance d from the emitter. Distances can be estimated by *gradients* [4], i.e., algorithms mapping a Boolean field of sources to the floating-point field of minimum distances from those sources. One gradient computation is not suffi-cient, because any device would compute the minimum distance from its nearest source. As dynamic field computations are required, aggregate processes can be used. If, at some round, pids is locally non-empty, corresponding processes are generated. Each time spawn is evaluated, function process is called for every aggregate process that is locally active—newly generated processes, those run (and preserved) in the previous round, or those acquired by neighbours. In this example, the `pids` can be tuples of the emitter ID and the message; the argument can be a field d of a distance threshold; and `process` can be defined as a field expression returning a tuple of (i) the message, and (ii) a Boolean stating whether the gradient value from the emitter is lower or equal d. When a process is generated at the emitter device, it spreads as follows:

- the emitter evaluates the process expression; the gradient from itself is 0, so it yields the result and propagates the process pid to all its neighbours;
- an emitter's neighbour evaluates the process expression; it computes the gradient from the emitter; if its distance is lower or equal d, it yields the expression result and propagates the process pid to all its neighbours in turn, otherwise it drops the process (which could still be re-evaluated in future if some neighbour keeps propagating the same pid).

By repeated application of these steps, a d-radius bubble from the emitter holding the message is set-up, with devices 1-hop beyond it evaluating but dropping the process. Such a continuous evaluation of the process border is essential for its expansion and retraction—more details, also regarding process shutdown, can be found in [15]. This example is very similar to what an `out` tuple operation must be like, except that its aggregate process must close when interaction with another aggregate process (of an `in` operation) leads to removal of the tuple.

4.2   Implementing Spatiotemporal Tuples via Aggregate Processes

We argue that aggregate processes are a suitable abstraction for implementing the Spatiotemporal Tuples model because: (i) they are based on and extend the FC, which is space-time universal [2] and a premier computational model for systems situated in space and time; (ii) they enable an aggregate to run a dynamic number of tuple operations concurrently; (iii) they define a tuple operation as a collective adaptive process that is carried out collaboratively, in a decentralised and self-organising way; and (iv) they enable each tuple operation to have a dynamic scope that depends on its intended spatiotemporal situation. In the following, we describe the essential elements of this implementation.

The basic idea is to map a tuple operation to a corresponding aggregate process, and define how these should behave and interact. Most specifically:

- the problem of scoping a tuple operation to a certain spatiotemporal region is mapped to the problem of scoping its aggregate process (i.e., specifying a Boolean field to control what devices must opt in the aggregate process);
- the problem of matching tuple operations and non-deterministically selecting tuples is mapped to the problem of letting aggregate processes interact and reaching internal consensus;
- the problem of unblocking operations is mapped the problem of controlling the *lifetime* of aggregate processes.

An implementation sketch is given in Fig. 3 (for the full sources, refer to the repository provided in Sect. 5). For details on the FC/ScaFi language, refer

```
def tupleOp(op: O)(arg: Map[O,R]): (R, Status) = op match {
  case Out(...) => outLogic(...); case In(...) => inLogic(...); ...
}
rep[Map[O,R]](Map.empty())(ops => spawn(tupleOp _, newLocalOps(), ops))
```

(a) SCAFI field-calculus expression for spawning and executing tuple operations.

```
def outLogic(pid,t,r,ops,leader) = {        def inLogic(pid,tt,r,ops,leader) = {
  val inside = computeRegion(r)               val inside = computeRegion(r)
  val p = workflow(Available){                val p = workflow(Waiting){
    case curr @ Available => {                  case curr @ Waiting => {
      val requests = C(leader, ∪, request())     val offers = C(leader,∪,outOffers(ops))
      val choice = requests.headOption()         val choice = offers.headOption()
      if(leader && choice.isPresent)             (if(leader && choice.isPresent)
        Serving(choice.get) else curr              Removing(choice.get) else curr)
    }                                              << Msg(Request(pid,choice))
    case curr @ Serving(inP) => {              }
      val ack = gossip(inLeaderAck())           case curr @ Removing(outP) => {
      (if(leader && ack) Done(inP) else curr)     val ack = gossip(outLeaderAck())
        << Msg(ReservedFor(pid,inP))             (if(leader && ack) Done(outP) else curr)
    }                                              << Msg(InAck(pid,outP))
    case curr @ Done(inP) =>                   }
      { curr << OutAck(pid,inP)  }             case Done(outP) => { /* no-op */ }
  }                                           }
  (R(t,p.msgs), runOrNot(inside,p))         (R(p.tupleIfAny(),p.msgs),runOrNot(inside,p))
}                                           }
```

(b) Excerpt of SCAFI code for outs.   (c) Excerpt of SCAFI code for ins.

Fig. 3. (Pseudo-)Implementation of tuple operations as SCAFI processes.

to [14,16]. The idea is to let the tuple operation processes evolve in collective behaviour phases (like in a state-machine), commanded by the leader, ensuring "transactional semantics", and to use messages (appended via << to the phase descriptor) to let *aggregate processes within an individual device* to interact. As shown in Fig. 3a, each aggregate process receives the overall map of processes and corresponding results (ops, remembered from round to round via rep) as an argument. Results R include a tuple (if any) and the messages. Function computeRegion uses region description r to call a proper SCAFI function yielding a Boolean field which is true only for the nodes that should belong to the region. E.g., if r denotes the region within a range ρ from the leader, then field expression gradient(mid()==leader)<=ρ is computed (where mid() returns the node ID); or, if R is a geographic area, then GPScoordinates() $\in$ R would do the job. Note that devices opt for the process (runOrNot) based on **inside** and phase p.

5   Evaluation

With the goal of checking correctness in dynamic environments, and to discuss applicability, in this section we evaluate the presented model and implementation by means of simulation, through synthetic experiments (Sect. 5.1) and a rescue case study (Sect. 5.2). For the simulations, we leverage the SCAFI

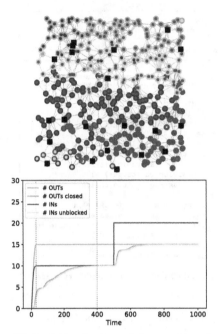

(a) A graphical view of the scenario as simulated in the SCAFI-Alchemist framework. The colours are used to denote different tuple operations (aggregate processes), though actually a single node may run several of them concurrently. The smaller coloured dots denote out processes, while the larger halos denote in processes. The black square symbols denote the devices that generated any tuple operation.

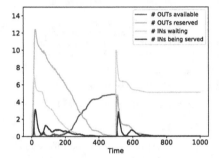

(b) Evolution in time of the number of outs and ins spawned and closed.

(c) Evolution in time of the number of outs and ins in the different phases.

Fig. 4. Evaluation

incarnation [13] of the Alchemist simulator [29]. Source code, tools, and instructions for reproducing the experiments can be found in the attached public repository[3].

5.1   Simulation-Based Evaluation

Setup. The scenario is shown in Fig. 4a. We configure a square arena with 400 mobile devices displaced in a $1\,km^2$ grid: they interact with neighbours within a 100-m connectivity range, and compute the SCAFI program asynchronously about once per second. We let the devices generate random tuple operations, either out or in operations, such that the system is engaged in multiple, concurrent operations that need to be carried out. Moreover, we generate tasks so that for $t < 400$ there are more outs than ins in the system, and for $t > 400$ there are more ins than outs. These operations have an extension of 450 m to promote high contention and are generated so that they intersect (otherwise they could not be matched). Then, we monitor the evolution of the system. We keep track of the number of spawned operations and terminated operations, as well as the phases that these transit on. We expect that a single in operation

---

[3] https://github.com/metaphori/experiment-2021-spatiotemporaltuples.

(a) Explorers start exploring and depositing breadcrumbs.

(b) Some explorers hit obstacles and become impaired.

(c) The followers managed to reach the victims.

Fig. 5. Snapshots of the simulated case study. Notation: black discs (explorers), cyan discs (followers), large blue dots (victims), large red squares (obstacles), small black dots (tactical network nodes), coloured halos (breadcrumbs), orange dots on the discs (impairment). (Larger pictures are available at the provided repository) (Color figure online)

pairs up with a single **out** operation, and vice versa. We perform 100 runs of the system, with different random seeds affecting the actual positions of nodes, the relative scheduling of the devices, and which devices generate the operations.

Results. The results, averaging the data produced in the 100 runs, are shown in Fig. 4. In Fig. 4b, we observe that the number of **out**s that get closed and the number of **in**s that are satisfied grow equally. All the operations are satisfied, provided there is still a matching one in the system, a condition that does not hold approximately for $t \in [200, 400]$ and $t > 550$ when no more **in** and **out** processes are alive, respectively. In Fig. 4c, we observe how the processes transit from their "waiting a match" phase to their "match found" phase. Note how the **out** processes immediately offer their tuple to a matching **in**, but as the **in**s are exhausted they become available again (approximately for $t = [150, 400]$).

5.2 Case Study: Rescue Scenario with Breadcrumbs

Like for Spatial Tuples, the Spatiotemporal Tuple model can be adopted in applications requiring various forms of spatial coordination. Example application scenarios providing motivation for this coordination approach can be found in [30]. A benefit of Spatiotemporal Tuples is streamlining decentralised implementation of such coordination patterns in logically ad-hoc or peer-to-peer networks.

Consider a simple rescue scenario: a set of rescuers have to explore a territory to find victims needing assistance; in the area, however, there are some hazardous elements (e.g., mines or blocks) that may impair the rescuers. The area is partially covered by a tactical mesh network. We consider two teams: explorers and followers. According to the *breadcrumb pattern* [30], the explorers navigate the area and, from time to time, leave a spatiotemporally-tagged tuple (a "breadcrumb") at their location to keep track of their paths. Some time later, the followers begin their expedition: they move by following the breadcrumbs left by the explorers; however, if the breadcrumbs-path interrupts, they take a random detour and, after that, start exploring in turn. Screenshots of the different phases of the simulation are in Fig. 5, showing how the spatial coordination pattern, backed by spatiotemporal tuples, allows the rescuers to succeed in reaching the victims (assuming no further obstacles impair them).

6   Conclusion and Future Work

In this paper, we propose a model for spatiotemporal tuples where tuple operations run on a *computational space-time structure* that *logically* bridges the situation domain with the computation domain. This choice has a twofold benefit: it enables locality and scalability of the tuple-based system and promotes straightforward implementation in the aggregate computing paradigm.

Finally, we discuss the following aspects, to be fully investigated in the future.

– *Properties and guarantees of the model and its implementations.* Basic properties of the model are given in Definition 5: these ensure safety and liveness of spatiotemporal tuple operations. A benefit of the proposed model with respect to Spatial Tuples [30] is that it provides a convenient basis for decentralised implementations where the tuple space is fragmented in a collection of local tuple spaces owned by the individual devices. It also promotes *scalability* through locality of tuples and operations: only the devices situated in the spatial region of a tuple operation would execute the aggregate process sustaining that operation. So, what about sparse networks or positioning tuples in areas not covered by any device? The idea is that a device should be aware of what tuple operations are where: it is sufficient that it knows the aggregate process IDs and it will play them once it belongs to their spatial region. So, for scalability, a decentralised middleware solution could propagate those IDs to a larger spatial region (still smaller than the entire application space), hence exploiting locality while ensuring operations are not lost. Moreover, a distributed implementation of the Spatiotemporal Tuple model has to decide how to deal with the *CAP theorem* [10], i.e., what kind of consistency and availability guarantees to provide when facing failure and network partitions. For instance, the relative level of consistency and availability (e.g., by introducing time-outs or priorities) might affect scalability [9]. Design decisions should be taken according to the levels of contention, variability (as induced by mobility, failure), and operation rates.

- *Spatiotemporal property verification and monitoring.* Potential for combining the coordination language with spatial and temporal logics for verification and monitoring, along the lines of [3], could also be investigated. Beside distributed runtime verification, statistical spatio-temporal model checking [18] may be adopted for verifying implementations in simulated settings.
- *Generality of the model w.r.t. deployments.* A major merit of the approach is that it supports both centralised, infrastructure-based deployments (cf. cloud- or server-based systems) and decentralised, infrastructureless deployments (cf. MANETs). Indeed, since aggregate computing systems can be partitioned into different deployment units (a notion also known as *pulverisation* [12]), applications can exploit available infrastructure and hosts to promote different levels of performance and CAP guarantees.

References

1. Alrahman, Y.A., Nicola, R.D., Loreti, M.: Programming interactions in collective adaptive systems by relying on attribute-based communication. Sci. Comput. Program. **192** (2020). https://doi.org/10.1016/j.scico.2020.102428
2. Audrito, G., Beal, J., Damiani, F., Viroli, M.: Space-time universality of field calculus. In: Di Marzo Serugendo, G., Loreti, M. (eds.) COORDINATION 2018. LNCS, vol. 10852, pp. 1–20. Springer, Cham (2018). https://doi.org/10.1007/978-3-319-92408-3_1
3. Audrito, G., Casadei, R., Damiani, F., Stolz, V., Viroli, M.: Adaptive distributed monitors of spatial properties for cyber-physical systems. J. Syst. Softw. **175** (2021). https://doi.org/10.1016/j.jss.2021.110908
4. Audrito, G., Casadei, R., Damiani, F., Viroli, M.: Compositional blocks for optimal self-healing gradients. In: 2017 IEEE 11th International Conference on Self-Adaptive and Self-Organizing Systems (SASO), pp. 91–100. IEEE (2017)
5. Audrito, G., Damiani, F., Viroli, M., Casadei, R.: Run-time management of computation domains in field calculus. In: IEEE International Workshops on Foundations and Applications of Self* Systems, pp. 192–197. IEEE (2016)
6. Audrito, G., Viroli, M., Damiani, F., Pianini, D., Beal, J.: A higher-order calculus of computational fields. ACM Trans. Comput. Log. **20**(1), 5:1–5:55 (2019). https://doi.org/10.1145/3285956
7. Beal, J., Dulman, S., Usbeck, K., Viroli, M., Correll, N.: Organizing the aggregate: languages for spatial computing. In: Formal and Practical Aspects of DSLs: Recent Developments, pp. 436–501. IGI Global (2013). http://arxiv.org/abs/1202.5509
8. Beal, J., Pianini, D., Viroli, M.: Aggregate programming for the Internet of Things. IEEE Comput. **48**(9), 22–30 (2015). https://doi.org/10.1109/MC.2015.261
9. Boix, E.G., Scholliers, C., De Meuter, W., D'Hondt, T.: Programming mobile context-aware applications with TOTAM. J. Syst. Softw. **92**, 3–19 (2014)
10. Brewer, E.: Cap twelve years later: how the "rules" have changed. Computer **45**(2), 23–29 (2012)
11. Busi, N., Gorrieri, R., Zavattaro, G.: On the expressiveness of Linda coordination primitives. Inf. Comput. **156**(1–2), 90–121 (2000)
12. Casadei, R., Pianini, D., Placuzzi, A., Viroli, M., Weyns, D.: Pulverization in cyber-physical systems: engineering the self-organizing logic separated from deployment. Future Internet **12**(11), 203 (2020)

13. Casadei, R., Pianini, D., Viroli, M.: Simulating large-scale aggregate MASs with Alchemist and Scala. In: 2016 Federated Conference on Computer Science and Information Systems (FedCSIS), pp. 1495–1504. IEEE (2016)
14. Casadei, R., Viroli, M., Audrito, G., Damiani, F.: FSCAFI: a core calculus for collective adaptive systems programming. In: Margaria, T., Steffen, B. (eds.) ISoLA 2020. LNCS, vol. 12477, pp. 344–360. Springer, Cham (2020). https://doi.org/10.1007/978-3-030-61470-6_21
15. Casadei, R., Viroli, M., Audrito, G., Pianini, D., Damiani, F.: Aggregate processes in field calculus. In: Riis Nielson, H., Tuosto, E. (eds.) COORDINATION 2019. LNCS, vol. 11533, pp. 200–217. Springer, Cham (2019). https://doi.org/10.1007/978-3-030-22397-7_12
16. Casadei, R., Viroli, M., Audrito, G., Pianini, D., Damiani, F.: Engineering collective intelligence at the edge with aggregate processes. Eng. Appl. Artif. Intell. **97**, 104081 (2021)
17. Casadei, R., Viroli, M., Ricci, A.: Collective adaptive systems as coordination media: the case of tuples in space-time. In: 1st IEEE International Conference on Autonomic Computing and Self-Organizing Systems, ACSOS, Companion Volume, pp. 139–144. IEEE (2020). https://doi.org/10.1109/ACSOS-C51401.2020.00045
18. Ciancia, V., Latella, D., Massink, M., Paškauskas, R., Vandin, A.: A tool-chain for statistical spatio-temporal model checking of bike sharing systems. In: Margaria, T., Steffen, B. (eds.) ISoLA 2016. LNCS, vol. 9952, pp. 657–673. Springer, Cham (2016). https://doi.org/10.1007/978-3-319-47166-2_46
19. Coulouris, G., Dollimore, J., Kindberg, T.: Distributed Systems: Concepts and Designs, 3rd edn. Addison-Wesley-Longman, Boston (2002)
20. DeHon, A., Giavitto, J., Gruau, F. (eds.): Computing Media and Languages for Space-Oriented Computation, Dagstuhl Seminar Proceedings, 03 September–08 September 2006, vol. 06361 (2007). http://drops.dagstuhl.de/portals/06361/
21. Gelernter, D.: Generative communication in Linda. ACM Trans. Program. Lang. Syst. (TOPLAS) **7**(1), 80–112 (1985)
22. Gelernter, D.: Multiple tuple spaces in Linda. In: Odijk, E., Rem, M., Syre, J.-C. (eds.) PARLE 1989. LNCS, vol. 366, pp. 20–27. Springer, Heidelberg (1989). https://doi.org/10.1007/3-540-51285-3_30
23. Loo, J., Mauri, J.L., Ortiz, J.H.: Mobile Ad Hoc Networks: Current Status and Future Trends. CRC Press, Boca Raton (2016)
24. Mamei, M., Zambonelli, F.: Programming pervasive and mobile computing applications: the TOTA approach. ACM Trans. Softw. Eng. Methodol. **18**(4), 1–56 (2009). https://doi.org/10.1145/1538942.1538945
25. Menezes, R., Wood, A.: The fading concept in tuple-space systems. In: Proceedings of the 2006 ACM Symposium on Applied Computing, pp. 440–444 (2006)
26. Merrick, I., Wood, A.: Scoped coordination in open distributed systems. In: Porto, A., Roman, G.-C. (eds.) COORDINATION 2000. LNCS, vol. 1906, pp. 311–316. Springer, Heidelberg (2000). https://doi.org/10.1007/3-540-45263-X_21
27. Murphy, A.L., Picco, G.P., Roman, G.C.: LIME: a coordination model and middleware supporting mobility of hosts and agents. ACM Trans. Softw. Eng. Methodol. **15**(3), 279–328 (2006). https://doi.org/10.1145/1151695.1151698
28. Pauty, J., Couderc, P., Banatre, M., Berbers, Y.: Geo-Linda: a geometry aware distributed tuple space. In: 21st International Conference on Advanced Information Networking and Applications (AINA 2007), pp. 370–377. IEEE (2007)
29. Pianini, D., Montagna, S., Viroli, M.: Chemical-oriented simulation of computational systems with Alchemist. J. Simul. **7**(3), 202–215 (2013). https://doi.org/10.1057/jos.2012.27

30. Ricci, A., Viroli, M., Omicini, A., Mariani, S., Croatti, A., Pianini, D.: Spatial tuples: augmenting reality with tuples. Expert. Syst. **35**(5), e12273 (2018)
31. Tolksdorf, R., Menezes, R.: Using swarm intelligence in Linda systems. In: Omicini, A., Petta, P., Pitt, J. (eds.) ESAW 2003. LNCS (LNAI), vol. 3071, pp. 49–65. Springer, Heidelberg (2004). https://doi.org/10.1007/978-3-540-25946-6_3
32. Viroli, M., Beal, J., Damiani, F., Audrito, G., Casadei, R., Pianini, D.: From distributed coordination to field calculus and aggregate computing. J. Log. Algebraic Methods Program. **109** (2019). https://doi.org/10.1016/j.jlamp.2019.100486
33. Viroli, M., Pianini, D., Beal, J.: Linda in space-time: an adaptive coordination model for mobile ad-hoc environments. In: Sirjani, M. (ed.) COORDINATION 2012. LNCS, vol. 7274, pp. 212–229. Springer, Heidelberg (2012). https://doi.org/10.1007/978-3-642-30829-1_15
34. Winskel, G.: An introduction to event structures. In: de Bakker, J.W., de Roever, W.-P., Rozenberg, G. (eds.) REX 1988. LNCS, vol. 354, pp. 364–397. Springer, Heidelberg (1989). https://doi.org/10.1007/BFb0013026

A Theory of Automated Market Makers in DeFi

Massimo Bartoletti[1] , James Hsin-yu Chiang[2]([envelope]) ,
and Alberto Lluch-Lafuente[2]

[1] Università degli Studi di Cagliari, Cagliari, Italy
bart@unica.it
[2] DTU Compute, Technical University of Denmark, Copenhagen, Denmark
{jchi,albl}@dtu.dk

Abstract. Automated market makers (AMMs) are one of the most prominent decentralized finance (DeFi) applications. They allow users to exchange units of different types of crypto-assets, without the need to find a counter-party. There are several implementations and models for AMMs, featuring a variety of sophisticated economic mechanisms. We present a theory of AMMs. The core of our theory is an abstract operational model of the interactions between users and AMMs, which can be concretised by instantiating the economic mechanisms. We exploit our theory to formally prove a set of fundamental properties of AMMs, characterizing both structural and economic aspects. We do this by abstracting from the actual economic mechanisms used in implementations and identifying sufficient conditions which ensure the relevant properties. Notably, we devise a general solution to the *arbitrage problem*, the main game-theoretic foundation behind the economic mechanisms of AMMs.

1 Introduction

Decentralized finance (DeFi) is emerging as an alternative to the traditional finance, boosted by blockchain-based crypto-tokens and smart contracts. One of the main DeFi applications are *Automated Market Makers (AMMs)*, which allow users to exchange crypto-tokens of different types without the intermediation of third parties. As of April 2021, the two AMM platforms leading by user activity, Uniswap [14] and Curve Finance [5], alone hold $8.1B and $6.2B worth of tokens, and process $1.5B and $210M worth of transactions daily [4,12].

AMMs are inherently hard to design, implement and understand, since they involve sophisticated economic incentive mechanisms. Although they generally only expose a handful of callable functions, interactions with AMMs are sensitive to transaction ordering [21,23,28,31]: thus, actors with the power to influence the order of transactions in the blockchain may be incentivized to do so for profit or to harm specific users. Thus, there exists a need for foundational work to devise formal models of AMMs which allow the study of their fundamental properties, transaction concurrency and the effect of economic incentives.

© IFIP International Federation for Information Processing 2021
Published by Springer Nature Switzerland AG 2021
F. Damiani and O. Dardha (Eds.): COORDINATION 2021, LNCS 12717, pp. 168–187, 2021.
https://doi.org/10.1007/978-3-030-78142-2_11

Current descriptions of AMMs are either economic models [17–19,24], which focus on the efficacy of incentive design, or the actual implementations. While economic models are useful to understand the macroscopic financial aspects of AMMs, they do not precisely describe the interactions between AMMs and their users. Still, understanding these interactions is crucial to determine possible deviations from the expected behaviour. Implementations, instead, reflect the exact behaviour of AMMs, but at a level of detail that hampers high-level understanding and reasoning. Moreover, the rich variety of implementations, proposals and models for AMMs, each featuring different sophisticated economic mechanisms, makes it difficult to establish comparisons between AMM designs or to provide a clear contour for the space of possible "well behaving" designs.

Contributions. In this paper we address these challenges by developing a theory of AMMs. The core of our theory is a formal model of AMMs (Sect. 2), based on a thorough inspection of leading AMM implementations like Uniswap [13], Curve [16], and Balancer [3], as well as existing models from the literature [1,31]. Our model precisely describes the interactions between users and AMMs, and their main economic features. An original aspect of our model is that it is parametric with respect to the key economic mechanism—the *swap invariant*—that algorithmically determines exchange rates between tokens. This makes our model general enough to encompass the mainstream implementations and models of AMMs. With respect to economic models, our theory considers implementation details that are crucial to guarantee (efficient) computability in practice. Our model features an *executable semantics*, which can support implementations and analysis tools. As a matter of fact, an open-source Ocaml implementation of our executable semantics is provided as a companion of this paper.[1]

Building upon our model, we prove a set of properties characterizing both structural (Sect. 3) and economic (Sect. 4) aspects of AMMs. With respect to previous works, which focus on specific economic mechanisms, all our results are parametric with respect to swap invariants. We identify indeed, for each property, a set of conditions on swap invariants that are sufficient for the property to hold. Our results include fundamental structural properties such as *net worth preservation* ("value cannot be created/destroyed"), *liquidity* ("assets cannot be frozen within an AMM"), and *transaction concurrency* ("two transactions can be executed in any order"), as well as fundamental economic properties such as *incentive-consistency*, which ensures an incentive feedback loop between deposits and swaps of tokens. Most notably, we generalize the formulation and the solution to the so-called *arbitrage problem*, the main game-theoretic foundation behind the economic aspects of AMMs. We show that users are incentivized to perform actions that keep the swap rates aligned with the exchange rates given by price oracles. Namely, if an AMM offers a better swap rate than the oracles' exchange rate, rational users will perform swaps to narrow the gap. Further, we show that, under certain conditions, deposits and swaps incentivize each other.

Overall, our theory encompasses and generalizes the main functional and economic aspects of the mainstream AMM implementations, providing solid grounds

---

[1] https://github.com/blockchain-unica/defi-workbench.

for the design of future AMMs. Due to space constraints, we provide the proofs of our statements in a separate technical report [26].

2   A Formal Model of Automated Market Makers

We introduce a formal, operational model of AMMs, focussing on the common features implemented by the main AMM platforms. We discuss in Sect. 6 the differences between these platforms and our model.

2.1   AMM States

Basics. We assume a set of **users** $\mathbb{A}$, ranged over by $A, A', \ldots$, and a set of **token types** $\mathbb{T}$, ranged over by $\tau, \tau', \ldots$. We denote with $\mathbb{T}_0 \subseteq \mathbb{T}$ a specific subset of token types that we call *initial* (they include, e.g., native blockchain tokens). The rest of the token types in $\mathbb{T}$ represent *minted* tokens, denoted as pairs (τ, τ') of distinct token types, and which represent shares in an AMM. We use v, v', r, r' to range over nonnegative real numbers $(\mathbb{R}_0^+)$, and we write $r : \tau$ to denote r units of token type τ. We denote with dom f the domain of a partial map f. We model the **wallet** of a user A as a term $A[\sigma]$, where the partial map $\sigma \in \mathbb{T} \rightharpoonup \mathbb{R}_0^+$ represents A's token holdings. We model an **AMM** as a pair of the form $(r_0 : \tau_0, r_1 : \tau_1)$, representing the fact that the AMM is holding, respectively, r_0 and r_1 units of token types τ_0 and τ_1.

States. We formalise the interaction between users and AMMs as a labelled transition system (LTS). Its labels $T, T', \ldots$ represent blockchain **transactions**, while the **states** $\Gamma, \Gamma', \ldots$ are compositions of wallets and AMMs:

$$A_1[\sigma_1] \mid \cdots \mid A_n[\sigma_n] \mid (r_1 : \tau_1, r'_1 : \tau'_1) \mid \cdots \mid (r_k : \tau_k, r'_k : \tau'_k)$$

where all A_i are distinct, and for all $i \neq j$: $\tau_i \neq \tau'_i$ (i.e., the token types in an AMM are *distinct*), and $(\tau_i = \tau_j \Rightarrow \tau'_i \neq \tau'_j) \wedge (\tau_i = \tau'_j \Rightarrow \tau'_i \neq \tau_j)$ (i.e., distinct AMMs cannot hold exactly the same token types). Two AMMs can indeed have a common token type τ, as in $(r_1 : \tau_1, r : \tau), (r' : \tau, r'_2 : \tau'_2)$, thus enabling indirect trades between token pairs not directly provided by any AMM. A state Γ is *initial* when it only contains wallets with initial tokens. We treat states as sets of terms (wallets/AMMs): hence, Γ and Γ' are equivalent when they contain the same terms; for a term Q, we write $Q \in \Gamma$ when $\Gamma = Q \mid \Gamma'$, for some Γ'.

Example 1. Figure 1 shows an execution trace in our model, that we will explain in detail later in Example 5. We write $\Gamma \xrightarrow{T} \Gamma'$ for a state transition from Γ to Γ', triggered by a transaction T. The first two states are initial, while the others contain an AMM for a token pair (τ_0, τ_1). ◻

$$A[70 : \tau_0, 80 : \tau_1] \mid B[30 : \tau_0]$$

$$\xrightarrow{A:xfer(B,10:\tau_1)} A[70 : \tau_0, 70 : \tau_1] \mid B[30 : \tau_0, 10 : \tau_1] \tag{1}$$

$$\xrightarrow{A:dep(70:\tau_0,70:\tau_1)} A[70 : (\tau_0, \tau_1)] \mid B[\cdots] \mid (70 : \tau_0, 70 : \tau_1) \tag{2}$$

$$\xrightarrow{B:swapL(30:\tau_0,20:\tau_1)} A[\cdots] \mid B[0 : \tau_0, 31 : \tau_1] \mid (100 : \tau_0, 49 : \tau_1) \tag{3}$$

$$\xrightarrow{B:swapR(29:\tau_0,21:\tau_1)} A[\cdots] \mid B[30 : \tau_0, 10 : \tau_1] \mid (70 : \tau_0, 70 : \tau_1) \tag{4}$$

$$\xrightarrow{B:rdm(30:(\tau_0,\tau_1))} A[30 : \tau_0, 30 : \tau_1, 40 : (\tau_0, \tau_1)] \mid B[\cdots] \mid (40 : \tau_0, 40 : \tau_1) \tag{5}$$

$$\xrightarrow{B:swapL(30:\tau_0,16:\tau_1)} A[\cdots] \mid B[0 : \tau_0, 27 : \tau_1] \mid (70 : \tau_0, 23 : \tau_1) \tag{6}$$

$$\xrightarrow{A:rdm(30:(\tau_0,\tau_1))} A[82 : \tau_0, 47 : \tau_1, 10 : (\tau_0, \tau_1)] \mid B[\cdots] \mid (18 : \tau_0, 6 : \tau_1) \tag{7}$$

Fig. 1. Interactions between two users and an AMM.

Token Supply. We define the **supply** of a token type τ in a state Γ as the sum of the balances of τ in all the wallets and the AMMs occurring in Γ. Formally:

$$sply_\tau(A[\sigma]) = \begin{cases} \sigma(\tau) & \text{if } \tau \in \text{dom } \sigma \\ 0 & \text{otherwise} \end{cases} \qquad sply_\tau(r_0 : \tau_0, r_1 : \tau_1) = \begin{cases} r_i & \text{if } \tau = \tau_i \\ 0 & \text{otherwise} \end{cases}$$

$$sply_\tau(\Gamma \mid \Gamma') = sply_\tau(\Gamma) + sply_\tau(\Gamma')$$

Example 2. Consider the first state in Fig. 1, $\Gamma_1 = A[70 : \tau_0, 80 : \tau_1] \mid B[30 : \tau_0]$. We have that $sply_{\tau_0}(\Gamma_1) = 70 + 30 = 100$, while $sply_{\tau_1}(\Gamma_1) = 80$. Observe that the supply of both token types remains constant in Fig. 1; we will show in Lemma 2 that the supply of initial token types is always preserved. □

Token Prices and Net Worth. Assume that initial tokens are priced by a global oracle $P^0 \in \mathbb{T}_0 \to \mathbb{R}_0^+$. We then define the **price** $P_\tau(\Gamma)$ of a token $\tau \in \mathbb{T}$ (either initial or minted) in a state Γ inductively as follows:

$$P_\tau(\Gamma) = P^0(\tau) \qquad\qquad \text{if } \tau \in \mathbb{T}_0$$

$$P_{(\tau_0,\tau_1)}(\Gamma) = \frac{r_0 \cdot P_{\tau_0}(\Gamma) + r_1 \cdot P_{\tau_1}(\Gamma)}{sply_{(\tau_0,\tau_1)}(\Gamma)} \qquad \text{if } (r_0 : \tau_0, r_1 : \tau_1) \in \Gamma \tag{8}$$

The main idea is that initial tokens are priced using directly the global oracle while minted tokens are priced under the assumption that they can be redeemed. Their price, hence, is obtained by (recursively) calculating the price of the tokens that can be obtained by redeeming them (i.e. the proportions of the reserves r_0 and r_1 given the current supply). This intuition will be further formalized later in Lemma 6.

Example 3. Let $\Gamma_7 = A[82 : \tau_0, 47 : \tau_1, 10 : (\tau_0, \tau_1)] \mid \cdots$ be the final state in Fig. 1. We have that $sply_{(\tau_0,\tau_1)}(\Gamma_7) = 10$. Assume that the prices of initial tokens are $P^0(\tau_0) = 5$ and $P^0(\tau_1) = 9$. The price of the minted token (τ_0, τ_1) is hence:

$$P_{(\tau_0,\tau_1)}(\Gamma_7) = \frac{1}{10}\Big(18 \cdot P_{\tau_0}(\Gamma_7) + 6 \cdot P_{\tau_1}(\Gamma_7)\Big) = \frac{18}{10} \cdot 5 + \frac{6}{10} \cdot 9 = 14.4 \qquad \square$$

We now define a key concept to understand the incentives for users to participate in AMMs, namely the **net worth** of a user A in a state Γ:

$$W_A(\Gamma) = \begin{cases} \sum_{\tau \in \text{dom } \sigma} \sigma(\tau) \cdot P_\tau(\Gamma) & \text{if } A[\sigma] \in \Gamma \\ 0 & \text{otherwise} \end{cases} \tag{9}$$

The **global net worth** $W(\Gamma)$ of a state Γ is the sum of the net worth in users' wallets. The token units held in AMMs are not accounted for by $W(\Gamma)$, because their value is already recorded by minted tokens held in users' wallets. Indeed, the equality $sply_{(\tau_0,\tau_1)}(\Gamma) \cdot P_{(\tau_0,\tau_1)}(\Gamma) = r_0 \cdot P_{\tau_0}(\Gamma) + r_1 \cdot P_{\tau_1}(\Gamma)$ between the net value of a minted token and the value of the AMM is a direct consequence of the definition of price in (8).

As we shall see later, one of the main goals of users is to maximize their net worth. This can be achieved through different interactions with the AMM (e.g., by investing tokens or trading units of differently priced token types).

Example 4. Recall from Fig. 1 the state $\Gamma_1 = A[70 : \tau_0, 80 : \tau_1] \mid B[30 : \tau_0]$, where τ_0 and τ_1 are initial tokens. Assume again that the prices are $P^0(\tau_0) = 5$ and $P^0(\tau_1) = 9$. The users' net worth in Γ_1 are then:

$$W_A(\Gamma_1) = 70 \cdot P^0(\tau_0) + 80 \cdot P^0(\tau_1) = 1070 \qquad W_B(\Gamma_1) = 30 \cdot P^0(\tau_0) = 150$$

In $\Gamma_7 = A[82 : \tau_0, 47 : \tau_1, 10 : (\tau_0, \tau_1)] \mid B[0 : \tau_0, 27 : \tau_1] \mid (18 : \tau_0, 6 : \tau_1)$ we have:

$$W_A(\Gamma_7) = 82 \cdot P_{\tau_0}(\Gamma_7) + 47 \cdot P_{\tau_1}(\Gamma_7) + 10 \cdot P_{(\tau_0,\tau_1)}(\Gamma_7) = 977$$
$$W_B(\Gamma_7) = 27 \cdot P_{\tau_1}(\Gamma_7) = 243$$

Note that the net worth of A has decreased w.r.t. the initial state, while the net worth of B has increased. One may think that B has been more successful than A, but this depends on the users' goals. Note, e.g., that A holds 10 units of the minted token (τ_0, τ_1), whose price may increase in the future. $\qquad \square$

2.2 AMM Semantics

We now formally describe the interactions of the AMM that give rise to state transitions. State transitions are triggered by the **transactions** in Table 1. We formalise below their behaviour, but we give before an overview of our running example from Fig. 1.

Table 1. AMM transactions.

$A : \mathsf{xfer}(B, v : \tau)$	A transfers $v : \tau$ to B
$A : \mathsf{dep}(v_0 : \tau_0, v_1 : \tau_1)$	A deposits $v_0 : \tau_0$ and $v_1 : \tau_1$ to an AMM ($r_0 : \tau_0, r_1 : \tau_1$), receiving in return some units of the minted token (τ_0, τ_1)
$A : \mathsf{swapL}(v_0 : \tau_0, v_1 : \tau_1)$	A tranfers $v_0 : \tau_0$ to an AMM ($r_0 : \tau_0, r_1 : \tau_1$), receiving in return *at least* v_1 units of τ_1
$A : \mathsf{swapR}(v_0 : \tau_0, v_1 : \tau_1)$	A tranfers $v_1 : \tau_1$ to an AMM ($r_0 : \tau_0, r_1 : \tau_1$), receiving in return *at least* v_0 units of τ_0
$A : \mathsf{rdm}(v : \tau)$	A redeems v units of minted token $\tau = (\tau_0, \tau_1)$ from an AMM ($r_0 : \tau_0, r_1 : \tau_1$), receiving in return some units of τ_0 and τ_1

Example 5. Figure 1 actually displays a sequence of transitions in the LTS of our model. To keep the example simple, we have used there the *constant product* swap invariant, which requires swap transactions to preserve the product between the amounts of the two tokens in the AMM; further, we have assumed no fees. In step (1), A transfers $10 : \tau_1$ from her wallet to B's. In step (2), A creates a new AMM, depositing $70 : \tau_0$ and $70 : \tau_1$; in return, she receives 70 units of the minted token (τ_0, τ_1). In step (3), B swaps 30 of his units of τ_0 for *at least* 20 units of τ_1. The actual amount of units of τ_1 received by B is 21: indeed, $(70 + 30) \cdot (70 - 21) = 70 \cdot 70$, hence 21 satisfies the constant product swap invariant. In step (4), B reverses his prior action by swapping 21 of his units of τ_1 for *at least* 29 units of τ_0. Here, the actual amount of units of τ_1 received by B is 30, which also satisfies the constant product swap invariant. In step (5), B redeems 30 units of the minted token (τ_0, τ_1), accordingly reducing the funds in the AMM. Note that the received tokens exhibit the same 1-to-1 ratio as in the initial deposit at step (2). In step (6), B swaps 30 of his units of τ_0 for *at least* 16 units of τ_1. Unlike in the previous swap at step (3), now the actual amount of τ_1 received by B is 17. Note that the implied *swap rate* between received τ_1 units and sent τ_0 units has deteriorated w.r.t. step (3), even if the pair (τ_0, τ_1) had the same 1-to-1 ratio of funds. This is caused by the reduction in funds resulting from A's redeem action: thus, the swap rate is sensitive to both the ratio of funds in the pair as well as their absolute balances, a key property of the incentive mechanisms, as we shall see later in Sect. 4. Finally, in step (7) A performs another redeem of 30 units of the minted token (τ_0, τ_1), thereby extracting 52 units of τ_0 and 17 units of τ_1 from the AMM. Note that the ratio of redeemed tokens is no longer 1-to-1 as in the previous redeem action (5), as the prior left swap has changed the ratio between the funds of τ_0 and τ_1 in the AMM. □

We now formalise the transition rules. We use the standard notation $\sigma\{v/x\}$ to update a partial map σ at point x: namely, $\sigma\{v/x\}(x) = v$, while $\sigma\{v/x\}(y) = \sigma(y)$ for $y \neq x$. Given a partial map $\sigma \in \mathbb{T} \rightharpoonup \mathbb{R}_0^+$, a token type $\tau \in \mathbb{T}$ and a partial operation $\circ \in \mathbb{R}_0^+ \times \mathbb{R}_0^+ \rightharpoonup \mathbb{R}_0^+$, we define the partial map $\sigma \circ v : \tau$ as follows:

$$\sigma \circ v : \tau = \begin{cases} \sigma\{\sigma(\tau) \circ v/\tau\} & \text{if } \tau \in \text{dom}\,\sigma \text{ and } \sigma(\tau) \circ v \in \mathbb{R}_0^+ \\ \sigma\{v/\tau\} & \text{if } \tau \notin \text{dom}\,\sigma \end{cases}$$

Token Transfer. A user A can transfer some of her tokens to another user B, provided that there are enough units of the token in A's wallet. Formally:

$$\frac{\sigma_\mathsf{A}(\tau) \geq v}{\mathsf{A}[\sigma_\mathsf{A}] \mid \mathsf{B}[\sigma_\mathsf{B}] \mid \Gamma \xrightarrow{\mathsf{A}:\mathsf{xfer}(\mathsf{B},v:\tau)} \mathsf{A}[\sigma_\mathsf{A} - v : \tau] \mid \mathsf{B}[\sigma_\mathsf{B} + v : \tau] \mid \Gamma} \text{ [XFER]}$$

A consequence of this rule is that tokens (both initial and minted) are *fungible*, i.e. individual units of the same token type are interchangeable. In particular, amounts of tokens of the same type can be split into smaller parts, and two amounts of tokens of the same type can be joined.

Deposit. Any user can create an AMM for a token pair (τ_0, τ_1) provided that such an AMM is not already present in the state. This is achieved by the transaction $\mathsf{A} : \mathsf{dep}(v_0 : \tau_0, v_1 : \tau_1)$, through which A transfers $v_0 : \tau_0$ and $v_1 : \tau_1$ to the new AMM. In return for the deposit, A receives a certain positive amount of units of a new token type (τ_0, τ_1), which is minted by the AMM. The exact amount of units received is irrelevant. In our model we choose v_0 but any other choice would be valid. We formalise this behaviour by the rule:

$$\frac{\sigma(\tau_i) \geq v_i > 0 \;\; (i \in \{0,1\}) \qquad \tau_0 \neq \tau_1 \qquad (\_ : \tau_0, \_ : \tau_1), (\_ : \tau_1, \_ : \tau_0) \notin \Gamma}{\mathsf{A}[\sigma] \mid \Gamma \xrightarrow{\mathsf{A}:\mathsf{dep}(v_0:\tau_0,v_1:\tau_1)}} \text{ [DEP0]}$$
$$\mathsf{A}[\sigma - v_0 : \tau_0 - v_1 : \tau_1 + v_0 : (\tau_0, \tau_1)] \mid (v_0 : \tau_0, v_1 : \tau_1) \mid \Gamma$$

Once an AMM is created, any user can deposit tokens into it, as long as doing so preserves the ratio of the token holdings in the AMM. When a user deposits $v_0 : \tau_0$ and $v_1 : \tau_1$ to an existing AMM, it receives in return an amount of minted tokens of type (τ_0, τ_1). This amount is the ratio between the deposited amount v_0 and the **redeem rate** of (τ_0, τ_1) in the current state Γ, i.e. the ratio between the amount r_0 of τ_0 stored in the AMM, and the total supply $sply_{(\tau_0,\tau_1)}(\Gamma)$ of the minted token in the state.

$$\frac{\sigma(\tau_i) \geq v_i > 0 \;\; (i \in \{0,1\}) \qquad r_1 v_0 = r_0 v_1 \qquad v = \frac{v_0}{r_0} \cdot sply_{(\tau_0,\tau_1)}(\Gamma)}{\Gamma = \mathsf{A}[\sigma] \mid (r_0 : \tau_0, r_1 : \tau_1) \mid \Gamma' \xrightarrow{\mathsf{A}:\mathsf{dep}(v_0:\tau_0,v_1:\tau_1)}} \text{ [DEP]}$$
$$\mathsf{A}[\sigma - v_0 : \tau_0 - v_1 : \tau_1 + v : (\tau_0, \tau_1)] \mid (r_0 + v_0 : \tau_0, r_1 + v_1 : \tau_1) \mid \Gamma'$$

Note that the premise $r_1 v_0 = r_0 v_1$ ensures that the ratio between the holdings of τ_0 and τ_1 in the AMM is preserved by the dep transaction, i.e.:

$$\frac{r_1 + v_1}{r_0 + v_0} = \frac{r_1}{r_0}$$

As we shall see in Sect. 4, users are incentivized to invest tokens into AMMs by the fact that trading operations (i.e., swaps) are subject to a fee mechanism that makes the redeem rate increase over time.

Swap. As shown in step (3) and on of Example 5, users can increase their net worth by swapping tokens. Any user A can swap units of τ_0 in her wallet for units of τ_1 in an AMM $(r_0 : \tau_0, r_1 : \tau_1)$ by firing a transaction $A : \mathsf{swapL}(v_0 : \tau_0, v_1 : \tau_1)$. Here, v_0 is the amount of τ_0 transferred from A's wallet to the AMM, while v_1 is a *lower bound* on the amount of τ_1 that A will receive in return. The actual amount v is determined by a **swap invariant** $I \in \mathbb{R}_0^+ \times \mathbb{R}_0^+ \to \mathbb{R}_0^+$, that must hold between the amounts of τ_0 and τ_1 held in the AMM before and after the swap. To determine v, the AMM requires a fraction $0 < \phi \leq 1$ of v_0; the rest is considered as a fee (the parameter ϕ is the **fee rate**). Formally:

$$\frac{\sigma(\tau_0) \geq v_0 > 0 \qquad I(r_0 + \phi\,v_0, r_1 - v) = I(r_0, r_1) \qquad 0 < v_1 \leq v \leq r_1}{\mathsf{A}[\sigma] \mid (r_0 : \tau_0, r_1 : \tau_1) \mid \Gamma \xrightarrow{A:\mathsf{swapL}(v_0:\tau_0,v_1:\tau_1)} \mathsf{A}[\sigma - v_0 : \tau_0 + v : \tau_1] \mid (r_0 + v_0 : \tau_0, r_1 - v : \tau_1) \mid \Gamma} \; [\textsc{SwapL}]$$

The effect of the fee is that the redeem rate of minted tokens increases; intuitively, the AMM retains a portion of the swapped amounts, but the overall reserve is still distributed among all minted tokens, thereby ensuring liquidity (as we shall formally establish liquidity later on in Lemma 4).

Although actual AMM implementations use a variety of different swap invariants, with the common aim to incentivize users to perform swaps, all these invariants share a few common design choices. A crucial one is that there exists *exactly* one v which satisfies the equation in the premise of [SwapL]; further, swapping 0 units of τ_0 results in 0 units of τ_1. Formally, for all $r_0, r_1 > 0$:

$$\forall v \in \mathbb{R}_0^+ : \exists! v' \in \mathbb{R}_0^+ : I(r_0 + v, r_1 - v') = I(r_0, r_1) \tag{10}$$

Hereafter, we assume that I always respects this condition. A common swap invariant, implemented e.g. by Uniswap [13] and Mooniswap [7] (and also used in Example 5), is the *constant product invariant*, which requires that the product of the amounts of τ_0 and τ_1 in the AMM remains constant, i.e. $I(r_0, r_1) = r_0 \cdot r_1$.

The rule [SwapR] allows for swaps in the other direction:

$$\frac{\sigma(\tau_1) \geq v_1 > 0 \qquad I(r_0 - v, r_1 + \phi\,v_1) = I(r_0, r_1) \qquad 0 < v_0 \leq v \leq r_0}{\mathsf{A}[\sigma] \mid (r_0 : \tau_0, r_1 : \tau_1) \mid \Gamma \xrightarrow{A:\mathsf{swapR}(v_0:\tau_0,v_1:\tau_1)} \mathsf{A}[\sigma + v : \tau_0 - v_1 : \tau_1] \mid (r_0 - v : \tau_0, r_1 + v_1 : \tau_1) \mid \Gamma} \; [\textsc{SwapR}]$$

where we assume that I enjoys the "right" version of the condition (10).

It is worth explaining why the swap transactions specify lower bounds for the amount of return tokens, instead of an exact amount. In practice, when a user emits a transaction, she cannot predict the exact state in which the transaction will be actually committed. This makes it unfeasible to guess the exact amount that will preserve the swap invariant: hence, users can only specify a lower bound that they are willing to accept.

Redeem. Any user can redeem units of a minted token (τ_0, τ_1), obtaining in return units of the underlying tokens τ_0 and τ_1. The redeemable amounts are determined by the redeem rate: each unit of (τ_0, τ_1) can be redeemed for equal fractions of τ_0 and τ_1 remaining in the AMM:

$$\frac{\sigma(\tau_0, \tau_1) \geq v > 0 \qquad v_0 = v \frac{r_0}{sply_{(\tau_0, \tau_1)}(\Gamma)} \qquad v_1 = v \frac{r_1}{sply_{(\tau_0, \tau_1)}(\Gamma)}}{\Gamma = A[\sigma] \mid (r_0 : \tau_0, r_1 : \tau_1) \mid \Gamma' \xrightarrow{A:rdm(v:(\tau_0, \tau_1))}} \quad [\text{RDM}]$$
$$A[\sigma + v_0 : \tau_0 + v_1 : \tau_1 - v : (\tau_0, \tau_1)] \mid (r_0 - v_0 : \tau_0, r_1 - v_1 : \tau_1) \mid \Gamma'$$

Example 6. Figure 2 shows the evolution of the AMM token holdings resulting from the trace in Fig. 1, presented with Example 5. Recall that we have assumed a constant product swap invariant $x \cdot y = k$, and no swap fees ($\phi = 1$). We refer to a state in Fig. 1 by the action number preceding it: the AMM $(70 : \tau_0, 70 : \tau_1)$ in state (2) is shown in Fig. 2. Subsequent left (3) and right (4) swaps result in a traversal along $k = 70 \cdot 70$ from $(70 : \tau_0, 70 : \tau_1)$ to $(100 : \tau_0, 49 : \tau_1)$, and back as the swap invariant must hold for swap actions. The redeem action (5) reduces the holdings of both tokens by the same factor to reach $(40 : \tau_0, 40 : \tau_1)$. A left swap (6) traverses $k' = 40 \cdot 40$ to reach $(70 : \tau_0, 23 : \tau_1)$ in state (6), which is then followed by another redeem (7) action, reducing both token holdings proportionally to $(18 : \tau_0, 6 : \tau_1)$.

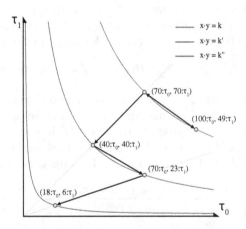

Fig. 2. Evolution of balances of AMM (τ_0, τ_1) along the trace in Fig. 1.

3   Structural Properties of AMMs

We now establish some structural properties of AMMs, which do not depend on the design of the economic mechanisms, i.e. on the choice of the swap invariant. We denote with $\rightarrow^*$ the reflexive and transitive closure of $\rightarrow$. Given a finite sequence of transactions $\lambda = T_1 \cdots T_k$, we write $\Gamma \xrightarrow{\lambda} \Gamma'$ when $\Gamma \xrightarrow{T_1} \cdots \xrightarrow{T_k} \Gamma'$. We say that a state Γ is *reachable* if $\Gamma_0 \rightarrow^* \Gamma$ for some initial Γ_0. We denote with $type(T)$ the type of T (i.e., $xfer, dep, \ldots$), with $wal(T)$ the set of wallets affected by T (e.g., $wal(\mathsf{A} : \mathsf{xfer}(\mathsf{B}, v : \tau)) = \{\mathsf{A}, \mathsf{B}\}$), and with $tok(\mathsf{T})$ the set of token types affected by T (e.g., $tok(\mathsf{A} : \mathsf{swapL}(v_0 : \tau_0, v_1 : \tau_1)) = \{\tau_0, \tau_1\}$).

First, we establish that the AMMs' LTS is deterministic. Note that, in swap rules, an unconstrained swap invariant I could admit different solutions to the equation in the premise: determinism is ensured by condition (10), which we assume to be true for all swap invariants.

Lemma 1 (Determinism). *If* $\Gamma \xrightarrow{\mathsf{T}} \Gamma'$ *and* $\Gamma \xrightarrow{\mathsf{T}} \Gamma''$, *then* $\Gamma' = \Gamma''$.

We can lift the statement to sequences of transactions by using a simple inductive argument. The same applies to other single-step results in this section.

Lemma 2 ensures that the supply of each *initial* token type τ is preserved by transitions (of any type). Note that preservation does not hold for *minted* tokens, as they can be created (by rule [DEP]) and destroyed (by rule [RDM]).

Lemma 2. *For all* $\tau \in \mathbb{T}_0$, *if* $\Gamma \to \Gamma'$ *then* $sply_\tau(\Gamma) = sply_\tau(\Gamma')$.

Lemma 3 ensures that the *global* net worth is preserved by transactions, whereas the user's net worth is preserved only by redeems/deposits.

Lemma 3 (Preservation of net worth). *Let* $\Gamma \xrightarrow{\mathsf{T}} \Gamma'$. *Then,* $W(\Gamma) = W(\Gamma')$. *Further, if* $type(\mathsf{T}) \in \{\mathsf{dep}, \mathsf{rdm}\}$ *or* $\mathsf{A} \notin wal(\mathsf{T})$, *then* $W_\mathsf{A}(\Gamma) = W_\mathsf{A}(\Gamma')$.

Lemma 4 ensures that funds cannot be *frozen* in an AMM, i.e. that users can always redeem arbitrary amounts of the tokens deposited in an AMM.

Lemma 4 (Liquidity). *Let* Γ *be a reachable state such that* $(r_0 : \tau_0, r_1 : \tau_1) \in \Gamma$ *with* $r_0 + r_1 > 0$. *Then: (a)* $sply_{(\tau_0, \tau_1)}(\Gamma) > 0$; *(b) for all* $r_0' \leq r_0$, *there exists* $r_1' \leq r_1$ *such that* $\Gamma \to^* (r_0' : \tau_0, r_1' : \tau_1) \mid \cdots$; *(c) for all* $r_1' \leq r_1$, *there exists* $r_0' \leq r_0$ *such that* $\Gamma \to^* (r_0' : \tau_0, r_1' : \tau_1) \mid \cdots$.

We now study the concurrency of transactions. Two finite sequences of transactions λ_0 and λ_1 are *observationally equivalent*, in denoted $\lambda_0 \sim \lambda_1$, when, for all states Γ, if $\Gamma \xrightarrow{\lambda_0} \Gamma_0$ and $\Gamma \xrightarrow{\lambda_1} \Gamma_1$ then $\Gamma_0 = \Gamma_1$. We say that two distinct transactions T, T' are *concurrent* (denoted, $\mathsf{T} \# \mathsf{T}'$) if $\mathsf{T}\mathsf{T}' \sim \mathsf{T}'\mathsf{T}$. Note that this does not mean that T and T' cannot disable each other as demanded by stricter notions of concurrency. Lemma 5 provides sufficient conditions for two transactions to be concurrent: intuitively, two non-swap transactions are always concurrent, while swap transactions are concurrent with xfer transactions, and with any transactions which do not affect the same token types.

Lemma 5. *Two distinct transactions* T_0, T_1 *are concurrent if, for* $i \in \{0, 1\}$, $type(\mathsf{T}_i) \in \{\mathsf{swapL}, \mathsf{swapR}\}$ *implies* $tok(\mathsf{T}_i) \cap tok(\mathsf{T}_{1-i}) = \emptyset$ *or* $type(\mathsf{T}_{1-i}) = \mathsf{xfer}$.

As we shall see later in Sect. 4, it is actually desirable, and crucial for the economic mechanism of AMMs, that swap transactions interfere with other transactions that trade the same token type.

The theory of Mazurkiewicz's trace languages [27] allows us to lift Lemma 5 to sequences of transactions. Let R be a symmetric and irreflexive relation on the set $\mathbb{X}$ of all transactions. The *Mazurkiewicz equivalence* $\sim_R$ is the least congruence in the free monoid $\mathbb{X}^*$ such that: $\forall \mathsf{T}, \mathsf{T}' \in \mathbb{X}$: $\mathsf{T} \, R \, \mathsf{T}' \implies \mathsf{T}\mathsf{T}' \sim_R \mathsf{T}'\mathsf{T}$. Theorem 1 states that the Mazurkiewicz equivalence constructed on the concurrency relation $\#$ is an observational equivalence.

Theorem 1 (Concurrent transactions can be reordered). $\sim_\# \subseteq \sim$.

A direct consequence of Theorem 1 is that we can transform a finite sequence of transactions into an observationally equivalent one by repeatedly exchanging adjacent concurrent transactions—provided that both sequences are executable in the LTS. For example, sequences of $\mathsf{A} : \mathsf{rdm}(\_)$ transactions can be freely reordered, resulting in the same, unique state. This is exploited in the following lemma, which supports the inductive definition of the price of minted tokens in (8): indeed, computing the net worth of a user A under that price definition corresponds to making A first redeem all her minted tokens, and then summing the price of the resulting initial tokens.

Lemma 6. *For all states Γ and users A, let $rdm_\mathsf{A}(\Gamma)$ be the unique state reached from Γ by performing only $\mathsf{A} : \mathsf{rdm}(\_)$ actions, such that A's wallet in $rdm_\mathsf{A}(\Gamma)$, only contains initial tokens. Then:*

$$W_\mathsf{A}(\Gamma) = \sum_{\tau \in \mathrm{dom}\,\sigma} \sigma(\tau) \cdot P^0(\tau) \qquad \text{if } \mathsf{A}[\sigma] \in rdm_\mathsf{A}(\Gamma)$$

Example 7. Recall from Example 4 that $W_\mathsf{A}(\Gamma_7) = 977$. Assume that A performs a further transaction to redeem all 10 units of (τ_0, τ_1) from her wallet. The resulting state is $\Gamma_8 = \mathsf{A}[100 : \tau_0, 53 : \tau_1] \mid \cdots$. We compute A's net worth in that state, using the oracle token prices: $W_\mathsf{A}(\Gamma_8) = 100 \cdot P_{(\tau_0)}(\Gamma_7) + 53 \cdot P_{(\tau_1)}(\Gamma_7) = 100 \cdot 5 + 53 \cdot 9 = 977$, as correctly predicted by Lemma 6. $\qquad \square$

4   Properties of AMM Incentives

We now study the incentive mechanisms of AMMs. We start in Sect. 4.1 by introducing a few notions of *exchange rate*, which are pivotal to understanding these mechanisms. In Sect. 4.2 we devise general conditions on swap invariants, overall named *incentive-consistency*, which guarantee that AMMs enjoy relevant economic properties. In Sect. 4.3 we study solutions to the *arbitrage problem*, which is the key to incentivize users to perform swap operations towards an ideal state where the AMM's exchange rates align with the exchange rates set by price oracles. Finally, in Sect. 4.4 we study the incentives to swap and deposit larger amounts.

4.1   Exchange Rates

The **exchange rate** between two token types is the number of units of one token needed to buy one unit of the other token at the current price. We define *Left* and *Right* versions of this notion, that reflect the direction of the exchange:

$$XL_\Gamma(\tau_0, \tau_1) = P_{\tau_0}(\Gamma)/P_{\tau_1}(\Gamma) \qquad XR_\Gamma(\tau_0, \tau_1) = P_{\tau_1}(\Gamma)/P_{\tau_0}(\Gamma) \qquad (11)$$

The **swap rate** between τ_0 and τ_1 upon a payment of $v_i : \tau_i$ (for $i \in \{0,1\}$) is the ratio between v and v_i, where v is the received amount of τ_{1-i} resulting from a swap action on an AMM $(r_0 : \tau_0, r_1 : \tau_1)$. We first introduce an auxiliary notion, parameterized over the balances r_0 and r_1, instead of the token types:

$$\begin{aligned} XL_\phi^{\mathsf{swap}}(v_0, r_0, r_1) &= v/v_0 \quad \text{if } I(r_0, r_1) = I(r_0 + \phi v_0, r_1 - v) \\ XR_\phi^{\mathsf{swap}}(v_1, r_0, r_1) &= v/v_1 \quad \text{if } I(r_0, r_1) = I(r_0 - v, r_1 + \phi v_1) \end{aligned} \qquad (12)$$

The swap rate is parameterized over the fee rate ϕ: the case where $\phi = 1$ represents an ideal scenario with no fees: in this case, we write just $XL^{\mathsf{swap}}(v_0, r_0, r_1)$. We define the swap rate in a state Γ such that $(r_0 : \tau_0, r_1 : \tau_1) \in \Gamma$ as follows:

$$XL_{\Gamma,\phi}^{\mathsf{swap}}(v_0, \tau_0, \tau_1) = XL_\phi^{\mathsf{swap}}(v_0, r_0, r_1) \qquad XR_{\Gamma,\phi}^{\mathsf{swap}}(v_1, \tau_0, \tau_1) = XR_\phi^{\mathsf{swap}}(v_1, r_0, r_1)$$

We also define the **redeem rate**. The left version is:

$$XL_\Gamma^{\mathsf{rdm}}(\tau_0, \tau_1) = r_0/sply_{(\tau_0, \tau_1)}(\Gamma) \qquad \text{if } (r_0 : \tau_0, r_1 : \tau_1) \in \Gamma \qquad (13)$$

4.2 General Properties of Swap Invariants

We now introduce a set of properties of swap invariants, called cumulatively *incentive-consistency*, which overall incentivize users to interact with AMMs by performing swap and deposit actions.

Swap-Rate Continuity. This property requires that, for all $r_0, r_1 > 0$:

$$\lim_{\varepsilon \to 0} XL^{\mathsf{swap}}(\varepsilon, r_0, r_1) = 1/\lim_{\varepsilon \to 0} XR^{\mathsf{swap}}(\varepsilon, r_0, r_1) \in \mathbb{R}^+ \qquad (14)$$

Figure 3 (left) illustrates this property, displaying the points (x, y) which satisfy the constant product invariant $x \cdot y = k$. The left swap rate limit for the constant product invariant and $\phi = 1$ is $\lim_{\varepsilon \to 0} XL^{\mathsf{swap}}(\varepsilon, r_0, r_1) = r_1/r_0$, while for the right swap we have $\lim_{\varepsilon \to 0} XR^{\mathsf{swap}}(\varepsilon, r_0, r_1) = r_0/r_1$. Coinciding left swap limit and right swap limit inverse are illustrated as the slope of the product constant curve at a selected point in Fig. 3 (left). The constant product invariant satisfies (14), i.e. it is swap-rate continuous.

Demand-Sensitivity. A swap invariant is demand-sensitive if the swap rate strictly decreases with demand. Formally, for all $r_0, r_1, r_0', r_1' > 0$:

$$I(r_0, r_1) = I(r_0', r_1') \wedge r_0' > r_0 \implies \lim_{\varepsilon \to 0} XL_\phi^{\mathsf{swap}}(\varepsilon, r_0, r_1) > \lim_{\varepsilon \to 0} XL_\phi^{\mathsf{swap}}(\varepsilon, r_0', r_1') \qquad (15)$$

We implicitly require that (15) and the subsequent properties stated for the left version of an exchange rate also hold for the right version.

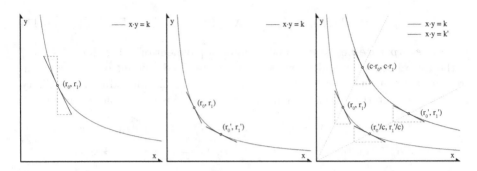

Fig. 3. The constant product invariant $I(x, y) = x \cdot y$ is swap-rate-consistent (left), demand-sensitive (center), non-depletable, funds-consistent (right) and swap-rate consistent (right).

Figure 3 (center) depicts two points (r_0, r_1), (r'_0, r'_1) on the constant product curve, which satisfy $x \cdot y = k$ for identical k. For the constant product invariant, the left swap limit can be expressed as $\lim_{\varepsilon \to 0} XL^{\mathsf{swap}}(\varepsilon, r_0, r_1) = \phi \cdot r_1/r_0$. For the given k and points in Fig. 3 (center):

$$\lim_{\varepsilon \to 0} XL^{\mathsf{swap}}_\phi(\varepsilon, r_0, r_1) = \phi \cdot k/r_0^2 \qquad \lim_{\varepsilon \to 0} XL^{\mathsf{swap}}_\phi(\varepsilon, r'_0, r'_1) = \phi \cdot k/r_0'^{\,2}$$

Thus for $r'_0 > r_0$, $\lim_{\varepsilon \to 0} XL^{\mathsf{swap}}_\phi(\varepsilon, r_0, r_1) > \lim_{\varepsilon \to 0} XL^{\mathsf{swap}}_\phi(\varepsilon, r'_0, r'_1)$: the constant product invariant is demand-sensitive.

Non-depletion. This property ensures that the balance of tokens within an AMM cannot be zeroed via swaps. Formally, I is non-depletable when, for all $r_0, r_1 > 0$ and $r'_0, r'_1 \geq 0$:

$$I(r_0, r_1) = I(r'_0, r'_1) \implies r'_0, r'_1 \neq 0 \tag{16}$$

Note that the constant product invariant trivially satisfies this property.

Funds-Consistency. Deposits to an AMM ensure higher swap rates for a given input amount v, whereas redeems will reduce the swap rates for v. This behaviour is formalized later on in Theorem 4, but is a consequence of the funds-consistency property of the swap invariant. Formally, we require that for all $r_0, r_1, r'_0, r'_1 > 0$:

$$\begin{aligned} I(r_0, r_1) \neq I(r'_0, r'_1) \iff \\ \exists! c \in \mathbb{R}^+ \setminus \{1\} : I(c \cdot r'_0, c \cdot r'_1) = I(r_0, r_1) \wedge I(\tfrac{r_0}{c}, \tfrac{r_1}{c}) = I(r'_0, r'_1) \end{aligned} \tag{17}$$

Figure 3 (right) illustrates funds-consistency for the constant product invariant. Here, $r_0 \cdot r_1 = k \neq k' = r'_0 \cdot r'_1$. We observe that there exists a unique $c > 0$ in $(c \cdot r_0) \cdot (c \cdot r_1) = r'_0 \cdot r'_1 = k'$: namely, $c = \sqrt{(r'_0 \cdot r'_1)/(r_0 \cdot r_1)}$. Conversely, $(r'_0/c) \cdot (r'_1/c) = r_0 \cdot r_1$, which holds for the same value of c.

Swap-Rate-Consistency. The design of AMMs aims to ensure that redeems and deposits do not interfere with the alignment of the swap rate towards the exchange rate. Since both deposits and redeems preserve the balance ratio of a token pair, we require swap rate limits for all balances of a given ratio to be constant. For all $r_0, r_1, c > 0$:

$$\lim_{\varepsilon \to 0} XL_\phi^{\mathsf{swap}}(\varepsilon, r_0, r_1) = \lim_{\varepsilon \to 0} XL_\phi^{\mathsf{swap}}(\varepsilon, c \cdot r_0, c \cdot r_1) \tag{18}$$

Figure 3 (right) illustrates equal swap rate limits for given r_0, r_1 and $c \cdot r_0, c \cdot r_1$. Here, $\lim_{\varepsilon \to 0} XL^{\mathsf{swap}}(\varepsilon, r_0, r_1) = \phi \cdot r_1/r_0 = \phi \cdot (c \cdot r_1)/(c \cdot r_0)$ for $c > 0$.

Finally, the following lemma establishes that the constant product swap invariant (the one used e.g. by Uniswap and Mooniswap) is indeed incentive-consistent. We conjecture that the same is true for the swap invariants implemented by the other mainstream AMM platforms.

Lemma 7. *The constant product swap invariant is incentive-consistent.*

4.3   The Arbitrage Game

We now study the incentive mechanisms of AMMs from a game-theoretic perspective. Indeed, AMMs can be seen as multi-player games where users collaborate or compete to achieve possibly conflicting goals. In such games the allowed moves of users are the interactions with other users and with AMMs, while their goal is typically to increase their net worth.

The **arbitrage problem** is an interesting example of an AMM game since it is directly linked to the incentive of swaps in a way that makes AMMs track exchange rates. The arbitrage problem has been formalized for specific swap invariants, namely the *weighted* and *constant product* swap invariant [17,19]. We generalize here the arbitrage problem to *arbitrary* swap invariants. We provide sufficient conditions for the existence of solutions, and we link the solutions to the expected relation between AMMs and exchange rates.

We model the arbitrage problem as a single-player, single-round game. The *initial game state* is $\Gamma_0 = \mathsf{A}[\sigma] \mid (r_1 : \tau_0, r_1 : \tau_1)$, where A is the only *player*. The *moves* of A are all the possible transactions fired by A; we also consider doing nothing as a possible move. The *goal* of A is to maximize her net worth, i.e. to maximize $W_\mathsf{A}(\Gamma) - W_\mathsf{A}(\Gamma_0)$, where Γ is the state resulting from executing the selected move. A *solution* to the game is a move that satisfies the goal, i.e. one of the optimal moves. We further assume that A holds no minted tokens containing (τ_0, τ_1) as a subterm (i.e., (τ_0, τ_1) itself, $((\tau_0, \tau_1), \tau_2)$, etc.). In this way, any change in A's net worth only depends on the exchange rate between τ_0 and τ_1, and on the transfer of value resulting from A's move.

Before presenting the solution to the game we examine the potential candidates for the solution. First, note that transfers are not valid solutions, as they can only decrease A's net worth. A second observation is that doing nothing, depositing or redeeming do not alter A's net worth (cf. Lemma 3). Hence, if one of such moves is a solution, so are the other two. The only moves that may affect A's net worth are swaps. For a swap to be a solution to the game, it must, first of all, result in a positive change of A's net worth. This happens when the swap rate is greater than the exchange rate. Theorem 2 presents the solution to the game. Note that if $\mathsf{swapL}(v_0 : \tau_0, v_1 : \tau_1)$ is a solution, then for all $v_1' \leq v_1$, also $\mathsf{swapL}(v_0 : \tau_0, v_1' : \tau_1)$ is a solution. Without loss of generality, our statement singles our the solution with the greatest v_1 (similarly for the right swap).

Theorem 2. *Let I be demand-sensitive and non-depletable, and let the initial state of the game be $\Gamma_0 = \mathsf{A}[\sigma] \mid (r_0 : \tau_0, r_1 : \tau_1)$, with $r_0, r_1 > 0$. Let $\sigma(\tau_0), \sigma(\tau_1)$ be large enough to enable any needed swap. Then, the solution to the game is:*

- $\mathsf{A} : \mathsf{swapL}(v_0 : \tau_0, v_1 : \tau_1)$ *if* $\Gamma_0 \xrightarrow{\ \mathsf{A:swapL}(v_0 : \tau_0, v_1 : \tau_1)\ } \Gamma$, *and:*

  (1) $\displaystyle\lim_{\varepsilon \to 0} XL_{\Gamma_0, \phi}^{\mathsf{swap}}(\varepsilon, \tau_0, \tau_1) > XL_{\Gamma_0}(\tau_0, \tau_1)$

  (2) $\displaystyle\lim_{\varepsilon \to 0} XL_\phi^{\mathsf{swap}}(\varepsilon, r_0 + \phi \cdot v_0, r_1 - v_1) = XL_\Gamma(\tau_0, \tau_1)$ *where* $\exists! \, \delta$:

  $$I(r_0, r_1) = I(r_0 + \phi \cdot v_0, r_1 - v_1) = I(r_0 + \phi \cdot (v_0 + \varepsilon), r_1 - (v_1 + \delta))$$

- $\mathsf{A} : \mathsf{swapR}(v_0 : \tau_0, v_1 : \tau_1)$ *if* $\Gamma_0 \xrightarrow{\ \mathsf{A:swapR}(v_0 : \tau_0, v_1 : \tau_1)\ } \Gamma$, *and:*

  (1) $\displaystyle\lim_{\varepsilon \to 0} XR_{\Gamma_0, \phi}^{\mathsf{swap}}(\varepsilon, \tau_0, \tau_1) > XR_{\Gamma_0}(\tau_0, \tau_1)$

  (2) $\displaystyle\lim_{\varepsilon \to 0} XR_\phi^{\mathsf{swap}}(\varepsilon, r_0 - v_0, r_1 + \phi \cdot v_1) = XR_\Gamma(\tau_0, \tau_1)$ *where* $\exists! \, \delta$:

  $$I(r_0, r_1) = I(r_0 - v_0, r_1 + \phi \cdot v_1) = I(r_0 - (v_0 + \delta), r_1 + \phi \cdot (v_1 + \varepsilon))$$

- *do nothing (or do any deposit or redeem), otherwise.*

Intuitively, condition (1) requires that the swap rate for infinitesimal amounts is greater than the exchange rate in the initial state; (2) requires that in the state Γ reached by performing the move of the solution, the swap rate for infinitesimal amounts tends to the exchange rate—thus achieving one of the main desiderata on AMMs. Note that Γ is an *equilibrium*: no move from there can improve A's net worth, i.e. doing nothing is a solution for the arbitrage problem in Γ.

Note that for the $\mathsf{swapL}/\mathsf{swapR}$ solutions, the swapped amounts are unique: this is a consequence on the assumption (10). An implicit desideratum on these solutions is that, given a specific instance of the swap invariant, they are efficiently computable: this is the case, e.g., for the constant product invariant [17].

For $\phi = 1$ we can observe by inspection of (14) that the do-nothing solution for Theorem 2 only holds for:

$$\lim_{\varepsilon \to 0} XL_{\Gamma_0}^{\mathsf{swap}}(\varepsilon, \tau_0, \tau_1) \ = \ 1/\lim_{\varepsilon \to 0} XR_{\Gamma_0}^{\mathsf{swap}}(\varepsilon, \tau_0, \tau_1) \ = \ XL_{\Gamma_0}(\tau_0, \tau_1) \tag{19}$$

Thus, the solution to the game results in the AMM tracking global exchange rates precisely: any infinitesimal deviation of the global exchange rate implies a swap action in the arbitrage game.

The assumption that the players' wallets are sufficiently large is common in formulations of the arbitrage problem. We note that any rational agent is incentivized to perform such a swap: the optimal solution to the arbitrage game can thus be approximated by multiple users exchanging smaller swap amounts. Furthermore, the availability of flash-loans [29,30] can provide up-front funds, and thus significantly reduce the balance requirements for arbitrage swaps.

Finally, we prove that a AMM deposits and redeems do not affect the solution type of the arbitrage game. If the arbitrage solution prior to a deposit or redeem is swapL, swapR or nothing, the arbitrage solution in the subsequent state should remain of the same type.

Theorem 3. *Let I be incentive-consistent. Let $(r_0 : \tau_0, r_1 : \tau_1) \in \Gamma$ with $r_0, r_1 > 0$. If $\Gamma \xrightarrow{\mathsf{T}} \Gamma'$, $\mathsf{type}(\mathsf{T}) \in \{\mathsf{dep}, \mathsf{rdm}\}$, then the arbitrage solutions in Γ and Γ' will have the same type or both be nothing.*

In other words, the design of AMMs aims to ensure that deposits and redeems do not interfere with the alignment of the swap rate towards the exchange rate.

Example 8. Consider the arbitrage game with player B and initial state $\Gamma_7 = \mathsf{B}[0 : \tau_0, 27 : \tau_1] \mid (18 : \tau_0, 6 : \tau_1) \mid \cdots$ resulting after the last step in Fig. 1. Assuming the constant product invariant and no fees (i.e., $\phi = 1$), we have that:

$$\lim_{\varepsilon \to 0} XL^{\mathsf{swap}}_{\Gamma_7}(\varepsilon, \tau_0, \tau_1) = r_1/r_0 = 6/18 < 5/9 = XL_{\Gamma_7}(\tau_0, \tau_1)$$

$$\lim_{\varepsilon \to 0} XR^{\mathsf{swap}}_{\Gamma_7}(\varepsilon, \tau_0, \tau_1) = r_0/r_1 = 18/6 > 9/5 = XR_{\Gamma_7}(\tau_0, \tau_1)$$

Hence, by Theorem 2 it follows that the optimal move is $\mathsf{swapR}(v_0 : \tau_0, v_1 : \tau_1)$, for suitable v_0 and v_1. To find these values, we must solve for v_0 and v_1 the equations in item (2) of Theorem 2, i.e.:

$$\lim_{\varepsilon \to 0} XR^{\mathsf{swap}}_{\phi}(\varepsilon, r_0 - v, r_1 + v_1) = XR_{\Gamma}(\tau_0, \tau_1) \qquad I(r_0, r_1) = I(r_0 - v_0, r_1 + v_1)$$

Solving these equations gives:

$$v_1 = \sqrt{\frac{5}{9} \cdot r_0 r_1} - r_1 \approx 1.74 \qquad v_0 = \frac{r_0 v_1}{r_1 + v_1} \approx 4$$

By performing $\mathsf{swapR}(v_0 : \tau_0, v_1 : \tau_1)$ with these values from Γ_7, we obtain:

$$\Gamma = \mathsf{B}[4 : \tau_0, 25.26 : \tau_1] \mid (14 : \tau_0, 7.74 : \tau_1) \mid \cdots$$

This action maximizes B's net worth: indeed, we have $W_{\mathsf{B}}(\Gamma_7) = 243$ and $W_{\mathsf{B}}(\Gamma) = 247.6$; any other action will result in a lower net worth for B. □

4.4   Incentivizing Deposits and Swaps

Theorem 2 ensures that incentive-consistent AMMs incentivize swaps to align to exchange rates. We now show that, under certain conditions, deposits and swaps incentivize each other. The intuition is that larger amounts of tokens in an AMM provide better swap rates, therefore attracting users interested in swaps. These swaps, in turn, result in increased redeem rates, making the AMM attractive for further deposits. Note that this behaviour relies on an underlying assumption of our model, i.e. that exchange rates are stable: oracle prices are fixed. In the wild, exchange rates can vary over time, possibly making the net worth of users holding minted AMM tokens decrease: this phenomenon is commonly referred to as *impermanent loss* [9].

The following theorem shows that deposits increase swap rates, hence incentivizing swaps, whilst redeems have the opposite effect.

Theorem 4. *Let I be incentive-consistent. Let $\Gamma = (r_0 : \tau_0, r_1 : \tau_1) \mid \cdots$, with $r_0, r_1 > 0$, and let $\Gamma \xrightarrow{A:\ell} \Gamma'$. Then, for all $v \in \mathbb{R}^+$:*

$$
\begin{aligned}
XL^{\mathsf{swap}}_{\Gamma,\phi}(v,\tau_0,\tau_1) \circ XL^{\mathsf{swap}}_{\Gamma',\phi}(v,\tau_0,\tau_1) \\
XR^{\mathsf{swap}}_{\Gamma,\phi}(v,\tau_0,\tau_1) \circ XR^{\mathsf{swap}}_{\Gamma',\phi}(v,\tau_0,\tau_1)
\end{aligned}
\quad where \circ =
\begin{cases}
< & if\ \ell = \mathsf{dep}(\_ : \tau_0, \_ : \tau_1) \\
> & if\ \ell = \mathsf{rdm}(\_ : (\tau_0, \tau_1))
\end{cases}
$$

We now show that, under certain conditions, swaps incentivize deposits. Intuitively, swaps contribute to higher redeem rates, which increase the net wealth of the holders of minted AMM tokens:

Theorem 5. *Let I be incentive-consistent. Let $\Gamma = (r_0 : \tau_0, r_1 : \tau_1) \mid \cdots$ and $\Gamma \to^* \Gamma'$, where $\Gamma' = (r'_0 : \tau_0, r'_1 : \tau_1) \mid \cdots$. If $r_1/r_0 = r'_1/r'_0$ then:*

$$
XL^{\mathsf{rdm}}_{\Gamma}(\tau_0,\tau_1) \leq XL^{\mathsf{rdm}}_{\Gamma'}(\tau_0,\tau_1) \qquad XR^{\mathsf{rdm}}_{\Gamma}(\tau_0,\tau_1) \leq XR^{\mathsf{rdm}}_{\Gamma'}(\tau_0,\tau_1)
$$

Recall that a user who deposits into an AMM $(r_0 : \tau_0, r_1 : \tau_1)$ in state Γ receives in return an amount of minted tokens. A consequence of Theorem 5 is that these minted tokens can be redeemed with a higher redeem rate in any subsequent state Γ' which preserves the funds ratio r_1/r_0. Note that swaps are the only actions that may affect the redeem rate along the run $\Gamma \to^* \Gamma'$. Therefore, performing swaps that eventually re-align the funds ratio to r_1/r_0 incentivizes deposits.

The condition of constant funds ratio in Theorem 5 is practically relevant. For instance, for stable exchange rates, such as in the case of exchanges between stable coins [6], the arbitrage game ensures stable fund ratios: users are hence incentivized to provide funds, as the redeem rate is likely to increase over time.

5 Related Work

To the best of our knowledge, our work is the first to study AMMs abstracting from the swap invariant. All works in literature consider concrete swap invariants; most of them focus on the constant product, popularized by Uniswap [13]. The arbitrage problem for constant-product swap invariants has been formalized in [17,19], which show that the solution can be efficiently computed, and suggest that constant product AMMs accurately tend towards exchange rates. Our work generalizes such results. Furthermore, as we have shown in Sect. 4.3 (19), the fee-rate ϕ determines how much AMMs deviate from global exchange rates: higher fees, however, also result in reduced swap amounts in arbitrage actions, negatively affecting fee accrual. In [24], the optimal fee-rate that maximizes the fee accrual for the depositing user is analytically derived.

A executable model of Uniswap [13] has been specified in [1] to analyze integer rounding errors in the Uniswap implementation.

A few alternatives to the constant product invariant have been proposed. Curve features a peculiar invariant [22] optimized for large swap volumes between *stable coins*, where the swap rate can support large amounts with small sensitivity. To efficiently compute swap invariant, implementations perform numerical approximations [15]. Should these approximations fail to converge, these implementations still guarantee that the AMM remains liquid. We conjecture that the invariants in [3, 22] are incentive-consistent. The work [25] proposes a constant product invariant that is adjusted dynamically based on the oracle price feed, thus reducing the need for arbitrage transactions, but at the cost of lower fee accrual. AMMs with *virtual* balances have been proposed [2] and implemented [7,8]. In these AMMs, the swap rate depends on past actions, besides the current funds balances in the AMM. This, similarly to [25], aims to minimize the need for arbitrage transactions to ensure the local AMM swap rate tends towards the exchange rates.

Some implementations [3] generalise AMM pairs to n-tokens, allowing users to swap any non-intersecting sets of token types. For example, the constant-product invariant becomes $I(r_0, \ldots, r_n) = r_0^{w_0} \cdot \ldots \cdot r_n^{w_n}$ where $\sum_{i=0}^{n} w^i = 1$.

6   Conclusions

We have proposed a theory of AMMs, featuring a model of their behaviour and a formally proven set of fundamental properties, characterizing both structural and economic aspects. Our theory is parametric w.r.t. platform-specific features (e.g., swap invariants), and it abstracts from implementation-specific features, and from the features that are orthogonal to the core functionality of AMMs (e.g., governance).

There are some differences between our model and the existing AMM platforms. Uniswap implements flash-loans as part of the swap actions: namely, the user can optionally borrow available pair funds [10] whilst returning these within the same *atomic group* of actions. Further, Uniswap implements an exchange rate oracle, allowing smart contracts to interpret (averages of) recent swap rates as exchange rates [11]. Balancer [3] extends token pairs to token *tuples*: a user can swap any two non-coinciding sets of supported tokens, such that the swap invariant is maintained. In all AMM implementations, token balances are represented as integers: consequently, they are subject to rounding errors [1]. AMM platforms frequently implement a governance logic, which allow "governance token" holders to coordinate changes to AMM fee-rates or swap invariant parameters.

AMM platforms like Uniswap [13] and Curve [22] have overtaken centralized cryptocurrency markets in size and usage. On the one hand, a better understanding of AMM design in cases where AMMs host the majority of the token's global swap volume is critical [18]. It would be interesting to investigate how our theory can be used to formally explain such behaviours. On the other hand, the growth of AMMs is making them more attractive for malicious users. Current research efforts [21,23,28,31] are devoted to understanding vulnerabilities and attacks, which we plan to investigate formally, exploiting our theory.

This paper, together with our work on formalizing another DeFi archetype called *lending pool* [20], is the first step towards a general theory of DeFi. We believe that a general theory encompassing interactions between different DeFi archetypes is crucial to be able to reason about their structural, economic and security aspects, as typical DeFi applications operate within a wider ecosystem, composed by a set of collaborating or competing agents, which interact through possibly separate execution environments.

Acknowledgements. Massimo Bartoletti is partially supported by Conv. Fondazione di Sardegna & Atenei Sardi project F74I19000900007 *ADAM*. James Hsin-yu Chiang is supported by the PhD School of DTU Compute. Alberto Lluch Lafuente is partially supported by the EU H2020-SU-ICT-03-2018 Project No. 830929 CyberSec4Europe (cybersec4europe.eu).

References

1. Formal specification of constant product market maker model & implementation (2018). https://github.com/runtimeverification/verified-smart-contracts/blob/uniswap/uniswap/x-y-k.pdf
2. Improving frontrunning resistance of x*y=k market makers (2018). https://ethresear.ch/t/improving-front-running-resistance-of-x-y-k-market-makers/1281
3. Balancer whitepaper (2019). https://balancer.finance/whitepaper/
4. Curve statistics (2020). https://www.curve.fi/dailystats
5. Curve (2020). https://www.curve.fi
6. Makerdao (2020). https://makerdao.com
7. Mooniswap implementation (2020). https://github.com/1inch-exchange/mooniswap/blob/02dccfab2ddbb8a409400288cb13441763370350/contracts/Mooniswap.sol
8. Mooniswap whitepaper (2020). https://mooniswap.exchange/docs/MooniswapWhitePaper-v1.0.pdf
9. Uniswap Documentation: Understanding Returns (2020). https://uniswap.org/docs/v2/advanced-topics/understanding-returns/
10. Uniswap flash loan implementation (2020). https://github.com/Uniswap/uniswap-v2-core/blob/4dd59067c76dea4a0e8e4bfdda41877a6b16dedc/contracts/UniswapV2Pair.sol#L172
11. Uniswap oracle template (2020). https://github.com/Uniswap/uniswap-v2-periphery/blob/dda62473e2da448bc9cb8f4514dadda4aeede5f4/contracts/examples/ExampleOracleSimple.sol
12. Uniswap statistics (2020). https://info.uniswap.org
13. Uniswap token pair implementation (2020). https://github.com/Uniswap/uniswap-v2-core/blob/4dd59067c76dea4a0e8e4bfdda41877a6b16dedc/contracts/UniswapV2Pair.sol
14. Uniswap (2020). https://www.uniswap.org

15. Curve computation of invariant constant (2021). https://github.com/curvefi/curve-contract/blob/a1b5a797790d3f5ef12b0e358892a0ce47c12f85/contracts/pool-templates/base/SwapTemplateBase.vy#L206

16. Curve token pair implementation (2021). https://github.com/curvefi/curve-contract/blob/a1b5a797790d3f5ef12b0e358892a0ce47c12f85/contracts/pool-templates/base/SwapTemplateBase.vy

17. Angeris, G., Chitra, T.: Improved price oracles: constant function market makers. In: ACM Conference on Advances in Financial Technologies (AFT), pp. 80–91. ACM (2020). https://doi.org/10.1145/3419614.3423251. https://arxiv.org/abs/2003.10001

18. Angeris, G., Evans, A., Chitra, T.: When does the tail wag the dog? Curvature and market making. arXiv preprint arXiv:2012.08040 (2020)

19. Angeris, G., Kao, H.T., Chiang, R., Noyes, C., Chitra, T.: An analysis of Uniswap markets. Cryptoeconomic Syst. J. (2019). https://ssrn.com/abstract=3602203

20. Bartoletti, M., Chiang, J.H., Lluch-Lafuente, A.: SoK: lending pools in decentralized finance. In: Workshop on Trusted Smart Contracts. LNCS. Springer (2021, to appear)

21. Daian, P., et al.: Flash boys 2.0: frontrunning in decentralized exchanges, miner extractable value, and consensus instability. In: IEEE Symposium on Security and Privacy, pp. 910–927. IEEE (2020). https://doi.org/10.1109/SP40000.2020.00040

22. Egorov, M.: Stableswap - efficient mechanism for stablecoin (2019). https://www.curve.fi/stableswap-paper.pdf

23. Eskandari, S., Moosavi, S., Clark, J.: SoK: transparent dishonesty: front-running attacks on blockchain. In: Bracciali, A., Clark, J., Pintore, F., Rønne, P.B., Sala, M. (eds.) FC 2019. LNCS, vol. 11599, pp. 170–189. Springer, Cham (2020). https://doi.org/10.1007/978-3-030-43725-1_13

24. Evans, A., Angeris, G., Chitra, T.: Optimal fees for geometric mean market makers (2021). https://web.stanford.edu/~guillean/papers/g3m-optimal-fee.pdf

25. Krishnamachari, B., Feng, Q., Grippo, E.: Dynamic curves for decentralized autonomous cryptocurrency exchanges. arXiv preprint arXiv:2101.02778 (2021)

26. Bartoletti, M., Chiang, J.H., Lluch-Lafuente, A.: A theory of Automated Market Makers in DeFi. arXiv preprint arXiv:2102.11350 (2021)

27. Mazurkiewicz, A.: Basic notions of trace theory. In: de Bakker, J.W., de Roever, W.-P., Rozenberg, G. (eds.) REX 1988. LNCS, vol. 354, pp. 285–363. Springer, Heidelberg (1989). https://doi.org/10.1007/BFb0013025

28. Qin, K., Zhou, L., Gervais, A.: Quantifying blockchain extractable value: how dark is the forest? (2021). https://arxiv.org/abs/2101.05511

29. Qin, K., Zhou, L., Livshits, B., Gervais, A.: Attacking the DeFi ecosystem with flash loans for fun and profit. In: Financial Cryptography (2021, to appear). https://arxiv.org/abs/2003.03810

30. Wang, D., et al.: Towards understanding flash loan and its applications in DeFi ecosystem. arXiv preprint arXiv:2010.12252 (2020)

31. Zhou, L., Qin, K., Torres, C.F., Le, D.V., Gervais, A.: High-frequency trading on decentralized on-chain exchanges. arXiv preprint arXiv:2009.14021 (2020)

ReGraDa: Reactive Graph Data

Leandro Galrinho[1], João Costa Seco[1,2(✉)], Søren Debois[3,5],
Thomas Hildebrandt[4], Håkon Norman[4,5], and Tijs Slaats[4]

[1] School of Science and Technology, NOVA University of Lisbon, Lisbon, Portugal
joao.seco@fct.unl.pt
[2] NOVA Laboratory for Computer Science and Informatics (NOVA LINCS),
Caparica, Portugal
[3] Computer Science Department, IT University Copenhagen, Copenhagen, Denmark
[4] SDPS Section, Department of Computer Science, University of Copenhagen,
Copenhagen, Denmark
[5] DCR Solutions (DCRSolutions.net), Copenhagen, Denmark

Abstract. Business processes, data, and run-time control state are all key elements in the design of enterprise applications. However, the different layers for processes, data, and control are usually represented using different technologies that must be explicitly combined and kept in sync.

We introduce ReGraDa, a process definition and programming language inspired by the declarative business process language Dynamic Condition Response Graphs and targeting the integrated description of business processes, data and run-time state as reactive graph data. ReGraDa processes compile directly to a data-centric graph-based system (*neo4j*/*cypher*), allowing for the database system to manage a process without the need for an external execution engine.

The underlying graph structure allows for the definition of native data relations between data elements that subsumes the integrity guaranties of relational and the semi-structured data models. Graph relationships are also used to represent data-dependency and control-flow in the database.

We present the reactive semantics of the language, a translation from ReGraDa to *cypher*, evaluate its performance, and briefly discuss future work and applications.

1 Introduction

Process-aware information systems [4] include both control-flow and data. The notions of control and data are, however, often treated separately: process models may refer to specific documents or data values to guide decision making, but data manipulation is largely handled outside the processes control. Moreover, as pointed out by several authors [16,17], even among notations that provide bindings for data and computation, it remains cumbersome or impossible to model

Supported by Innovation Fund Denmark (EcoKnow.org & DREAM), Independent Research Fund Denmark (PAPRiCAS), EU MSCA-RISE BehAPI (ID: 778233), NOVA LINCS UID/CEC/04516/2013, and GOLEM Lisboa-01-0247-Feder-045917.

F. Damiani and O. Dardha (Eds.): COORDINATION 2021, LNCS 12717, pp. 188–205, 2021.
https://doi.org/10.1007/978-3-030-78142-2_12

complex data models and dependencies between data and activities belonging to multiple instances of processes.

These difficulties hinder both representation and reasoning about the full process behaviour, and form a practical barrier to adoption of system implementations based on formal workflow models.

Recent formalisms attempt to address these difficulties in combining data-modeling and declarative process-modeling, in various ways. The Case Management Model and Notation (CMMN) [7] makes data a first class citizen and arbiter of activity availability. The Object-Centric Behavioural Constraints (OCBC) [17] formalism cleverly ties together DECLARE and ER-modelling, explaining, e.g., how the satisfaction of a response constraint requires the creation of a data object. Extensions of Petri nets with identifiers [12,18] model the interplay of information and processes and model the influence of process transitions in the data model using first-order logic over finite sets. Finally, the Reactive Semi-structured Data Formalism removes the distinction between "activity" and "data" in a constraint-based language [13].

The present work advances this research agenda in two directions at once: First, we **introduce graph data and queries**, most notably aggregating queries, into the language of RESEDA [13] and relaxing the semi-structured data, resulting in the more general language REGRADA, short for Reactive Graph Data. While other data-centric process models use loosely coupled data relations (values as keys), which provide weak data-integrity guarantees, REGRADA provides a declarative definition of processes, graph data modeling, queries, and reactive computation. We formally define the syntax and semantics of the language and then focus on its pragmatics. The formal results on liveness properties of processes are out of the scope of this work, as they conservatively extend the results already obtained in REGRADA.

Second, we **provide a high-performance implementation** of this language via a translation of REGRADA programs into a contemporary graph database engine query language, specifically the query language *cypher* [6] of the graph database *neo4j*. The database computation capabilities and reactive mechanisms (triggers) are strong enough to not only implement the reactive embedded query language of REGRADA, but also its process semantics: Process execution is fully and autonomously realised in the database. We provide an initial exploratory empirical study of the performance of translated REGRADA programs in the latter section of this paper; initial results are encouraging.

REGRADA (and RESEDA) are inspired by both the declarative Dynamic Condition Response (DCR) graph process notation [1,8,15] and the widely used reactive model of data and behaviour used in spreadsheets [3,14] and provide a unified specification of data, behaviour, and run-time execution state. However, REGRADA differs from DCR Graphs in several ways. Firstly, it introduces a distinction between *input* and *computation* events, here called data elements. Secondly, REGRADA allows data elements to be related in a general labelled graph structure and to be referenced in computation expressions, either directly or by using graph query expressions. Similarly, control relations (edges) between data elements in REGRADA are dynamic. They are defined between sets of data elements given by graph query expressions and guarded by boolean expressions over the graph state.

Overview. We proceed as follows. We present REGRADA informally by example in Sect. 2; then provide formal syntax and semantics in Sect. 3 and 4. In Sect. 5 we present the translation of REGRADA to cypher/*neo4j*. In Sect. 6 we report on exploratory empirical studies of the performance characteristics of the translation. Finally, we briefly conclude and provide directions for future work in Sect. 7.

2 ReGraDa: Programming with Reactive Graph Data

In this section, we informally illustrate the syntax and semantics of REGRADA by giving an example of managing authors, books and book loans in a library.

A REGRADA process defines simultaneously the process, the data and the control flow of a software system. Consider the process below comprising three main sections separated by semicolon symbols. The first section (line 1) declares all instances of data elements in the process, i.e. the nodes of the graph. The second section (line 3–15) defines control relations. The third section after the semicolon in line 16 declares data relations, i.e. the edges in the graph data. This section is initially empty in this example.

```
1   (createAuthor:Input) [?: { authorName:String }]
2   ;
3   createAuthor -->> {
4     (author:Author) [{ name:@trigger.value.authorName }],
5     (createBook:Input) [?:{ bookTitle:String, isbn:String }]
6     ;
7     createBook -->> {
8       (book:Book) [{bookTitle:@trigger.value.bookTitle,
9                     isbn:@trigger.value.isbn,
10                    author:author.value.name }]
11      ; ;
12      author -[:WROTE]-> book
13    }
14    ;
15  }
16  ;
```

Line 1 declares an input data element that accepts values as input of type record {authorName:String}. Line 3 defines a spawn relation, which is a control relation that, whenever the input data element in line 1 is executed, triggers the creation of the elements contained in the sub-process defined in line 4–15. The sub-process creates two new data elements (line 4–5): author and createBook. The two data elements are implicitly associated with each other due to a syntactic dependency through a nested spawn relation (lines 7–13). The expression enclosed in declaration of data element author, of type record, denotes the

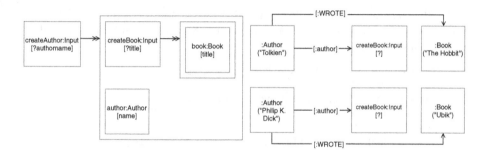

Fig. 1. Process state after the creation of two authors and two books.

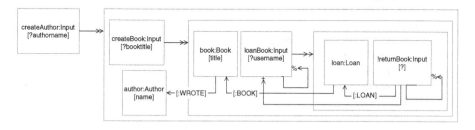

Fig. 2. Complete representation of the example.

new value given to the new data element, where @trigger is evaluated once in a call-by-value strategy (copying the value of the createAuthor data-element triggering the spawn reaction). Notice that each data element author will be explicitly associated to all book data elements created by its, implicitly associated, createBook input data element. From this, we can see that each author will have a distinct and direct entry point in the system to create their own books in the database. In our pragmatic approach, the entry points for input data elements are implemented in a companion system following REST conventions to identify the target element. Also, notice that the value of name author in the expression of data element book is associated to the data element statically associated with createBook. The sub-process spawned by the rule in line 7, when the createBook input data element is executed, it introduces a data element book and a new data relation, with label WROTE, between the data element author defined in the outer scope and the new data element book. The resulting graph is a flat structure of data elements, all created at the process's top level. So, after executing input data element createAuthor twice – with values ''Tolkien'' and "Philip K. Dick" – and "adding" one book for each one of the authors, we can observe that the process now includes the elements visually depicted in Fig. 1. Notice that the data relation above is introduced between the two newly created instances of the data elements. REGRADA also allows for the definitions of more general control and data relations between sets of data elements, which are denoted by graph queries.

To illustrate other control flow constraints we define the input data element `loanBook` in the sub-process of each book (line 8), and the sub-process that it triggers (lines 12–17).

```
1   (createAuthor:Input) [?: {authorName:String}] ;
2   createAuthor -->> {
3     (author:Author) [{name:@trigger.value.authorName}],
4     (createBook:Input) [?:{bookTitle:String, isbn:String}] ;
5     createBook -->>{
6       (book:Book) [{bookTitle:@trigger.value.bookTitle,
7                     isbn:@trigger.value.isbn, author:author.value.name}],
8       (loanBook:Input) [?:{username:String}] ;
9       loanBook -->% loanBook,
10      author -[:WROTE]-> book
11      loanBook -->>{
12        (loan:Loan) [{user:@trigger.value.username}],
13        !(returnBook:Input) [?:()] ;
14        returnBook -->% returnBook,
15        returnBook -->+ loanBook ;
16        loan -[:BOOK]-> book,
17        returnBook -[:LOAN]-> loan
18      } ;
19    } ;
20  } ;
```

This inner process makes more use of DCR constructs, in particular the notions of a data element being *included, excluded,* and *pending.*

Intuitively, an *excluded* data element is considered temporarily excluded from the process: We pretend that it, its contents, and the relations to or from it are "not there". The notion of exclusion is dynamic: data elements can switch states from included to excluded and back again. In the example, the relation `-->%` indicates such a dynamic exclusion: Whenever the data element on the left is executed, the one on the right is so excluded.

Similarly, a data element may become *pending* as consequence of another executing via the "response" relation `*-->`. Intuitively, a pending element must at some later point execute (or be excluded) in order for the program to terminate.

In this inner process, `loanBook` is executed given a user's name, and it excludes itself from the process (`-->%`, line 9), thus executing only once until it is explicitly included again; it also spawns the elements in a sub-process (line 11): a new data element `loan` that stores the user's name, and an input data element `returnBook` that is used when the user wants to terminate a loan in the library. Notice that data element `returnBook` is declared using an exclamantion mark as annotation. This means that this input data element must be executed, or excluded, in order to complete the process. The example also declares data relations to link data element `loan` to its corresponding `book` element. The sub-process introduces new control relations to self-exclude `returnBook`, i.e. it cannot happen twice, and to include `loanBook` back into the process, allowing for new loans to happen. Figure 2 depicts the final state in our example. For the

$$P \quad ::= \overline{D} \; ; \; \overline{R} \; ; \; \overline{Y} \qquad\qquad\qquad\qquad\qquad \text{Processes}$$

$$D \quad ::= (n_\rho : \ell)[?{:}T]{:}(h,i,r,v) \; | \; (n_\rho : \ell)[E]{:}(h,i,r,v) \qquad \text{Data Elements}$$

$$R \quad ::= \phi\text{–}[E]{\rightarrow}\bullet\ \phi \; | \; \phi\text{–}[E]{\rightarrow}\!\!\ast\ \phi \; | \; \phi\bullet\text{–}[E]{\rightarrow}\phi$$
$$\qquad | \; \phi\text{–}[E]{\rightarrow}+\ \phi \; | \; \phi\text{–}[E]{\rightarrow}\%\ \phi \; | \; \phi\text{–}[E]{\twoheadrightarrow}P \qquad \text{Control Relations}$$

$$Y \quad ::= \phi\text{ –}[n : \ell]{\rightarrow}\ \phi \qquad\qquad\qquad\qquad\qquad\quad \text{Data Relations}$$

$$T \quad ::= \mathsf{Unit} \; | \; \mathsf{String} \; | \; \mathsf{Number} \; | \; \mathsf{Boolean} \; | \; \mathsf{List}\ T \; | \; \{\ \overline{x : T}\ \} \quad \text{Data Types}$$

$$\phi \quad ::= \psi\ \mathsf{RETURN}\ E \; | \; n \qquad\qquad\qquad\qquad\qquad \text{Node Queries}$$

$$\psi \quad ::= \ \mathsf{MATCH}\ Q\ \mathsf{WHERE}\ E$$
$$\qquad | \ \mathsf{MATCH}\ Q\ \mathsf{WHERE}\ E\ \mathsf{WITH}\ pipe\ \mathsf{WHERE}\ E \qquad \text{Match Expressions}$$

$$E \quad ::= c \; | \; n \; | \; Q \; | \; \phi \; | \; \psi \; | \; E{:}attr \; | \; f(E_1, ..., E_n)$$
$$\qquad | \ \{\ \overline{x = E}\ \} \; | \; E.\ell \; | \; [E] \; | \; \mathsf{hd}(E) \; | \; \mathsf{tl}(E) \qquad\quad \text{Expressions}$$

$$c \quad ::= numbers \; | \; strings \; | \; \mathsf{true} \; | \; \mathsf{false} \; | \; 1 \; | \; \bot \qquad\quad \text{Literals}$$

$$pipe ::= agg\ \mathsf{AS}\ n \; | \; n\ \mathsf{AS}\ n \qquad\qquad\qquad\qquad\quad \text{Pipeline Term}$$

$$agg \; ::= n \; | \; \mathsf{COUNT}(E) \; | \; \mathsf{MAX}(E) \; | \; \mathsf{MIN}(E) \; | \; \mathsf{SUM}(E) \quad \text{Aggregating Functions}$$

$$attr ::= value \; | \; executed \; | \; included \; | \; pending \qquad\qquad \text{Attributes}$$

Fig. 3. Syntax of ReGraDa

sake of space, we omit from this diagram the implicit data dependencies between data elements that are necessary to implement the reactive computation.

This section illustrates, by example, the dynamic spawning of data and control elements, and also the dynamic inclusion and exclusion of data elements in the process. We have omitted the details of how the run-time state of each data element is represented, i.e. the value assigned to an input data element, whether an event is included or excluded and whether it is pending or not. This is explained and made formal in the next two sections.

3   Formal Syntax of ReGraDa

The abstract syntax of ReGraDa is given by the grammar in Fig. 3. In this grammar, we assume given enumerable sets of names (ranged over by n, a, b, c and the reserved keyword *trigger*), of unique data element identifiers (ranged over by ρ), and labels for data elements and relations (ℓ). We use the notation $\overline{x}$ to denote a sequence $x_1, ..., x_n$ and elide concrete syntax separators and the number of elements in the sequence. Distinctively, names abstract data elements in the scope of a process, very much like variables in a program. Identifiers are global and uniquely denote data elements in a process, like a key of a record in a database or the memory heap allocated regions. Labels work like classes for data elements, playing an important role in queries on the graph of data elements.

Analysing the syntax topdown, we have that a ReGraDa process P defines data, control relations and runtime state simultaneously as seen in the example using the concrete syntax given in the previous section. It comprises a sequence $\overline{D}$ of data element definitions (D), followed by a sequence $\overline{R}$ of control relation definitions (R) and a sequence $\overline{Y}$ of data relation definitions (Y). Both control and data relation definitions use query expressions over graphs of data elements denoting sets of data elements (ϕ) and expressions (E) that manipulate the usual set of datatypes, comprising types for unit, strings, numbers, boolean values, lists, and records.

As exemplified in the previous section, REGRADA processes define a nested structure of process definitions (P), via the spawn control relation ($\phi-[E]\twoheadrightarrow P$). Data elements D declare a local identifier (n) in the scope of the current process definition and its corresponding sub-processes; a label (ℓ), visible globally; and a unique runtime identifier (ρ), the latter is a runtime constant that is added to the data elements when they are created.

Data elements can be of one of two kinds: an input data element or a computation data element. Input data elements, such as the `createAuthor:Book` element in the previous section, has the form $(n_\rho{:}\ell)[?{:}T]{:}(h,i,r,v)$ and define system entry points of type (T), that can be linked, to web services, web forms, or any other form of input to the process.

Computation data elements, of the form $(n_\rho{:}\ell)[E]{:}(h,i,r,v)$, define nodes in the graph that compute and store values denoted by their expressions E. Such expression may refer to values stored in other data elements by using their identifiers or the reserved name `@trigger` that refers to the data element triggering a spawn control relation as used in the `author` and `book` data elements in the previous section. Expressions may also explicitly query the graph. For instance, the expression

```
1   (authorCount:Stats)[MATCH (1:Author) COUNT(1)]
```

declares a computation data element that if executed computes the number of author elements in the graph.

Following the typical structure of Dynamic Condition Response (DCR) graphs [2,8,9,13], the run-time state of a data element, referred to as the marking, is defined using the four properties (h,i,r,v) associated to each data element (and so far ignored in our examples):

1. a boolean value h (`executed` in the concrete syntax) that signals that the event was previously executed (happened). A data element can be executed multiple times, this property only registers the first execution.
2. a boolean i (`included`) indicating whether the data element is currently included. A data element not included, also referred to as excluded, is considered irrelevant: it cannot execute and cannot prevent execution of others;
3. a boolean r (`pending`) indicating whether the data element is currently pending. A pending element is required to be subsequently updated (or become excluded) at some point in the future to let a process reach a final state; and finally,
4. a value v of any type admissible in the language (`value`) indicating the current value of the data element, or the undefined value ($\bot$) if the data element has not yet been executed/received a value and has no initial value.

For instance, the `createAuthor:Input` data element in the previous section will initially have the state

```
1   (createAuthor:Input)[?:{authorName:String}](false,true,false,⊥)
```

representing that the element has not been executed, is included, is not pending, and has the value ⊥ because no value has been given yet. After executing it inputting the value "Tolkien", the data element will have the state

```
1   (createAuthor:Input)[?:{authorName:String}](true,true,false,"Tolkien")
```

Control relations (R) range over a set of six different kinds of relations stemming from the declarative process model of DCR graphs. All relations are guarded by a boolean expression E, that may refer all identifiers in scope or use queries to refer to the global state of the graph.

1. **condition** ($\phi\!-\![E]\!\mapsto\!\bullet\ \phi$) (-->* in the concrete syntax), defining that if the expression E evaluates to true, then the data-elements denoted by the query on the right-hand side cannot execute unless all data elements denoted by the query on the left-hand side are either marked not included or executed;
2. **milestone** ($\phi\!-\![E]\!\mapsto\!\diamond\ \phi$) (--<>), defining that if the expression E evaluates to true, then the data elements denoted by the query on the right cannot execute unless all data elements denoted by the query on the left-hand side are marked not included or not pending;
3. **response** ($\phi\!\bullet\!-\![E]\!\mapsto\!\phi$) (*-->), defining that if the expression E evaluates to true, then whenever some data element denoted by the query on the left-hand side executes, all data elements denoted by the query on the right-hand side become marked pending;
4. **inclusion** ($\phi\!-\![E]\!\rightarrow\!+\ \phi$) (-->+), defining that if the expression E evaluates to true, then whenever some data element denoted by the query on the left-hand side executes, all data elements denoted by the query on the right-hand side become marked included;
5. **exclusion** ($\phi\!-\![E]\!\rightarrow\!\%\ \phi$) (-->%), defining that if the expression E evaluates to true, then whenever some data element denoted by the query on the left-hand side executes, all data elements denoted by the query on the right-hand side become excluded; and finally,
6. **spawn** relation ($\phi\!-\![E]\!\mapsto\ P$) (-->>), defining that if the expression E evaluates to true, then whenever some data element denoted by the query on the left hand side executes, the data elements and rules in the sub-process P on the right-hand side are instantiated in the current process. The reserved name *trigger* denotes the left-hand side element that caused the spawning of the sub-process, in all expressions in the new elements.

Just like in [8], one important semantic property of data elements is whether they are enabled or not. We say that a data-element is *enabled* iff (i) it is included, (ii) every other element preceding it by a condition is either executed or not included, (iii) every element preceding it by a milestone is either not included or not pending. An enabled element may *execute*, modifying its marking by making it executed and not pending, and possibly assigning it a new value. This execution causes toggling the included state of every element succeeding the executed one by an inclusion or exclusion, and by making pending all elements succeeding the executed one by a response relation. In all cases, both for enabledness and execution, a relation is considered only if it either has no guard, or that guard evaluates to true.

We already saw examples of the spawn, include and exclude relations constraining the loanBook and returnBook input actions in the previous section. As an example of the guard expression E, we can use a guarded inclusion relation

```
1    returnBook -[ MATCH (1:Loan)-[r:BOOK]->(book)
2                  WITH COUNT(1) as n WHERE n<50   ]->+ loanBook
```

to only include it if a book has not reached its lifespan, e.g. 50 loans. If the query returns an empty set of nodes that satisfy the condition, the relation is disabled.

As examples of the condition, milestone and response, consider the relations

```
1    createAuthor *--> authorCount
2    createAuthor -->* authorCount
3    authorCount --<> createAuthor
```

The response control relation means that the authorCount computation event becomes pending when a new author is created, and the reactive semantics of REGRADA will then ensure that the author count is updated whenever an author is added. The condition control relation ensures that the authorCount can not be executed before any author has been added. Finally, the milestone relation ensures that a new author cannot be created if authorCount is pending, i.e. it has not yet been updated after the last creation of an author.

The data relations (Y) of the form $\phi -[n : \ell]\rightarrow \phi$ create a native data link between all combinations of nodes resulting from the queries on the left and right-hand side. Data relations (Y) and, in particular, match expressions (ϕ) closely resemble the notation of *cypher* [6] for node relationships and graph queries respectively, identifying nodes and relations via patterns (Q), filtering and aggregating results (ψ). This approach contrasts with, but can encode, the semi-structured data style of RESEDA, and the relational schema of approaches like [17]. For instance, the example given in the previous section introduced simple data relations like

```
1    tolkien -[:WROTE]-> hobbit
```

Where tolkien and hobbit are identifiers denoting data elements. Finally, the expression language in REGRADA includes the usual set of constructor and destructor expressions for all the base datatypes considered. It also includes the use of match expressions to enable the runtime manipulation of data elements and their attributes as already illustrated above.

4   Semantics

Following the tradition of DCR graphs [2,8,10,13], we define the semantics of REGRADA by means of a transition system, where states are processes comprising data elements, the corresponding relations, and including their *marking* information. Each transition, written $P \xrightarrow{\rho} P'$, corresponds to the execution (i.e. value update) of a data element ρ. The execution of an input data element $P \xrightarrow{\rho(v)} P'$ requires a value v to be provided in the transition. To formally define the transition system, we must first define two auxiliary functions. Section 4.1 defines function $\mathsf{enabled}_P(\rho)$, that determines, for a given REGRADA program state, if a given data element ρ is currently executable (enabled). Section 4.3 defines function $\mathsf{effects}_P(\overline{R})$ that determines, for given a REGRADA program state and a set of control rules $\overline{R}$, what are the effects of those rules that allow us to compute the next state of the process. For the sake of space, we omit the semantics of expressions, $(\!|E|\!)_P$, and query expressions, $[\![\phi]\!]_P$, which are straightforwardly defined on the structure of the expression or graph, respectively. We finally define the two allowed transitions in our semantics.

4.1 Enabledness

For a data element ρ in process P to be enabled it must be the case that (i) the data element ρ must itself be included; (ii) every data element ρ' that is a condition (where E evaluates to true) for ρ must be either excluded or previously executed; (iii) every data element ρ' that is a milestone (where E evaluates to true) for ρ must be either excluded or not pending. We define function $\mathsf{enabled}_P(\rho)$, that checks if the data element ρ is enabled in process $P = (\overline{D}; \overline{R}; \overline{Y})$.

$$
\begin{aligned}
\mathsf{enabled}_P(\rho) \triangleq{}& \rho[\mathsf{included}] \\
&\wedge \forall \phi\text{-}[E]\!\!\rightarrow\!\!\bullet\ \phi' \in \overline{R}.\ \rho \in [\![\phi']\!]_P \wedge (\!|E|\!)_P = \mathsf{true} \Longrightarrow \\
&\qquad ([\![\phi[\mathsf{included}]]\!]_P = [\![\phi[\mathsf{included} \wedge \mathsf{executed}]]\!]_P) \\
&\wedge \forall \phi\text{-}[E]\!\!\rightarrow\!\!\diamond\ \phi' \in \overline{R}.\ \rho \in [\![\phi']\!]_P \wedge (\!|E|\!)_P = \mathsf{true} \Longrightarrow \\
&\qquad ([\![\phi[\mathsf{included}]]\!]_P = [\![\phi[\mathsf{included} \wedge \neg\mathsf{pending}]]\!]_P)
\end{aligned}
$$

4.2 Effects

The effect of executing a data element ρ in the context of a global process P can be computed from the current state and given a value in the case of input data elements. Effects are gathered by iterating the set of control rules (excluding conditions and milestones) in the process as defined below

$$
\mathsf{effects}_P(\rho) \triangleq \cup_{R \in \overline{R}}\ \mathsf{effects}'_P(R, \rho) \ \text{with}\ P = \overline{D}; \overline{R}; \overline{Y}
$$

$$
\begin{aligned}
\mathsf{effects}'_P(\phi\bullet\text{-}[E]\!\!\mapsto\!\!\phi', \rho) &\triangleq \{(\mathsf{pend}, \rho') \mid (\rho, \rho') \in [\![\phi]\!]_P \times [\![\phi']\!]_P \wedge (\!|E|\!)_P = \mathsf{true}\} \\
\mathsf{effects}'_P(\phi\text{-}[E]\!\!\rightarrow\!\!\%\ \phi', \rho) &\triangleq \{(\mathsf{excl}, \rho') \mid (\rho, \rho') \in [\![\phi]\!]_P \times [\![\phi']\!]_P \wedge (\!|E|\!)_P = \mathsf{true}\} \\
\mathsf{effects}'_P(\phi\text{-}[E]\!\!\rightarrow\!\!+\ \phi', \rho) &\triangleq \{(\mathsf{incl}, \rho') \mid (\rho, \rho') \in [\![\phi]\!]_P \times [\![\phi']\!]_P \wedge (\!|E|\!)_P = \mathsf{true}\} \\
\mathsf{effects}'_P(\phi\text{-}[E]\!\!\mapsto\!\!P', \rho) &\triangleq \{(\mathsf{spawn}(P'\{^{\rho}/_{\mathsf{trigger}}\})) \mid \rho \in [\![\phi]\!]_P \wedge (\!|E|\!)_P = \mathsf{true}\}
\end{aligned}
$$

4.3   Transitions

Finally, we present below the transition rules that define the complete labelled transition system. The execution of a computation data element ($P \xrightarrow{\rho} P'$) is possible from a state where the given element is enabled, and to a state where the value of the element is refreshed based on the values of other references, given by function $\mathsf{compute}_P(\rho)$, and where the effects of the execution are applied by operation ($P' \lhd \delta$).

$$\frac{\mathsf{enabled}_P(\rho) \quad P' = \mathsf{compute}_P(\rho) \quad \delta = \mathsf{effects}_{P'}(\rho)}{P \xrightarrow{\rho} P' \lhd \delta}$$

In the case of an input data element, a transition may occur if the element is enabled, and to a state where the element's value is updated ($\mathsf{update}_P(\rho, v)$) to the value v given in the transition label as input, and after applying the corresponding effects.

$$\frac{\mathsf{enabled}_P(\rho) \quad P' = \mathsf{update}_P(\rho, v) \quad \delta = \mathsf{effects}_{P'}(\rho)}{P \xrightarrow{\rho(v)} P' \lhd \delta}$$

We omit the definition of function $\mathsf{compute}_P(\rho)$ which is the straightforward application of the expression semantics to the enclosed expression in computation data elements, with relation to other data elements, and the definition of function $\mathsf{update}_P(\rho, v)$ which simply updates the value of the data element with the incoming value. The application of the effects consists in changing the state of the given data element and the creation of new elements in the case of spawn relations, thus providing fresh identifiers and binding the triggering data element to the new data elements and relations.

$$\overline{D}, (n_\rho : \ell)[?{:}T]{:}(h, i, p, v));\overline{R};\overline{Y} \lhd (\mathsf{pend}, \rho) \triangleq (\overline{D}, (n_\rho : \ell)[?{:}T]{:}(h, i, \mathsf{t}, v));\overline{R};\overline{Y}$$
$$(\overline{D}, (n_\rho : \ell)[E]{:}(h, i, p, v));\overline{R};\overline{Y} \lhd (\mathsf{excl}, \rho) \triangleq (\overline{D}, (n_\rho : \ell)[E]{:}(h, \mathsf{f}, p, v));\overline{R};\overline{Y}$$
$$(\overline{D}, (n_\rho : \ell)[E]{:}(h, i, p, v));\overline{R};\overline{Y} \lhd (\mathsf{incl}, \rho) \triangleq (\overline{D}, (n_\rho : \ell)[E]{:}(h, \mathsf{t}, p, v));\overline{R};\overline{Y}$$
$$\overline{D};\overline{R};\overline{Y} \lhd (\mathsf{spawn}(\overline{D'};\overline{R'};\overline{Y'}), \rho) \triangleq D, \overline{D'}\sigma; R, \overline{R'}\sigma; Y, \overline{Y'}\sigma$$

Substitution σ, used above, replaces the free names of $\overline{D'}$ with fresh event identifiers, assigns new node identifiers and replaces identifier *trigger* by ρ. The set of free names of $\overline{R'}$ and $\overline{Y'}$, except *trigger*, is a subset of the free names of $\overline{D'}$.

5   From ReGraDa to Cypher

We now define the compilation procedure of REGRADA to *cypher*, the query language of the *neo4j* database. For want of space, we omit an introduction *cypher* here, and refer the reader to the introductory work [6] and the *neo4j* official documentation[1].

---

[1] https://neo4j.com/.

```
1  (a:A)[?:Number], (b:B)[a.value+1] ;
2  b -->% a,
3  a -->> {
4    (c:C)[ {x:a.value+b.value, y:@trigger.value} ] ;
5    c -->> { (d:D)[c.value.x+c.value.y+a.value] ; ; } ;
6  } ;
```

Fig. 4. Toy example illustrating compilation of ReGraDa to *cypher*

Our encoding uses the native capabilities of the database system as much as possible to allow for an almost standalone execution of the process and embeds the reactive behaviour of the process to independent data modifications. Our approach is to translate a ReGraDa process to a set of update queries and triggers in the database and let data elements, their properties, and data relationships act as the data model of an external application to be freely queried and modified. We next present the compilation procedure that systematically transforms a simple ReGraDa process into *cypher*.

The structure of our target code is a list of trigger definitions and a *cypher* script, which is a flat list of node and relationship declarations, graph queries and update commands. To transform the nested structure of ReGraDa processes into the flat structure of *cypher* code we resolve all names with a standard static resolution of names and representing syntactic dependencies with data relationships between nodes in the database graph.

So, in the general case, a ReGraDa process is translated into a four-part *cypher* script containing: (1) a list of queries that is used to fetch and bind all related nodes from other contexts to be used in local (or inner) definitions, this list is empty at the top-level; (2) a set of node definitions that map the definitions in the current process of input and computation data elements; (3) a set of node relationship definitions that map data dependencies, control relations, and data relations defined in the current process; and finally, (4) (in the case of triggers associated to a computation data element), one update command that (re)evaluates the node's expression with relation to the nodes it depends on.

We use a simplified example, in Fig. 4, to illustrate the compilation procedure. It contains all main cases of a ReGraDa process (data dependencies, nested processes, and sub-processes). The *cypher* code emitted for this example is presented step by step in this section.

First, the top-level data elements are translated to node definitions that include the defined name (alpha renamed), their labels, and default values for the markings. We add an extra field that identifies the source element in the code (`reda_id`). Notice that node names are only visible in the current script.

```
1  CREATE (a_0:A{reda_id="a_0", executed:0, included:true, pending:false})
2  CREATE (b_1:B{reda_id="b_0", executed:0, included:true, pending:false})
```

Both nodes are initialized without an attribute for its value. This attribute is left uninitialized since the data elements were not executed and therefore cannot be referred or evaluated at this stage. Also, we alpha-renamed names and identifiers (a_0, b_1) to avoid name clashing between different declaration contexts.

Consider the syntactic dependencies between data elements a and b in Fig. 4, created by the expression of data element b, and also because a spawns a sub-process using b. The static resolution of names in REGRADA is mapped onto explicit node relations that define a name substitution inside the sub-process in the spawn relation of line 3 in Fig. 4. Three relationships are needed in *neo4j*

```
3   CREATE (a_0)-[:a]->(a_0)
4   CREATE (a_0)-[:a]->(b_1)
5   CREATE (b_1)-[:b]->(a_0)
```

Lines 3 and 4 mean that node a_0 in this context is the correct substitution for the free name a in all sub-processes (and expression) of node a_0 and b_1.

The data dependency of b on a is reified into control relations (condition and response) as follows. Clearly we cannot execute b without first having executed— and thus gotten a value for—a; and equally clearly, whenever the value of a changes, we must re-compute b to reflect that change in the value of b. That is, we add the following condition and response relations:

```
6   CREATE (a_0)-[:condition]->(b_1)
7   CREATE (a_0)-[:response]->(b_1)
```

These relations establish the essence of the reactive behaviour of REGRADA, similarly to the semantics of RESEDA. (The mechanics here is akin to spreadsheet semantics: updating "cell" a forces a recompute of the value of b.)

We next translate the control relation (excludes) on line 3 almost verbatim.

```
8   CREATE (b_1)-[:excludes]->(a_0)
```

Other control relations are translated directly to relations between node instances. This concludes the translation of node and relation top-level declarations. Next, we present the main trigger that checks for the enabledness of data elements prior to execution, and applies the effects of control relations (inclusion, exclusion, responses) after a successful execution.

```
9    CALL apoc.trigger.add('EVERYWERE',
10   'UNWIND apoc.trigger.propertiesByKey($assignedNodeProperties,"executed")
11     as prop WITH prop.node as n WHERE n.executed>0
12
13     CALL apoc.util.validate(
14       n.included=false, "EVENT IS NOT INCLUDED", [])
15     CALL apoc.util.validate(
16       EXISTS((n)<-[:condition]-({included:true, executed:0})),
17       "EVENT HAS A CONDITION UNSATISFIED", [])
18     CALL apoc.util.validate(
19       EXISTS((n)<-[:milestone]-({included:true, pending:true})),
20       "EVENT HAS A MILESTONE UNSATISFIED", [])
21
22     SET n.pending=false WITH n
23     OPTIONAL MATCH (n)-[:response]->(t) SET t.pending = true WITH n
24     OPTIONAL MATCH (n)-[:excludes]->(t) SET t.included = false WITH n
25     OPTIONAL MATCH (n)-[:includes]->(t) SET t.included = true
```

```
26   RETURN 1 ', {phase:'before'});
```

The *enabledness* validation is translated into explicit validations (lines 13–20) that check if any preceding element (using a relation with tag `:condition` or `:milestone`) is included, and not executed in the case of condition relations or pending in the case of milestone relations. The effects of *execution* via the response, includes and excludes relations are translated to *cypher* update queries that search for this kind of relations between node instances and modifies the marking of the target node accordingly (lines 23–25). The enabledness check and the subsequent execution of effects is performed here in a way that aborts any transaction in case of error.

The remaining behaviour, including the spawning of sub-processes is represented in triggers generated for each one of the data elements statically declared in the program. Such triggers are fired whenever the associated `executed` property is changed. These triggers contain the compiled code for all the actions that need to be executed when related nodes are (re)evaluated. Consider the example of node `a_0`, compiled from the computation node `a` in the example. The trigger is the following

```
27   CALL apoc.trigger.add('When a_0 happens',
28   'UNWIND apoc.trigger.propertiesByKey($assignedNodeProperties,"executed")
29   as prop WITH prop.node as n WHERE n.reda_id="a_0" AND n.executed>0
30
31   MATCH (a_0)-[:a]->(n)
32   MATCH (b_1)-[:b]->(n)
33   CREATE (c_2:C{reda_id="c_2", executed:0, included:true,
34                            pending:false, value_y:n.value})
35   CREATE (a_0)-[:a]->(c_2)
36   CREATE (b_1)-[:b]->(c_2)
37   CREATE (c_2)-[:c]->(c_2)
38   CREATE (b_1)-[:condition]->(c_2)
39   CREATE (b_1)-[:response]->(c_2)
40   CREATE (a_0)-[:condition]->(c_2)
41   CREATE (a_0)-[:response]->(c_2)
42   RETURN 1 ', {phase:'before'});
```

This trigger starts by instantiating the free names of the sub-process of `a_0`, reifying the nested structure of the process. It queries the nodes that represent identifiers `a` and `b` in this context (lines 31–32). These relations match the relations created at the top-level (lines 3–5). Line 33 includes the local definition for data element `c`, here alpha-renamed to `c_2`, and includes the partial evaluation of expression `{x:a.value+b.value, y:@trigger.value}`, in this case for field `y` which depends on the triggering data element. Lines 35–37 repeat the static resolution of names for the inner scope of sub-processes and expressions as described at the top level. Notice that identifiers `a` and `b` cross more than one syntactic context level and direct links are created at all stages. Lines 38–41 create the control relations created by the sub-process.

The trigger that handles node `b` is quite simpler since it is not used to spawn any sub-process. The value of node `b` depends on the value of node `a`, so its trigger basically (re)computes the value of `b` whenever the node is executed.

```
43   CALL apoc.trigger.add('When b_1 happens',
44    'UNWIND apoc.trigger.propertiesByKey($assignedNodeProperties,"executed")
45    as prop WITH prop.node as n WHERE n.reda_id="b_1" AND n.executed>0
46
47    MATCH (a_0)-[:a]->(n)
48    SET n.value=a_0.value+1
49    RETURN 1 ', {phase:'before'});
```

Line 47 retrieves the substitution for identifier a_0 in this context and updates the value attribute of node b_1 (line 45). Notice that each instance of b may be associated with a different instance of a. We omit the handlers for nodes c_2 and d_3, that are similar to the handlers of nodes a_0 and b_1 depicted above (lines 27 and 43). Notice also that field x of the record in data element c_2 should be computed in the corresponding trigger since it depends on other elements.

The resulting target code comprises a set of top-level definitions, and a set of triggers: a main trigger, and a trigger associated to each definition of data elements that contains computations or spawns sub-processes.

6   Empirical Experiments

To study the performance and scalability of the resulting code, and thus the translation strategy presented in this paper, we tested the prototype using thousands of data elements and relationships between them. Note that the number of triggers is statically determined by the process definition and remains constant throughout all executions. We designed two case studies for this purpose: an "expected" program and a worst-case scenario. These programs were developed to grow linearly in an experiment with twenty-five executions, each one executed ten times. They were executed using *neo4j* 4.1.1 with APOC 4.1.0.2, Windows 8.1, and an Intel Core i7-4510U CPU @ 2.00 GHz 2.60 GHz with 8 GB RAM.

The "expected" case scenario consists of a program where nodes and relationships are split amongst different clusters. This case study starts with only two data-elements belonging to one cluster, with each further execution adding an arbitrary number (eighty-seven) of new data-elements that are then split uniformly into three clusters. Each data-element will either have either no relationships, acting as spawner input data-elements, or will have a number of relationships between one and the third of the number of existing data-elements. As depicted in Fig. 5, the time difference between the request and the response tends to grow in a somewhat linear to sub-linear fashion with each execution. However, in the worst-case scenario, where we have one giant cluster where data-elements are highly dependent on each other, the time difference between the requests and responses tends to grow in a linear to super-linear fashion, as depicted in Fig. 6. Pre-determined sequences of requests were used in the tests.

To conclude, triggers are many times the source of performance issues in database systems. With this in mind, we made every effort to encode all the reactivity and behavior of REGRADA into static triggers, remaining constant in number throughout all execution. There are at most two triggers activated each time a specific data-element is executed: (i) the trigger regarding that

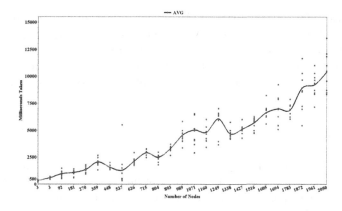

Fig. 5. Expected case scenario.

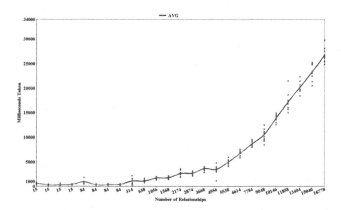

Fig. 6. Worst case scenario.

specific data-element, containing the specific behavior defined in the process; and (ii) the `main_trigger` that is always activated despite the data-element being executed, guaranteeing that the language rules like the `enabledness` verification or the application of DCR effects are being followed. With this information and the results of our case study, we can infer that the main cause for performance deterioration is the number of control relationships on each node being executed. This comes from the need to process each of the relations in the `main_trigger` to reach the next REGRADA process state.

7   Conclusions and Future Work

We introduced REGRADA, a language for REactive GRAph DAta based on the declarative DCR graph language, and evaluated the language in a prototype implementation using the graph-database *neo4j*, with promising performance characteristics of the first early tests. As future work we also plan to research the transfer of DCR results to REGRADA, e.g. refinement [2] and choreographies [11], providing guarantees for deadlock freedom by design. Also, we plan to investigate the use of REGRADA as target language for multi-instance process mining of complex ERP and EIM systems and the relation between REGRADA models and the recent work in [5].

References

1. Debois, S., Hildebrandt, T., Slaats, T.: Hierarchical declarative modelling with refinement and sub-processes. In: Sadiq, S., Soffer, P., Völzer, H. (eds.) BPM 2014. LNCS, vol. 8659, pp. 18–33. Springer, Cham (2014). https://doi.org/10.1007/978-3-319-10172-9_2

2. Debois, S., Hildebrandt, T.T., Slaats, T.: Replication, refinement and reachability: complexity in dynamic condition-response graphs. Acta Informatica 55(6), 489–520 (2018)

3. Domingues, M., Seco, J.C.: Type safe evolution of live systems. In: Workshop on Reactive and Event-based Languages and Systems (REBLS 2015) (2015)

4. Dumas, M., Van der Aalst, W.M., Ter Hofstede, A.H.: Process-Aware Information Systems: Bridging People and Software Through Process Technology. Wiley, New York (2005)

5. Esser, S., Fahland, D.: Multi-dimensional event data in graph databases. J. Data Semant. (2021)

6. Francis, N., et al.: Cypher: an evolving query language for property graphs. In: Proceedings of the 2018 International Conference on Management of Data, SIGMOD 2018, New York, pp. 1433–1445. Association for Computing Machinery (2018)

7. Object Management Group. Case Management Model and Notation V 1.1. (2016)

8. Hildebrandt, T., Mukkamala, R.R.: Declarative event-based workflow as distributed dynamic condition response graphs. In: Post-Proceedings of PLACES 2010, volume 69 of EPTCS, pp. 59–73 (2010)

9. Hildebrandt, T., Mukkamala, R.R., Slaats, T., Zanitti, F.: Contracts for cross-organizational workflows as timed Dynamic Condition Response Graphs. JLAP 82(5), 164–185 (2013)

10. Hildebrandt, T.T., Mukkamala, R.R.: Declarative event-based workflow as distributed dynamic condition response graphs. arXiv:1110.4161 (2011)

11. Hildebrandt, T.T., Slaats, T., López, H.A., Debois, S., Carbone, M.: Declarative choreographies and liveness. In: Pérez, J.A., Yoshida, N. (eds.) FORTE 2019. LNCS, vol. 11535, pp. 129–147. Springer, Cham (2019). https://doi.org/10.1007/978-3-030-21759-4_8

12. Polyvyanyy, A., van der Werf, J.M.E.M., Overbeek, S., Brouwers, R.: Information systems modeling: language, verification, and tool support. In: Giorgini, P., Weber, B. (eds.) CAiSE 2019. LNCS, vol. 11483, pp. 194–212. Springer, Cham (2019). https://doi.org/10.1007/978-3-030-21290-2_13

13. Seco, J.C., Debois, S., Hildebrandt, T.T., Slaats, T.: RESEDA: declaring live event-driven computations as REactive SEmi-Structured DAta. In: 22nd IEEE International Enterprise Distributed Object Computing Conference, EDOC 2018, pp. 75–84 (2018)

14. Sestoft, P.: Spreadsheet Implementation Technology. Basics and Extensions. MIT Press, Cambridge (2014)

15. Slaats, T.: Flexible Process Notations for Cross-organizational Case Management Systems. Ph.D. thesis, IT University of Copenhagen, January 2015
16. Su, J., Wen, L., Yang, J.: From data-centric business processes to enterprise process frameworks. In: 21st IEEE International Enterprise Distributed Object Computing Conference, EDOC 2017, pp. 1–9 (2017)
17. van der Aalst, W., Artale, A., Montali, M., Tritini, S.: Object-centric behavioral constraints: integrating data and declarative process modelling. In: DL 2017, International Workshop on Description Logics, vol. 1879 (2017)
18. van der Werf, J.M.E.M., Polyvyanyy, A.: The information systems modeling suite. In: Janicki, R., Sidorova, N., Chatain, T. (eds.) PETRI NETS 2020. LNCS, vol. 12152, pp. 414–425. Springer, Cham (2020). https://doi.org/10.1007/978-3-030-51831-8_22

Modelling: Structures and Implementations

The Structure of Concurrent Process Histories

Chad Nester[✉]

Tallinn University of Technology, Tallinn, Estonia

Abstract. We identify the algebraic structure of the material histories generated by concurrent processes. Specifically, we extend existing categorical theories of resource convertibility to capture concurrent interaction. Our formalism admits an intuitive graphical presentation via string diagrams for proarrow equipments.

1 Introduction

Concurrent systems are abundant in computing, and indeed in the world at large. Despite the large amount of attention paid to the modelling of concurrency in recent decades (e.g., [1, 10, 16–18]), a canonical mathematical account has yet to emerge, and the basic structure of concurrent systems remains elusive.

In this paper we present a basic structure that captures what we will call the *material* aspect of concurrent systems: As a process unfolds in time it leaves behind a material history of effects on the world, like the way a slug moving through space leaves a trail of slime. This slime is captured in a natural way by *resource theories* in the sense of [4], in which morphisms of symmetric monoidal categories – conveniently expressed as string diagrams – are understood as transformations of resources.

From the resource theoretic perspective, objects of a symmetric monoidal category are understood as collections of resources, with the unit object denoting the empty collection and the tensor product of two collections consisting of their combined contents. Morphisms are understood as ways to transform one collection of resources into another, which may be combined sequentially via

---

This research was supported by the ESF funded Estonian IT Academy research measure (project 2014-2020.4.05.19-0001).

F. Damiani and O. Dardha (Eds.): COORDINATION 2021, LNCS 12717, pp. 209–224, 2021.
https://doi.org/10.1007/978-3-030-78142-2_13

composition, and in parallel via the tensor product. For example, the process of baking bread might generate the following material history:

meaning that the baking process involved kneading dough and baking it in an oven to obtain bread (and also the oven).

This approach to expressing the material history of a process has many advantages: It is general, in that it assumes minimal structure; canonical, in that monoidal categories are well-studied as mathematical objects; and relatively friendly, as it admits an intuitive graphical calculus (string diagrams). However, it is unable to capture the interaction between components of a concurrent process. For example, consider our hypothetical baking process and suppose that the kneading and baking of the dough are handled by separate subsystems, with control of the dough being handed to the baking subsystem once the kneading is complete. Such interaction of parts is a fundamental aspect of concurrency, but is not expressible in this framework – we can only describe the effects of the system as a whole.

We remedy this by extending a given resource theory to allow the decomposition of material histories into concurrent components. Specifically, we augment the string diagrams for symmetric monoidal categories with *corners*, through which resources may flow between different components of a transformation.

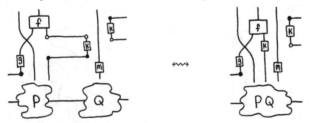

Returning to our baking example, we might express the material history of the kneading and baking subsystems *separately* with the following diagrams, which may be composed horizontally to obtain the material history of the baking process as a whole.

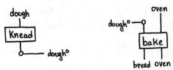

These augmented diagrams denote cells of a single object double category constructed from the original resource theory. The corners make this double category into a proarrow equipment, which turns out to be all the additional structure we need in order to express concurrent interaction. From only this structure, we obtain a theory of exchanges – a sort of minimal system of behavioural types – that conforms to our intuition about how such things ought to work remarkably well.

Our approach to these concurrent material histories retains the aforementioned advantages of the resource-theoretic perspective: We lose no generality, since our construction applies to any resource theory; It is canonical, with proarrow equipments being a fundamental structure in formal category theory – although not usually seen in such concrete circumstances; Finally, it remains relatively friendly, since the string diagrams for monoidal categories extend in a natural way to string diagrams for proarrow equipments [11].

1.1 Contributions and Related Work

Related Work. Monoidal categories are ubiquitous – if often implicit – in theoretical computer science. An example from the theory of concurrency is [15], in which monoidal categories serve a purpose similar to their purpose here. String diagrams for monoidal categories seem to have been invented independently a number of times, but until recently were uncommon in printed material due to technical limitations. The usual reference is [12]. We credit the resource-theoretic interpretation of monoidal categories and their string diagrams to [4]. Double categories first appear in [6]. Free double categories are considered in [5] and again in [7]. The idea of a proarrow equipment first appears in [22], albeit in a rather different form. Proarrow equipments have subsequently appeared under many names in formal category theory (see e.g., [9,20]). String diagrams for double categories and proarrow equipments are treated precisely in [11]. We have been inspired by work on message passing and behavioural types, in particular [2], from which we have adopted our notation for exchanges.

Contributions. Our main contribution is the resource-theoretic interpretation of certain proarrow equipments, which we call *cornerings*, and the observation that they capture exactly the structure of concurrent process histories. Our mathematical contributions are minor, most significantly the identification of crossing cells in the free cornering of a resource theory and the corresponding Lemma 2, which we believe to be novel. We do not claim the other lemmas of the paper as significant mathematical contributions. Instead, they serve to flesh out the structure of the free cornering.

1.2 Organization and Prerequisites

Prerequisites. This paper is largely self-contained, but we assume some familiarity with category theory, in particular with monoidal categories and their string diagrams. Some good references are [8,14,19].

Organization. In Sect. 2 we review the resource-theoretic interpretation of symmetric monoidal categories. We continue by reviewing the theory of double categories in Sect. 3, specialized to the single object case. In Sect. 4 we introduce cornerings of a resource theory, in particular the free such cornering, and exhibit the existence of crossing cells in the free cornering. In Sect. 5 we show how the free cornering of a resource theory inherits its resource-theoretic interpretation while enabling the concurrent decomposition of resource transformations. In Sect. 6 we conclude and consider directions for future work.

2   Monoidal Categories as Resource Theories

Symmetric strict monoidal categories can be understood as theories of resource transformation. Objects are interpreted as collections of resources, with $A \otimes B$ the collection consisting of both A and B, and I the empty collection. Arrows $f : A \to B$ are understood as ways to transform the resources of A into those of B. We call symmetric strict monoidal categories *resource theories* when we have this sort of interpretation in mind.

For example, let $\mathfrak{B}$ be the free symmetric strict monoidal category with generating objects

$$\{\texttt{bread}, \texttt{dough}, \texttt{water}, \texttt{flour}, \texttt{oven}\}$$

and with generating arrows

$$\texttt{mix} : \texttt{water} \otimes \texttt{flour} \to \texttt{dough} \qquad \texttt{knead} : \texttt{dough} \to \texttt{dough}$$

$$\texttt{bake} : \texttt{dough} \otimes \texttt{oven} \to \texttt{bread} \otimes \texttt{oven}$$

subject to no equations. $\mathfrak{B}$ can be understood as a resource theory of baking bread. The arrow $\texttt{mix}$ represents the process of combining water and flour to form a bread dough, $\texttt{knead}$ represents kneading dough, and $\texttt{bake}$ represents baking dough in an oven to obtain bread (and an oven).

The structure of symmetric strict monoidal categories provides natural algebraic scaffolding for composite transformations. For example, consider the following arrow of $\mathfrak{B}$:

$$(\texttt{bake} \otimes 1_{\texttt{dough}}); (1_{\texttt{bread}} \otimes \sigma_{\texttt{oven}, \texttt{dough}}; \texttt{bake})$$

of type

$$\texttt{dough} \otimes \texttt{oven} \otimes \texttt{dough} \to \texttt{bread} \otimes \texttt{bread} \otimes \texttt{oven}$$

where $\sigma_{A,B} : A \otimes B \xrightarrow{\sim} B \otimes A$ is the braiding. This arrow describes the transformation of two units of dough into loaves of bread by baking them one after the other in an oven.

It is often more intuitive to write composite arrows like this as string diagrams: Objects are depicted as wires, and arrows as boxes with inputs and outputs. Composition is represented by connecting output wires to input wires, and we represent the tensor product of two morphisms by placing them beside one another. Finally, the braiding is represented by crossing the wires involved. For the morphism discussed above, the corresponding string diagram is:

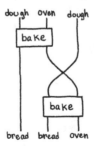

Notice how the topology of the diagram captures the logical flow of resources.

Given a pair of parallel arrows $f, g : A \rightarrow B$ in some resource theory, both f and g are ways to obtain B from A, but they may not have the same effect on the resources involved. We explain by example: Consider the parallel arrows $1_{\text{dough}}, \text{knead} : \text{dough} \rightarrow \text{dough}$ of $\mathfrak{B}$. Clearly these should not be understood to have the same effect on the dough in question, and this is reflected in $\mathfrak{B}$ by the fact that they are not made equal by its axioms. Similarly, knead and $\text{knead} \circ \text{knead}$ are not equal in $\mathfrak{B}$, which we understand to mean that kneading dough twice does not have the same effect as kneading it once, and that in turn any bread produced from twice-kneaded dough will be different from once-kneaded bread in our model.

Consider a hypothetical resource theory constructed from $\mathfrak{B}$ by imposing the equation $\text{knead} \circ \text{knead} = \text{knead}$. In this new setting we understand kneading dough once to have the same effect as kneading it twice, three times, and so on, because the corresponding arrows are all equal. Of course, the sequence of events described by knead is not the one described by $\text{knead} \circ \text{knead}$: In the former the dough has been kneaded only once, while in the latter it has been kneaded twice. The equality of the two arrows indicates that these two different processes would have the same effect on the dough involved. We adopt as a general principle in our design and understanding of resource theories that transformations should be equal if and only if they have the same effect on the resources involved.

For the sake of further illustration, observe that by naturality of the braiding maps the following two resource transformations are equal in $\mathfrak{B}$:

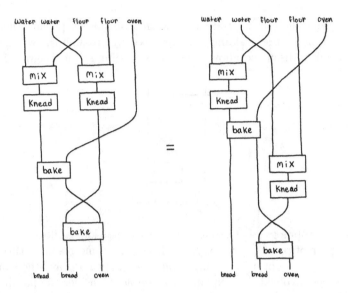

Each transformation gives a method of baking two loaves of bread. On the left, two batches of dough are mixed and kneaded before being baked one after the other. On the right, first one batch of dough is mixed, kneaded and baked and only then is the second batch mixed, kneaded, and baked. Their equality tells us that, according to $\mathfrak{B}$, the two procedures will have the same effect, resulting in the same bread when applied to the same ingredients with the same oven.

3   Single Object Double Categories

In this section we set up the rest of our development by presenting the theory of *single object double categories*, being those double categories $\mathbb{D}$ with exactly one object. In this case $\mathbb{D}$ consists of a *horizontal edge monoid* $\mathbb{D}_H = (\mathbb{D}_H, \otimes, I)$, a *vertical edge monoid* $\mathbb{D}_V = (\mathbb{D}_V, \otimes, I)$, and a collection of *cells*

$$X \xrightarrow{\hspace{0.3cm}} \boxed{\alpha} \xrightarrow{\hspace{0.3cm}} Y$$

where $A, B \in \mathbb{D}_H$ and $X, Y \in \mathbb{D}_V$. Given cells α, β where the right boundary of α matches the left boundary of β we may form a cell $\alpha|\beta$ – their *horizontal composite* – and similarly if the bottom boundary of α matches the top boundary of β we may form $\frac{\alpha}{\beta}$ – their *vertical composite* – with the boundaries of the composite cell formed from those of the component cells using $\otimes$. We depict horizontal and vertical composition, respectively, as in:

Horizontal and vertical composition of cells are required to be associative and unital. We omit wires of sort I in our depictions of cells, allowing us to draw horizontal and vertical identity cells, respectively, as in:

$$x \longrightarrow x \qquad \text{and} \qquad \begin{array}{c} A \\ \Big\uparrow \\ A \end{array}$$

Finally, the horizontal and vertical identity cells of type I must coincide – we write this cell as $\square_I$ and depict it as empty space, see below on the left – and vertical and horizontal composition must satisfy the interchange law. That is, $\frac{\alpha}{\beta}\big|\frac{\gamma}{\delta} = \frac{\alpha|\gamma}{\beta|\delta}$, allowing us to unambiguously interpret the diagram below on the right:

Every single object double category $\mathbb{D}$ defines strict monoidal categories $\mathbf{V}\mathbb{D}$ and $\mathbf{H}\mathbb{D}$, consisting of the cells for which the $\mathbb{D}_H$ and $\mathbb{D}_V$ valued boundaries respectively are all I, as in:

$$\begin{array}{c} A \\ \mathtt{I} \ \boxed{\alpha} \ \mathtt{I} \\ B \end{array} \qquad \text{and} \qquad \begin{array}{c} \mathtt{I} \\ x - \boxed{\beta} - y \\ \mathtt{I} \end{array}$$

That is, the collection of objects of $\mathbf{V}\mathbb{D}$ is $\mathbb{D}_H$, composition in $\mathbf{V}\mathbb{D}$ is vertical composition of cells, and the tensor product in $\mathbf{V}\mathbb{D}$ is given by horizontal composition:

$$\begin{array}{c} A \\ \boxed{\alpha} \\ B \end{array} \otimes \begin{array}{c} A' \\ \boxed{\beta} \\ B' \end{array} = \begin{array}{cc} A & A' \\ \boxed{\alpha} & \boxed{\beta} \\ B & B' \end{array}$$

In this way, **VD** forms a strict monoidal category, which we call the category of *vertical cells* of $\mathbb{D}$. Similarly, **HD** is also a strict monoidal category (with collection of objects $\mathbb{D}_V$) which we call the *horizontal cells* of $\mathbb{D}$.

4   Cornerings and Crossings

Next, we define cornerings, our primary technical device. In particular we discuss the free cornering of a resource theory, which we show contains special crossing cells with nice formal properties. Tersely, a cornering of a resource theory $\mathbb{A}$ is a single object proarrow equipment with $\mathbb{A}$ as its vertical cells. Explicitly:

Definition 1. *Let $\mathbb{A}$ be a symmetric strict monoidal category. Then a cornering of $\mathbb{A}$ is a single object double category $\mathbb{D}$ such that:*

(i) *The vertical cells of $\mathbb{D}$ are $\mathbb{A}$. That is, there is an isomorphism of categories* $\mathbf{V}\mathbb{D} \cong \mathbb{A}$.

(ii) *For each A in $\mathbb{A}_0 \cong \mathbb{D}_H$, there are distinguished elements A° and $A^\bullet$ of $\mathbb{D}_V$ along with distinguished cells of $\mathbb{D}$*

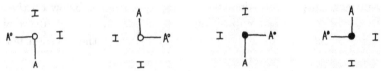

called $\circ$-corners and $\bullet$-corners respectively, which must satisfy the yanking *equations:*

$$\begin{array}{ccccc} \raisebox{0pt}{$\multimap$} = \raisebox{0pt}{$-$} & \quad & \raisebox{0pt}{$\looparrowright$} = \Big| = \raisebox{0pt}{$\looparrowleft$} & \quad & \raisebox{0pt}{$-$} = \raisebox{0pt}{$\rotatebox{180}{$\multimap$}$} \end{array}$$

Intuitively, A° denotes an instance of A moving from left to right, and $A^\bullet$ denotes an instance of A moving from right to left (see Sect. 5).

Of particular interest is the free cornering of a resource theory:

Definition 2. *Let $\mathbb{A}$ be a resource theory. Then the free cornering of $\mathbb{A}$, written $\ulcorner\!\mathbb{A}\!\lrcorner$, is the free single object double category defined as follows:*

– *The horizontal edge monoid $\ulcorner\!\mathbb{A}\!\lrcorner_H = (\mathbb{A}_0, \otimes, I)$ is given by the objects of $\mathbb{A}$.*
– *The vertical edge monoid $\ulcorner\!\mathbb{A}\!\lrcorner_V = (\mathbb{A}_0 \times \{\circ, \bullet\})^*$ is the free monoid on the set $\mathbb{A}_0 \times \{\circ, \bullet\}$ of polarized objects of $\mathbb{A}$ – whose elements we write A° and $A^\bullet$.*
– *The generating cells consist of corners for each object A of $\mathbb{A}$ as above, subject to the yanking equations, along with a vertical cell $\ulcorner\!f\!\lrcorner$ for each morphism $f : A \to B$ of $\mathbb{A}$ subject to equations as in:*

$$\mathrm{I} \ \begin{array}{c} \uparrow A \\ \ulcorner\!f\!\lrcorner \\ \downarrow B \end{array} \ \mathrm{I} \qquad \begin{array}{c} \ulcorner\!f\!\lrcorner \\ \ulcorner\!g\!\lrcorner \end{array} = \ulcorner\!fg\!\lrcorner \qquad \ulcorner\!1\!\lrcorner = \Big| \qquad \ulcorner\!f\!\lrcorner\ulcorner\!g\!\lrcorner = \ulcorner\!f\!\lrcorner\ulcorner\!g\!\lrcorner$$

For a precise development of free double categories see [7]. In brief: cells are formed from the generating cells by horizontal and vertical composition, subject to the axioms of a double category in addition to any generating equations. The free cornering is free both in the sense that it is freely generated, and in the sense that for any cornering $\mathbb{D}$ of $\mathbb{A}$ there is exactly one double functor $\ulcorner\mathbb{A}\urcorner \to \mathbb{D}$ that sends corner cells to corner cells and restricts to the identity on $\mathbb{A} \cong \mathbf{V}\mathbb{D}$. That is, diagrams in $\ulcorner\mathbb{A}\urcorner$ have a canonical interpretation in any cornering of $\mathbb{A}$.

Proposition 1. $\ulcorner\mathbb{A}\urcorner$ *is a cornering of* $\mathbb{A}$.

Proof. Intuitively $\mathbf{V}\ulcorner\mathbb{A}\urcorner \cong \mathbb{A}$ because in a composite vertical cell every wire bent by a corner must eventually be un-bent by the matching corner, which by yanking is the identity. The only other generators are the cells $\ulcorner f \urcorner$, and so any vertical cell in $\ulcorner\mathbb{A}\urcorner$ can be written as $\ulcorner g \urcorner$ for some morphism g of $\mathbb{A}$. A more rigorous treatment of corner cells can be found in [11], to the same effect.

$\square$

Before we properly explain our interest in $\ulcorner\mathbb{A}\urcorner$ we develop a convenient bit of structure: *crossing cells*. For each B of $\ulcorner\mathbb{A}\urcorner_H$ and each X of $\ulcorner\mathbb{A}\urcorner_V$ we define a cell

of $\ulcorner\mathbb{A}\urcorner$ inductively as follows: In the case where X is A° or $A^\bullet$, respectively, define the crossing cell as in the diagrams below on the left and right, respectively:

in the case where X is I, define the crossing cell as in the diagram below on the left, and in the composite case define the crossing cell as in the diagram below on the right:

We prove a technical lemma:

Lemma 1. *For any cell* α *of* $\ulcorner\mathbb{A}\urcorner$ *we have*

218   C. Nester

Proof. By structural induction on cells of $\ulcorner A\urcorner$. For the ∘-corners we have:

$$\text{(diagram)}$$

and for the •-corners, similarly:

$$\text{(diagram)}$$

the final base cases are the $\ulcorner f\urcorner$ maps:

$$\text{(diagram)}$$

There are two inductive cases. For vertical composition, we have:

$$\text{(diagram)}$$

Horizontal composition is similarly straightforward, and the claim follows by induction. □

From this we obtain a "non-interaction" property of our crossing cells, similar to the naturality of braiding in symmetric monoidal categories:

Corollary 1. *For cells α of $\mathbf{V}\ulcorner A\urcorner$ and β of $\mathbf{H}\ulcorner A\urcorner$, the following equation holds in $\ulcorner A\urcorner$:*

$$\text{(diagram)}$$

These crossing cells greatly aid in the legibility of diagrams corresponding to cells in $\ulcorner A\urcorner$, but also tell us something about the categorical structure of $\ulcorner A\urcorner$, namely that it is a monoidal double category in the sense of [21]:

Lemma 2. *If $\mathbb{A}$ is a symmetric strict monoidal category then $\ulcorner A\urcorner$ is a monoidal double category. That is, $\ulcorner A\urcorner$ is a pseudo-monoid object in the strict 2-category* $\mathbf{VDblCat}$ *of double categories, lax double functors, and vertical transformations.*

Proof. We give the action of the tensor product on cells:

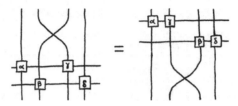

This defines a pseudofunctor, with the component of the required vertical transformation given by exchanging the two middle wires as in:

Notice that $\otimes$ is strictly associative and unital, in spite of being only pseudofunctorial.

□

5   Concurrency Through Cornering

We next proceed to extend the resource-theoretic interpretation of some symmetric strict monoidal category $\mathbb{A}$ to its free cornering $\ulcorner\mathbb{A}\lrcorner$. Interpret elements of $\ulcorner\mathbb{A}\lrcorner_V$ as $\mathbb{A}$-*valued exchanges*. Each exchange $X_1 \otimes \cdots \otimes X_n$ involves a left participant and a right participant giving each other resources in sequence, with A° indicating that the left participant should give the right participant an instance of A, and $A^\bullet$ indicating the opposite. For example say the left participant is Alice and the right participant is Bob. Then we can picture the exchange $A^\circ \otimes B^\bullet \otimes C^\bullet$ as:

$$\text{Alice} \rightsquigarrow \quad \overset{\xrightarrow{\quad A^\circ \quad}}{\underset{\xleftarrow{\quad C^\bullet \quad}}{\xleftarrow{\quad B^\bullet \quad}}} \quad \rightsquigarrow \text{Bob}$$

Think of these exchanges as happening *in order*. For example the exchange pictured above demands that first Alice gives Bob an instance of A, then Bob gives Alice an instance of B, and then finally Bob gives Alice an instance of C.

We interpret cells of $\ulcorner\mathbb{A}\lrcorner$ as *concurrent transformations*. Each cell describes a way to transform the collection of resources given by the top boundary into that given by the bottom boundary, via participating in $\mathbb{A}$-valued exchanges along the left and right boundaries. For example, consider the following cells of $\ulcorner\mathfrak{B}\lrcorner$:

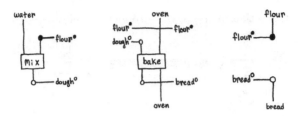

From left to right, these describe: A procedure for transforming `water` into nothing by `mixing` it with `flour` obtained by exchange along the right boundary, then sending the resulting `dough` away along the right boundary; A procedure for transforming an `oven` into an `oven`, receiving `flour` along the right boundary and sending it out the left boundary, then receiving `dough` along the left boundary, which is `baked` in the `oven`, with the resulting `bread` sent out along the right boundary; Finally, a procedure for turning `flour` into `bread` by giving it away and then receiving `bread` along the left boundary. When we compose these concurrent transformations horizontally in the evident way, they give a transformation of resources in the usual sense, i.e., a morphism of $\mathbb{A} \cong \mathbf{V}\ulcorner\mathbb{A}\urcorner$:

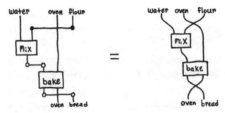

We understand equality of cells in $\ulcorner\mathbb{A}\urcorner$ much as we understand equality of morphisms in a resource theory: two cells should be equal in case the transformations they describe would have the same effect on the resources involved. In this way, cells of $\ulcorner\mathbb{A}\urcorner$ allow us to break a transformation into many concurrent parts. Note that with the crossing cells, it is possible to exchange resources "across" cells.

Consider the category $\mathbf{H}\ulcorner\mathbb{A}\urcorner$ of horizontal cells. If the vertical cells $\mathbf{V}\ulcorner\mathbb{A}\urcorner$ are concerned entirely with the transformation of resources, then our interpretation tells us that the horizontal cells are concerned entirely with exchange. Just as isomorphic objects in $\mathbf{V}\ulcorner\mathbb{A}\urcorner \cong \mathbb{A}$ can be thought of as equivalent collections of resources – being freely transformable into each other – we understand isomorphic objects in $\mathbf{H}\ulcorner\mathbb{A}\urcorner$ as *equivalent exchanges*. For example, There are many ways for `Alice` to give `Bob` an A and a B: Simultaneously, as $A \otimes B$; one after the other, as A and then B; or in the other order, as B and then A. While these are different sequences of events, they achieve the same thing, and are thus equivalent. Similarly, for `Alice` to give `Bob` an instance of I is equivalent to nobody doing anything. Formally, we have:

Lemma 3. *In* $\mathbf{H}\ulcorner\mathbb{A}\urcorner$ *we have for any* A, B *of* $\mathbb{A}$:

(i) $I^\circ \cong I \cong I^\bullet$.

(ii) $A^\circ \otimes B^\circ \cong B^\circ \otimes A^\circ$ and $A^\bullet \otimes B^\bullet \cong B^\bullet \otimes A^\bullet$.

(iii) $(A \otimes B)^\circ \cong A^\circ \otimes B^\circ$ and $(A \otimes B)^\bullet \cong A^\bullet \otimes B^\bullet$

Proof. (i) For $I \cong I^\circ$, consider the ∘-corners corresponding to I:

we know that these satisfy the yanking equations:

which exhibits an isomorphism $I \cong I^\circ$. Similarly, $I \cong I^\bullet$. Thus, we see formally that exchanging nothing is the same as doing nothing.

(ii) The ∘-corner case is the interesting one: Define the components of our isomorphism to be:

then for both of the required composites we have:

and so $A^\circ \otimes B^\circ \cong B^\circ \otimes A^\circ$. Similarly $A^\bullet \otimes B^\bullet \cong B^\bullet \otimes A^\bullet$. This captures formally the fact that if Alice is going to give Bob an A and a B, it doesn't really matter which order she does it in.

(iii) Here it is convenient to switch between depicting a single wire of sort $A \otimes B$ and two wires of sort A and B respectively in our string diagrams. To this end, we allow ourselves to depict the identity on $A \otimes B$ in multiple ways, using the notation of [3]:

Then the components of our isomorphism $(A \otimes B)^\circ \cong A^\circ \otimes B^\circ$ are:

and, much as in (ii), it is easy to see that the two possible composites are both identity maps. Similarly, $(A \otimes B)^\bullet \cong (A^\bullet \otimes B^\bullet)$. This captures formally the fact that giving away a collection is the same thing as giving away its components.

□

For example, we should be able to compose the cells on the left and right below horizontally, since their right and left boundaries, respectively, indicate equivalent exchanges:

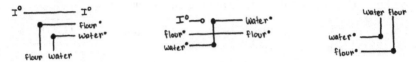

Our lemma tells us that there will always be a canonical isomorphism, as above in the middle, making composition possible.

It is worth noting that we *do not* have $A^\circ \otimes B^\bullet \cong B^\bullet \otimes A^\circ$:

Observation 1. *There is a morphism $d_\bullet^\circ : A^\circ \otimes B^\bullet \to B^\bullet \otimes A^\circ$ in one direction, defined by*

$$
\begin{array}{c}
A^\circ \\ B^\bullet
\end{array}
\!\!-\!\!\!\!\!\!-\!\!
\begin{array}{c}
B^\bullet \\ A^\circ
\end{array}
\quad = \quad
\begin{array}{c}
A^\circ \qquad B^\bullet \\
\times \\
B^\bullet \qquad A^\circ
\end{array}
\quad = \quad
\begin{array}{c}
A^\circ \\ B^\bullet
\end{array}
\!\!-\!\!\!\!\!\!-\!\!
\begin{array}{c}
B^\bullet \\ A^\circ
\end{array}
$$

but there is need not be a morphism in the other direction, and this is not in general invertible. In particular, $\mathbf{H}\ulcorner A \urcorner$ is monoidal, but need not be symmetric.

This observation reflects formally the intuition that if I receive some resources before I am required to send any, then I can send some of the resources that I receive. However, if I must send the resources first, this is not the case. In this way, $\mathbf{H}\ulcorner A \urcorner$ contains a sort of causal structure.

6   Conclusions and Future Work

We have shown how to decompose the material history of a process into concurrent components by working in the free cornering of an appropriate resource theory. We have explored the structure of the free cornering in light of this interpretation and found that it is consistent with our intuition about how this sort of thing ought to work. We do not claim to have solved all problems in the modelling of concurrency, but we feel that our formalism captures the material aspect of concurrent systems very well.

We find it quite surprising that the structure required to model concurrent resource transformations is precisely the structure of a proarrow equipment. This structure is already known to be important in formal category theory, and we are appropriately intrigued by its apparent relevance to models of concurrency

– a far more concrete setting than the usual context in which one encounters proarrow equipments!

There are of course many directions for future work. For one, our work is inspired by the message passing logic of [2], which has its categorical semantics in *linear actegories*. Any cornering defines an category – although not quite a *linear* actegory – and we speculate that cornerings are equivalent to some class of actegories, which would connect our work to the literature on behavioural types. Another direction for future work is to connect our material histories to a theory of concurrent processes – the slugs to our slime – with the goal of a formalism accounting for both. The category of spans of reflexive graphs, interpreted as open transition systems, seems especially promising here [13]. More generally, we would like to know how the perspective presented here can be integrated into other approaches to modelling concurrent systems.

References

1. Abramsky, S.: What are the fundamental structures of concurrency? we still don't know! CoRR abs/1401.4973 (2014)
2. Cockett, J.R.B., Pastro, C.: The logic of message-passing. Sci. Comput. Program. **74**, 498–533 (2009)
3. Cockett, J.R.B., Seely, R.A.G.: Proof theory of the cut rule. In: Landry, E. (ed.) Categories for the Working Philosopher, pp. 223–261. Oxford University Press, Oxford (2017)
4. Coecke, B., Fritz, T., Spekkens, R.W.: A mathematical theory of resources. Inf. Comput. **250**, 59–86 (2016)
5. Dawson, R., Paré, R.: What is a free double category like? J. Pure Appl. Algebra **168**(1), 19–34 (2002)
6. Ehresmann, C.: Catágories structurées. Annales scientifiques de l'École Normale Supérieure **80**(4), 349–426 (1963)
7. Fiore, M., Paoli, S., Pronk, D.: Model structures on the category of small double categories. Algebraic Geometric Topol. **8**(4), 1855–1959 (2008)
8. Fong, B., Spivak, D.I.: Seven Sketches in Compositionality: An Invitation to Applied Category Theory (2018)
9. Grandis, M., Pare, R.: Adjoint for double categories. Cahiers de Topologie et Géométrie Différentielle Catégoriques **45**(3), 193–240 (2004)
10. Hoare, C.A.R.: Communicating sequential processes. Commun. ACM **21**(8), 666–677 (1978)
11. Myers, D.J.: String Diagrams For Double Categories and Equipments. arXiv e-prints (2016)
12. Joyal, A., Street, R.: The geometry of tensor calculus, I. Adv. Math. **88**(1), 55–112 (1991)
13. Katis, P., Sabadini, N., Walters, R.F.C.: Span(Graph): a categorical algebra of transition systems. In: Johnson, M. (ed.) AMAST 1997. LNCS, vol. 1349, pp. 307–321. Springer, Heidelberg (1997). https://doi.org/10.1007/BFb0000479
14. Mac Lane, S.: Categories for the Working Mathematician. Springer, New York (1971). https://doi.org/10.1007/978-1-4612-9839-7
15. Meseguer, J., Montanari, U.: Petri nets are monoids. Inf. Comput. **88**(2), 105–155 (1990)

16. Milner, R. (ed.): A Calculus of Communicating Systems. LNCS, vol. 92. Springer, Heidelberg (1980). https://doi.org/10.1007/3-540-10235-3
17. Milner, R.: Communicating and Mobile Systems: The Pi-Calculus. Cambridge University Press, Cambridge (1999)
18. Petri, C.A.: Communication with automata (1966)
19. Selinger, P.: A survey of graphical languages for monoidal categories. In: New Structures for Physics, pp. 289–355. Springer, Heidelberg (2010). https://doi.org/10.1007/978-3-642-12821-9_4
20. Shulman, M.: Framed bicategories and monoidal fibrations. Theory Appl. Categories **20**(18), 650–738 (2008)
21. Shulman, M.A.: Constructing symmetric monoidal bicategories. arXiv e-prints (2010)
22. Wood, R.J.: Abstract pro arrows I. Cahiers de Topologie et Géométrie Différentielle Catégoriques **23**(3), 279–290 (1982)

A Clean and Efficient Implementation of Choreography Synthesis for Behavioural Contracts

Davide Basile[(⊠)] [ID] and Maurice H. ter Beek[ID]

Formal Methods and Tools Lab, ISTI–CNR, Pisa, Italy
{davide.basile,maurice.terbeek}@isti.cnr.it

Abstract. The Contract Automata Tool is an open-source tool for the specification, composition and synthesis of coordination of service contracts, including functionalities to deal with modalities and configurations. We discuss an implementation of the abstract parametric synthesis algorithm firstly introduced in our COORDINATION 2019 paper, comprehending most permissive controller, orchestration and choreography synthesis. The tool's source code has been redesigned and refactored in Java 8, and we show the resulting gain in computational efficiency.

Keywords: Service Computing · Contract Automata · Controller Synthesis · Orchestration · Choreography

1 Introduction

Orchestration and choreography are two coordination policies for service composition [14,16,40]. The specifications of services can be provided as behavioural contracts [5] that expose the interface to other services and are used to compute contract-based coordination policies.

Contract automata [10] formalise behavioural service contracts in terms of service offer actions and service request actions that need to match to achieve agreement among a composition of contracts. Modalities are used to indicate when an action must be matched (necessary) and when it can be withdrawn (permitted) in the synthesised coordination [6]. Composing contracts and synthesising a coordination, by refining a spurious composition, are the two main operations supporting contracts. Synthesis builds upon results from supervisory control theory [17,26,41] for synthesising the most permissive controller (mpc for short), duly revisited for synthesising orchestrations and choreographies in [9]. We are aware of only one other approach to coordinating services by supervisory control theory [2]. Contract automata have been equipped with a proof-of-concept tool [7] to show the feasibility of the proposed theoretical approach.

Motivation. According to a recent survey on formal methods among high-profile experts [23], the debate between "leaving the development of professional

Published by Springer Nature Switzerland AG 2021
F. Damiani and O. Dardha (Eds.): COORDINATION 2021, LNCS 12717, pp. 225–238, 2021.
https://doi.org/10.1007/978-3-030-78142-2_14

tools to industry" and "academia should invest effort to develop and consolidate usable tools" has no clear winner. In support of the latter, there is a shared belief that "academia should invest effort to develop and consolidate usable tools" because "this is the only way to provide technological transfer to industry, [as] in most cases efficient implementation requires to know a bit about the underlying theory". Indeed, according to [21,24], tool deficiencies (e.g., ease of use) are rated as one of the top obstacles for the adoption of formal methods by industry. However, to achieve this industrial transfer, in [30] it is recommended that "universities need to find ways to incentives industrial collaboration by adjusting its system of academic and career credits" and "research support and funding agencies need to actively encourage tool development and maintenance beyond prototyping" and "develop flexible funding schemes (in-cash or in-kind) to support the engineering work that is necessary to transform a prototype implementation into a demonstrable implementation". In support of the former, quite some academics believe that "we should not spend time on polishing the things that matter for acceptance in industry, such as user interfaces, have round-the-clock available help desks, liability, etc.", because "there is no business case for long term support of (academic) tools; industry needs stability and performance, academics need to innovate". In fact, it is evident that few research groups manage to work for decades on one tool and have it applied successfully in industry. We note, however, a gap between going beyond prototyping (e.g., by providing well-designed, clean and efficient implementations) and going as far as providing industry-ready tools (e.g., with help desks, industrial certification and floating licenses). Indeed, as also reported in [23], "the tools we develop should be usable (and extensible) by researchers in our own community" and "effort should be devoted to open-source community efforts". To this aim, we present a clean and efficient implementation of theoretical results presented in [9], providing an open-source tool [18] beyond the prototypical level, which can be reused as an API (and extended) by other researchers and developers in service coordination, rather than an off-the-shelf tool, ready to be adopted in industry.

Contribution. In this paper, we discuss improvements in the design and implementation of the contract automata tool [18]. It has been redesigned according to the principles of model-based systems engineering (MBSE for short) [29,42] and those of writing clean and readable code [15,36], which are known to improve reliability and understandability and facilitate maintainability and reuse. The tool has moreover been refactored using lambda expressions and Java Streams as available in Java 8 [25,43], exploiting parallelism. We are not aware of any other synthesis algorithm that uses big data-like parallel operations as Java Streams. The implementation of the abstract parametric synthesis algorithm from [9] and the mpc, orchestration and choreography synthesis are presented. We recompute the contracts of the case study in [9] to demonstrate the gain in computational efficiency of the new implementation, and we briefly address the gain in code readability and maintainability.

Outline. The paper is organised as follows. In Sect. 2, we briefly discuss the tool's new design. In Sect. 3, we recall theoretical results on the abstract synthesis algorithm. In Sect. 4, we present in detail the refactored synthesis implementation and discuss its adherence to the specification. In Sect. 5, we evaluate the improvement, both in absolute terms and in performance gain. In Sect. 6, we present related work whilst Sect. 7 concludes the paper.

2   Design

The tool's architecture has been redesigned with the MBSE tool Sparx Enterprise Architect[1] (EA for short) and Eclipse. EA allows to import Eclipse projects to generate documentation and UML diagrams. The UML class diagram concerning the main package of the tool, displayed in Fig. 1, has been generated by EA. For readability, only fields that are relevant for this paper are visible for each class.

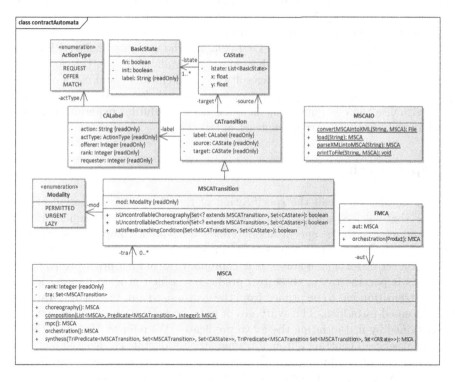

Fig. 1. The class diagram of the contract automata tool [18]

The standard UML class diagram is self-explanatory. The input/output functionalities are grouped in a stand-alone class MSCAIO, used by the application.

---

[1] https://sparxsystems.com/products/ea/.

The core of the implementation resides in the class MSCA that contains methods for composing and synthesising contracts, discussed below. The decorator pattern is used for the class FMCA, which adds the functionality of synthesising an orchestration for a specific configuration (called a product, cf. [6]).

Another package of the tool, family, concerns the aforementioned functionalities, discussed in [6], regarding the possibility of synthesising an orchestration of a product line (also called family) of service contracts, where each configuration is in a (partial) ordering relation with other configurations. The functionalities of this package have not been refactored in Java 8 yet, and do not concern the contribution discussed in this paper. The repository is available at [18].

The GUI Application. One of the advantages of adopting a widely used language such as Java is the availability of many resources. In particular, we implemented a GUI application, publicly available in [19]. This application is importing and using both our CAT library discussed in this paper and the mxGraph library [37] that provides features for displaying interactive diagrams and graphs. We specialised the GraphEditor example of the library to develop the GUI of the tool. We wish to emphasise the separation of concerns between the tool's usability for end users, addressed by the GUI [19], and the usability of the API offered to other developers, addressed in this paper and available in [18]. Developers can use our library as back-end to other software, and efficiency and clean design of the implementation are our primary concern. Nevertheless, being able to graphically visualise the computed contracts has been helpful for experimenting new developments in the theory of contract automata.

3 Specification

In this section, we recall the specification of the abstract synthesis algorithm from [9] that will be useful to provide some evidence that the implementation in Sect. 4 adheres with the specification. This is a fix-point computation where at each iteration the set of transitions of the automaton is refined (pruning predicate ϕ_p) and a set of forbidden states R is computed (forbidden predicate ϕ_f). The synthesis is parametric on these two predicates, which provide information on when a transition has to be pruned from the synthesised automaton or a state has to be deemed forbidden. The syntheses of mpc, orchestration and choreography are obtained by instantiating these two predicates. We refer to MSCA as the set of (modal service) contract automata, where the set of states is denoted by Q and the set of transitions by T (with $T^\square$ denoting the set of necessary transitions). For an automaton $\mathcal{A}$, the predicate $Dangling(\mathcal{A})$ contains those states that are not reachable from the initial state or that cannot reach any final state.

Definition 1 (Abstract synthesis [9]). *Let $\mathcal{A}$ be an MSCA, and let $\mathcal{K}_0 = \mathcal{A}$ and $R_0 = Dangling(\mathcal{K}_0)$. Given two predicates $\phi_p, \phi_f : T \times MSCA \times Q \to Bool$, we let the* abstract synthesis function $f_{(\phi_p, \phi_f)} : MSCA \times 2^Q \to MSCA \times 2^Q$ *be defined as follows:*

$$f_{(\phi_p,\phi_f)}(\mathcal{K}_{i-1},R_{i-1}) = (\mathcal{K}_i,R_i), with$$
$$T\mathcal{K}_i = T\mathcal{K}_{i-1} \setminus \{\, t \in T\mathcal{K}_{i-1} \mid \phi_p(t,\mathcal{K}_{i-1},R_{i-1}) = true \,\}$$
$$R_i = R_{i-1} \cup \{\, q \mid (q \rightarrow) = t \in T_A^{\square},\ \phi_f(t,\mathcal{K}_{i-1},R_{i-1}) = true \,\} \cup Dangling(\mathcal{K}_i)$$

The abstract controller is defined in Eq. 1 below as the least fixed point (cf. Theorem 5.2 [9]) where, if the initial state belongs to $R_s^{(\phi_p,\phi_f)}$, then the controller is empty, otherwise it is the automaton with the set of transitions $T_{\mathcal{K}_s^{(\phi_p,\phi_f)}}$ and without states in $R_s^{(\phi_p,\phi_f)}$.

$$(\mathcal{K}_s^{(\phi_p,\phi_f)}, R_s^{(\phi_p,\phi_f)}) = sup(\{\, f_{(\phi_p,\phi_f)}^n(\mathcal{K}_0,R_0) \mid n \in \mathbb{N} \,\}) \tag{1}$$

4   Implementation

The implementation has been refactored in Java 8, the latest major feature release[2] including lambda expressions and streaming API. Streams are used for big data-style processing of data structures, incorporating MapReduce-like operations [20]. Streams can be easily parallelised, abstracting from the underlying realisation with parallel threads. Although a parallel stream can be obtained with a simple method (`parallelStream()`), if not carefully used issues may be encountered, e.g., race conditions. Indeed, the usage of Java 8 Streams is currently under investigation [31–33]. Based on the analysis of 34 Java projects, two important findings listed in [33] are: "Stream parallelization is not widely used", and "Although streams feature performance improving parallelism, developers tend to struggle with using streams efficiently". This seems to confirm the finding of [35], "indicating the difficulty of reasoning [on] concurrent execution by programmers", while in [31,32], focusing on evaluating refactoring, it is noted that "using streams efficiently requires many subtle considerations".

In our implementation, parallel streams are carefully used to speed-up the computation of the set of transitions and forbidden states at each iteration. We both provide an informal argument on the correctness of our implementation below, confirmed by testing our implementation on the case studies in [9] and [6], as well as experimental evidence on the efficiency of the new implementation in Sect. 5. We start by discussing the parametric synthesis method below.

Lines 2–3 show the two parameters of the method. Both predicates take three arguments: the transition under scrutiny, the set of transitions and the set of forbidden states computed so far. Lines 5–6 are used to store references to the transitions, states and initial state, which could be lost during the synthesis. Initially, the set of forbidden states R is composed of dangling states (line 7). A Boolean flag `update` is used to flag when the least fixed point is reached. At each iteration (lines 9–20), the set of transitions is refined with a parallel stream filtering away those transitions satisfying the pruning predicate (lines 11–13).

---

[2] https://www.oracle.com/java/technologies/java8.html.

Similarly, the set R is updated by adding dangling states due to pruned transitions (line 14). Source states of transitions satisfying the forbidden predicate are computed using a parallel stream (considering also transitions previously pruned) and added to R (lines 15–18). Finally, when the fixed point is reached the dangling transitions are removed (line 21), and if the initial state is not forbidden (line 25) the synthesised MSCA is returned (line 26).

```
1    public MSCA synthesis(
2      TriPredicate<MSCATransition, Set<MSCATransition>, Set<CAState>> pruningPred,
3      TriPredicate<MSCATransition, Set<MSCATransition>, Set<CAState>> forbiddenPred)
4    {
5      Set<MSCATransition> trbackup = new HashSet<MSCATransition>(this.getTransition());
6      Set<CAState> statesbackup= this.getStates();  CAState init = this.getInitial();
7      Set<CAState> R = new HashSet<CAState>(this.getDanglingStates(statesbackup,init)); //R0
8      boolean update=false;
9      do{ final Set<CAState> Rf = new HashSet<CAState>(R);
10         final Set<MSCATransition> trf= new HashSet<MSCATransition>(this.getTransition())
11         if (this.getTransition().removeAll(this.getTransition().parallelStream()
12                           .filter(x->pruningPred.test(x,trf, Rf))
13                           .collect(Collectors.toSet())))) //Ki
14            R.addAll(this.getDanglingStates(statesbackup,init));
15         R.addAll(trbackup.parallelStream()
16                           .filter(x->forbiddenPred.test(x,trf, Rf))
17                           .map(MSCATransition::getSource)
18                           .collect(Collectors.toSet())); //Ri
19         update=Rf.size()!=R.size()|| trf.size()!=this.getTransition().size();
20      } while(update);
21      this.removeDanglingTransitions();
22      if (R.contains(init)) return null;
23      return this;
24    }
```

Correctness. We provide an informal argument on the adherence of the implementation with respect to the specification provided in Sect. 3. Thanks to the high-level constructs provided by Java, this is quite straightforward since the distance between the implementation and the specification is narrow.

As already stated, the fix-point computation is implemented as a simple do while loop, where the Boolean variable update (line 19) is used to check that the computed sets have not been modified by the last iteration. This is done by simply checking that their size has not changed. Indeed, only instructions for removing transitions or adding states to R are invoked at each iteration. The functional interface TriPredicate is used to type both pruning and forbidden predicates as functions taking three arguments and returning a Boolean. The set R_0 of Definition 1 is computed by the instruction in line 7, using the method getDanglingStates that implements the predicate $Dangling$. This method basically performs a forward and backward visit of the automaton. Here the correspondence with Definition 1 is obtained by simply observing that $\mathcal{K}_0 = \mathcal{A}$. Indeed, the predicate $Dangling$ of Definition 1 takes as arguments the automaton to which the dangling states are computed. In the implementation, such automaton is the object this to which the method getDanglingStates is invoked (basically, $\mathcal{K}_i$ in Definition 1 is the object this).

The instructions in lines 11–12 perform the set difference on the set of transitions, by removing the transitions satisfying the pruning predicate. This is basically the same as Definition 1. As already stated, the computation of the set of forbidden states R starts in line 14 by adding the dangling states. In case no transition has been removed, the set of dangling states is unchanged.

Sources of transitions satisfying the forbidden predicate are added in lines 15–18. Here there is a slight divergence from Definition 1: the abstract synthesis algorithm only checks the forbidden predicate on necessary transitions. Since the notion of necessary transition varies depending on whether we are synthesising an mpc, an orchestration or a choreography, in the implementation this check will be implemented by the forbidden predicate passed as argument to the **synthesis** method (see below). Due to the well-known state-explosion problem, it is expected that, for an average composition, the set of transitions is not of a small size. Thus, parallel streams are used to efficiently process each element separately and independently from the other threads, with no concurrency issues.

Instructions in lines 21–22 finalise the automaton to be returned as discussed in Sect. 3.

Mpc Synthesis. Concerning the synthesis of the mpc below, the property of agreement is enforced, i.e., no request shall be left unmatched. Thus, a state is forbidden if it has an outgoing uncontrollable request. Indeed, in the mpc synthesis, necessary requests are uncontrollable, according to the standard notion of uncontrollability in supervisory control theory, called *urgent* in contract automata.

```
1    public MSCA mpc(){
2      return synthesis((x,t,bad) -> bad.contains(x.getTarget()) || x.getLabel().isRequest(),
3                  (x,t,bad) -> !t.contains(x) && x.isUrgent());
4    }
```

The synthesis of the mpc is obtained by instantiating the pruning and forbidden predicates. The pruning predicate checks if a transition has a forbidden target state or is a request (line 2). The forbidden predicate selects source states of necessary transitions (i.e., urgent) that have been previously removed (line 3).

Orchestration Synthesis. The synthesis of the orchestration below is similar to the one of the mpc, apart from the different notion of necessary request.

```
1    public MSCA orchestration(){
2      return synthesis((x,t,bad) -> bad.contains(x.getTarget())|| x.getLabel().isRequest(),
3            (x,t,bad) -> x.isUncontrollableOrchestration(t, bad));
4    }
```

In the orchestration, necessary requests are semi-controllable (line 3): basically, a necessary request becomes uncontrollable if there exists no execution in which that request is matched, otherwise it is controllable. Intuitively, in an orchestration of service contracts the order (among possible interleavings) in which the necessary requests are matched does not matter, as long as there exists at least one execution in which the match takes place. The orchestrator is in charge of driving the services towards executions in agreement [9].

Choreography Synthesis. The orchestration assumes the presence of an implicit orchestrator driving the executions toward safe behaviour. In a choreography, instead, contract automata are supposed to be able to interact safely on their own, without resorting to a central orchestrator. To do so, the property to be enforced is called *strong agreement*, i.e., all requests and offers have to be matched (this property is also referred to as absence of orphan messages). A property called *branching condition* must hold: automata must be able to send offers independently from the state of other automata. In the choreographic framework, requests are always permitted, whereas offers can also be necessary. Necessary offers use semi-controllability for choreographies, which is weaker than uncontrollability yet stronger than the semi-controllable notion used in the synthesis of orchestration. Indeed, compared to orchestrations, an additional constraint must hold: the transitions matching the necessary offer must share the same source state. This is because the automata must be able to interact correctly by only using local information.

```
1    public MSCA choreography(){
2      MSCA aut; MSCATransition toRemove= null;
3      Set<String> violatingBC = new HashSet<>();
4      do {
5      aut=this.clone().synthesis((x,t,bad)->!x.getLabel().isMatch()||bad.contains(x.getTarget())
6             ||violatingBC.contains(x),(x,t,bad) -> x.isUncontrollableChoreography(t, bad));
7      if (aut==null) break;
8      final Set<MSCATransition> trf = aut.getTransition();
9      toRemove=(aut.getTransition().parallelStream()
10              .filter(x->!x.satisfiesBranchingCondition(trf, new HashSet<CAState>()))
11              .findAny().orElse(null));
12     } while (violatingBC.add(toRemove));
13     return aut;
14   }
```

The choreography synthesis algorithm iteratively calls the synthesis method using semi-controllability for choreographies in the forbidden predicate and strong agreement in the pruning predicate (lines 5–6). After reaching the fixed point, a transition that violates the branching condition is non-deterministically selected (lines 9–11). Depending on which transition is selected and removed, different choreographies can be obtained. The synthesis abstracts away from the way in which transitions violating the branching condition are selected. Notably, removing only one such transition at each synthesis invocation allows to remove a smaller number of transitions than, for example, removing all of them at the first iteration. The iteration continues until there are no transitions violating the branching condition. An alternative implementation could contain only one call to the synthesis method, similarly to the orchestration and mpc methods. It would suffice to only use the instructions in lines 6–7 by moving the branching condition check in line 10 inside the pruning predicate in line 5. In this way, transitions violating the branching condition would be pruned at each step of the called synthesis algorithm, and this method would compute a smaller, possibly empty choreography. The specification did not fix any strategy for selecting which transition violating the branching condition should be pruned and when. This indeed could be decided according to different criteria.

Table 1. Improvement in computational runtime (ms) of the current tool version [18]. All experiments run on a machine with Processor Intel(R) Core(TM) i7-8500Y CPU at 1.50 GHz, 1601 Mhz, 2 Core(s), 4 Logical Processor(s), 16 GB RAM, 64-bit Windows 10.

	composition			orchestration			choreography		
	runtime in [9]	current runtime	runtime speedup	runtime in [9]	current runtime	runtime speedup	runtime in [9]	current runtime	runtime speedup
A_1	65594	1312	49.99x	715216	2872	249.03x	–	–	–
A_2	66243	1006	65.85x	–	–	–	459311	1604	286.35x

5 Evaluation

A rough measure of the improvement for what concerns code readability and maintainability can be obtained by comparing the lines of source code (LOC for short) with those used in the previous prototypical implementation [22]. The previous choreography synthesis used 211 LOC, while the current implementation uses only 14 (choreography) + 24 (synthesis) LOC. Similarly, the previous orchestration synthesis used 178 LOC, which have been refactored in 2 (orchestration) + 24 (synthesis) LOC. The synthesis method is factorised for orchestration, choreography and mpc, which was not possible before, so reducing code duplication. Finally, UML diagrams (cf. Fig. 1) provide the benefits of graphical documentation of the architecture of the tool that was not previously available.

To evaluate the gain in efficiency of the current implementation [18], we compare its performance with that of the previous implementation [22], which was programmed using quick incremental patches over the years and without parallelism. In [9], the previous implementation was applied to a case study, with the performances reported in Examples 2.5, 3.4 and 4.6 and recalled in Table 1. Table 1 also reports the data of applying the current implementation and the speedup, showcasing the improvement obtained thanks to redesigning the tool, cleaning the code and refactoring the algorithms by using parallel streams.

6 Related Work

The literature offers several approaches to the problem of synthesising a choreography of interacting components, with supporting tools. Recently, a tool chain for choreographic design has been proposed in [28]. Choreographies are designed using a kind of BPMN2 Choreography Diagrams, but equipped with a formal semantics. The operation of closure at the semantic level is used to insert missing behaviour, which can be suggested as amendments to be validated by a human. Our approach is completely automatised. Our choreography synthesis is based on the synthesis of the mpc that *refines* the composition by removing rather than adding behaviour. The composition can be computed automatically, starting from local components, to represent all their possible interactions independently from the selected communication pattern (e.g., non-blocking output, blocking output). The composition could also be the starting point, in this case representing a global choreography to be realised, if possible. Our algorithm is non-deterministic and accounts for necessary and permitted actions.

In [3], the synthesis of so-called coordination delegates is discussed. Coordination delegates are used to enforce the behaviour prescribed by a choreography designed as a BPMN2 Choreography Diagram, and are additional components that interact with each other and with the services identified by the choreography to enforce the prescribed behaviour. A mature tool for software development according to this proposal is presented in [4]. Similarly, in [38], BPMN2 Choreography Diagrams are used to automatically derive a conformant choreography-based software architecture. Informal diagrams are mapped to coloured Petri nets, specifying the coordination logic. Coordination delegates are synthesised to fulfill the inferred coordination logic that is needed to enforce the realisability of the choreography. They communicate with the participants they are supervising or among themselves. These delegates are synthesised using the approach described in [12] to either relax or restrict the original behaviour. This is obtained by introducing extra communications performed by the delegates.

These approaches to the synthesis of coordination delegates are similar to the synthesis of distributed controllers in [34], which studies the fundamental problem of supervisory control synthesis for local controllers interacting among them through a coordinator.

Compared to the above work, our approach to choreography synthesis does not introduce any intermediate component, nor additional behaviour. This is not the case for our orchestration synthesis that assumes the presence of an orchestrator dictating the overall execution by interacting with local components. Since contract automata are *composable* and our synthesised choreography is again a contract automaton, we conjecture that similar results could be obtained by (i) partitioning the composition, (ii) separately synthesising a choreography for each partition, and (iii) computing the orchestration of the composition of the choreographies. The conditions under which such partitions can be computed to obtain non-empty choreographies need to be investigated, perhaps exploiting existing research on requirements splitting for supervisory control synthesis [27].

A static analyser for Go programs that uses a global session graph synthesis tool to detect communication deadlocks is discussed in [39]. From Go programs, communicating finite state machines (CFSM for short) are extracted, and used to synthesise a global choreography that represents deadlock-freeness in the original program. Our synthesised choreography has also been interpreted in the framework of CFSM [11], and the composition of contract automata enables to proceed bottom-up by composing local components into a choreography. Notably, if such choreography cannot be realised by composing local components, our algorithm automatically detects which portion of behaviour is to be pruned, if possible, to synthesise a deadlock-free choreography. We conjecture that this result could be used to suggest amendments to the original Go program.

The authors of this paper have gained experience in applying other tools for controller synthesis, viz., CIF 3 [13] and UPPAAL STRATEGO [8]. It would be interesting to investigate an encoding of the coordination syntheses discussed in this paper in the tools discussed in this section, to draw a comparison.

Since our implementation is cleanly designed, efficient and implemented in a widely used language in few lines of code, we hope that it will be exploited in other tools as a further option to the synthesis problem for orchestration, choreographies and most permissive controllers.

7   Conclusion

We have presented recent improvements in the contract automata tool. The source code has been redesigned using MBSE techniques, and refactored in Java 8 exploiting parallel streams, including the novel choreography synthesis. The correspondence between the formal specification and the implementation is discussed. The obtained improvements are emphasised by comparisons with the previous tool version.

Future Work. In the future, we would like to formally prove that the implementation respects its specification using, e.g., the theorem prover KeY [1] that adopts specifications written in Java Modeling Language. While this is the state-of-the-art for Java, there is no support for Java Streams and lambda expressions to date, leaving this as a long-term goal. Also, the current version of our tool supports product lines of orchestrations but not of choreographies, which we plan to investigate, together with real-time support. Our approach refines a spurious composition to a choreography, in the style of controller synthesis. As discussed in Sect. 6, other approaches propose to add additional behaviour during synthesis. A full-fledged comparison with other approaches is a matter of future investigation. It is also interesting to exploit the compositionality offered by contract automata to combine choreography and orchestration synthesis with the goal of maximising the set of contracts that can correctly interact whilst minimising the overhead of the orchestration.

Acknowledgments. We acknowledge funding from the MIUR PRIN 2017FTXR7S project IT MaTTerS (Methods and Tools for Trustworthy Smart Systems).

References

1. Ahrendt, W., Beckert, B., Bubel, R., Hähnle, R., Schmitt, P.H., Ulbrich, M. (eds.): Deductive Software Verification - The KeY Book: From Theory to Practice. LNCS, vol. 10001. Springer, Cham (2016). https://doi.org/10.1007/978-3-319-49812-6
2. Atampore, F., Dingel, J., Rudie, K.: Automated service composition via supervisory control theory. In: Proceedings of the 13th International Workshop on Discrete Event Systems (WODES 2016), pp. 28–35. IEEE (2016). https://doi.org/10.1109/WODES.2016.7497822

3. Autili, M., Inverardi, P., Perucci, A., Tivoli, M.: Synthesis of distributed and adaptable coordinators to enable choreography evolution. In: de Lemos, R., Garlan, D., Ghezzi, C., Giese, H. (eds.) Software Engineering for Self-Adaptive Systems III. Assurances. LNCS, vol. 9640, pp. 282–306. Springer, Cham (2017). https://doi.org/10.1007/978-3-319-74183-3_10

4. Autili, M., Salle, A.D., Gallo, F., Pompilio, C., Tivoli, M.: CHOReVOLUTION: service choreography in practice. Sci. Comput. Program. **197** (2020). https://doi.org/10.1016/j.scico.2020.102498

5. Bartoletti, M., Cimoli, T., Zunino, R.: Compliance in behavioural contracts: a brief survey. In: Bodei, C., Ferrari, G.-L., Priami, C. (eds.) Programming Languages with Applications to Biology and Security. LNCS, vol. 9465, pp. 103–121. Springer, Cham (2015). https://doi.org/10.1007/978-3-319-25527-9_9

6. Basile, D., et al.: Controller synthesis of service contracts with variability. Sci. Comput. Program. **187** (2020). https://doi.org/10.1016/j.scico.2019.102344

7. Basile, D., ter Beek, M.H., Gnesi, S.: Modelling and analysis with featured modal contract automata. In: Proceedings of the 22nd International Systems and Software Product Line Conference (SPLC 2018), vol. 2, pp. 11–16. ACM (2018). https://doi.org/10.1145/3236405.3236408

8. Basile, D., ter Beek, M.H., Legay, A.: Strategy synthesis for autonomous driving in a moving block railway system with UPPAAL STRATEGO. In: Gotsman, A., Sokolova, A. (eds.) FORTE 2020. LNCS, vol. 12136, pp. 3–21. Springer, Cham (2020). https://doi.org/10.1007/978-3-030-50086-3_1

9. Basile, D., ter Beek, M.H., Pugliese, R.: Synthesis of orchestrations and choreographies: bridging the gap between supervisory control and coordination of services. Log. Methods Comput. Sci. **16**(2) (2020). https://doi.org/10.23638/LMCS-16(2:9)2020

10. Basile, D., Degano, P., Ferrari, G.L.: Automata for specifying and orchestrating service contracts. Log. Methods Comput. Sci. **12**(4:6), 1–51 (2016). https://doi.org/10.2168/LMCS-12(4:6)2016

11. Basile, D., Degano, P., Ferrari, G.L., Tuosto, E.: Relating two automata-based models of orchestration and choreography. J. Log. Algebr. Meth. Program. **85**(3), 425–446 (2016). https://doi.org/10.1016/j.jlamp.2015.09.011

12. Basu, S., Bultan, T.: Automated choreography repair. In: Stevens, P., Wąsowski, A. (eds.) FASE 2016. LNCS, vol. 9633, pp. 13–30. Springer, Heidelberg (2016). https://doi.org/10.1007/978-3-662-49665-7_2

13. ter Beek, M.H., Reniers, M.A., de Vink, E.P.: Supervisory controller synthesis for product lines using CIF 3. In: Margaria, T., Steffen, B. (eds.) ISoLA 2016, Part I. LNCS, vol. 9952, pp. 856–873. Springer, Cham (2016). https://doi.org/10.1007/978-3-319-47166-2_59

14. ter Beek, M.H., Bucchiarone, A., Gnesi, S.: Web service composition approaches: from industrial standards to formal methods. In: Proceedings of the 2nd International Conference on Internet and Web Applications and Services (ICIW 2007). IEEE (2007). https://doi.org/10.1109/ICIW.2007.71

15. Boswell, D., Foucher, T.: The Art of Readable Code. O'Reilly, Sebastopol (2011)

16. Bouguettaya, A., et al.: A service computing manifesto: the next 10 years. Commun. ACM **60**(4), 64–72 (2017). https://doi.org/10.1145/2983528

17. Caillaud, B., Darondeau, P., Lavagno, L., Xie, X. (eds.): Synthesis and Control of Discrete Event Systems. Springer, New York (2002). https://doi.org/10.1007/978-1-4757-6656-1

18. https://github.com/davidebasile/ContractAutomataLib

19. https://github.com/davidebasile/ContractAutomataApp
20. Dean, J., Ghemawat, S.: MapReduce: simplified data processing on large clusters. Commun. ACM **51**(1), 107–113 (2008). https://doi.org/10.1145/1327452.1327492
21. Ferrari, A., Mazzanti, F., Basile, D., ter Beek, M.H., Fantechi, A.: Comparing formal tools for system design: a judgment study. In: Proceedings of the 42nd International Conference on Software Engineering (ICSE 2020), pp. 62–74. ACM (2020). https://doi.org/10.1145/3377811.3380373
22. https://github.com/davidebasile/ContractAutomataLib/blob/old-backup/src/ FMCA/FMCA.java#L1200 . Lines 1200–1378 contain the orchestration synthesis, lines 1385–1596 the choreography synthesis (the utility methods are not counted)
23. Garavel, H., Beek, M.H., van de Pol, J.: The 2020 expert survey on formal methods. In: ter Beek, M.H., Ničković, D. (eds.) FMICS 2020. LNCS, vol. 12327, pp. 3–69. Springer, Cham (2020). https://doi.org/10.1007/978-3-030-58298-2_1
24. Gleirscher, M., Marmsoler, D.: Formal methods in dependable systems engineering: a survey of professionals from Europe and North America. Empir. Softw. Eng. **25**(6), 4473–4546 (2020). https://doi.org/10.1007/s10664-020-09836-5
25. Goetz, B., Peierls, T., Bloch, J., Bowbeer, J., Holmes, D., Lea, D.: Java Concurrency in Practice. Addison-Wesley, Amsterdam (2006)
26. Goorden, M.A., et al.: The road ahead for supervisor synthesis. In: Pang, J., Zhang, L. (eds.) SETTA 2020. LNCS, vol. 12153, pp. 1–16. Springer, Cham (2020). https://doi.org/10.1007/978-3-030-62822-2_1
27. Goorden, M., van de Mortel-Fronczak, J., Reniers, M., Fokkink, W., Rooda, J.: The impact of requirement splitting on the efficiency of supervisory control synthesis. In: Larsen, K.G., Willemse, T. (eds.) FMICS 2019. LNCS, vol. 11687, pp. 76–92. Springer, Cham (2019). https://doi.org/10.1007/978-3-030-27008-7_5
28. Guanciale, R., Tuosto, E.: PomCho: a tool chain for choreographic design. Sci. Comput. Program. **202** (2021). https://doi.org/10.1016/j.scico.2020.102535
29. Henderson, K., Salado, A.: Value and benefits of model-based systems engineering (MBSE): evidence from the literature. Syst. Eng. **24**(1), 51–66 (2021). https://doi. org/10.1002/sys.21566
30. Huisman, M., Gurov, D., Malkis, A.: Formal methods: from academia to industrial practice. A travel guide. arXiv:2002.07279 [cs.SE], February 2020. https://arxiv. org/abs/2002.07279
31. Khatchadourian, R., Tang, Y., Bagherzadeh, M.: Safe automated refactoring for intelligent parallelization of Java 8 streams. Sci. Comput. Program. **195** (2020). https://doi.org/10.1016/j.scico.2020.102476
32. Khatchadourian, R., Tang, Y., Bagherzadeh, M., Ahmed, S.: Safe automated refactoring for intelligent parallelization of Java 8 streams. In: Proceedings of the 41st International Conference on Software Engineering (ICSE 2019), pp. 619–630. IEEE (2019). https://doi.org/10.1109/ICSE.2019.00072
33. Khatchadourian, R., Tang, Y., Bagherzadeh, M., Ray, B.: An empirical study on the use and misuse of Java 8 streams. In: Wehrheim, H., Cabot, J. (eds.) FASE 2020. LNCS, vol. 12076, pp. 97–118. Springer, Cham (2020). https://doi.org/10. 1007/978-3-030-45234-6_5
34. Komenda, J., Masopust, T., van Schuppen, J.H.: Supervisory control synthesis of discrete-event systems using a coordination scheme. Automatica **48**(2), 247–254 (2012). https://doi.org/10.1016/j.automatica.2011.07.008

35. Lu, S., Park, S., Seo, E., Zhou, Y.: Learning from mistakes – a comprehensive study on real world concurrency bug characteristics. In: Proceedings of the 13th International Conference on Architectural Support for Programming Languages and Operating Systems (ASPLOS 2008), pp. 329–339. ACM (2008). https://doi.org/10.1145/1346281.1346323
36. Martin, R.C.: Clean Code. Prentice Hall, Upper Saddle River (2008)
37. https://jgraph.github.io/mxgraph/java/index.html
38. Najem, T.: A formal semantics for supporting the automated synthesis of choreography-based architectures. In: Proceedings of the 13th European Conference on Software Architecture (ECSA 2019), vol. 2, pp. 51–54. ACM (2019). https://doi.org/10.1145/3344948.3344949
39. Ng, N., Yoshida, N.: Static deadlock detection for concurrent go by global session graph synthesis. In: Proceedings of the 25th International Conference on Compiler Construction (CC 2016), pp. 174–184. ACM (2016). https://doi.org/10.1145/2892208.2892232
40. Peltz, C.: Web services orchestration and choreography. IEEE Comput. **36**(10), 46–52 (2003). https://doi.org/10.1109/MC.2003.1236471
41. Ramadge, P.J., Wonham, W.M.: Supervisory control of a class of discrete event processes. SIAM J. Control. Optim. **25**(1), 206–230 (1987). https://doi.org/10.1137/0325013
42. Tockey, S.: How to Engineer Software: A Model-Based Approach. Wiley, Hoboken (2019)
43. Warburton, R.: Java 8 Lambdas: Pragmatic Functional Programming. O'Reilly, New York (2014)

A Practical Tool-Chain for the Development of Coordination Scenarios
Graphical Modeler, DSL, Code Generators and Automaton-Based Simulator

Eva Maria Kuehn[✉]

Faculty of Informatics, Compilers and Languages Group, TU Wien, Vienna, Austria
eva.kuehn@tuwien.ac.at
http://www.complang.tuwien.ac.at/eva/

Abstract. Coordination scenarios have high demands on concurrency and interaction. However, these are typical sources for flaws in both design and implementation. A modeling approach enables reasoning about distributed algorithms and finding deficiencies right from the beginning. The Peer Model has been introduced as a modeling tool for distribution, concurrency and blackboard-based collaboration and coordination, relying on known foundations like tuple spaces, Petri Nets and Actor Model. A runtime system exists that serves Java developers for prototyping, but still a feasible tool-chain was missing, like for most academic systems.

This paper presents a practical new tool-chain for the Peer Model consisting of a graphical modelling tool, building on a drawing program that exports XML. A translator parses the XML and translates it into a newly developed domain specific language that is the basis for code generation. One target is a new, formal automaton-based runtime written in the Go programming language. It allows systematic simulation runs of user models. The demo shows a peer competition scenario, where several players play a game, a global state holds the players' scores, and in addition each peer maintains a decentralized state. Before taking a move in the game, a peer asserts its current local state to be the same like the global one. If this is the case, it carries out its action and distributes the information about it to all other players for further verification. The scenario captures core coordination mechanisms found in blockchain systems.

Keywords: Peer Model · tool-chain · coordination modelling · coordination simulation

1 Introduction to the Peer Model Tool-Chain

The *Peer Model* [17,18] is a modelling notation that relies on know concepts from Petri Nets [5,14,23,24], tuple spaces [11,12] and the Actor model [7]. Distributed *Peers* collaborate with each other by asynchronous message sending (cf. Actor model). The behaviour of a Peer is indeterministic and modelled by

© IFIP International Federation for Information Processing 2021
Published by Springer Nature Switzerland AG 2021
F. Damiani and O. Dardha (Eds.): COORDINATION 2021, LNCS 12717, pp. 239–254, 2021.
https://doi.org/10.1007/978-3-030-78142-2_15

means of *wirings* which relate to transitions in Petri Nets. All wirings of a Peer run concurrently and synchronize themselves via transactional operations on two tuple spaces: one is termed *PIC* (Peer input container) and the other one *POC* (Peer output container).

The Peer Model supports domain specific abstractions as higher-level modeling constructs which lead to easy to understand models, like automatic flow correlation [15,18], abstraction of asynchronous message sending [15,18], timing constraints for all resources [15], and transactions [16]. The original specification of the Peer Model can be found in [17].

Targeted application areas are scenarios with high concurrency and decentralized coordination. Some selected application examples are:

Smart Contracts which realize distributed application logic on a blockchain. They were made popular by Ethereum [1], which introduced a new language termed "Solidity". The result must be deterministic, meaning that eventually all blockchain nodes must achieve a consensus on the result. Also, the execution must terminate. A smart contract holds an internal state and is triggered by an external event. It forms an automatized, formalized contract among multiple parties based on complex conditions.

Complex coordination patterns [15] like distributed, heterogeneous transactions, distributed consensus algorithms, distributed voting, collaboration, load balancing, load clustering and peer clustering.

Embedded systems especially in the domain of traffic management systems (train [13], truck, and air), and other autonomous cyber physical systems.

So far, a Java-based runtime system has been developed for the Peer Model in the context of a diploma thesis [8] and a doctoral thesis [9] which also added a security model to the Peer Model. This system is open source and can be used by system developers who are experienced in Java programming. However there are the following drawbacks: There is no tool support yet for graphical modeling, and a formal analysis tool is still missing. The motivation of this work was therefore to provide a practical tool-chain for the modeling and analysis of complex coordination scenarios with the Peer Model. It consists of the components highlighted in gray color in Fig. 1.

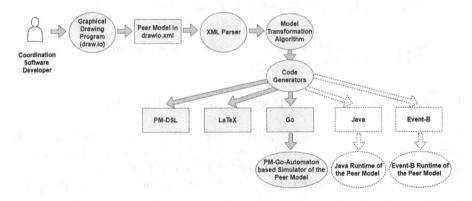

Fig. 1. Peer Model Tool-Chain.

As front end serves a graphical drawing program[1], for which dedicated shapes were designed for all Peer Model artefacts. An extended language notation is introduced that supports types for Peer Model artefacts to enable their reuse as patterns [15,19]. Moreover it provides context properties, a notation for range, for all and exists expressions, and the specification of configurations. Developers employ the new shapes to model coordination scenarios.

The resulting XML model is parsed and transformed into an intermediate format on which a model transformation algorithm (MTA) is applied. The MTA interprets the newly introduced language concepts and statically resolves them for the code generators. These form the next step in the tool-chain. The here considered code generator translates the model into Go code that is understood by the Peer Model Concurrent State Automate System written in the Go programming language, termed the *PM-Go-Automaton* for short. This is a new formal analysis tool, based on state machines (see Sect. 3). Other code generators comprise the compilation into the XML-based PM-DSL (Peer Model Domain Specific Language), and also into LaTeX drawings that can be easily included into publications. Planned for the future are code generators for the existing Java runtime system, as well as for the Event-B-based [6] verification system for the Peer Model, which is currently under development [20].

According to our proposal of a hybrid verification approach [10] also further target systems will be considered in future work. Basically the hybrid verification approach suggests to integrate several verification tools in the Peer Model tool-chain. Each Peer Model is a complete model from which also production code for the Java runtime can be generated. It does not suppress important information, which is sometimes the case with abstract models. Therefore, one can formulate assertions and invariants based on the (respectively extended) Peer Model query language, as proposed in [21], and map them to the most suitable verification tool with a focus to verify certain properties of the system. For example, timed automate [4] will be used to reason about timing properties, for which Event-B is less suited, and Colored Petri Net tools [3] shall be exploited to verify deadlock and reachability properties.

2 Peer Model in a Nutshell

This section summarizes the already published concepts of the Peer Model (see Sect. 2.1) and describes the newly introduced features (see Sect. 2.2).

2.1 Core Concepts

The *Peer Model* serves for the modelling of coordination logic as concurrent, timed, distributed flows. Its design was influenced by the tuple space paradigm to achieve a high decoupling of components, by Petri Nets that inspired the modelling of concurrency by means of *wirings*, and by the Actor Model that

---

[1] The open source tool Draw.io [2] was selected, that can export XML.

motivated asynchronously communicating Peers that implement a behaviour. The main artefacts are: Peer, entry, container, wiring, link and service.

Peer. A peer is a named resource with behaviour. It possesses two tuple spaces, termed *containers*, that store tuples, termed *entries*.

Entry. An entry is a typed message with properties. A property has a name and a value. Entries consist of user and system properties (e.g., `ttl` is the time-to-live, `fid` is a flow identifier, and `type` denotes the entry type).

Container. The Peer's containers are termed peer-in-container (*PIC*) and peer-out-container (*POC*). Containers represent the system state. They support transactional operations to `read`, `take`, `create` and `delete` entries.

Wiring. *Wirings* model the Peer's behaviour. A wiring specifies a transaction on containers. It consists of *links* which are either *guards* or *actions*, and an internal container (*WIC*) to temporarily hold entries retrieved by guard links.

Link. A *link* issues space operations on containers. The source of a guard is either the PIC or the POC of the peer, and its target is the WIC; for actions it is the other way round. Link kinds are named after their operation on the source: READ and TAKE links select entries from source and write them to target, whereby the TAKE links also remove the entries from the target. DELETE links remove entries from the target. CREATE links create new entries and write them to the target. NOOP links do not access entries. The specification of which entries are to be selected or created consists of an entry type, an entry count (an exact number, an interval, or the keyword `ALL`), and a query on entry properties and variables. Assignments between entry properties and user variables serve to either set entry properties or to pass entry properties between links. The scope of user variables, which start with $ and are written in lower case, is the current wiring instance. System variables start with $$ and are written in upper case (e.g. `$PID` is the identifier of the local Peer, and `$FID` holds the current flow identifier). Finally, a link possesses properties; e.g., `ttl` defines how long a link shall wait until it can be fulfilled (default=`infinite`), `mandatory` defines if the link is obligatory (default=`on`), `flow` says if the flow correlation shall be applied (default=`on`), and `dest` on an action link asynchronously delivers all entries via an i/o Peer to the Peer denoted by the property value. All links are numbered.

Service. In between guard and action execution, wirings may call a service. It encapsulates application logic which is considered as "black box" from point of view of the Peer Model.

The operational semantics is that all wirings of a peer run concurrently. A wiring executes sequentially in the specified order: guards, the optional service, and actions. If a mandatory link cannot be fulfilled then the current wiring execution fails, a rollback takes place and depending on the `repeat_count` property of the wiring, a next instance of this wiring is started. Further properties of a wiring are `ttl` (maximum allowed execution time for this wiring instance) and `tts` (time to wait until the next wiring instance may start).

2.2   Newly Introduced Concepts

For more modelling convenience, in this paper, the following new modelling concepts are introduced. They are implemented by the Translator component of the tool-chain (see Sect. 3):

Types. Abstract types for entries, wirings, Peers and the Peer Model Meta Model (PMMM).

User-defined wiring, Peer and PMMM properties. So far, only entries had user-defined properties. This concept is extended to wirings, Peers and the PMMM. In type declarations, default property values can be specified.

Configuration. Instantiation of a PMMM, defining the required Peers, based on Peer types, and properties for all artefacts.

INIT entry. As a convention, a system entry of type INIT is written into the PIC of each instantiated Peer. This serves to signal a Peer that it has been started and is useful if it has to carry out initializations.

Reference data type. An array data type, using # as access operator, provides indirect referencing of user-defined properties.

RANGE, FORALL, and EXISTS. With RANGE it is possible to iterate within a range over the array type, using an INDEX. FORALL and EXISTS are to be used in queries; they also use an INDEX that iterates over an interval, and translate to AND respectively to OR expressions.

3   Implementation of the Toolchain

Design Principles: The leading principles were: A graphical user interface shall be supported to make the Peer Model more usable. An existing tool shall be employed for implementing the graphical modeller. The tool-chain shall be practical and realizable with "one woman's power" in reasonable time, like the already developed PM-Go-Automaton. The PM-Go-Automaton should not have to be changed, i.e. all new concepts (see Sect. 2.2) must be translated to the core concepts (see Sect. 2.1) that the PM-Go-Automaton can execute. A domain specific language shall be provided, termed the PM-DSL, represented as XML.

Graphical Modelling Tool: The requirements on the drawing program were that it is easy to use, provides an open source license, allows the definition of shapes, and can export the designed user models as readable XML code where dedicated shapes can be identified. Eventually, draw.io was selected, where shapes can be tagged to make their recognition in the XML code possible. For each core and newly introduced Peer Model artefact a shape was designed. However, for practical reasons, the originally proposed graphical notation [17] of the Peer Model – where links are arcs connecting PIC and WIC, respectively WIC and POC, and where link features are specified as labels on these arcs – had to adapted, because this could not be realized by means of draw.io shapes. Instead, a link is now represented by a box that specifies the link's features as a form to be filled in. This form also denotes the PIC or the POC, and by means of an unlabelled arc it is connected to the WIC of the wiring to which it belongs.

All elements of the link are grouped and tagged, so they can be identified as belonging together in the XML.

One draw.io file represents one PMMM type including several configurations of it. It consists of several drawing sheets (tabs), following certain naming conventions. E.g., the name of a drawing containing a Peer Type must start with "PeerType:" followed by the type name of the Peer; analogously the prefixes "EntryTypes:", "WiringTypes:", "PmmmType:", and "Config:" were introduced. The layout with many drawing sheets contributes to structure the model.

Translator: The translator is written in Java and consists of three parts, where parsers respectively code generators can be exchanged by means of the builder design pattern.

XML Parser. There are two parsers supported so far: One reads the XML exported by draw.io, and the other one the XML-based PM-DSL and translates it to an internal data representation.

Model Transformation Algorithm (MTA). The MTA operates on the internal data representation and consist of several passes: recognition of tokens, type evaluation, and transformation of the newly introduced modelling concepts.

Code Generator. Finally, code for the target runtime system is generated. Three code generators have been developed so far: One compiles the model into Go code for the PM-Go-Automaton, one generates PM-DSL (which in turn can be parsed by the respective XML Parser), and one produces LaTeX code – representing the model in the original Peer Model graphical notation – that is useful for inclusion in publications.

The generated PM-DSL code of the Peer type Player and its GameOver wiring (see Fig. 6) is shown in Fig. 2 and the Go code (for one Peer instance, and with comments stripped) in Fig. 3; at "..." are the other wirings of this Peer (type) generated. Note that without the tool-chain, developers would have to write this Go code manually, but now they can either use the graphical interface or the PM-DSL to specify their models.

```
<PeerType name="Player">
 <Wiring name="gameOver" service="Watch">
  <Guard number="1" container="PIC" op="TAKE" entryType="matchball" count="1">
   <Query>EXISTS INDEX.1 IN 1..PMMM.nPlayers -> scores#INDEX.1 >= PMMM.max</Query>
  </Guard>
  <Action number="1" container="POC" op="TAKE" entryType="matchball" count="1">
   <VarPropsSetGet>gameOverFlag=true;</VarPropsSetGet>
   <PropsDefinition>dest=PMMM.gameController</PropsDefinition>
  </Action>
 </Wiring>
 ...
</PeerType>
```

Fig. 2. PM-DSL code snippet.

```
p = NewPeer("player")
w = NewWiring("gameOver")
w.AddServiceWrapper("SID_Watch", NewServiceWrapper(Watch,  "Watch"))
w.AddGuard("", PIC, TAKE,
  Query{Typ: SEtype("matchball"), Count: IVal(1),
  Sel: XValP(XVal(XVal(IArrayLabel(DynArrayRef("scores", IVal(1))), GREATER_EQUAL, IVal(10)),
    OR, XVal(IArrayLabel(DynArrayRef("scores", IVal(2))), GREATER_EQUAL, IVal(10))),
    OR, XVal(IArrayLabel(DynArrayRef("scores", IVal(3))), GREATER_EQUAL, IVal(10)))},
  LProps{},
  EProps{},
  Vars{})
w.AddSin(TAKE, Query{Typ: SVal("*"), Count: IVal(ALL)}, "SID_Watch", LProps{}, EProps{}, Vars{})
w.AddScall("SID_Watch", LProps{}, EProps{}, Vars{})
w.AddSout(Query{Typ: SVal("*"), Count: IVal(ALL)}, "SID_Watch", LProps{}, EProps{}, Vars{})
w.AddAction("", POC, TAKE,
  Query{Typ: SEtype("matchball"), Count: IVal(1)},
  LProps{"dest": SUrl("arbiter"), "commit": BVal(true)},
  EProps{"gameOverFlag": BVal(true)},
  Vars{})
...
p.AddWiring(w)
...
ps.AddPeer(p)
```

Fig. 3. Go code snippet.

PM-Go-Automaton: The PM-Go-Automaton is written in the Go programming language ("Golang[2]" for short). Golang supports convenient mechanisms to program concurrency, like go routines, mutexes, channels. This was the reason why it was chosen to implement the highly concurrent state machines of the PM-Go-Automaton.

The entire Peer Model specification [17] is mapped to formal state automata, so there is a separation into a framework that implements the concurrent state machines, the Peer Model specification and the application model. This way changes and extensions in either part can be carried out independently. A controller component coordinates the concurrency of the re-entrant machines, which support leave and enter mechanisms. At least if a machine waits for an event, e.g. an entry to arrive in a PIC, it gives up its control. The controller selects the next machine according to a configurable execution mode. E.g. it may take the machine that waits longest for execution; check specification-defined waiting conditions; repeatedly perform indeterministic simulation runs; or try out all possible inter-leavings defined by the possible leave-points up to a configurable bound. These different modi are helpful in finding bugs in the user model at an early design stage. At the moment it is possible to model run-time assertions [21] manually; in future work it is planned to support a declarative notation for assertions and invariants, based on the existing query syntax of the Peer Model.

Implementation Notes: Some implementation facts: Currently, the Translator consists of 23K LOCs written in Java, and the PM-Go-Automaton (framework and Peer Model specification) has 24,5K LOCs written in Golang. The generated Go code for the Peer Competition example has 2,2K LOCs.

---

[2] https://golang.org/.

4   Use Case Example

As demonstrator, a game has been invented, where concurrent peers catch and throw a matchball. Whoever receives the ball next is indeterministic. Every ball catching/throwing gives a plus point and whoever reaches a defined high score first is the winner. Every move is broadcasted to all peers in the network who build up their own view of the network-wide "truth". The score of each peer is recorded on the matchball which represents the global state. In addition, each peer updates its own local statistics, based on the broadcasted game moves. This local view serves to verify, whether the global state of the matchball is correct.

This example reflects basic mechanisms found in blockchain applications: Every peer verifies the truth on its own and does the next game move only if its verification succeeds. For this it uses a runtime assertion [21] the violation of which causes the system to stop, as no move is possible any more[3]. Many games may run concurrently, using different matchballs. The correlation of Players' actions with the right game is accomplished with the flow concept of the Peer Model: Entries belonging to the same game are stamped with the same flow identifier (fid). A wiring transaction treats only entries with compatible flow.

Figures 4, 5, 6 and 7, which are drawn with the new draw.io shapes for the Peer Model, present the Player Peer. In addition there is an Arbiter Peer (see Appendix A2, Fig. 8), and an exchangeable Broadcaster Peer (not shown, as it is not part of the use case). The Arbiter Peer's responsibilities are to init itself (see wiring init), to start the game (see wiring startGame), to recognize the end of the game (see wiring endGame) and then to decide about the winner (see wiring decision). There is one decision wiring for each player that checks if this very player is the winner. Note that the fid is needed to correlate the matchball with the individual statistics of the Players and with the result.

Figure 4 declares entry and types entries that are used by and/or shared between the Peers: matchball (global game state that is passed around), createGame (created by the Arbiter Peer who starts the game and creates a flow id), gameInfo (info about a new game sent by the Arbiter Peer to all Player Peers), winner (result about who has won the game), actionInfo (sent by each Player Peer to all other Peers, saying is has taken a game move), statistics (local view of each Player Peer on the game, i.e. the current scores of all Peers), and decide (used by the Arbiter Peer for the decision about the winner).

Figure 5 and Fig. 6 specify the Player Peer type. Wirings are either directly modeled, or configured based on wiring types. As convention, each Peer receives a system entry termed INIT in its PIC at the beginning. The Player Peer just removes this entry (see deleteInit wiring) There is a concurrent and competing doGameAction wiring for each possible next player. This models the indeterminism of who will get the ball next. Specifically mentioned must also be guard 1 of this wiring, where the runtime assertion that verifies local versus global state is modeled. Note the usage of the flow id (fid) to correlate all components of a game. The wiring playerInit creates a local entry for the Peer's statistics. Every

---

[3] E.g., in case of Byzantine errors [22], the assertion might be violated.

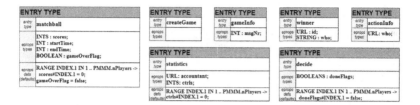

Fig. 4. Entry Types.

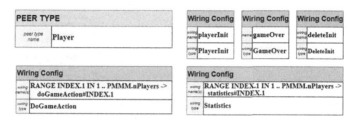

Fig. 5. Peer Type "Player".

time a Peer receives an `actionInfo` entry, it updates its bookkeeping (see wiring `statistics`). There is a concurrent `statistics` wiring for each Player, responsible to update the control counter for this very Player. Finally, the `gameOver` checks the matchball, if there exists one Player who has reached a certain high score, which is configured as property `max` in the Peer Model Meta Model.

Figure 7 shows the Peer Model Meta Model (PMMM) type. It defines a default `max` of 100. It also shows a PMMM configuration for up to 5 Player Peers and a high score of 5. The property `nPlayers` holds the actual number of players and is set to 3. For each Player an array property termed `players` is set in the PMMM.[4] The Arbiter Peer configuration defines the number of balls and the player who gets the matchball first.

5   Evaluation

Simulation Runs: For the evaluation, a simulation run of the Peer Competition use case is shown in Appendix A1. The game was carried out with three players, three matchballs and a high score of five. Please note that there is no limit for the amount of players, matchballs and the maximum to be reached that the simulation is able to cope with. The wiring traces, produced by "Watch" services, show the Players' moves, and the final global state of the entire system, which consists of the PIC and POC containers of all Peers. This way, it is possible to verify, if the output reflects an allowed result. Due to the indeterminism of map access to data structures (e.g. like machine controls, container entries etc.) and

---

[4] `gameInfo` serves only to make game runs more appealing by giving the players real names.

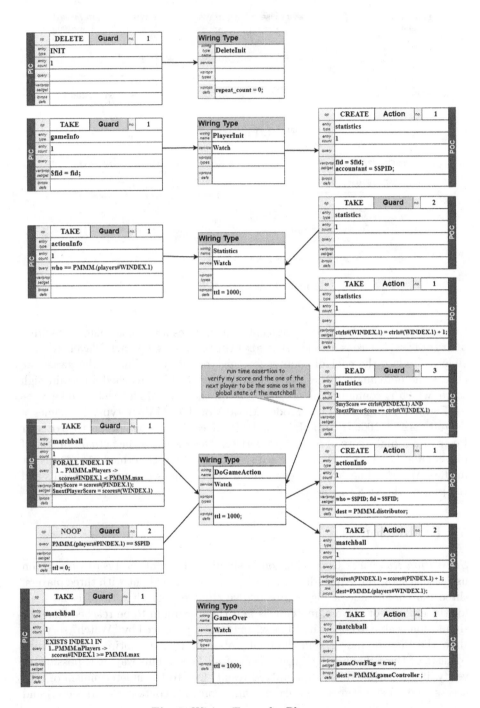

Fig. 6. Wiring Types for Player.

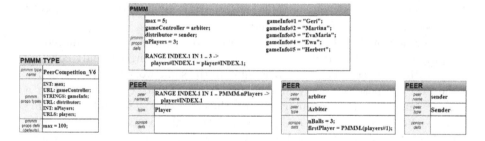

Fig. 7. PMMM Type (left) and Configuration (right).

the concurrent modelling of the machines in the PM-Go-Automaton, the result of a simulation run is not deterministic – another simulation run will result in other winners of the game. In addition, there exists a "model-checking" mode that systematically tries out all possible interleavings of the machines of the PM-Go-Automaton. These interleavings are determined by the enter/leave points of the re-entrant machines.

Variety of Application Possibilities: The Peer Model is a useful and feasible methodology that – as a proof-of-concept – has been employed to model a variety of use cases, reaching from embedded systems to enterprise scenarios in research as well as industrial scenarios. The Peer Model examples published in our papers so far, were verified with the PM-Go-Automaton, which has proven to be helpful to detect bugs in the designs. The graphical modeller of the new tool-chain has been tested already in several scenarios, like a simplified triage scenario of a hospital, a client/server pattern, some factory 4.0 scenarios, an armed gate, a producer/consumer pattern, and currently a blockchain use case is under development.

Graphical Modeller versus PM-DSL or Go Code: Whether developers prefer a graphical notation over a code-based one, depends on his/her educational background. In [20] we found out, that there was a slight preference for the (original) graphical notation of the Peer Model over an Event-B notation, which addressed rather mathematically oriented developers.

In any case, a graphical notation is a contribution that developers can discuss their models with their end users (clients). Even if a non-expert, like a client, will not be able to model a use case by him/herself, he/she can understand graphical models to a certain degree so that the communication between developer and end user is eased this way: For sure, this will not be possible with PM-DSL or Go code or any other notation that requires programming experience.

Usability and Scalability of Designs. The usability and scalability of models primarily depends on the semantics of the Peer Model modelling constructs themselves. The objective of its domain specific abstractions was to gain models without unnecessary, low-level "ballast" (see [18]). This means that models are compact and therefore it was possible to depict the *entire* and complete model of the peer competition use case including its configuration in this paper. E.g., the correlation of data belonging to one workflow can be simply achieved by stamping the related entries with a flow identifier. A wiring will only consider entries with compatible flows, i.e. belonging to the same workflow. For example, in the peer competition, many matchballs can be around, each representing a separate game that does not interfere with the other ones: The Statistics wiring in Fig. 6 correlates the current action info with the right local book-keeping entry termed statistics; The DoGameAction wiring in Fig. 6 correlates the matchball with the local statistics and the next action carried out by the player (by setting the flow id property on the actionInfo entry in Action 1).

An analysis how good designs with the Peer Model's (original) graphical notation scale is given in [18]. Especially when it comes to more dynamic scenarios, the Peer Model is advantageous. The here introduced types for Peer Model artefacts also contribute to the scalability of designs, as well as the fact that the model is structured into many diagrams in the draw.io file. In the future, also the pattern-based concept proposed in [19] will be implemented.

With regard to usability, the number of concepts that a developer must learn play a major role [25]. There are only 14 draw.io shapes that a developer must comprehend, whereby, however, for convenience the single concept of a link has been explicitly "flatted" into 6 separate shapes for (PIC/POC/NOOP × action/guard), which gives 6 shapes instead of 1.

6   Conclusion and Future Work

The contribution of this work is a new tool-chain and an improved modelling notation for the Peer Model, which is translated by a model transformation algorithm to code for the simulator. The objective is to support the design of complex coordination algorithms involving high concurrency and many Peers. The new tool-chain has been demonstrated by means of an example whose full specification is given in the paper. Currently we apply the tool-chain for the verification of smart contracts of blockchain applications, as well as for consensus protocols on the infrastructure layer.

In future work the methodology shall be extended by invariants, hybrid verification tools and more sophisticated pattern support. Also planned are the visualization of the results of simulation runs, and in the long-term of the run-time behaviour of a Peer Model by showing the states of the containers and how entries are moved between them.

Appendix

A1: Simulation Run

```
player#1_playerInit_SID_Watch_SIC____M8: WATCH:
    <Id=e90, type=gameInfo, fid=''f1''>
player#1_doGameAction#3_SID_Watch_SIC____M16: WATCH:
    <Id=e86, type=matchball, fid=''f1'', gameOverFlag=false, scores#1=0, scores#2=0, scores#3=0, startTime=46>
    <Id=e123, type=statistics, accountant=''player#1'', ctrls#1=0, ctrls#2=0, ctrls#3=0, fid=''f1''>
player#2_playerInit_SID_Watch_SIC____M22: WATCH:
    <Id=e92, type=gameInfo, fid=''f1''>
player#3_playerInit_SID_Watch_SIC____M31: WATCH:
    <Id=e94, type=gameInfo, fid=''f1''>
player#3_doGameAction#3_SID_Watch_SIC____M30: WATCH:
    <Id=e126, type=matchball, fid=''f1'', gameOverFlag=false, scores#1=1, scores#2=0, scores#3=0, startTime=46>
    <Id=e204, type=statistics, accountant=''player#3'', ctrls#1=0, ctrls#2=0, ctrls#3=0, fid=''f1''>
player#1_playerInit_SID_Watch_SIC____M8: WATCH:
    <Id=e158, type=gameInfo, fid=''f2''>
player#1_doGameAction#1_SID_Watch_SIC____M11: WATCH:
    <Id=e103, type=matchball, fid=''f2'', gameOverFlag=false, scores#1=0, scores#2=0, scores#3=0, startTime=58>
    <Id=e217, type=statistics, accountant=''player#1'', ctrls#1=0, ctrls#2=0, ctrls#3=0, fid=''f2''>
player#2_playerInit_SID_Watch_SIC____M22: WATCH:
    <Id=e160, type=gameInfo, fid=''f2''>
player#3_playerInit_SID_Watch_SIC____M31: WATCH:
    <Id=e162, type=gameInfo, fid=''f2''>
player#1_playerInit_SID_Watch_SIC____M8: WATCH:
    <Id=e175, type=gameInfo, fid=''f3''>
player#1_doGameAction#2_SID_Watch_SIC____M12: WATCH:
    <Id=e115, type=matchball, fid=''f3'', gameOverFlag=false, scores#1=0, scores#2=0, scores#3=0, startTime=73>
    <Id=e254, type=statistics, accountant=''player#1'', ctrls#1=0, ctrls#2=0, ctrls#3=0, fid=''f3''>
player#2_playerInit_SID_Watch_SIC____M22: WATCH:
    <Id=e177, type=gameInfo, fid=''f3''>
player#3_playerInit_SID_Watch_SIC____M31: WATCH:
    <Id=e179, type=gameInfo, fid=''f3''>
player#2_doGameAction#2_SID_Watch_SIC____M25: WATCH:
    <Id=e257, type=matchball, fid=''f3'', gameOverFlag=false, scores#1=1, scores#2=0, scores#3=0, startTime=73>
    <Id=e364, type=statistics, accountant=''player#2'', ctrls#1=0, ctrls#2=0, ctrls#3=0, fid=''f3''>
player#3_doGameAction#3_SID_Watch_SIC____M30: WATCH:
    <Id=e207, type=matchball, fid=''f1'', gameOverFlag=false, scores#1=2, scores#2=0, scores#3=1, startTime=46>
    <Id=e391, type=statistics, accountant=''player#3'', ctrls#1=1, ctrls#2=0, ctrls#3=1, fid=''f1''>
player#1_doGameAction#2_SID_Watch_SIC____M12: WATCH:
    <Id=e220, type=matchball, fid=''f2'', gameOverFlag=false, scores#1=1, scores#2=1, scores#3=0, startTime=58>
    <Id=e418, type=statistics, accountant=''player#1'', ctrls#1=1, ctrls#2=0, ctrls#3=0, fid=''f2''>
player#2_doGameAction#2_SID_Watch_SIC____M25: WATCH:
    <Id=e367, type=matchball, fid=''f3'', gameOverFlag=false, scores#1=1, scores#2=1, scores#3=0, startTime=73>
    <Id=e550, type=statistics, accountant=''player#2'', ctrls#1=1, ctrls#2=1, ctrls#3=0, fid=''f3''>
...
player#3_doGameAction#2_SID_Watch_SIC____M34: WATCH:
    <Id=e1934, type=matchball, fid=''f1'', gameOverFlag=false, scores#1=4, scores#2=4, scores#3=4, startTime=46>
    <Id=e2026, type=statistics, accountant=''player#3'', ctrls#1=3, ctrls#2=4, ctrls#3=4, fid=''f1''>
player#2_gameOver_SID_Watch_SIC____M18: WATCH:
    <Id=e2029, type=matchball, fid=''f1'', gameOverFlag=false, scores#1=4, scores#2=4, scores#3=5, startTime=46>

*** SYS INFO ------ SYSTEM TTL 100000 exceeded -------------------------------------------------- CLOCK=101189
*** SYS INFO ------ Controler EXIT ------------------------------------------------------------------ CLOCK=101189

-------------------- SPACE at CLOCK=101189 --------------------
arbiter_POC updateEvtTime=2083 = {
    <Id=e1540, type=matchball, endTime=1735, fid=''f3'', gameOverFlag=true, scores#1=2, scores#2=5, scores#3=2, startTime=73>,
    <Id=e1730, type=matchball, endTime=1920, fid=''f2'', gameOverFlag=true, scores#1=5, scores#2=3, scores#3=2, startTime=58>,
    <Id=e2029, type=matchball, endTime=2080, fid=''f1'', gameOverFlag=true, scores#1=4, scores#2=4, scores#3=5, startTime=46>,
    <Id=e1825, type=winner, fid=''f3'', id=''player#2'', who=''!!! the winner is Martina !!!''>,
    <Id=e1976, type=winner, fid=''f2'', id=''player#1'', who=''!!! the winner is Geri !!!''>,
    <Id=e2127, type=winner, fid=''f1'', id=''player#3'', who=''!!! the winner is EvaMaria !!!''>}
player#1_POC updateEvtTime=2029 = {
    <Id=e1944, type=statistics, accountant=''player#1'', ctrls#1=5, ctrls#2=3, ctrls#3=2, fid=''f2''>,
    <Id=e1766, type=statistics, accountant=''player#1'', ctrls#1=2, ctrls#2=5, ctrls#3=2, fid=''f3''>,
    <Id=e2089, type=statistics, accountant=''player#1'', ctrls#1=4, ctrls#2=4, ctrls#3=5, fid=''f1''>}
player#2_POC updateEvtTime=2044 = {
    <Id=e1949, type=statistics, accountant=''player#2'', ctrls#1=5, ctrls#2=3, ctrls#3=2, fid=''f2''>,
    <Id=e1771, type=statistics, accountant=''player#2'', ctrls#1=2, ctrls#2=5, ctrls#3=2, fid=''f3''>,
    <Id=e2096, type=statistics, accountant=''player#2'', ctrls#1=4, ctrls#2=4, ctrls#3=5, fid=''f1''>}
player#3_POC updateEvtTime=2057 = {
    <Id=e1958, type=statistics, accountant=''player#3'', ctrls#1=5, ctrls#2=3, ctrls#3=2, fid=''f2''>,
    <Id=e1778, type=statistics, accountant=''player#3'', ctrls#1=2, ctrls#2=5, ctrls#3=2, fid=''f3''>,
    <Id=e2103, type=statistics, accountant=''player#3'', ctrls#1=4, ctrls#2=4, ctrls#3=5, fid=''f1''>}
    ------------------------------------------------------------------
```

A2: Arbiter Peer Type

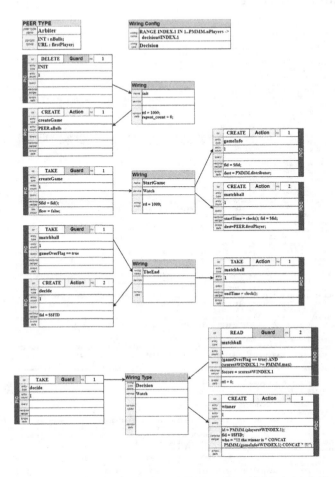

Fig. 8. Peer Type "Arbiter" (above) and Wiring Types for Arbiter (below).

References

1. Ethereum. https://www.ethereum.org/. Accessed 01 Apr 2019
2. Flowchart marker and online diagram software (draw.io). https://app.diagrams. net/. Accessed 20 Feb 2020
3. GreatSPN 3, Universita di Torino, http://www.di.unito.it/greatspn/
4. UPPAAL 4.015, Uppsala University Sweden (2019). https://uppaal.org/
5. High-level Petri Nets - Concepts, Definitions and Graphical Notation. Tech. rep., Final Draft International Standard ISO IEC 15909, V. 4.7.1 (2000)

6. Abrial, J.R.: Modeling in Event-B: System and Software Engineering. Cambridge University Press (2010)
7. Agha, G.A.: ACTORS: A Model Of Concurrent Computation in Distributed Systems. MIT Press (1990)
8. Cejka, S.: Enabling scalable collaboration by introducing platform-independent communication for the Peer Model. Master's thesis, TU Wien (2019)
9. Craß, S.: Secure coordination through fine-grained access control for space-based computing middleware. Ph.D. thesis, TU Wien (2020)
10. Elaraby, N., Kühn, E., Messinger, A., Radschek, S.T.: Towards a hybrid verification approach. In: Mazzara, M., Ober, I., Salaün, G. (eds.) STAF 2018. LNCS, vol. 11176, pp. 367–386. Springer, Cham (2018). https://doi.org/10.1007/978-3-030-04771-9_27
11. Gelernter, D.: Generative communication in Linda. ACM Trans. Program. Lang. Syst. 7(1), 80–112 (1985)
12. Gelernter, D., Carriero, N.: Coordination languages and their significance. Commun. ACM (CACM) 35(2), 96–107 (1992)
13. Group, E.E.U.: Hybrid ertms/etcs level 3: principles. Technical Report, Ref: 16E042, version 1A, Hybrid-ERTMS-ETCS-Level-3 (2017)
14. Jensen, K., Kristensen, L.M., Wells, L.: Coloured Petri Nets and CPN Tools for modelling and validation of concurrent systems. Int. J. Softw. Tool Technol. Transfer (STTT) 9, 213–254 (2007)
15. Kuehn, E.: Reusable coordination components: reliable development of cooperative information systems. Int. J. Cooperative Inf. Syst. 25(4), 1740001:1–1740001:32 (2016)
16. Kühn, E.: Flexible transactional coordination in the peer model. In: Dastani, M., Sirjani, M. (eds.) FSEN 2017. LNCS, vol. 10522, pp. 116–131. Springer, Cham (2017). https://doi.org/10.1007/978-3-319-68972-2_8
17. Kühn, E.: Peer Model: Agile Middleware and Programming Model for the coordination of parallel and distributed flows. Tech. rep, TU Wien, Institute of Computer Languages (2012)
18. Kühn, E., Craß, S., Joskowicz, G., Marek, A., Scheller, T.: Peer-based programming model for coordination patterns. In: De Nicola, R., Julien, C. (eds.) COORDINATION 2013. LNCS, vol. 7890, pp. 121–135. Springer, Heidelberg (2013). https://doi.org/10.1007/978-3-642-38493-6_9
19. Kühn, E., Craß, S., Schermann, G.: Extending a peer-based coordination model with composable design patterns. In: 23rd Euromicro International Conference on Parallel, Distributed, and Network-Based Processing, PDP. IEEE (2015)
20. Kühn, E., Radschek, S.T.: An initial user study comparing the readability of a graphical coordination model with event-B Notation. In: Cerone, A., Roveri, M. (eds.) SEFM 2017. LNCS, vol. 10729, pp. 574–590. Springer, Cham (2018). https://doi.org/10.1007/978-3-319-74781-1_38
21. Kuehn, E., Radschek, S.T., Elaraby, N.: Distributed coordination runtime assertions for the Peer Model. In: Di Marzo Serugendo, G., Loreti, M. (eds.) COORDINATION 2018. LNCS, vol. 10852. pp. 200–219, Springer, Cham (2018). https://doi.org/10.1007/978-3-319-92408-3_9
22. Lamport, L., Shostak, R., Pease, M.: The byzantine generals problem. ACM Trans. Program. Lang. Syst. 4(3), 382–401 (1982)
23. Petri, C.A.: Kommunikation mit automaten. Ph.D. thesis, Technische Hochschule Darmstadt (1962)

24. Ratzer, A.V., et al.: CPN tools for editing, simulating, and analysing coloured petri nets. In: van der Aalst, W.M.P., Best, E. (eds.) ICATPN 2003. LNCS, vol. 2679, pp. 450–462. Springer, Heidelberg (2003). https://doi.org/10.1007/3-540-44919-1_28

25. Scheller, T., Kuehn, E.: Automated measurement of API usability: the API concepts framework. Inf. Softw. Technol. **61**, 145–162 (2015)

Microservices

PHOTOGRAPHS

Microservice Dynamic Architecture-Level Deployment Orchestration

Lorenzo Bacchiani[1(✉)], Mario Bravetti[1,2], Saverio Giallorenzo[1,2],
Jacopo Mauro[3], Iacopo Talevi[1], and Gianluigi Zavattaro[1,2]

[1] Università di Bologna, Bologna, Italy
lorenzo.bacchiani2@unibo.it
[2] Focus Team, Inria, Sophia Antipolis, France
[3] University of Southern Denmark, Odense, Denmark

Abstract. We develop a novel approach for run-time global adaptation of microservice applications, based on synthesis of architecture-level reconfiguration orchestrations. More precisely, we devise an algorithm for automatic reconfiguration that reaches a target system Maximum Computational Load by performing optimal deployment orchestrations. To conceive and simulate our approach, we introduce a novel integrated timed architectural modeling/execution language based on an extension of the actor-based object-oriented Abstract Behavioral Specification (ABS) language. In particular, we realize a timed extension of SmartDeployer, whose ABS code annotations make it possible to express architectural properties. Our Timed SmartDeployer tool fully integrates time features of ABS and architectural annotations by generating timed deployment orchestrations. We evaluate the applicability of our approach on a realistic microservice application taken from the literature: an Email Pipeline Processing System. We prove its effectiveness by simulating such an application and by comparing architecture-level reconfiguration with traditional local scaling techniques (which detect scaling needs and enact replications at the level of single microservices). Our comparison results show that our approach avoids cascading slowdowns and consequent increased message loss and latency, which affect traditional local scaling.

1 Introduction

Inspired by service-oriented computing, microservices structure software applications as highly modular and scalable compositions of fine-grained and loosely-coupled services [16,22]. These features support modern software engineering practices, like continuous delivery/deployment [28] and application autoscaling [7]. A significant problem in these practices consists of the automated deployment of the microservice application: optimal distribution of the fine-grained components over the available Virtual Machines (VMs), and dynamic reconfiguration to cope, e.g., with positive or negative peaks of user requests.

Although these practices are already beneficial, they can be further improved by exploiting the interdependencies within an architecture (interface functional

F. Damiani and O. Dardha (Eds.): COORDINATION 2021, LNCS 12717, pp. 257–275, 2021.
https://doi.org/10.1007/978-3-030-78142-2_16

dependences), instead of focusing on the single microservice. Indeed, w.r.t. traditional local scaling techniques, architecture-level dynamic deployment orchestration can:

- Avoid "domino" effects of unstructured scaling, i.e. single services scaling one after the other (cascading slowdowns) due to local workload monitoring.
- Quickly restore an acceptable performance in terms of message loss and latency.

In this paper, we first introduce a novel *integrated timed architectural modeling/execution language* based on an extension of the actor-based object-oriented Abstract Behavioral Specification (ABS) language [4]. The extension that we devise crucially exploits the double nature of ABS, which is both a process algebra (it has a probabilistic/timed formal semantics) and a programming language (it is compiled and executed, e.g. with the Erlang backend). In particular, we realize a *timed* extension of SmartDeployer [13,14], whose ABS code *annotations* make it possible to express: *architectural properties* of the modeled distributed system (global architectural invariants and allowed reconfigurations), of its VMs (their characteristics and the resource they provide) and of its software components/services (their resource/functional requirements). Such annotations are read by SmartDeployer that, at compile-time, checks them for satisfiability (accounting for requirements and architectural invariants) and synthesizes deployment orchestrations that build the system architecture and each of its specified reconfigurations. SmartDeployer generates optimal deployment and undeployment code by using ABS itself as an orchestration language and by making it available via methods with conventional names. Such methods can be invoked by the ABS code of services, thus realizing run-time adaptation. Here we introduce the *Timed SmartDeployer tool* that fully realizes the integration between timed ABS execution language and architectural annotations by generating *timed deployment orchestrations*. Such orchestrations also manage time aspects, dynamically setting VM speeds (based on virtual cpu cores that are actually being used) and overall startup time for the deployed architectural reconfiguration.

One of our main motivations in having a model encompassing architectural invariants/reconfigurations is to anticipate at the modeling level deployment orchestration related issues. This indeed fosters an approach where analysis of the consequences of deployment decisions are available early on: Timed Smart-Deployer checks (at compile-time) the synthesizability of deployment orchestrations that, at run-time, will ensure the system to be always capable of adapting in case of positive/negative peaks of user requests. On the contrary run-time deployment decisions, if left to loosely-coupled reactive scaling policies, could lead to a chaotic behavior in the system.

Moreover, in this paper we contribute an algorithm for architecture-level run-time adaptation that overcomes the shortcomings of the traditional local scaling approach. We could conceive and simulate it thanks to the above architectural modeling/execution language. Such an algorithm finds application in the context of cloud-computing platforms endowed with orchestration engines. The algorithm reaches, by performing global reconfigurations, a target system

Maximum Computational Load (MCL), i.e. the maximum supported frequency for inbound requests. The idea is that, by monitoring at run-time the inbound workload, our algorithm causes the system to be always in the reachable configuration that better fits such a workload (and that has the minimum number of deployed microservice instances). In particular, global reconfigurations are targeted at guaranteeing a given increment (or decrement) of the system MCL. Moreover, we show how such an overall system MCL can be computed by the MCL of single service instances. In turn, they are mathematically calculated based on: the microservice data rate (we use, e.g., real data in [32] for Nginx servers) and the role it plays in the application architecture (which determines the mean number and size of its requests for each incoming message). As we will see, the timed features of deployment orchestrations synthesized by our Timed SmartDeployer tool are essential to model, in an MCL consistent way, adaptation actions enacted by our algorithm (dynamic speed of VMs and their overall startup time).

Finally, we evaluate the applicability of our approach on a realistic microservice application: an Email Pipeline Processing System taken from Iron.io [23]. Its model is built by considering: static aspects of the architecture (annotations) and ABS code modeling the behavior of services. We simulate system execution using inbound traffic inspired to two different real datasets in [24,29], representing the frequency of emails entering the system. In order to show the effectiveness of our architecture-level adaptation algorithm, we compare it with traditional local scaling techniques. In particular, we produce two ABS programs: one implementing our algorithm (using 4 Timed SmartDeployer synthesized orchestrations) and one just dealing with scaling needs at the level of single microservices. Our comparison results show that our algorithm actually avoids cascading slowdowns and consequent increased message loss and latency that affect traditional local scaling. The obtained code fully exploits the expressive power of ABS, e.g. using both its timed and probabilistic features.[1]

Wrapping up the novel contributions of this paper (e.g. compared to our previous work in [13,14]) are: (i) a novel integrated timed architectural modeling/execution language based on a timed extension of SmartDeployer that, differently from the previous version, exploits timed instructions of ABS to automatically generate timed deployment orchestrations, (ii) an architecture-level run-time adaptation algorithm that reaches any target system MCL, (iii) mathematical calculation of service MCL and MCL-based scaling configurations and (iv) ABS code implementing system service execution/scaling mechanism for the Email Pipeline Processing System [23].

The paper is structured as follows. In Sect. 2 we briefly recall the microservice model, the ABS language and the SmartDeployer tool. Then, in Sect. 3 we present the Email Processing Pipeline case study, mathematical calculation of system properties like MCL, and we introduce the novel timed architectural

---

[1] Complexity of our ABS process algebraic models is also witnessed by the fact that they led us to discover an error in the Erlang backend: it caused interferences in time evolution between unrelated VMs (it was solved thanks to our code).

modeling/execution language based on our Timed SmartDeployer. In Sect. 4, we present our global scaling algorithm and its mathematical foundations. Finally, in Sect. 5 we present simulation of our case study, discussing comparison results, and in Sect. 6 we conclude the paper and discuss related work.

2   Preliminaries

In this section we present the microservice model, as formalized in [13,14], the ABS language [4] and the SmartDeployer tool [13,14].

2.1   The Microservice Model

The work in [13,14] formalizes component-based software systems (where components are deployed on VMs) and the automated deployment problem: synthesis of deployment orchestrations that reach a given target system configuration. In particular, the deployment life-cycle of each component type is formalized by means of a finite-state automaton, whose states denote a deployment stage. Each state is associated with a set of provided ports (operations exposed by the component that can be used by other components) and a set of required ports (operations of other components needed for the component to work in that deployment stage). More specifically, [13,14] consider the case of microservices: components whose deployment life cycle consists of just two phases: (i) creation, which entails *mandatorily* establishing initial connections, via so-called *strongly required ports*, with already available microservices, and (ii) subsequent *optional* binding/unbinding, via so-called *weakly required ports*, with other microservices. The two phases make it possible to manage circular dependencies among microservices. These concepts are inspired by Docker Compose [20], a language for defining multi-container Docker applications, that makes it possible for users to specify different relationships among microservices using, e.g. the depends_on (resp. external_links) modalities that impose (resp. do not impose) a specific startup order, in the same way as strong (resp. weak) dependencies.

In addition [13,14] consider resource/cost-aware deployments modeling the memory and computational resources: number of virtual CPU cores (vCores in Azure), sometimes simply called virtual CPUs as in Amazon EC2 and Kubernetes [25]. In particular, both microservice specifications and VM descriptions are enriched with the amount of resources they, respectively, need and supply.

A microservice *deployment orchestration* is a program in an *orchestration language* that includes primitives for (i) creating/removing a certain microservice together with its strongly required bindings and (ii) adding/removing weak-required bindings between some created microservices. Given an initial microservice system, a set of available VMs and a new target set of microservices to be deployed, the *optimal deployment problem* is the problem of finding the deployment orchestration that: satisfies core and memory requirements, leads to a new system configuration including target microservices and optimizes resource usage in case of multiple solutions.

Differently from the case of components with arbitrary deployment life-cycles [18], the optimal deployment problem has been shown to be decidable for microservices. In particular, [13,14] present a constraint-solving algorithm whose result is the new system configuration, i.e. the microservices to be deployed, their distribution over the VMs and the bindings to be established among their strong/weak require and provide ports.

2.2 Abstract Behavioral Specification Language

Abstract Behavioral Specification [4] is an actor-based object-oriented specification language (a process algebra) offering algebraic user-defined data types, side effect-free functions and immutable data. The ABS toolchain [5] makes it possible to write ABS process algebraic models by conveniently using a programming language syntax and to execute them by means, e.g., of the ABS Erlang backend. ABS objects are organized into Concurrent Object Groups (COGs) representing software components or services. Objects belonging to different COGs communicate with each other using asynchronous method calls [12], expressed as *object!method(...)* instructions. Asynchronicity is realized by means of the future mechanism: asynchronous method calls return a future that can be used to wait for the result using the *await* statement. *Timed ABS* is an extension to the ABS core language that introduces a notion of *abstract time*. In particular, evolution of time in ABS is modeled by means of discrete time: during execution system time is expressed as the number of *time units* that have passed since system start. The modeler decides what a time unit represents for a specific application. Such a feature makes it possible to perform simulations analysing the time-related behavior of systems. Timed ABS has also *probabilistic* features that allow modelers to create uniform distributions, e.g. the average number of attachments per email in our case study.

To represent VMs (and simulate them, e.g., inside the Erlang backend) ABS introduces the notion of Deployment Component (DC) as a *location* where a COG can be deployed. As VMs, ABS DCs are associated with several kinds of resources. In particular virtual cpu speed is represented in ABS by the DC *speed*: it models the amount of *computational resource* per time unit a DC can supply to the hosted COGs. This resource is consumed by ABS instructions that are marked with the *Cost* tag, e.g. *[Cost: 30] instruction*. COG instructions tagged with a cost consume the hosting DC computational resource still available for the current time unit (the instruction above consumes 30 from the DC speed resource): if not enough computational resource is left in the current time unit, then the instruction terminates its execution in the next one.

Concerning the microservice model, in ABS we represent microservice types as classes and instances as objects, each executed in an independent COG. Moreover, we represent strong dependencies as mandatory parameters required by class constructors: such parameters contain the references to the objects corresponding to the microservices providing the strongly required ports. Weak required ports are expressed by means of specific methods that allow an existing object to receive the references to the objects providing them.

2.3   SmartDeployer

SmartDeployer implements the algorithm described at the end of Sect. 2.1 to perform automated deployment of microservice applications, i.e. synthesis of deployment orchestrations that reach a given target system configuration. In particular, it exploits the constraint solver Zephyrus2 [3]. The input to Smart-Deployer is expressed by means of an ABS source file from which it extracts:

- ABS annotations *[SmartDeployCost : JSONstring]* to *classes* representing microservice types. They describe, in JSON format, the functional dependencies (provided and weak/strong required ports) and the resources (number of cores, amount of memory) they need.
- A global *[SmartDeployCloudProvider : JSONstring]* ABS annotation. It defines, in JSON format, the types of Deployment Components and their associated resources (e.g. number of cores, amount of memory, speed).
- A global *[SmartDeploy : JSONstring]* ABS annotation. It describes, in JSON format, the desired properties of the target configuration, e.g. microservice types (possibly with multiple instances) we want to be included in such configuration.

In output it produces the synthesized *deployment orchestration*: the set of *orchestration language* instructions (expressed as ABS code) that cause the system to reach a deployment configuration with the desired properties. It also produces the *undeployment orchestration* to undo such deployment operations.

3   Timed Architectural Modeling/Execution Language

In this section we introduce our integrated timed architectural modeling/execution language based on the novel *Timed SmartDeployer tool*. Our tool fully realizes the integration between timed ABS execution language and architectural annotations by generating *timed deployment orchestrations*. For ease of presentation, we make use of a case study: the Email Pipeline Processing System taken from Iron.io [23]. With its help we introduce the concept of microservice Multiplicative Factor (MF) and Maximum Computational Load (MCL). We show that in our integrated timed language it is possible to model microservice MCL in a way that is consistent with timed deployment orchestrations. As we will see in Sect. 4, this allows us to give a mathematical foundation to the calculation of: the base system configuration and the target ones used by Timed SmartDeployer to synthesize scaling orchestrations (global adaptation algorithm). We present the necessary modeling steps and calculations in a conceptual/mathematical way, so that they can be applied to any other microservice application.

3.1   Case Study and Timed Characteristics of Microservice Systems

In Fig. 1 (similar to that in [13,14]) we show the Email Pipeline Processing System of [23]: it is composed of 12 types of microservices, each one having its

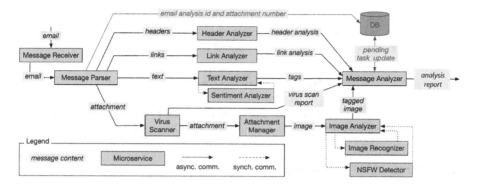

Fig. 1. Microservice Architecture for the Email Processing Pipeline Case Study.

own load balancer. The latter is used to distribute requests over a set of instances (connected to weakly required ports) that are incremented/decremented at need.

Recall that in our approach we consider virtual CPU cores, both for machines (providing them) and for microservices (requiring them), see Sect. 2.1. In particular, in our case study, we assume microservices to be deployed on Amazon EC2 VMs of type *large*, *xlarge*, *2xlarge* and *4xlarge*. They respectively provide 2, 4, 8 and 16 virtual CPU cores (following the Azure vCore terminology), simply called vCPUs in Amazon EC2. Notice that we model computational resources supplied by VMs (and required by microservices) by means of *virtual* cores with some specified speed, as commonly done by cloud providers to abstract underlying hardware. The cloud provider itself takes care of mapping virtual cores into physical ones by delegating to the runtime (the VM/OS) the scheduling of instructions to make maximal use of real processors. Each microservice type is characterized by a *number of required virtual cores*. Assigning such a number to obtain some expected microservice performance (e.g., an expected throughput) is a problem orthogonal to that investigated in this paper. While in practice this is usually done as guesswork informed by the experience of the programmers/operators (as in our case), techniques like instruction counting [10] and profiling [11] can help in providing objective estimations of the required cores.

The case study architecture can be divided into four pipelines analyzing different parts of an email. Messages enter the system through the *MessageReceiver*, which forwards them to the *MessageParser*. This microservice, in turn, extracts data from the email and routes them to a proper sub-pipeline. Once each email component is processed, entailing a specific working time, analysis data is collected by the *MessageAnalyzer* that produces an analysis report.

Based on system architecture, we observe that each microservice type is also characterized by: (*i*) a Maximum Computational Load (MCL), i.e. the maximum number of requests that a microservice instance of that type can handle within a second and (*ii*) a Multiplicative Factor (MF) i.e. the mean number of requests that a single email entering the system generates for that microservice type.

From a timing viewpoint, considering microservice type MCL and MF is important because it allows us to calculate the minimum number of instances of that type needed to guarantee a given overall system MCL sys_MCL, i.e.[2]

$$N_{instances} = \lceil \frac{sys\_MCL \cdot MF}{MCL} \rceil$$

As we will see in Sect. 4, this is an important system timed characteristic that plays a fundamental role in our global adaptation algorithm.

3.2   Microservice MF and MCL Calculation

The MF of a microservice type is determined from the case study architecture, i.e. from the role played by the microservice and the email part it receives. As a consequence it is strictly related to the (average) structure of emails entering the system. In particular we estimate an email to have: (i) A single header. (ii) A set of links (treated collectively as a single information, received by the *Link-Analyser*). (iii) A single text body (received by the *TextAnalyser*), which is split, on average, into $N_{blocks} = 2.5$ text blocks (individually analysed by *Sentiment-Analyser*). (iv) on average $N_{attachments} = 2$ attachments (individually sent to the attachment sub-pipeline starting with the *VirusScanner*), each having average size of $size_{attachment} = 7MB$ and containing a virus with probability $P_V = 0.25$ (which determines whether a virus scan report is sent to the *MessageAnalyser* or, in case of no virus, the attachment is forwarded to the *AttachmentManager*).

The average numbers above are estimated ones: the MF of microservices can be easily recomputed in case different numbers are considered. In particular, MFs are calculated as follows. Since emails have a single header, a set of links that are sent together and a single text body, the microservices that analyze these elements, i.e. *HeaderAnalyser, LinkAnalyser* and *TextAnalyser*, have $MF = 1$. As text blocks and attachments are individually sent, each of them generates a request to the *Sentiment Analyser* and the *Virus Scanner*, therefore they have $MF = N_{blocks}$ and $MF = N_{attachments}$ respectively. The microservices that follow the *VirusScanner* in the architecture, i.e. *AttachmentManager, ImageAnalyzer, ImageRecognizer* and *NSFWDetector* have a MF equal to the number of virus-free attachments, which can be computed as $MF = N_{attachments} \cdot (1 - P_V)$. Finally, the MF of the *MessageAnalyser* is the sum of the email parts (1 header, 1 set of links, 1 text body and $N_{attachments}$ attachments).

The MCL of a microservice is computed as follows:

$$MCL = 1/(\frac{size_{request}}{data\_rate} + pf)$$

where $size_{request}$ is the average request size of the microservice in MB. Moreover, data_rate is the microservice rate in MB/sec for managing request data. We determine such a value, based on the number of microservice requested cores, from Nginx server data in [32] (considering Nginx servers with that number of

---

[2] $\lceil x \rceil$ is the ceil function that takes as input a real number and gives as output the least integer greater than or equal to x.

vCPUs). Finally, pf is a penalty factor that expresses an additional amount of time that a microservice needs to manage its requests: e.g. the *ImageRecognizer*, which needs Machine Learning techniques to fulfill its tasks.

We compute microservice $\text{size}_{\text{request}}$ as follows. For all microservices receiving attachments, but the *MessageAnalyser* we have:

$$\text{size}_{\text{request}} = N_{\text{attach\_per\_req}} \cdot \text{size}_{\text{attachment}}$$

where $N_{\text{attach\_per\_req}} = N_{\text{attachments}}$ for microservices receiving entire emails and $N_{\text{attach\_per\_req}} = 1$ for the others. For *HeaderAnalyser, LinkAnalyser* and *Text-Analyser* we consider $\text{size}_{\text{request}}$ to be neglectable, thus (since their pf is also 0) their MCL is infinite. Concerning *MessageAnalyser* request size, we compute the average size of the MF requests that en email entering the system generates (since we consider only attachments to have a non-negligible size), i.e.

$$\text{size}_{\text{request\_MA}} = \frac{N_{\text{attachments}} \cdot (1 - P_V) \cdot \text{size}_{\text{attachment}}}{MF}.$$

3.3   Timed SmartDeployer

Our timed architectural modeling/execution language fully integrates timed ABS and architectural annotations thanks to the novel *Timed SmartDeployer*. Such a tool extends SmartDeployer [13] with synthesis of *timed* deployment orchestrations: they additionally encompass dynamic management of overall Deployment Component (DC) *startup time* and DC *speed* (computational resources per time unit, see Sect. 2.2), based on the number of DC virtual cores that are actually used by some microservice after enacting the synthesized deployment sequence. As we will show, this allows us to correctly model time (microservice MCL).

The original SmartDeployer implicitly handles time by simply assigning all properties of DCs, copying them from annotations. The effect of this on timed ABS was to *statically* assign a speed and a startup_time to each DC. Concerning speed, this caused microservices, deployed in a DC with unused cores, to unrealistically proceed faster: as if they could exploit the computational power of unused cores. Our solution is to dynamically evaluate, during orchestration, the number of DC cores that are actually used by deployed services, and to adjust each DC speed to: speed - speed_per_core · unused_cores. Concerning startup_time, since in synthesized orchestrations DCs are sequentially created, in timed ABS the overall startup time turned out to be the *sum* of that of individual DCs. To have a more realistic modeling of virtual machine provisioning (where VMs are contemporaneously acquired), our solution is to dynamically set such a time to the *maximum* of their startup time. The above was realized by automatically synthesizing orchestrations, whose language additionally includes (w.r.t. SmartDeployer) two primitives *explicitly* managing time aspects

- One to decrement the speed of a DC: *decrementResources(. . .)* in ABS.
- One to set overall the startup time of created DCs: *duration(. . .)* in ABS.

3.4   Modeling Service MCL

We now show how Time SmartDeployer allows us to correctly simulate the service MCL we want to model (see Sect. 3.2), independently of the VM (DC) in which it is deployed. An example is considering, as we do in our case study, the ABS time unit to be 1/30 s and setting VMs to supply 5 speed_per_core. In the ABS code of a service we implement its MCL by using the *Cost* instruction tag (see Sect. 2.2). E.g., for the *ImageRecognizer*, which requires 6 cores to be deployed, we obtain the MCL of 91 requests per second as follows:

```
1    class ImageRecognizer() implements ImageRecognizerInterface {
2      Int mcl = 91;
3      String recognizeImage(String image, ImageRecognizer_LoadBalancerInterface balancer){
4        [Cost: 5 * 6 * 30 / mcl] balancer!removeMessage();
5        Int category = random(9);
6        return "Category Recognized: " + toString(category);}}
```

where the method *recognizeImage(...)* is executed at each request.

Due to our SmartDeployer timed extension, the amount of VM speed used by *ImageRecognizer* is always $5 \cdot 6$ (speed_per_core · cores_required), independently of the VM in which it is deployed: i.e. *ImageRecognizer* can use up to $5 \cdot 6$ computational resources per time unit. The *Cost* tag above causes each request to consume speed_per_core · cores_required · 30/MCL computational resources. Therefore, since MCL/30 is the *ImageRecognizer* MCL expressed in requests per time unit, this realizes the desired (deployment independent) service MCL.

4   Global Run-Time Adaptation

In this section, we present our algorithm for global run-time adaptation, which is totally independent from the case study (and from the ABS language itself).

4.1   Calculation of Scaling Configurations

We consider a base **B** system configuration, see Table 1, which guarantees a system MCL of 60 emails/sec. In the corresponding column of Table 1 we present the number of instances for each microservice type, calculated according to the formula in Sect. 3.1. Moreover, we consider four incremental configurations $\Delta 1$, $\Delta 2$, $\Delta 3$ and $\Delta 4$, synthesized via Timed SmartDeployer, each adding a number of instances to each microservice type, see Table 1. Those incremental configurations are used as target configurations for deployment/undeployment orchestration synthesis in order to perform run-time architecture-level reconfiguration. As shown in Table 2, $\Delta 1$, $\Delta 2$, $\Delta 3$ and $\Delta 4$ are used, in turn, to build (summing up them element-wise as arrays) the incremental configurations Scale1, Scale2, Scale3 and Scale4 that guarantee an additional system MCL of +60, +150, +240 and +330 emails/sec, respectively.

The reason for not considering our Scales as monolithic blocks and defining them as combinations of the Δ incremental configurations is the following. Let us suppose the system to be, e.g., in a **B** + Scale1 configuration and the increase in incoming workload to require the deployment of Scale2 and the undeployment of

Table 1. Base **B** ($60\ \frac{emails}{sec}$) and incremental Δ configurations.

Microservice	B	$\Delta 1$	$\Delta 2$	$\Delta 3$	$\Delta 4$	Microservice	B	$\Delta 1$	$\Delta 2$	$\Delta 3$	$\Delta 4$
Message Receiver	1	+1	+0	+1	+1	Virus Scanner	1	+1	+2	+1	+2
Message Parser	1	+1	+0	+1	+1	Attachment Manager	1	+0	+1	+0	+1
Header Analyser	1	+0	+0	+0	+0	Image Analyser	1	+0	+1	+0	+1
Link Analyser	1	+0	+0	+0	+0	NSFW Detector	1	+1	+2	+1	+2
Text Analyser	1	+0	+0	+0	+0	Image Recognizer	1	+1	+2	+1	+2
Sentiment Analyser	2	+1	+3	+2	+2	Message Analyser	1	+1	+2	+1	+2

Table 2. Incremental Scale configurations.

Scale 1 ($+60\ \frac{emails}{sec}$)	Scale 2 ($+150\ \frac{emails}{sec}$)	Scale 3 ($+240\ \frac{emails}{sec}$)	Scale 4 ($+330\ \frac{emails}{sec}$)
$\Delta 1$	$\Delta 1 + \Delta 2$	$\Delta 1 + \Delta 2 + \Delta 3$	$\Delta 1 + \Delta 2 + \Delta 3 + \Delta 4$

Scale1. If we had not introduced Δ configurations and we had synthesized orchestrations directly for Scale configurations, we would have needed to perform an undeployment of Scale1 followed by a deployment of Scale2. With Δ configurations, instead, we can simply additionally deploy $\Delta 2$. Moreover, notice that dealing with such an incoming workload increase by naively deploying another Scale1 additional configuration, besides the already deployed one, would not lead the system MCL to be increased of another +60 emails/sec. This is because the maximum number of email per seconds that can be handled by individual microservices composing the obtained **B**+2·Scale1 configuration would be unbalanced. Such an effect worsens if the system incoming workload keeps slowly increasing and further additional Scale1 configurations are deployed. Since Scale1 for some microservices (*AttachmentManager, ImageAnalyser*) does not provide additional instances, such microservices would eventually become the bottleneck of the system and the system MCL would no longer increase. Moreover, Δ configurations yield, w.r.t. monolithic Scale ones, a finer granularity that makes SmartDeployer orchestration synthesis faster.

For each microservice type, the number of additional instances considered in Tables 1 and 2 for the Scale configurations have been calculated as follows. Given the additional system MCL to be guaranteed, the number $N_{deployed}$ of instances of that microservice already deployed and its MF and MCL, we have:

$$N_{instances} = \left\lceil \frac{(\text{base\_MCL} + \text{additional\_MCL}) \cdot \text{MF}}{\text{MCL}} - N_{deployed} \right\rceil$$

In the following section we will present the algorithm for global adaptation. The algorithm is based on the principles described here, i.e. it has the following *invariant* property: if N Scale configurations are considered (N = 4 in our case study) and are indexed in increasing order of additional system MCL they guarantee, the system configuration reached after adapting to the monitored inbound workload is either **B** or **B** + (n · ScaleN) + scale, for some scale $\in$ {Scale1, Scale2, . . . , ScaleN} and n $\geq$ 0. The invariant property indeed shows, as we explained above, that the deployment of sequences of the same Scale configuration is not allowed, except for sequences of ScaleN. This is because, the biggest configuration ScaleN should be devised, for the system being monitored, in such a way that the inbound workload rarely yields to additional scaling needs. Moreover, even if a sequence of ScaleN occurs, the system would be sufficiently balanced. This is because, differently from smaller Scale configurations, ScaleN is assumed to add, at least, an instance for each microservice having non-infinite MCL (as for Scale4 in our case study).

4.2 Scaling Algorithms

For comparison purposes, we realized two algorithms, for local and global adaptation. In both of them we use a scaling condition on monitored inbound workload involving two constants called K and k. K is used to leave a margin under the guaranteed MCL, so to make sure that the system can handle the inbound workload. k is used to prevent fluctuations, i.e. sequences of scale up and down.

The condition for scaling up is (inbound_workload + K) − total_MCL > k and the one for scaling down is total_MCL − (inbound_workload + K) > k. The interpretation of such conditions changes, depending on whether they are used for the local or global adaptation algorithm. In the case of local adaptation the conditions are applied by monitoring a single microservice type: inbound_workload is the number of requests per second received by the microservice load balancer and total_MCL is the MCL of a microservice instance of that type (calculated as explained in Sect. 3.2) multiplied by the number of deployed instances. In the case of global adaptation the conditions are applied by monitoring the whole system: inbound_workload is the number of requests (emails in our case study) per second entering the system and total_MCL is the system MCL.

Concerning global adaptation, we have a single monitor that periodically executes (e.g. every 10 s in our case study) the code excerpt below. The code uses constants numScales, representing the number of Scale configurations (4 in our case study), and scaleComponents: an array[3] of numScales elements (corresponding to Table 2 in our case study) that stores in each position an array representing a Scale configuration (i.e. specifying, for each microservice, the number of additional instances to be deployed). Moreover, the code uses the variables sys_MCL, containing the current system MCL (assumed to be initially set to the **B** configuration MCL, see Table 1 in our case study), and deployedDeltas: an array of numScales numbers that keeps track of the number of currently deployed Δ incremental configurations (assumed to be initially empty, i.e. with all 0 values). Both variables are updated by the code in case of scaling. First of all the code applies the above described scale up/down conditions. Then it loops, starting from the **B** configuration in variable config (an array that stores, for each microservice, the number of instances we currently consider), and selecting Scale configurations to add to config, until a configuration c is found such that its

---

[3] The ABS instructions nth(a, i) and length(a) retrieve the i-th element and the length of the a array, respectively.

system MCL satisfies sys_MCL − (inbound_workload + K) ≥ 0. The system MCL of a configuration c is calculated with method *mcl*, which yields

$$\min_{1 \leq i \leq \text{length(config)}} \text{nth}(\text{config}, i-1) \cdot \text{MCL}_i / \text{MF}_i$$

with $\text{MCL}_i / \text{MF}_i$ denoting the MCL/MF of the i-th microservice. More precisely the algorithm uses an external loop updating variables config and configDeltas according to the incremental Scale selected by the internal loop: configDeltas is an array with the same structure of deployedDeltas, which is initially empty and, every time a Scale configuration is selected, is updated by incrementing the amount of corresponding Δ configurations (as described in Table 2 in our case study). The internal loop selects a Scale configuration by looking for the first one that, added to config, yields a candidate configuration whose system MCL satisfies the condition above. If such Scale configuration is not found then it just selects the last (the biggest) Scale configuration (Scale4 in our case study), thus implementing the invariant presented in Sect. 4.1.

```
1    if((inbound_workload+kbig)-sys_MCL>k || (sys_MCL-(inbound_workload+kbig)>k){
2      List<Int> configDeltas = this.createEmpty(numScales);
3      List<Int> config = baseConfig;
4      sys_MCL = this.mcl(config);
5      Bool configFound = sys_MCL-(inbound_workload+kbig)>=0;
6      while(!configFound) {
7        List<Int> candidateConfig = baseConfig;
8        Int i = -1;
9        while(i<numScales-1 && !configFound){
10         i=i+1;
11         candidateConfig = this.vectorSum(config,nth(scaleComponents,i));
12         sys_MCL = this.mcl(candidateConfig);
13         configFound = sys_MCL-(inbound_workload+kbig)>=0;}
14       config = candidateConfig;
15       configDeltas = this.addDeltas(i,configDeltas);}
16     this.reconfigureSystem(deployedDeltas,configDeltas);
17     deployedDeltas = configDeltas;}
```

Finally, as we show in the method *reconfigureSystem* below, given the target Δ configurations configDeltas to be reached and the current deployedDeltas ones, we perform the difference between them so to find the Δ orchestrations that have to be (un)deployed.

```
1    Unit reconfigureSystem(List<Int> deployedDeltas, List<Int> configDeltas) {
2      Int i = 0;
3      while(i<numScales) {
4        Int diff = nth(configDeltas,i)-nth(deployedDeltas,i);
5        Rat num = abs(diff);
6        while(num>0) {
7          if (diff>0) {nth(orchestrationDeltas,i)!deploy();}
8          else {nth(orchestrationDeltas,i)!undeploy();}
9          num = num-1;}
10         i = i+1;}}
```

We use methods *deploy/undeploy* of the object in the position $i-1$ of the array orchestrationDeltas to execute the orchestration of the i-th Δ configuration. In our model such an orchestration is the ABS code generated by Timed SmartDeployer at compile-time: it makes use of ABS primitives *duration(...)* and *decrementResources(...)* to *dynamically* set, respectively, the overall startup time to the maximum of those of deployed DCs and the speed of such DCs accounting for the virtual cores actually being used (by decrementing the DC static speed, see Sect. 3.3). In this way we are guaranteed that each microservice always preserves the desired fixed MCL we want to model (see Sect. 3.4). Moreover, we remind that, besides speed, also constraints related to other resources (memory) are considered in the SmartDeployer synthesis process.

5   Simulation with ABS

In this section we present simulation results obtained with our ABS programs [1] modeling local and global scaling (via Timed SmartDeployer orchestrations) for our case study. Such programs encompass, besides static aspects of the case study architecture (annotations), also the code representing service/adaptation behavior *under an inboud workload*: they fully implement what we explained in Sects. 3 and 4. In particular, we implement by means of *monitoring services*: our algorithm for global adaptation (a single system monitor) and the one for local adaptation (a monitor for each load balancer) by just detecting scaling needs and enacting replications at the level of single microservices. Monitors are implemented by dedicated ABS services that run on a separate (simulated) VM. For these services we do not model the computing resources: we assume that monitors are part of the deployment infrastructure, which is also responsible for enacting the scaling strategies (as it happens, e.g., with Kubernetes autoscaling).

To make scaling operations realistic, it is important to explicitly represent VM overall startup time and, within load balancers, request queues of a fixed size. This explicit management not only provides a realistic model, but is also crucial for preventing the system from over-loading. Indeed, without these queues, the system wouldn't refuse any message and when the inbound workload grows up, it would overload the system with no possibility of restoring acceptable performances even if scaling actions occur. Moreover, queues allow us to model message loss and to use it for comparing the behavior of local and global scaling. In our modeling, we assume microservices not to fail and messages to be eventually delivered unless the receiver queue is overloaded (in this case they are dropped).

We decided to test our approach using both a real diurnal load pattern inspired to that in [24], see Fig. 2a, and part of an IMAPS email traffic similar to that in [29] (accounting for the fact that here email attachments are also considered), see Fig. 3a. We implemented such inbound workloads by means of an *email generating service*. The ABS code is executed with the Erlang backend.

5.1   Simulation Results

We compare the simulation of our approach based on global scaling with the classical one (based on local scaling) by focusing on the following aspects: (i) latency comparison, (ii) message loss comparison and (iii) number of microservices comparison.

The first metric to be analyzed, in order to evaluate the performance of our new scaling approach, is the *latency*. We consider the latency as the average time for completely processing an email that enters the system. As shown by Figs. 2b and 3b (the latter considers monitoring time to be 40 min instead of 10 s), our approach, represented by the red dashed line, is outperforming the classical one. Considering the different peaks of incoming messages present in the chosen workloads, it is clear the extent of the improvement introduced by our new approach: our global adaptation makes the system adapt much faster than the classic approach. This is caused by the ability of the global adaptation strategy of detecting in advance the scaling needs of all system microservices.

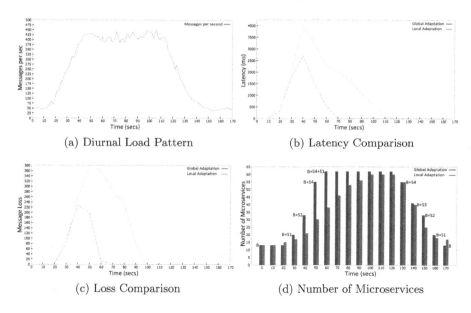

(a) Diurnal Load Pattern

(b) Latency Comparison

(c) Loss Comparison

(d) Number of Microservices

Fig. 2. Comparison results under the real diurnal load pattern.

The above observation is confirmed by analyzing system *message loss*. Observing Figs. 2c and 3c, it is possible to see that our approach always stops losing messages earlier than the classic approach. This means that message queues start to empty and latency can start to decrease.

Finally, comparing the *number of deployed microservices* helps to have a deeper understanding of the reasons why the global adaptation performs better. As shown by Figs. 2d and 3d (where we also label the diagram with the structure of configurations in the case of global scaling), our approach reaches the target configuation, needed to handle the maximum inbound workload, faster than the classical approach. As expected this increments the adaptation responsiveness to higher workloads. The local adaptation slowness in reaching such a target configuration is caused by a *scaling chain effect*: local monitors periodically check the workload, thus single services scale one after the other. Hence, w.r.t. global adaptation, in which microservices in the target configuration are deployed together, the number of instances grows slower. For example, considering the attachment pipeline in Fig. 1, the first microservice to become a bottleneck is the *VirusScanner*: it starts losing messages, which will never arrive to the *AttachmentManager*. Therefore, this component will not perceive the increment in the inbound emails until the *VirusScanner* will be replicated, thus causing a scaling chain effect that delays adaptation. This is the main cause for the large deterioration in performances observed. On the other hand, the local approach requires, in total, less resources: this is particularly visible in Fig. 2d. Due, however, to optimal resource allocation of SmartDeployer reconfigurations, this does not necessarily imply a significant increase in VM costs.

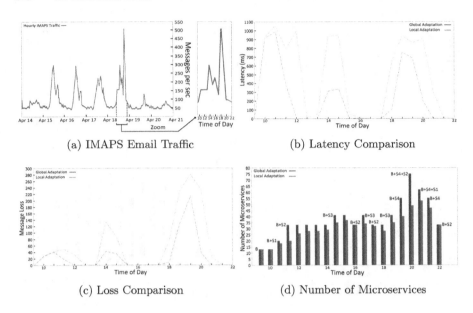

(a) IMAPS Email Traffic   (b) Latency Comparison

(c) Loss Comparison   (d) Number of Microservices

Fig. 3. Comparison results under the IMAPS email traffic.

6 Related Work and Conclusion

We introduced an integrated timed architectural modeling/execution language that correctly deals with service Maximum Computational Load (MCL). Moreover, we proposed a novel global scaling algorithm that optimally chooses deployment orchestrations, so to keep the system in a configuration that better fits the inbound workload (with the minimum number of instances). Finally, we performed a comparison between our global scaling algorithm and a classical local one by simulating, under two real workloads, a microservice application.

We now discuss related literature by first comparing with our previous work. In [13,14] initial ideas about applying SmartDeployer generated orchestrations to the case study of [23] were discussed, but (apart from annotations modeling static aspects of the architecture) no actual ABS code implementing system service execution/scaling mechanism was presented. Moreover, [13,14] draft some scaling configurations just for exemplifying the idea of global adaptation via deployment orchestrations (without presenting any actual scaling algorithm). Such manually drafted scaling configurations are completely different from those here presented in Sect. 4.1, which are precisely calculated (based on service MCL) via a formula yielding the additional number of instances. As explained in Sect. 4.1, the novel idea of relying on service MCL (and to its mathematical evaluation, see Sect. 3.2) makes it possible to effectively use such configurations in the context of a global scaling algorithm that is guaranteed to reach any target system MCL. Finally, here we introduce the novel non-monolithic Δ scales and provide the implementation of the global scaling algorithm. Such algorithm avoids bottlenecks by keeping the system balanced (w.r.t. microservice instance number), thanks to the ability of the novel Timed SmartDeployer of correctly dealing with service MCL, see Sect. 3.4.

We then consider additional related work on SmartDeployer. While [19] just exemplifies the execution of deployment orchestrations for a specific system reconfiguration and [9] additionally deals with selection among different scaling actions based on human suggestions, we devise: a general methodology for designing a set of deployment orchestrations based on target incremental system MCLs (hence having a mathematical foundation) and an auto-scaling algorithm that makes human intervention unneeded. Moreover, w.r.t. [9,19], we correctly model real aspects such as deployment time and MCL-preserving core-based VM speed computation (thanks to our Timed SmartDepoyer) and we also test the effectiveness of our algorithm, by comparing it with classical local adaptation.

Regarding related work on auto-scaling, there are several solutions [6,8,21,25] supporting the automatic system reconfiguration, by incrementing or decrementing of the number of instances at the service/container level, when some conditions (e.g., CPU average load greater than 80%) are met. Our work shows how we can go beyond such local horizontal scaling policies (analyzed, e.g., in [15]).

A strand of work sees the predictive capabilities of machine learning applied to auto-scaling. Below, we cite a few relevant examples, but we point the interested reader to the survey in [30] for a more comprehensive view on the field. In [27] a scheduling system is proposed, which is based on deep reinforcement learning. There, the scheduler interacts with the deployment environment to learn scheduling strategies without any prior knowledge of both the environment and the services. Similarly, [26] attacks the problem of defining optimal thresholds for scaling policies with a reinforcement-learning algorithm that automatically and dynamically adjusts the thresholds without user configuration. Finally, [2] proposes an approach that uses a predictive autoscaling model trained on a dataset generated from simulations of reactive rule-based autoscaling. W.r.t. work on workload prediction, such as [2], our global adaptation algorithm ability of detecting in advance service scaling needs is not based on guessing workload by means of logged data, but on mathematically calculating service MCL from system MCL (thanks to service Multiplicative Factor and current number of instances, see formula in Sect. 3.1). The two approaches are, thus, orthogonal: our approach avoids the negative consequences of the scaling chain effect, but it just passively waits for the triggering event (significant increment in the inbound workload). The integration of machine learning techniques with our approach could further soften the impact of such an event leading to a better Quality of Service (e.g. latency and message loss).

Concerning future work, besides realizing the above described integration, we plan to improve system simulation by accounting for failures (e.g., network partitioning, computing hardware failures) and their impact on the deployed system. To this aim, we could evaluate the system following the practice of Chaos Engineering [17], simulating the failures in ABS and making sure that the available resources are enough to guarantee a given level or robustness and resilience. Moreover, to improve the portability of our approach, we also plan to base our system modeling using a workflow language/notation that also includes data flow besides standard control flow, such as BPMN [31]. This will make it possible to automatically calculate microservice MCL and Multiplicative Factor according to formulae such as those used in our case study.

References

1. Code repository for the email processing examples. https://github.com/LBacchiani/ABS-Simulations-Comparison
2. Abdullah, M., Iqbal, W., Mahmood, A., Bukhari, F., Erradi, A.: Predictive autoscaling of microservices hosted in fog microdata center. IEEE Syst. J. 1–12 (2021)
3. Ábrahám, E., Corzilius, F., Johnsen, E.B., Kremer, G., Mauro, J.: Zephyrus2: on the fly deployment optimization using SMT and CP technologies. In: Fränzle, M., Kapur, D., Zhan, N. (eds.) SETTA 2016. LNCS, vol. 9984, pp. 229–245. Springer, Cham (2016). https://doi.org/10.1007/978-3-319-47677-3_15
4. ABS. ABS documentation. http://docs.abs-models.org/
5. ABS. ABS toolchain. https://abs-models.org/laboratory/
6. Amazon. Amazon cloudwatch. https://aws.amazon.com/cloudwatch/
7. Amazon. AWS auto scaling. https://aws.amazon.com/autoscaling/
8. Apache. Apache mesos. http://mesos.apache.org/
9. Bezirgiannis, N., de Boer, F., de Gouw, S.: Human-in-the-loop simulation of cloud services. In: De Paoli, F., Schulte, S., Broch Johnsen, E. (eds.) ESOCC 2017. LNCS, vol. 10465, pp. 143–158. Springer, Cham (2017). https://doi.org/10.1007/978-3-319-67262-5_11
10. Binder, W., Hulaas, J., Camesi, A.: Continuous bytecode instruction counting for CPU consumption estimation. In: Third International Conference on the Quantitative Evaluation of Systems-(QEST 2006), pp. 19–30. IEEE (2006)
11. Binder, W., Hulaas, J., Moret, P., Villazón, A.: Platform-independent profiling in a virtual execution environment. Softw. Prac. Experience **39**(1), 47–79 (2009)
12. Bravetti, M., Carbone, M., Zavattaro, G.: Undecidability of asynchronous session subtyping. Inf. Comput. **256**, 300–320 (2017)
13. Bravetti, M., Giallorenzo, S., Mauro, J., Talevi, I., Zavattaro, G.: Optimal and automated deployment for microservices. In: Hähnle, R., van der Aalst, W. (eds.) FASE 2019. LNCS, vol. 11424, pp. 351–368. Springer, Cham (2019). https://doi.org/10.1007/978-3-030-16722-6_21
14. Bravetti, M., Giallorenzo, S., Mauro, J., Talevi, I., Zavattaro, G.: A formal approach to microservice architecture deployment. Microservices, pp. 183–208. Springer, Cham (2020). https://doi.org/10.1007/978-3-030-31646-4_8
15. Bravetti, M., Gilmore, S., Guidi, C., Tribastone, M.: Replicating web services for scalability. In: Barthe, G., Fournet, C. (eds.) TGC 2007. LNCS, vol. 4912, pp. 204–221. Springer, Heidelberg (2008). https://doi.org/10.1007/978-3-540-78663-4_15
16. Bravetti, M., Zavattaro, G.: On the expressive power of process interruption and compensation. Math. Struc. Comput. Sci. **19**(3), 565–599 (2009)
17. Casey Rosenthal, N.J.: Chaos Engineering. O'Reilly Media Inc, 1 edition (2020)

18. Di Cosmo, R., Zacchiroli, S., Zavattaro, G.: Towards a formal component model for the cloud. In: Eleftherakis, G., Hinchey, M., Holcombe, M. (eds.) SEFM 2012. LNCS, vol. 7504, pp. 156–171. Springer, Heidelberg (2012). https://doi.org/10.1007/978-3-642-33826-7_11

19. de Gouw, S., Mauro, J., Zavattaro, G.: On the modeling of optimal and automatized cloud application deployment. J. Logical Algebraic Methods Programm. **107**, 108–135 (2019)

20. Docker. Docker compose documentation. https://docs.docker.com/compose/

21. Docker. Docker swarm. https://docs.docker.com/engine/swarm/

22. Dragoni, N., et al.: Microservices: yesterday, today, and tomorrow. Present and Ulterior Software Engineering, pp. 195–216. Springer, Cham (2017). https://doi.org/10.1007/978-3-319-67425-4_12

23. Fromm, K.: Thinking Serverless! How New Approaches Address Modern Data Processing Needs. https://urlread.acloud.guru/thinking-serverless-how-new-approaches-address-urlmodern-data-processing-needs-part-1-af6a158a3af1

24. Gan, Y., et al.: An open-source benchmark suite for microservices and their hardware-software implications for cloud & edge systems. In Proceedings of the Twenty-Fourth International Conference on Architectural Support for Programming Languages and Operating Systems, ASPLOS 2019, pp. 3–18, New York (2019)

25. Hightower, K., Burns, B., Beda, J.: Kubernetes: Up and Running Dive into the Future of Infrastructure. O'Reilly Media Inc, 1st edition (2017)

26. Horovitz, S., Arian, Y.: Efficient cloud auto-scaling with sla objective using q-learning. In: 2018 IEEE 6th International Conference on Future Internet of Things and Cloud (FiCloud), pp. 85–92. IEEE (2018)

27. Huang, J., Xiao, C., Wu, W.: Rlsk: a job scheduler for federated kubernetes clusters based on reinforcement learning. In: 2020 IEEE International Conference on Cloud Engineering (IC2E), pp. 116–123. IEEE (2020)

28. Humble, J., Farley, D.: Continuous Delivery: Reliable Software Releases Through Build, Test, and Deployment Automation. Addison-Wesley Professional (2010)

29. Karamollahi, M., Williamson, C.: Characterization of IMAPS email traffic. In: 27th IEEE International Symposium on Modeling, Analysis, and Simulation of Computer and Telecommunication Systems, MASCOTS 2019, Rennes, France, October 21–25, pp. 214–220. IEEE Computer Society (2019)

30. Lorido-Botran, T., Miguel-Alonso, J., Lozano, J.A.: A review of auto-scaling techniques for elastic applications in cloud environments. J. Grid Comput. **12**(4), 559–592 (2014)

31. OMG. Business Process Model and Notation (BPMN), Version 2.0. http://www.omg.org/spec/BPMN/2.0 (2011)

32. Rawdat, A.: Testing the performance of nginx and nginx plus web servers (2017). https://www.nginx.com/blog/testing-the-performance-of-nginx-and-nginx-plus-web-servers/

Jolie and LEMMA: Model-Driven Engineering and Programming Languages Meet on Microservices

Saverio Giallorenzo[1,2]($\boxtimes$) ⓘ, Fabrizio Montesi[3] ⓘ, Marco Peressotti[3] ⓘ,
Florian Rademacher[4] ⓘ, and Sabine Sachweh[4]

[1] Universitá di Bologna, Bologna, Italy
saverio.giallorenzo2@unibo.it
[2] Inria, Sophia Antipolis, France
[3] University of Southern Denmark, Odense, Denmark
{fmontesi,peressotti}@imada.sdu.dk
[4] University of Applied Sciences and Arts Dortmund, Dortmund, Germany
{florian.rademacher,sabine.sachweh}@fh-dortmund.de

Abstract. In microservices, Model-Driven Engineering (MDE) has emerged as a powerful methodology for architectural design. Independently, the community of programming languages has investigated new linguistic abstractions for effective microservice development. Here, we present the first preliminary study of how the two approaches can cross-pollinate, taking the LEMMA framework and the Jolie programming language as respective representatives. We establish a common ground for comparing the two technologies in terms of metamodels, discuss practical enhancements that can be derived from the comparison, and present some directions for future work that arise from our new viewpoint.

1 Introduction

In microservices, applications emerge as compositions of independently-executable components (*microservices*, or briefly, services), which communicate via message passing [12]. Building microservice systems poses a series of challenges for both design and development, which has motivated two prolific strands of research.

On the side of design, Model-Driven Engineering (MDE) [17] has become a prominent methodology for the specification of service architectures [2]. Frameworks such as LEMMA, MicroBuilder, and MDSL offer modelling languages to design service components that abstract from concrete implementations [21,32,33].

On the side of development, new linguistic abstractions for programming languages are emerging as powerful tools to effectively express the configuration and coordination of microservices. Ballerina and Jolie are examples of such

Work partially supported by Independent Research Fund Denmark, grant no. 0135-00219.

F. Damiani and O. Dardha (Eds.): COORDINATION 2021, LNCS 12717, pp. 276–284, 2021.
https://doi.org/10.1007/978-3-030-78142-2_17

languages [27,29]. In particular, Jolie incorporates ideas from process calculi to ease the programming of workflows and it offers "polyglot" constructs to integrate services written in foreign languages (e.g., Java) [25,27].

So far, results on microservices by the MDE and programming communities have evolved prolifically, yet separately. This is unfortunate since previous research showed great potential in combining programming language and MDE techniques [6,11,13]. In part, we deem this phenomenon due to the few opportunities the two communities have to interact. Case in point, the authors come from the different two communities and met only recently, at the last two editions of the International Conference on Microservices (an event organised specifically to bridge sub-communities of traditional fields that share an interest in microservices). Seminars from both parts evidenced that MDE methodologies and programming languages for microservices share a common conceptual foundation that has never been properly made precise nor leveraged [16,30].

This article is the first step towards bridging conceptually MDE frameworks and programming languages for microservices. As grounding, we take LEMMA [31,32] and Jolie [27] as respective representatives of the two approaches.

The main challenge is that MDE frameworks come with specifications—like LEMMA's metamodels [31,32]—distant from those given for programming languages—some parts of Jolie are described by using process calculi [19,26], and for others there is a reference implementation [1,24]. To address this, we develop the first conceptual metamodel of the Jolie language, drawing from our experience with its formalisations [10,19,26] and reference implementation [1,24].

Having metamodels for both Jolie (from this paper) and LEMMA (from [31,32]) allows for comparing them. We identify some key shared concepts and differences. Interestingly, the differences are complementary perspectives on common concerns, providing fertile ground for future evolutions of both approaches: we sketch extensions of LEMMA induced by Jolie, and vice versa.

The common footing we establish brings us closer to an ecosystem that coherently combines MDE and programming abstractions to offer a tower of abstractions [23] that supports a step-by-step refinement process from the abstract specification of a microservice architecture (MSA) to its implementation.

2   A Structured Comparison of Jolie and LEMMA

The conceptual metamodels of Jolie (new in this article) and LEMMA (a simplification of the metamodel in [32]) are respectively displayed in Fig. 1a and b, in UML format. As a basis for comparison, we classify their elements in the three categories commonly found in characterisation and specifications of (micro)services in [3,14,35]: Application Programming Interfaces (APIs) ① and Access Points ②, which, combined, define the public contract of a microservice, and the private internal behaviour ③ that a microservice enacts. We proceed by explaining the metamodels and our comparison following these categories.

2.1   Application Programming Interfaces (APIs)

APIs—originally introduced to provide hardware independence to programs [8]—specify *what* functionalities a microservice offers to clients [12]. Besides loosing coupling, APIs contribute to technology agnosticism, especially when minimising the assumptions made on the technologies used to implement behaviours.

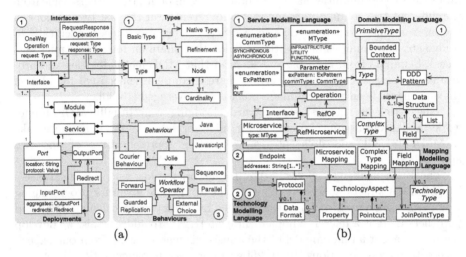

(a)   (b)

Fig. 1. Core meta-models of Jolie (a) and LEMMA (b).

Jolie conceptualises APIs into Interfaces. An Interface is a collection of Operations, each having its own name and being either: a OneWay operation, where the sender delivers its message to the service but does not wait for it to be processed by the service's behaviour; or a RequestResponse operation, where the sender delivers its message and waits for the receiving service's behaviour to reply with a response. Operations include types for the data structures that can be exchanged through them. A Jolie Type is a tree-shaped data type made of two components: (i) a Basic Type that describes the type of the root of the tree and (ii) a set of Nodes that define the fields of the data structure. Basic Types include a Native Type (primitives like boolean, integer, char, string) and a Refinement that specifies further restrictions on the native type [18]. Nodes are arrays with specified ranges of lengths (Cardinality). Jolie data types, and thus interfaces, are technology agnostic: they model Data Transfer Objects that build on native types generally available in most architectures [9].

LEMMA captures APIs as characterising components of a given Microservice though its Service Modelling Language [32]. Conceptually, a Microservice is a composition of Interfaces, each clustering one or more Operations. LEMMA distinguishes three types of microservices. Functional and utility ones realise domain-specific business logic and reusable generic functionality, respectively.

Infrastructure microservices provide technical capabilities, e.g., for service discovery [4]. In LEMMA, a microservice operation is a collection of Parameters, each defined by an exchange pattern (either incoming or outgoing), a communication type (synchronous or asynchronous), and a Type, expressed in the Domain Modelling language. Types can specify some Domain-Driven Design (DDD) semantics in the form of DDD patterns, e.g., the Entity pattern [15] which defines the identifying traits of the Type's inhabitants, e.g., a Person with a name and birthdate but uniquely identified by its social security number.

From the above descriptions—also remarked with the colours of the partitions in Fig. 1a and b, tagged with ①—APIs are captured similarly in Jolie and LEMMA: they both attribute a paradigm to each operation, either request-response/synchronous or notification/asynchronous, although Jolie at the level of operations and LEMMA at the level of parameters. Types in the two models differ, but, besides LEMMA's DDD semantics, the differences are mostly technical. We exploit the vicinity of views on APIs between Jolie and LEMMA to propose in Sect. 3 an extension of Jolie that captures DDD patterns of LEMMA's Types. At the conceptual level, Jolie and LEMMA interpret API design from different perspectives. Jolie defines APIs as reusable artefacts, separately from services (a service can then refer to API definitions). In LEMMA, APIs are part of a service definition. This difference makes for an interesting point for building a reference metamodel for microservices, as discussed in Sect. 3.

2.2   Access Points

When a microservice implements an API, it must make a technological commitment on *where* and *how* its clients can interact with the API. Access points fulfil this need, complementing the public APIs of a microservice with the specification and configuration of the technologies used to (i) format data (how data are structured/marshalled for transmission, e.g., JSON); and (ii) transmit data (where microservices can contact each other and how data are transported among them, e.g., an IP address). Access points are the main elements that increase coupling between microservices, as providers expect clients to include in their technology stacks the technologies used at providers' access points.

Jolie integrates the Port concept (cf. Fig. 1a) to support access point definition and configuration. A Jolie Port determines the *location* of an access point in the form of a URI [5] and associates it with a *protocol*. Furthermore, a Port clusters one or more Jolie Interfaces, which define the operations available at that access point (and also complete the public contract of the given microservice).

Jolie distinguishes between InputPorts and OutputPorts (cf. Fig. 1a). InputPorts expose a public contract to clients while OutputPorts define access points used in behaviours (cf. Sect. 2.3) to invoke other microservices.

LEMMA provides the Endpoint concept (cf. Fig. 1b) to model locations and technologies of access points, as part of a microservice API. To cope with *technology heterogeneity* in MSA [28], LEMMA treats technology information as a dedicated concern in microservice modelling. Indeed, it provides two modelling languages to (i) organise technology information in dedicated *technology models*; and (ii) assign this information to service models within dedicated *mapping models*. In the context of access points, technology models cluster Protocols and DataFormats (cf. Fig. 1b) and make them available to mapping models for determining the technical endpoint characteristics.

Both Jolie and LEMMA support the specification of inbound access points: Jolie InputPorts and LEMMA Endpoints include the definition of the technological choices that define the location and the data formats of access points. However, Jolie and LEMMA differ in how they describe outbound access points: (i) Jolie uses OutputPorts to specify, in behaviours, the interaction with the access points of other microservices. (ii) LEMMA uses the RefMicroservice concept to specify dependencies among microservices—LEMMA leaves to model processors how to interpret RefMicroservices, e.g., defining deployment precedence.

2.3 Behaviours

Behaviours specify the internal business logic of a microservice, including when the microservice accepts requests from clients and when it invokes other microservices. Jolie allows developers to use Java, JavaScript or Jolie Behaviours to express the behaviour of microservices. Jolie Behaviours are a fragment of the Jolie Language (herein, Jolie Behavioural Language), where microservice behaviours are first-class citizens that, starting from the basic service invocation, one can compose into complex behaviours via high-level *workflow operators* such as Sequence, Parallel, and Guarded Replication. The choice of these operators comes from process calculi and the study of core languages for service-oriented computing [20,27]. In this sense, the Jolie Behavioural Language is a full-fledged specification language for microservices behaviour and, borrowing LEMMA's conceptual organisation, the Jolie Interpreter as its default technology.

LEMMA does not support (yet) complete specifications of microservice behaviours. However, one can use LEMMA's malleable technology modelling language in this direction, defining a suite of technology aspects for declaring general behaviours (e.g., that a microservice is guarded by a circuit breaker) and programming new code generators to produce microservice skeletons.

3 Cross-Fertilisation and Conclusion

The conceptual similarities between Jolie and LEMMA regarding APIs, Access Points and Behaviours identified in this work open the door to cross-fertilisation.

Behaviours in LEMMA. As discussed in Sect. 2.3, LEMMA does not support complete and general specifications of microservice behaviours. We propose to extend LEMMA with hosting of languages for programming behaviours like the Jolie Behavioural Language. In general, one can envision a suite of such guest languages that users can select from or extend. The snippet below illustrates a typical instance of this scenario where a programmer extends a microservice specification with a behaviour for operation1. To this end, the programmer imports a behaviour modelling language and a suitable technology for it, in this case, the Jolie Behavioural Language and the Jolie Interpreter.

```
import microservices from "example.services" as ExampleServices
import behaviour_language from "jolie.behaviour_language" as jolie
import technology from "jolie.technology" as jolie_interpreter

@behaviour_language(jolie)
@technology(jolie_interpreter)
ExampleServices::org.example.Microservice {
  operation1() { /* programmed using the given behavioural language */ }
}
```

This requires a conceptual and technological infrastructure for language integration in some regards similar to quotation [7,22]: APIs modelled in LEMMA need to be rendered available to the guest language and aspects of behaviour interaction and composition need to be made available to LEMMA. This observation suggests that this integration infrastructure could be founded over the core concepts and behaviour operators for service-oriented programming of process calculi that already constitute the foundation of the Jolie Behavioural Language.

DDD Patterns in Jolie. As mentioned in Sect. 2.1, we can augment LEMMA's Types with DDD semantics, i.e., constraints imposed by the domain on data structures. Equipping Jolie with such a feature can increase its expressiveness in useful ways, which we discuss briefly below. Comment annotations can capture DDD patterns in Jolie. For example, we can express the Entity pattern (cf. Sect. 2.1) via the annotation @entity below, which associates the property identity of the pattern with two sub-nodes of the Person type (SSN and country):

```
/// @entity { identity = [ SSN, country ] }
type Person { SSN: string, country: string( length(3) ), name: string }
```

An immediate result is using DDD patterns to improve documentation, by attaching plain-text explanations of the intended usage of types—in unison with the additional constraints expressed by refinements (cf. length(3) above). More advanced integrations can elevate DDD patterns at the level of types, opening the door to runtime and static utilities. For instance, we can have operations "governed" by the semantics of patterns, e.g., to verify entity equality through a unique assertEquals operation that checks equality of the components defined in the identity annotation of the entity's type. Similarly, patterns can indicate static constraints on types, e.g., there cannot be two Persons, identified by SSN and country, whose names differ. Pattern-aware execution engines can enforce static constraints at runtime, e.g., keeping track of the (privacy-preserving) "signature" of each identified entity and its correlated immutable values.

Reference Metamodel. Jolie and LEMMA are in remarkable conceptual proximity despite their distant origins—namely Programming Languages and MDE. This close match in their conceptual foundations hints at the existence of a reference metamodel for MSAs to be uncovered. This reference metamodel should identify the main concepts of MSA including their basic properties and relationships to each other. Furthermore, it should emerge from the analysis of various existing, yet fragmented bodies of MSA knowledge ranging from pattern collections, over best practices and reference solutions for certain challenges in MSA, to more formal approaches like metamodels for programming and modelling languages. Recent efforts in the area of software deployment automation [34] reveal the potential of reference metamodels as they (i) reify and organise knowledge about a specific subject area; (ii) enable the comparison and reasoning about alternative approaches to the same issue; and (iii) allow identification of migration paths and cost estimation for technology choices. We believe that a reference metamodel for MSAs would be valuable to organise efforts and unify the great number of ad-hoc solutions for recurring challenges and the heterogeneity of MSAs.

References

1. Jolie website (2020). https://www.jolie-lang.org
2. Ameller, D., Burgués, X., Collell, O., Costal, D., Franch, X., Papazoglou, M.P.: Development of service-oriented architectures using model-driven development: a mapping study. Inf. Softw. Technol. **62**, 42–66 (2015)
3. Andrews, T., et al.: Business process execution language for web services (2003)
4. Balalaie, A., Heydarnoori, A., Jamshidi, P.: Migrating to cloud-native architectures using microservices: an experience report. In: Celesti, A., Leitner, P. (eds.) ESOCC Workshops 2015. CCIS, vol. 567, pp. 201–215. Springer, Cham (2016). https://doi.org/10.1007/978-3-319-33313-7_15
5. Berners-Lee, T., Fielding, R.T., Masinter, L.: Uniform Resource Identifier (URI): Generic syntax. RFC 3986, RFC Editor (2005)
6. Butting, A., Eikermann, R., Kautz, O., Rumpe, B., Wortmann, A.: Modeling language variability with reusable language components. In: SPLC 2018, p. 65–75. Association for Computing Machinery, New York (2018)
7. Cheney, J., Lindley, S., Radanne, G., Wadler, P.: Effective quotation: relating approaches to language-integrated query. In: PEPM, pp. 15–26. ACM (2014)
8. Cotton, I.W., Greatorex Jr, F.S.: Data structures and techniques for remote computer graphics. In: Proceedings of the December 9–11, 1968, fall joint Computer Conference, Part I, pp. 533–544 (1968)
9. Daigneau, R.: Service Design Patterns, 1st edn. Addison-Wesley, Boston (2012)
10. Dalla Preda, M., Gabbrielli, M., Guidi, C., Mauro, J., Montesi, F.: Interface-based service composition with aggregation. In: De Paoli, F., Pimentel, E., Zavattaro, G. (eds.) ESOCC 2012. LNCS, vol. 7592, pp. 48–63. Springer, Heidelberg (2012). https://doi.org/10.1007/978-3-642-33427-6_4
11. Deantoni, J.: Modeling the behavioral semantics of heterogeneous languages and their coordination. In: 2016 Architecture-Centric Virtual Integration (ACVI), pp. 12–18 (2016)
12. Dragoni, N.: Microservices: yesterday, today, and tomorrow. In: Present and Ulterior Software Engineering, pp. 195–216. Springer, Cham (2017). https://doi.org/10.1007/978-3-319-67425-4_12
13. Erdweg, S., Giarrusso, P.G., Rendel, T.: Language composition untangled. In: LDTA 2012. Association for Computing Machinery, New York (2012)
14. Erl, T.: Service-Oriented Architecture: Concepts, Technology, and Design. Pearson Education, New Delhi (2005)

15. Evans, E.: Domain-Driven Design, 1st edn. Addison-Wesley, Boston (2004)
16. Fernando, A., et al.: Ballerina and Jolie: connecting two frontiers of microservice programming. In: Microservices 2020 (2020)
17. Frankel, D.S.: Model Driven Architecture: Applying MDA to Enterprise Computing. Wiley, Hoboken (2003)
18. Freeman, T., Pfenning, F.: Refinement types for ML. In: Proceedings of the ACM SIGPLAN 1991 Conference on Programming Language Design and Implementation, pp. 268–277 (1991)
19. Guidi, C., Lanese, I., Montesi, F., Zavattaro, G.: Dynamic error handling in service oriented applications. Fundam. Informaticae **95**(1), 73–102 (2009)
20. Guidi, C., Lucchi, R., Gorrieri, R., Busi, N., Zavattaro, G.: SOCK: a calculus for service oriented computing. In: Dan, A., Lamersdorf, W. (eds.) ICSOC 2006. LNCS, vol. 4294, pp. 327–338. Springer, Heidelberg (2006). https://doi.org/10.1007/11948148_27
21. Kapferer, S., Zimmermann, O.: Domain-driven service design. In: Dustdar, S. (ed.) SummerSOC 2020. CCIS, vol. 1310, pp. 189–208. Springer, Cham (2020). https://doi.org/10.1007/978-3-030-64846-6_11
22. McCarthy, J.: Recursive functions of symbolic expressions and their computation by machine, part I. Commun. ACM **3**(4), 184–195 (1960)
23. Milner, R.: The tower of informatic models. From semantics to Computer Science (2009)
24. Montesi, F.: JOLIE: a Service-oriented Programming Language. Master's thesis, University of Bologna, Department of Computer Science (2010). http://amslaurea.cib.unibo.it/1226/
25. Montesi, F.: Process-aware web programming with Jolie. Sci. Comput. Program. **130**, 69–96 (2016)
26. Montesi, F., Carbone, M.: Programming services with correlation sets. In: Kappel, G., Maamar, Z., Motahari-Nezhad, H.R. (eds.) ICSOC 2011. LNCS, vol. 7084, pp. 125–141. Springer, Heidelberg (2011). https://doi.org/10.1007/978-3-642-25535-9_9
27. Montesi, F., Guidi, C., Zavattaro, G.: Service-Oriented Programming with Jolie, pp. 81–107. Springer, New York (2014). https://doi.org/10.1007/978-1-4614-7518-7_4
28. Newman, S.: Building Microservices: Designing Fine-Grained Systems, 1st edn. O'Reilly, Beijing (2015)
29. Oram, A.: Ballerina: A Language for Network-Distributed Applications, 1st edn. O'Reilly, Boston (2019)
30. Rademacher, F.: A non-intrusive approach to extend microservice modeling languages with architecture pattern support. In: Microservices 2020 (2020)
31. Rademacher, F., Sachweh, S., Zündorf, A.: Aspect-oriented modeling of technology heterogeneity in Microservice Architecture. In: 2019 IEEE International Conference on Software Architecture (ICSA), pp. 21–30. IEEE (2019)
32. Rademacher, F., Sorgalla, J., Wizenty, P., Sachweh, S., Zündorf, A.: Graphical and textual model-driven microservice development. In: Microservices, pp. 147–179. Springer, Cham (2020). https://doi.org/10.1007/978-3-030-31646-4_7
33. Terzić, B., Dimitrieski, V., Kordić, S., Milosavljević, G., Luković, I.: Development and evaluation of microBuilder: a model-driven tool for the specification of REST microservice software architectures. Enterpr. Inf. Syst. **12**(8–9), 1034–1057 (2018)

34. Wurster, M., et al.: The essential deployment metamodel: a systematic review of deployment automation technologies. SICS Softw. Intens. Cyber-Phys. Syst. 63–75 (2019). https://doi.org/10.1007/s00450-019-00412-x
35. Zimmermann, O.: Microservices tenets. Comput. Sci. Res. Dev. **32**(3), 301–310 (2017)

SCAFI-WEB: A Web-Based Application for Field-Based Coordination Programming

Gianluca Aguzzi$^{(\boxtimes)}$, Roberto Casadei⬤, Niccolò Maltoni, Danilo Pianini⬤, and Mirko Viroli⬤

Alma Mater Studiorum–Università di Bologna, Cesena, Italy
{gianluca.aguzzi,roby.casadei,niccolo.maltoni,
danilo.pianini,mirko.viroli}@unibo.it

Abstract. Field-based coordination is a model for expressing the coordination logic of large-scale adaptive systems, composing functional blocks from a global perspective. As for any coordination model, a proper toolchain must be developed to support its adoption across all development phases. Under this point of view, the SCAFI toolkit provides a coordination language (field calculus) as a DSL internal in the SCALA language, a library of reusable building blocks, and an infrastructure for simulation of distributed deployments. In this work, we enrich such a toolchain by introducing SCAFI-WEB, a web-based application allowing in-browser editing, execution, and visualisation of SCAFI programs. SCAFI-WEB facilitates access to the SCAFI coordination technology by flattening the learning curve and simplifying configuration and requirements, thus promoting agile prototyping of field-based coordination specifications. In turn, this opens the door to easier demonstrations and experimentation, and also constitutes a stepping stone towards monitoring and control of simulated/deployed systems.

Keywords: Field-based coordination · Aggregate Programming · Online Playground

1 Introduction

Emerging trends such as the Internet of Things (IoT) and Cyber-Physical Systems (CPS) foster a vision of large-scale coordinated systems of situated devices that operate in a dynamic environment and seamlessly collaborate to reach global goals. When designing such systems, one key engineering challenge is mapping the intended global and adaptive behaviour that the system should exhibit to the local behaviour and interaction of its components. To tackle this issue, research often looked at nature for inspiration: (bio)chemistry [34], ecosystems [36], ethology [30], and fields in physics [24,25]. Accordingly, several approaches in the literature proposed the idea of programming coordination and adaptation through reusable abstractions [13,20] and interaction structures [1,22,23]. Recently, *aggregate computing* [8] has emerged as a paradigm,

ⓒ IFIP International Federation for Information Processing 2021
Published by Springer Nature Switzerland AG 2021
F. Damiani and O. Dardha (Eds.): COORDINATION 2021, LNCS 12717, pp. 285–299, 2021.
https://doi.org/10.1007/978-3-030-78142-2_18

stemming from *field-based coordination* [33], fostering a top-down and global-to-local approach to the specification of the collective adaptive behaviour of a system. The idea is to exploit the *(computational) field* abstraction – a "collective" data structure mapping any device of the system to a corresponding value – to program the system as a whole; namely, the program expressing the behaviour of the collective takes the form of a composition of functions from input fields (*e.g.*, sensor fields) to output fields (*e.g.*, value and actuation fields) [5]. Aggregate programming is supported by several various domain-specific languages (DSL), including Proto [7], a Scheme-based DSL; Protelis [28], a Java-interoperable stand-alone DSL; FCPP [2], a lightweight native implementation; and SCAFI [18], a modern SCALA-based DSL.

Language-based approaches often enjoy solid formal foundations and demonstrable properties [33], but in turn require the user a potentially steep learning curve which includes learning a paradigm, a language, and a development toolset. In the case of languages for distributed systems, a further element of complexity exists: programs should be executed on a *network of devices*. Due to the costs and impracticality of real deployments, a typical approach for studying, testing, and developing applications with distributed programming languages consists in using *simulators*. However, this introduces further practical issues to the setup of a development environment; such accidental complexity could hinder accessibility.

Along the line of pioneering platforms such as Web Proto [31], this paper presents SCAFI-WEB, an online playground for the SCAFI aggregate programming DSL, featuring an intuitive web-based graphical user interface (GUI), an integrated simulation environment with zero-configuration overhead from the user, and a guided tour of the key language features. The paper continues as follows: Sect. 2 discusses motivation and related work; Sect. 3 provides background on SCAFI and field calculus; Sect. 4 covers the SCAFI-WEB platform (the tool at the core of this contribution) and its use cases; finally, Sect. 5 presents the conclusions and points out directions for future work.

2   Motivation and Related Work

Learning a new language may not be trivial, especially when it involves learning new paradigms and/or new development tools. The literature on learning computational concepts suggests that two key elements for effectively introducing novel programming concepts are *simplicity* and *visibility* [12], intended, respectively, as the number of interacting parts that should be understood to realise how the system works, and as the possibility to isolate and inspect such parts. Also, in [11] four critical dimensions are identified:

1. *orientation*, namely finding out what a programming language is for and which class of problems it applies well to;
2. *understanding of the notional machine*, namely understanding how changes in the program affect results;

3. *notation*, namely getting acquainted with the syntax and the underlying semantics; and finally

4. *pragmatics*, including all skills related to assemble and use an environment supporting development, testing, and debugging.

To tackle the problem, it is common practice to provide graphical tools that enable the user to kickstart a project. Typically, however, these tools have prerequisites (runtimes, editors, integrated development environments, plugins, custom software modules) that require an investment of time and effort to begin the learning process. This initial investment, usually easily tolerated by the experienced practitioner or the committed learner, could be costly enough to discourage occasional users from experimenting with a novel tool or language. For this reason, all major modern general-purpose languages have adopted the strategy of providing web-based programming playgrounds with the sole prerequisite of a modern web browser, using no third-party tool at all. A purely browser-based tool has several advantages over a classic application:

- *portability* – experimentation can happen from any device equipped with a modern browser, thus including devices usually not supported by classic development stacks (gaming consoles, smart TVs, set-top boxes, and the like), as well as niche operating systems;
- *future-proofness* – any future software environment with a standard-compliant web browser will be able to run the application;
- *zero-permission* – the absence of any part to be locally installed implies that the experimentation can happen entirely in userspace, while very often a correct local installation of a runtime environment should be performed by a system administrator;
- *zero-time experimentation* – executing a simple experiment is as easy as opening a browser tab and typing the program, as opposed to manually using compilers or starting a stand-alone application.

Well-designed web playgrounds hide many of the issues related to the *pragmatics* of learning a language, postponing them and hence allowing developers to focus on other dimensions first. Also, by presenting a carefully designed learning path of increasingly complex exercises and examples, these platforms increase *simplicity* and favour the *understanding of the notional machine*, ultimately promoting *self-orientation* as well. Examples of web playgrounds for modern programming languages include Kotlin Koans[1], ScalaFiddle[2], and Rust Playground[3].

Web Proto [31] pioneered the approach for languages dedicated to distributed systems by providing:

- an online editor,
- an interpreter for the Proto [7] language for spatial computing based on emscripten[4],

---

[1] https://play.kotlinlang.org/koans.

[2] https://scalafiddle.io/.

[3] https://play.rust-lang.org/.

[4] https://emscripten.org/.

– an in-browser simulated environment, and
– the possibility to share code between different users.

Unfortunately though, Proto is no longer maintained (as it has been replaced by Protelis [28][5], which has no web environment at the time of writing); and Web Proto, to the best of our knowledge, is no longer reachable, and there is no plan to deploy it again. The approach proposed in Web Proto inspired the tool at the centre of this paper: SCAFI-WEB, which directly supports modern aggregate programming tools like SCAFI (see Sect. 3), provides a cleaner and clever web-based technical solution (see Sect. 4), and has well-defined pedagogical use cases (see Sect. 4.2). Unlike Web Proto, which is a JAVASCRIPT re-implementation of Proto, this project fully reuses the mainline SCAFI code through transpilation into a browser-compatible target, considerably reducing maintenance and enabling feature parity with the classic version. Indeed, the DSL and the simulator provided by SCAFI have been successfully brought into the JAVASCRIPT world leveraging SCALA.JS, with no special changes or disruptive adaptations of the original code. Furthermore, while Web Proto was designed to support only one language, several SCAFI-WEB components (primarily, the visualisation section) are agnostic to the aggregate language of choice, in the spirit of supporting different languages and platforms (distributed or simulated) in the future.

3   The SCAFI Aggregate Programming Toolchain

SCAFI[6] (SCAla FIeld) is a modular SCALA-based toolchain for aggregate computing. It provides *(i)* a DSL implementation of the field calculus [18,33] designed to simplify embedding in common general-purpose languages; *(ii)* a library of reusable aggregate behaviour functions; *(iii)* simulation support for logical networked systems driven by SCAFI programs (*aggregate systems*), through an internal engine or a plug-in for the Alchemist simulator [27,35]; and *(iv)* an actor-based platform [17] to deploy aggregate systems in real-world clusters. SCAFI has been used as a framework for experimenting with new field calculus constructs [19] and for building decentralised algorithms and applications in large-scale computing scenarios ranging from trust-based collaborative systems [15] to resource coordination in IoT and edge computing [16]. In a typical aggregate application development workflow, a developer iteratively constructs a SCAFI program, performs a set of simulations and tests to evaluate how the system performs in a range of target environments, iterates until sufficient confidence on correctness is achieved, and finally deploys the program to a set of nodes running an aggregate computing middleware (such as the SCAFI actor-based platform), when further maintenance, monitoring, and control is generally required. SCAFI, with respect to other aggregate programming languages, benefits from being an internal DSL, enabling reuse of the toolchain available for its host language (SCALA).

---

[5] https://bit.ly/3uRZYgp.
[6] https://scafi.github.io.

3.1   Field Calculus and the SCAFI DSL

Field Calculus. The field calculus [5] is a core language that captures the essential aspects for programming self-organising systems. In this language, programs – also called *field programs* or *aggregate programs* – consist of expressions that conceptually manipulate distributed state. The distributed state is modelled by the *computational field* abstraction, which is essentially a map from any device of a system domain to computational values. For instance, globally querying a "temperature sensor" in a sensor network would yield a field of temperatures, which maps each device with the corresponding temperature that it read. The field calculus is based on a minimal set of operators such as the following.

- *Stateful field evolution*: expression $rep(e_1)\{(x) \Rightarrow e_2\}$ describes a field evolving in time. e_1 imposes the initial field value, and function $(x) \Rightarrow e_2$ declares how the field changes at each execution.
- *Neighbour interaction*: expression $nbr\{e\}$ builds a *neighbouring field*, a view of the field values in the surroundings of each device where neighbours are mapped to their evaluations of e.
- *Domain partitioning*: expression $if(e_0)\{e_1\}\{e_2\}$ splits the computational field into two non-communicating zones hosting isolated subcomputations: e_1 where e_0 is $true$, and e_2 where e_0 is $false$.

System Model and Execution Model. The logical structure of an aggregate system merely consists of a network of nodes connected through a *neighbouring relationship*. The network semantics of the field calculus [5] defines what local execution protocol any device belonging to the aggregate system should follow so that an aggregate program leads to the designed collective behaviour. The basic idea is that any device should "continuously" sense, coordinate, and act over its local context. Therefore, every device performs *asynchronous rounds of execution*, where each round consists of the following steps:

1. *context gathering*—the device retrieves sensor data, messages from neighbours, and its previous state;
2. *computation*—the device evaluates the aggregate program, which yields an output as well as a coordination message – called an *export* – meant to be shared with neighbours;
3. *context action*—the device runs actuations and broadcasts the export to its neighbours.

Following this protocol, a collective execution of a field program can lead to self-organising behaviour, in a powerful, emergent way—cf. the channel example in Sect. 3.2.

The SCAFI Aggregate Programming Language. The SCAFI DSL implements a field calculus variant, called FScaFi [18], in which nbr does not directly yield a computational field but rather must be evaluated while folding over neighbourhoods (through a function $foldhood$, described next). The core language constructs are captured in SCALA through the following trait:

```
trait Constructs {
  def nbr[A](expr: => A): A
  def rep[A](init: =>A)(fun: (A) => A): A
  def foldhood[A](init: => A)(aggr: (A, A) => A)(expr: => A): A
  // Contextual, but foundational
  def mid(): ID
  def sense[A](name: LSNS): A
  def nbrvar[A](name: NSNS): A
}
```

In particular, `mid` is a built-in sensor that provides the identifier (ID) of the running node, whereas **sense** and **nbrvar** are two operators included for interacting with the environment. The former abstracts a local sensor queries (*e.g.*, the value of a temperature sensor), and the latter instead produces a field of local sensor readings that are *relative to* neighbours. A typical example of **nbrvar** is **nbrRange**, an "environmental sensor" that creates a field of distances mapping every neighbour with its relative distance from the running node. Moreover, the field calculus `if` expression became branch in SCALA, because `if` is a reserved keyword. Now, we provide a brief tutorial on SCAFI. As a very trivial example, a local value such as

```
true
```

can be used to represent a uniform and constant field in the system (indeed, any node evaluates such expression to **true**). Using `rep`, we can evolve state, *e.g.*, to implement a local round counter:

```
rep(0){ _ + 1 } // _ + 1 is a Scala shorthand for function x => x + 1
```

This code snippet describes a field that starts from 0 and then evolves by increasing by one. To pass from purely local to global computations, we need devices to interact. This is possible by combining the `nbr` and `foldhood` operators:

```
foldhood(mid()) { Math.min } { nbr(mid()) }
```

The `foldhood` operator accepts three arguments: *(i)* an initial value *(ii)* an accumulator, i.e. a strategy used to combine a neighbour's value to the partial accumulation, and *(iii)* an expression to be evaluated against any neighbour. In this example, we gather the neighbours' IDs, folding over them to take the minimum ID in the neighbourhood. We can combine `rep` and `foldhood` to build fields progressively constructed and refined by coordination of all the nodes. For instance, expression

```
rep(mid()){ minId => foldhood(minId) { Math.min } { nbr(mid()) } }
```

represents a gossip process that will produce a field eventually tending to the minimum ID of the whole system.

The key idea of aggregate computing is to find recurrent patterns and then use the functional abstraction to create reusable building blocks [32]. One of these is G, which generalises *gradient* computations [4] to allow propagation of information form a node outwards:

```
G[F](source: Boolean, field: F, accumulator: F => F, metric: Metric)
```

G diffuses information by accumulating `field` data while ascending a potential field centred where `source` is `true`. Graphically, Fig. 1 shows the operator behaviour. On top of G, we can build other significant functions as `distanceTo` (i.e., a self-healing version of the Bellman-Ford algorithm [26]),

```
def distanceTo(source: Boolean, metric: Metric = nbrRange): Double = {
  val field = if(source){ 0.0 } { Double.PositiveInfinity }
  G(source, field, _ + metric(), metric)
}
```

and `distanceBeetwen` (i.e. the network-propagated self-healing minimum distance between source and target nodes):

```
def distanceBetween(source: Boolean,target: Boolean,
  metric: Metric = nbrRange
): Double =
  G(source, distanceTo(target, metric), v => v, metric = metric)
```

Finally, using only this subset of operators, it is possible to build non-trivial examples, such as the self-healing channel explained below.

G(source, f, acc, metric)

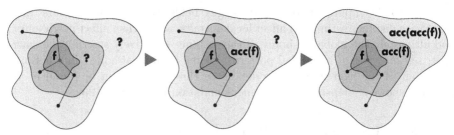

Fig. 1. Evolution in time of G. Red color marks the source node. The links express a neighbour relation between nodes. The time flows from the left to the right. Initially, the source node computes its value as `f` (initial value). The potential field will be created following the metric passed. Step by step, `f` will be shared through the accumulator function.

3.2 The Channel Example

A paradigmatic example of aggregate computing is the *channel*, an algorithm yielding a self-healing Boolean field that is (eventually) `true` along the minimal hop-by-hop path from a `source` to a `target` device (as identified also by Boolean

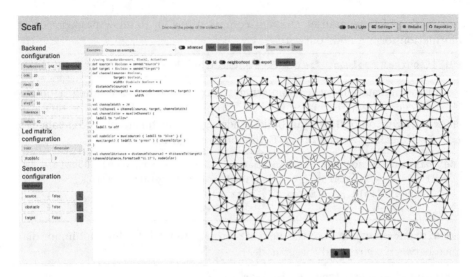

Fig. 2. SCAFI-WEB (https://scafi.github.io/web) running the channel example.

fields). Self-healing field means that the channel structure recovers itself after failures, without human interaction. This can be used *e.g.* for navigating people or streaming information towards target locations. An implementation leverages distance estimations (based on gradients [4]) and the triangular inequality:

```
distanceTo(source) + distanceTo(target) <= distanceBetween(source,target)
```

Changes to the inputs (`source` and `target` fields, topology, neighbours' messages with distance estimates) affect local outputs, which then affect neighbours', and ultimately the global response of the system—effectively steering the emergent, *self-organising* (i.e. global patterns emerge from local node's interactions) behaviour of the aggregate. More details on this example can be found in [6]. Figure 2 shows a snapshot of a channel simulation in SCAFI-WEB.

3.3 SCAFI **Programming in Practice**

Programming in SCAFI requires building a model of the system, writing a field-based program assuming that model, and finally deploying and running the corresponding application. However, setting up a (simulated) system requires familiarity with a set of tools and notions, including: build automation and dependency management tools (such as SBT or Gradle) to import SCAFI modules as dependencies, integrated-development environments (such as IntelliJ Idea) for editing programs, library and framework APIs for configuring and integrating several components. In particular, some boilerplate code or configuration files may be needed: the program expressing the system behaviour, the structure of the simulated system, the dynamics of the simulated system (cf. scheduling, failure injection, interaction) and the environment, simulation parameters (*e.g.*, for reproducibility and control of scenarios), as well as inspection and visualisation aspects (*e.g.*, of the graphical evolution of the system and the data produced by its components).

Therefore, any support reducing the gap from the aggregate specification to a graphical representation of a running system can be useful to promote accessibility, learning, and experimentation—hence motivating ScaFi-Web.

4   ScaFi-Web

ScaFi-Web[7] is an online playground for learning the ScaFi toolkit, experimenting with it, and monitoring executions in a browser. It features:

- an interactive editor for writing ScaFi programs;
- a guided tour of the most prominent features, kickstarting development;
- a set of increasingly complex examples;
- an in-browser simulated network of devices hosting the execution;
- visualisation, inspection, and interaction tools integrated with the simulated environment.

Besides flattening the learning curve of a novel paradigm and allowing first-hand experimentation with zero configuration, ScaFi-Web also provides a stepping stone towards a monitoring and control system for aggregate computing deployments. In the following sections, we explain the architecture in detail, motivating design choices and exposing some relevant use cases and opportunities.

4.1   Architecture Details

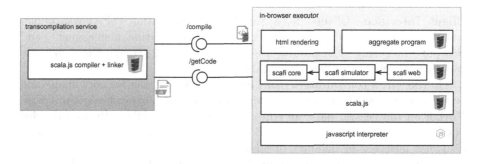

Fig. 3. Architecture of ScaFi-Web, with the involved technologies.

ScaFi-Web finds its novelty in the capability of running the whole aggregate program inside the runtime of the browser. Most modern browsers can execute a limited number of code targets, mostly JavaScript and WebAssembly

---

[7] https://scafi.github.io/web.

(WASM) [29]. SCALA, the language hosting the SCAFI DSL, primarily targets the Java Virtual Machine (JVM), whose execution on browser platform was deprecated[8] years ago and is no longer supported.

To be able to execute SCAFI code (and thus SCALA code) client-locally, a transcompilation from SCALA to one of the aforementioned languages is required; JAVASCRIPT has been selected as the only web target currently supported by the SCALA native compiler[9]. User-written SCALA code can be transcompiled into JAVASCRIPT on-the-fly and injected into the simulator, leveraging the `scalac` compiler with SCALA.JS [21]. The SCALA compiler, however, currently requires to be executed in a JVM, and hence off-browser (despite being written mostly in SCALA, there is no JAVASCRIPT version of `scalac` at the time of writing). Consequently, the SCAFI-WEB architecture has been designed with two components: a frontend hosting the interpreter, simulator, and user interface; and a transcompilation service, in charge of producing JAVASCRIPT code for the aggregate specifications written in SCALA.

Transcompilation Service. The remote service instance, depicted on the left of Fig. 3, exposes the transcompilation service via RESTful HTTP APIs. The route `/compile` accepts POST requests containing the SCAFI code to be transcompiled. Leveraging the SCALA compiler, it creates a REST resource identified by a UUID with the transpiled JAVASCRIPT code. The identifier returned to the client can be used on the `/getCode/{UUID}` API via GET requests to download the transpiled code.

The service is platform-agnostic and can be executed on all operating systems and runtimes that can host a JVM. To simplify the deployment of SCAFI-WEB instances, the service has been made publicly available[10] in a containerised [14] fashion as a Docker image, deployable on any compatible container runtime.

Client Interface. Client-side, a Single-Page Application (SPA) was implemented to manage *(i)* programs execution, *(ii)* simulation management, and *(iii)* page rendering. The interface, as visible in Fig. 2, is structured in three parts, each exposing a different logical control.

On the left, a configuration panel enables control of the network shape and device sensors, enabling users to design their own deployment configurations. Moving on the central part, an editor is available to fiddle with the provided examples or write fresh new code. Editing can be performed in two flavours: *simplified* (selected by default), or *advanced*.

In simplified mode, inspired by the interaction typical of REPL interpreters [10], the editor hides all the boilerplate code, allowing for a very straightforward hands-on with the core language mechanisms. In advanced mode, instead, these details are exposed, bridging the gap towards full-fledged development environments.

---

[8] http://openjdk.java.net/jeps/289.

[9] https://archive.is/SaV6B.

[10] https://hub.docker.com/r/gianlucaaguzzi/scafi-web.

Finally, the program can be executed with the controls available on the rightmost section of the page. Pressing the play button causes the application to transpile under-the-hood the code in the editor (by leveraging the aforementioned remote service), injecting the resulting JAVASCRIPT in the browser-hosted SCAFI simulator.

4.2   Usage Scenarios

Learning and Education. Web-based playgrounds are a trending way to experiment with languages, they are well accepted as they lower the adoption and learning curves. SCAFI-WEB guides the user to an understanding of field-based coordination by *(i)* exposing an environment with minimal requirements (a modern browser); *(ii)* including a tour of its functions; *(iii)* presenting a sequence of guided examples of increasing complexity that can be simulated immediately; *(iv)* providing simplified access to the simulated sensors and actuators (*e.g.* for controlling movement and colour of devices).

Fast Prototyping. Programming complex coordination logic is challenging, even with paradigms that promote collective behaviour abstractions to first-class: robust specifications usually result from an iterative, incremental process where SCAFI programs are progressively refined. Simulation has a key role in this development workflow, as it allows for observing and controlling the software in a variety of scenarios (different network structures, dynamics, and perturbations) without the issues related to actual deployment. SCAFI-WEB supports this kind of workflow, by providing an out-of-the-box web-based simulation environment with zero installation overhead.

4.3   Roadmap to Monitoring and Control of Deployed Systems

The monitoring and control of distributed systems is a prominent practical issue. In the context of field-based coordination, automated runtime verification approaches have been recently investigated, whereby spatial or temporal logics are mapped to field calculus programs to directly encode the behaviour of decentralised monitors [3]. However, these techniques are complementary to monitoring and control activities carried out by humans, which may need remote frontends to inspect and act over a running system. The SCAFI-WEB's frontend has been designed to be adaptable to different backends; indeed, the UI is completely separated from the underlying aggregate execution system (called Support in SCAFI-WEB). We plan to evolve SCAFI-WEB into a platform for remote monitoring and control of aggregate systems. In particular, we aim to:

1. define a middleware in charge of both retrieving values from the different nodes in the system, injecting aggregate code and sending well-defined commands;
2. create a new Support able to communicate with the aforementioned middleware (*e.g.* via WebSocket);

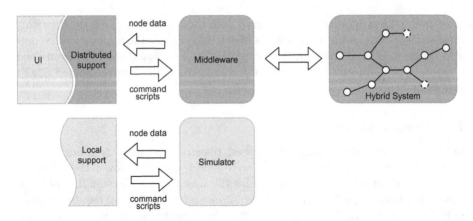

Fig. 4. This figure shows the logical components currently available (yellow) and those that have to be developed to support a full-fledged monitoring and control solution. Notice the separation between UI and support (Notation: nodes with dotted border are purely simulated.)

3. create a Support-to-UI component that understands and manages the aggregate computing languages of the new Support;
4. establish a simulation-to-middleware component that can inspect the overall system status;
5. realise tests upon real systems;
6. introduce the opportunity to orchestrate hybrid real-virtual systems, in which real devices can interact with virtual devices managed by a simulation platform.

Figure 4 summarises the general idea of the final product. With the proposed architecture, it will be possible to inject new behaviours by either specific commands (*e.g.* move the alpha node to X,y) or by injecting new aggregate programs (*e.g.* to verify a property at runtime, as in [3]). Finally, given the hybrid nature of the system, it can be interesting to spawn new simulated nodes at runtime. This can be useful, for instance, to improve the performance of programs performing density-sensitive operations [9] when executing in low-device-density conditions.

5   Conclusion and Future Work

In this paper, we have presented SCAFI-WEB, a web-based playground and frontend for simulated aggregate computing systems, enabling seamless and universal access to the SCAFI aggregate programming toolchain. It provides an environment with zero-installation overhead and pedagogical support for learning, exploratory testing, and easy application deployment.

As a future work, we would like to extend SCAFI-WEB with out-of-the-box support for monitoring and control of deployed systems. Additionally, it would be nice to provide a graphical DSL allowing the creation of aggregate specifications by the composition of algorithmic blocks, hence simplifying application development.

References

1. Arbab, F.: A behavioral model for composition of software components. Obj. Logiciel Base données Réseaux **12**(1), 33–76 (2006). https://doi.org/10.3166/objet.12.1.33-76
2. Audrito, G.: FCPP: an efficient and extensible field calculus framework. In: IEEE International Conference on Autonomic Computing and Self-Organizing Systems, ACSOS 2020, Washington, DC, USA, 17–21 August 2020, pp. 153–159. IEEE (2020). https://doi.org/10.1109/ACSOS49614.2020.00037
3. Audrito, G., Casadei, R., Damiani, F., Stolz, V., Viroli, M.: Adaptive distributed monitors of spatial properties for cyber–physical systems. J. Syst. Softw. **175**, 110908 (2021). https://doi.org/10.1016/j.jss.2021.110908
4. Audrito, G., Casadei, R., Damiani, F., Viroli, M.: Compositional blocks for optimal self-healing gradients. In: 11th IEEE SASO 2017, pp. 91–100. IEEE Computer Society (2017). https://doi.org/10.1109/SASO.2017.18
5. Audrito, G., Viroli, M., Damiani, F., Pianini, D., Beal, J.: A higher-order calculus of computational fields. ACM Trans. Comput. Log. **20**(1), 5:1–5:55 (2019). https://doi.org/10.1145/3285956
6. Bachrach, J., Beal, J., McLurkin, J.: Composable continuous-space programs for robotic swarms. Neural Comput. Appl. **19**(6), 825–847 (2010). https://doi.org/10.1007/s00521-010-0382-8
7. Beal, J., Bachrach, J.: Infrastructure for engineered emergence on sensor/actuator networks. IEEE Intell. Syst. **21**(2), 10–19 (2006). https://doi.org/10.1109/MIS.2006.29
8. Beal, J., Pianini, D., Viroli, M.: Aggregate programming for the Internet of Things. Computer **48**(9), 22–30 (2015). https://doi.org/10.1109/MC.2015.261
9. Beal, J., Viroli, M., Pianini, D., Damiani, F.: Self-adaptation to device distribution in the Internet of Things. ACM Trans. Auton. Adapt. Syst. **12**(3), 12:1–12:29 (2017). https://doi.org/10.1145/3105758
10. van Binsbergen, L.T., Merino, M.V., Jeanjean, P., van der Storm, T., Combemale, B., Barais, O.: A principled approach to REPL interpreters. In: Proceedings of the 2020 ACM SIGPLAN International Symposium on New Ideas, New Paradigms, and Reflections on Programming and Software. ACM, November 2020. https://doi.org/10.1145/3426428.3426917
11. du Boulay, B.: Some difficulties of learning to program. J. Educ. Comput. Res. **2**(1), 57–73 (1986). https://doi.org/10.2190/3lfx-9rrf-67t8-uvk9
12. du Boulay, B., O'Shea, T., Monk, J.: The black box inside the glass box: presenting computing concepts to novices. Int. J. Hum. Comput. Stud. **51**(2), 265–277 (1999). https://doi.org/10.1006/ijhc.1981.0309
13. Bures, T., Gerostathopoulos, I., Hnetynka, P., Keznikl, J., Kit, M., Plasil, F.: DEECO: an ensemble-based component system. In: CBSE 2013, pp. 81–90. ACM (2013). https://doi.org/10.1145/2465449.2465462
14. Butzin, B., Golatowski, F., Timmermann, D.: Microservices approach for the Internet of Things. In: 21st IEEE ETFA 2016, pp. 1–6. IEEE (2016). https://doi.org/10.1109/ETFA.2016.7733707

15. Casadei, R., Aldini, A., Viroli, M.: Towards attack-resistant aggregate computing using trust mechanisms. Sci. Comput. Program. (2018). https://doi.org/10.1016/j.scico.2018.07.006

16. Casadei, R., Tsigkanos, C., Viroli, M., Dustdar, S.: Engineering resilient collaborative edge-enabled IoT. In: 2019 IEEE International Conference on Services Computing (SCC), pp. 36–45, July 2019. https://doi.org/10.1109/SCC.2019.00019

17. Casadei, R., Viroli, M.: Programming actor-based collective adaptive systems. In: Ricci, A., Haller, P. (eds.) Programming with Actors. LNCS, vol. 10789, pp. 94–122. Springer, Cham (2018). https://doi.org/10.1007/978-3-030-00302-9_4

18. Casadei, R., Viroli, M., Audrito, G., Damiani, F.: FSCAFI : a core calculus for collective adaptive systems programming. In: Margaria, T., Steffen, B. (eds.) ISoLA 2020. LNCS, vol. 12477, pp. 344–360. Springer, Cham (2020). https://doi.org/10.1007/978-3-030-61470-6_21

19. Casadei, R., Viroli, M., Audrito, G., Pianini, D., Damiani, F.: Engineering collective intelligence at the edge with aggregate processes. Eng. Appl. Artif. Intell. **97**, 104081 (2021). https://doi.org/10.1016/j.engappai.2020.104081

20. Denti, E., Natali, A., Omicini, A.: Programmable coordination media. In: Garlan, D., Le Métayer, D. (eds.) COORDINATION 1997. LNCS, vol. 1282, pp. 274–288. Springer, Heidelberg (1997). https://doi.org/10.1007/3-540-63383-9_86

21. Doeraene, S.: Cross-platform language design in scala.js (keynote). In: Erdweg, S., d. S. Oliveira, B.C. (eds.) Proceedings of the 9th ACM SIGPLAN International Symposium on Scala, SCALA@ICFP 2018, St. Louis, MO, USA, 28 September 2018, p. 1. ACM (2018). https://doi.org/10.1145/3241653.3266230

22. Fernandez-Marquez, J.L., Serugendo, G.D.M., Montagna, S., Viroli, M., Arcos, J.L.: Description and composition of bio-inspired design patterns: a complete overview. Nat. Comput. **12**, 43–67 (2013). https://doi.org/10.1007/s11047-012-9324-y

23. Frey, S., Diaconescu, A., Menga, D., Demeure, I.: A holonic control architecture for a heterogeneous multi-objective smart micro-grid. In: 2013 IEEE 7th International Conference on Self-Adaptive and Self-Organizing Systems. IEEE, September 2013. https://doi.org/10.1109/saso.2013.11

24. Mamei, M., Zambonelli, F.: Programming pervasive and mobile computing applications with the TOTA middleware. In: PerCom 2004, pp. 263–276. IEEE Computer Society (2004). https://doi.org/10.1109/PERCOM.2004.1276864

25. Mamei, M., Zambonelli, F., Leonardi, L.: Co-fields: towards a unifying approach to the engineering of swarm intelligent systems. In: Petta, P., Tolksdorf, R., Zambonelli, F. (eds.) ESAW 2002. LNCS (LNAI), vol. 2577, pp. 68–81. Springer, Heidelberg (2003). https://doi.org/10.1007/3-540-39173-8_6

26. Mo, Y., Dasgupta, S., Beal, J.: Robustness of the adaptive bellman-ford algorithm: global stability and ultimate bounds. IEEE Trans. Autom. Control. **64**(10), 4121–4136 (2019). https://doi.org/10.1109/TAC.2019.2904239

27. Pianini, D., Montagna, S., Viroli, M.: Chemical-oriented simulation of computational systems with Alchemist. J. Simul. (2013). https://doi.org/10.1057/jos.2012.27

28. Pianini, D., Viroli, M., Beal, J.: Protelis: practical aggregate programming. In: Proceedings of the 30th Annual ACM Symposium on Applied Computing, Salamanca, Spain, 13–17 April 2015, pp. 1846–1853. ACM (2015). https://doi.org/10.1145/2695664.2695913

29. Rossberg, A., et al.: Bringing the web up to speed with webassembly. Commun. ACM **61**(12), 107–115 (2018). https://doi.org/10.1145/3282510

30. Trianni, V., Nolfi, S., Dorigo, M.: Evolution, self-organization and swarm robotics. In: Blum, C., Merkle, D. (eds.) Natural Computing Series, pp. 163–191. Springer, Heidelberg (2008). https://doi.org/10.1007/978-3-540-74089-6_5

31. Usbeck, K., Beal, J.: Web Proto: aggregate programming for everyone. In: 7th IEEE SASOW, 2013, pp. 17–18. IEEE Computer Society (2013). https://doi.org/10.1109/SASOW.2013.12

32. Viroli, M., Audrito, G., Beal, J., Damiani, F., Pianini, D.: Engineering resilient collective adaptive systems by self-stabilisation. ACM Trans. Model. Comput. Simul. **28**(2), 16:1–16:28 (2018)

33. Viroli, M., Beal, J., Damiani, F., Audrito, G., Casadei, R., Pianini, D.: From distributed coordination to field calculus and aggregate computing. J. Log. Algebraic Methods Program. **109** (2019). https://doi.org/10.1016/j.jlamp.2019.100486

34. Viroli, M., Casadei, M.: Biochemical tuple spaces for self-organising coordination. In: Field, J., Vasconcelos, V.T. (eds.) COORDINATION 2009. LNCS, vol. 5521, pp. 143–162. Springer, Heidelberg (2009). https://doi.org/10.1007/978-3-642-02053-7_8

35. Viroli, M., Casadei, R., Pianini, D.: Simulating large-scale aggregate mass with alchemist and Scala. In: Proceedings of FedCSIS 2016. Annals of Computer Science and Information Systems, vol. 8, pp. 1495–1504. IEEE (2016). https://doi.org/10.15439/2016F407

36. Zambonelli, F., et al.: Developing pervasive multi-agent systems with nature-inspired coordination. Pervasive Mob. Comput. **17**, 236–252 (2015). https://doi.org/10.1016/j.pmcj.2014.12.002

Author Index

Printed in the United States
by Baker & Taylor Publisher Services